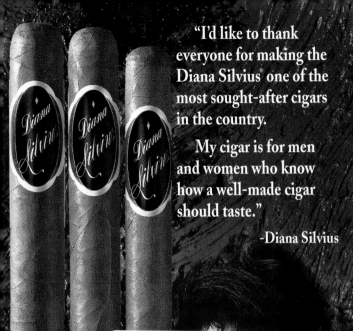

"I'd like to thank everyone for making the Diana Silvius® one of the most sought-after cigars in the country.

My cigar is for men and women who know how a well-made cigar should taste."

-Diana Silvius

D1521587

Diana Silvius® Diamond Vintage Cigars are hand-rolled in the Dominican Republic by Arturo Fuente's master rollers. Connecticut shade wrapper and fine, aged Dominican tobaccos are used to create a superb smoke that's mild-bodied yet rich in flavor.

THE BENCHMARK FOR FINE CIGARS
The Aroma and Taste
of High Style
A TRADITION OF EXCELLENCE
TROYA
TROYA
Lignum 2 • Casa Real

Happy 40th Danny-Boy!

Enjoy!

Perelman's Pocket Cyclopedia of Cigars

Vinnie & Anne 2-8-97

1997 edition

Compiled by
Richard B. Perelman

Published by
PERELMAN PIONEER & COMPANY

Los Angeles, California

$ 9.95 U.S.

ISBN 0-9649258-3-4

Published in Los Angeles, California, USA. First printing 1996. Printed by Pace Lithographers, Inc. of Industry, California. Cover photograph by Long Photography, Inc. of Los Angeles, California.

Please address inquiries to:

PERELMAN PIONEER & COMPANY

POST OFFICE BOX 67B99
CENTURY CITY STATION
LOS ANGELES, CALIFORNIA 90067 USA

Perelman's Pocket Cyclopedia of Cigars

1997 edition

TABLE OF CONTENTS

TABLE OF CONTENTS

Please send comments, inquiries, questions and suggestions to the author at:

PERELMAN, PIONEER & COMPANY
POST OFFICE BOX 67B99
CENTURY CITY STATION
LOS ANGELES, CALIFORNIA 90067 USA

Telephone: (213) 965-4905
Facsimile: (213) 965-4919

INTRODUCTION

The cigar explosion that has swept the United States and is now spreading to Asia, Europe and beyond has gone well past even the imagination of most everyone who has been involved with the cigar trade.

Our goal is to try to bring some discipline to the classification of the hundreds of brands on the U.S. market today in this, our third annual compilation.

We are very grateful for the wonderful support of our readers of the first two editions and hope that this new volume will be as well received.

A few comments are in order, about this book, and about the cigar scene as 1996 comes to an end:

About this book:
We have provided critical details on a lot of cigars. A total of 659 brands are profiled, comprising more than 5,000 different models; compare this with 457 brands in the 1996 edition or 370 brands in our first edition and you can see the kind of growth that the cigar industry has enjoyed.

Our listing represents virtually every brand marketed nationally, although the reader may find some brands which are not listed here, but which are available at his or her local tobacconist. These brands are very likely:

► Private label, unbranded cigars offered in bundles by major manufacturers, on which store names are placed for local sale;

► House brands produced for individual retailers, which are not generally available through wholesalers for national distribution to tobacco stores;

- ▸ Cigars produced in limited quantities by small, local factories and marketed regionally;

- ▸ New lines introduced after this book was completed;

- ▸ Close-outs or discontinued brands which are no longer available from manufacturers.

This should not dissuade readers from trying or enjoying these cigars. We actively encourage everyone to try new cigars and refrain from the kind of "cigar snobbery" which is so easy for premium cigar smokers to fall into. ***The best cigar you will ever smoke might be the next one you try.***

That's how I have discovered many of my favorite brands; I try to keep up with new products by buying one or two cigars of a new brand and note my reaction to it on a small index card. After a while, some of these "new" cigars become favorites that are integrated into the rotation of brands that I already like - an experience that would have been missed if the opportunity to try new brands was dismissed.

About the brands:
Cigar enthusiasts world-wide know about the shortage of many brands as demand has outstripped supplies. As regards our listings, this situation has had an important impact in many ways:

- ▸ There are a lot less "seconds" these days. Virtually any cigar which appears to be of reasonable quality upon manufacture is being sold as first-line goods. This does

INTRODUCTION

not mean that a box of your favorite brand includes second-quality cigars; most manufacturers of premium brands are as picky as ever about what goes in their boxes. But it does mean that private-labeled or bundled cigars sometimes give way to secondary brands marketed in boxes at a higher price than in the past. Is this wrong? Hardly. But if you're having a hard time finding your favorite "specials," now you know why.

▸ We have tried to list, for each premium brand, the country of origin of the wrapper, filler and binder. While we have received wonderful cooperation from the manufacturers and distributors, more than one executive has told us something like, "This is what we would like to use, but if we can't get it, we will blend in something else."

In most cases, this should *not* be of great concern. After all, most consumers buy specific cigars based on an expectation of taste and draw, not on the ingredients. And recent history shows that master blenders have little difficulty re-configuring their brands with different tobaccos to achieve the same taste and quality of construction.

The most outstanding example of this is the recent switch by Consolidated Cigar Corporation from Cameroon to Indonesian wrappers on some of their highest-profile brands, including such household names as H. Upmann, Montecruz and Royal Jamaica. Recognizing upcoming problems in procuring Cameroon leaf, Consolidated's master blenders were able to re-blend these brands and produce a virtually identical product without any delays in production and without so much as a murmur from the consumer, a brilliant achievement.

The old adage, "the proof of the pudding is in the tasting" applies equally to cigars. Those who actually smoke cigars (as opposed to those who "wear" them as a fashion accessory as seen in some high-profile cigar lounges) and enjoy them should be fully content whether the wrapper is Connecticut-seed or actually grown in Connecticut's Windsor Valley.

About the shapes:
The clear trend is toward cigars with larger and larger ring gauges. Where lonsdales were considered large cigars in years past, we now see robustos, churchills and double coronas as standard smokes for many. As the desire for more and more complex flavors grows, we will continue to see this trend expand.

Where smaller cigars are being introduced, however, they are still getting bigger . . . in length. The avalanche of new brands saw a bevy of long panatelas to go along with churchills, double coronas or giant cigars.

Another trend is toward shaped cigars, such as perfectos, torpedos and pyramids. Even wilder is the introduction of the "barber pole" or "candy cane" cigar which features a double wrapper for a striped effect. The standard brand in this style is the Hugo Cassar Diamond Mystique line from the Dominican Republic and Honduras, for which a whole series of shapes is available. A list of the brands which feature this style is listed in section 2.04, along with a list of brands which are artificially flavored.

INTRODUCTION

Cuban cigars:
Because of our concentration on cigars available in the U.S., listings of cigars produced in Cuba are not included. In response to many requests for this information, however, we have produced a companion volume, *Perelman's Pocket Cyclopedia of Havana Cigars,* available through your local tobacconist or by writing to us directly.

The future:
Although we have been careful to include as many brands as possible, the explosion of interest in cigars in the United States has led to the introduction of hundreds of new brands in the last few years. This trend will continue and many new brands will be coming into the market in 1997; these will be cataloged in our 1998 edition.

With our thanks:
This book could not have been produced without a tremendous amount of help from many people in and around the cigar industry. Representatives of most every manufacturer and distributor in the country endured many telephone calls requesting information, and virtually everyone we contacted was not only forthcoming, but enthusiastic about the project.

I would like to express special thanks to individuals whose efforts went far beyond the norm; without them, this book would not have been produced: Jules Abbosh, Brian Dewey, Alan Edwards, Mark Estrin, Dickson Farrington, John Geohagen, Dr. Steve Nathan, Ph.C., and his "wife," Liz Facchiano, Brad Part, Janelle Rosenfeld, Sherwin Seltzer and Brad Weinfeld. And the help of our in-house staff, notably Bruce Dworshak, Mitchel Sloan and Bruce Tenen, who made it possible to finish this effort.

INTRODUCTION

I hope that our readers will enjoy our work; if you have suggestions on how to make this book better, we would be pleased to hear from you; our address follows the Table of Contents.

We will also be pleased to meet our readers in person at our LE CIGAR NOIR festivals which we produce in cooperation with our friends at *Smoke* magazine. A schedule of our 1997 shows is included on page 14. I hope to see you in a smoke-filled room soon!

RICHARD B. PERELMAN
Los Angeles, California
November 1996

1.
CIGAR BASICS

1.01 ABOUT CIGARS

The joy of smoking rolled tobacco leaves began in the Americas hundreds of years ago and was introduced to Europeans after Christopher Columbus' return from his first voyage in 1492.

In the ensuing years, the popularity and sophistication of tobacco products has grown and the 1990s has brought a significant increase in the popularity of cigars in the United States. Despite much controversy, the status of cigars as a luxury product in American culture is secure.

The important technical elements to be appreciated in cigars include their construction and the many shapes and sizes.

1.02 CONSTRUCTION

What goes into cigars? The answer to this question is the key to assessing the quality of a specific cigar. All but the thinnest cigars include three elements: (1) the filler tobacco at the center, (2) a binder leaf which holds the filler together and (3) the outer wrapper, which is rolled around the binder.

Cigars which are made by hand use "long filler" tobacco: leaves which run the length of a cigar. In a handmade, the filler, binder and wrapper are combined manually to create a cigar.

Machine-made cigars utilize high-speed machinery to combine "short filler" tobacco - usually scraps or pieces of tobacco - with a binder and wrapper. Because of the

CIGAR BASICS

tension placed on the tobacco by the machines, the binders and wrappers are usually made of a homogenized tobacco product which is stronger than natural leaves and can be produced in a variety of flavors, strengths and textures.

A few brands combine machine-bunching (using long-filler tobacco) with hand-rolled wrappers; this practice has been very properly dubbed "hand-rolled" as opposed to handmade by cigar expert Rick Hacker in *The Ultimate Cigar Book*. And some larger cigars use "mixed" or "combination" filler of long-filler and short-filler tobaccos.

The most obvious characteristic of most cigars is the color of the exterior wrapper. While not the only factor in the taste of a cigar, it is an important element and a key in many people's purchase of specific cigars. Although manufacturers have identified more than 100 different wrapper shades, six major color classifications are used herein, as noted below:

Color	Abbrev.	Description
Double Claro	"DC"	Also known as "American Market Selection" [AMS] or "Candela," this is a green wrapper. Once popular, it is rarely found today.
Claro	"Cl"	This is a very light tan color, almost beige in shade; usually from Connecticut.
Colorado Claro	"CC"	A medium brown found on many cigars, this category covers many descriptions. The most popular are "Natural" or "English Market Selection."[EMS] Tobaccos in this shade are grown in many countries.
Colorado	"Co"	This shade is instantly recognizable by the obvious reddish tint.

CIGAR BASICS

Color	Abbrev.	Description
Colorado Maduro	"CM"	Darker than Colorado Claro in shade, this color is often associated with African tobacco, such as wrappers from Cameroon, or with Havana Seed tobacco grown in Honduras.
Maduro	"Ma"	Very dark brown or black; this category also includes the deep black "Oscuro" shade. Tobacco for Maduro wrappers is grown in Connecticut, Mexico, Nicaragua and Brazil.

The listing of cigar brands in this book assumes that, unless otherwise noted, handmade cigars utilize long-filler tobacco and machine-made cigars use short-filler.

1.03 SHAPES AND SIZES

There are cigars of every shape and every size for every occasion. From tiny, cigarette-like cigarillos to giant monsters resembling pool cues, there is a wide variety to choose from.

Certain sizes and shapes which have gained popularity over the years and have become widely recognized, even by non-smokers. Cigar shape names such as "corona" or "panatela" have specific meanings to the cigar industry, although there is no formally agreed-to standard for any given size.

The following table lists 19 well-known shapes, and is adapted from Paul Garmirian's explanation of sizes in *The Gourmet Guide to Cigars.* The "classical" measurements for which this shape is known are given, along with a size and girth range for each size for classification purposes:

Shape	*Classical Lngth. x Ring*	*Length range*	*Ring range*
Giant	9 x 52	8 & up	50 & up
Double Corona	7¾ x 49	6¾-7¾	49-54
Churchill	7 x 47	6¾-7⅞	46-48
Pyramid	7 x 36⇒54	all	flared
Torpedo	6½ x 52	all	tapered
Toro	6 x 50	5⅝-6⅝	48-54
Robusto	5 x 50	4½-5½	48-54
Grand Corona	6½ x 46	5⅝-6⅝	45-47
Corona Extra	5½ x 46	4½-5½	45-47
Giant Corona	7½ x 44	7½ & up	42-45
Lonsdale	6½ x 42	6½-7¼	40-44
Long Corona	6 x 42	5⅞-6⅜	40-44
Corona	5½ x 42	5¼-5¾	40-44
Petit Corona	5 x 42	4-5	40-44
Long Panatela	7½ x 38	7 & up	35-39
Panatela	6 x 38	5½-6⅞	35-39
Short Panatela	5 x 38	4-5⅜	35-39
Slim Panatela	6 x 34	5 & up	30-34
Small Panetela	5 x 33	4-5	30-34
Cigarillos	4 x 26	6 & less	29 & less

For the purposes of classification, the cigar models of the 659 brands profiled have been separated into these 19 major groups. Other shapes worth noting include:

- Culebras, which is made up of three small cigars twisted together. Hoyo de Monterrey is the only brand offering this shape on the U.S. market today.

▶ Perfecto, which has two tapered ends. Until recently, there were just a few cigars which offered Perfecto "tips" on the foot, but true Perfectos are making a comeback. Check out the Arturo Fuente Hemingway Series or the Ashton Vintage Cabinet Selection nos. 10, 20 and 30 for modern-day examples. For the bold, take a look at the Cuba Aliados Diademas (7½ inches long by 60 ring) to see a true "pot-bellied" cigar.

▶ Torpedo, which was traditionally a fat cigar with two fully closed, pointed ends, but has now come to mean a cigar with an open foot and a straight body which tapers to a closed, pointed head. This "new" torpedo was popularized by the Montecristo (Havana) No. 2.

The Torpedo differs from "Pyramid"-shaped cigars, which flare continuously from the head to the foot, essentially forming a triangle.

Like the Torpedo, whose meaning has changed over time, the Royal Corona or Rothschild title is seen less and less on cigars now known as "Robustos." This change has been rapid over the past 4-5 years, but some manufacturers still label their shorter, thicker cigars as Rothschilds or even as a "Rothchild" (an incorrect spelling of the famous German banking family name).

Many other shape names are used by manufacturers; some cigars even have multiple names. For the sake of convenience, the many types of small, very thin cigars are grouped under the "Cigarillo" title rather than distributed over a long list of names such as "Belvederes," "Demi-Tasse" and others.

CIGAR BASICS

1.04   ENJOYING CIGARS

The enjoyment of cigars is a personal pleasure, which is as varied as the 659 brands profiled. However, there are certain matters which should be considered carefully by all smokers and which require attention.

- ▸ Foremost among these is storage and the usefulness of a humidor in proper working condition cannot be underestimated. The death of a quality cigar due to a lack of care is a sad occurrence indeed.

- ▸ For those carrying cigars on the go, travel humidors or leather cigar cases are important items to keep your cigars safe and in good smoking condition.

- ▸ Finally, the proper tools for cutting and lighting your cigar are necessary accessories for full enjoyment.

Other authors have written extensively on these topics and references to leading books on cigars are listed in section 9. Each offers many suggestions on how to enjoy and store cigars and many details about the history and manufacture of cigars.

In addition, an important but often under-utilized resource for the cigar smoker is the many outstanding local tobacco shops and cigar dealers in their area. These merchants are experienced, knowledgeable and can get answers to questions from a national selection of experts, manufacturers and the Retail Tobacco Dealers of America trade association. Use their expertise to help you!

SMOKE PRESENTS

LE CIGAR NOIR

4 GREAT CITIES, 4 FABULOUS EVENTS!

A UNIQUE EXPERIENCE OF PLEASURES AND PASSIONS

- CHICAGO, ILLINOIS
  DECEMBER 3, 1996
- NEW ORLEANS, LOUISIANA
  FEBRUARY 26, 1997
- BEVERLY HILLS, CALIFORNIA
  APRIL 30, 1997
- THE HAMPTONS, NEW YORK
  SUMMER, 1997

❈ More than a dozen brands of premium hand-made cigars in your own travel case
❈ Four glorious courses of food ❈ Premium wines and spirits
❈ One-on-one talk with cigar manufacturers and marketers ❈ Live entertainment

Attendance is limited for your enjoyment.

Admission: US$ 129 per person 30 days prior to event; $145 thereafter.
For tickets, please call (213) 965-4905

2.
THE CIGAR ALMANAC

Here are facts, figures and a little fun about the 659 brands (493 handmades, 115 mass-market and 51 small cigars) profiled in this year's edition:

2.01   BIRTHS AND DEATHS

The cigar renaissance has led to an explosion of 170 new handmade brands introduced since our 1996 edition, contrasted with 56 new handmades listed in last year's Cyclopedia:

Handmade (170):

Abreu Anillo de Oro
Al-Capone
Alta Gracia
Anillo de Oro
AZ
Ballena Suprema
Big Butt
Blair
C.A.O. Gold
Caonabo
Capote
Cara Mia
Carbonell
Casa Blanca Reserve
Casa Buena
Cerdan
Chairman's Choice
Charles the Great
Cifuentes
Cleopatra
Cojimar
Coloniales
Conucos
Creston Prestige Cuvee
Crispin Patino
Cristal de Leon
Cubana La Tradicion Cabinet

Cusano Hermanos
Cusano Romani
Da Vinci
Daniel Marshall Sigature Series
Defiant
Diamond Crown
Dominican Specials
Domino Park
Don Alberto
Don Armando
Don Barco
Don Fife
Don Leo
Don Manolo
Don Melo Centenario
Don Quijote
Don Rene de Cuba
Don Salvador
Don Tito
Don Tonioli
Don Tuto Habanos
Don Vito
Don Xavier
Don Yanes
Doña Elba
El Incomparable
El Sabinar

El Tigre
El Unicornio
El Valle
Escudo Cubano
Espanola
Estrella Fina
Evelio
Excelsior
F.D. Grave
Fat Cat
Flor Cubana
Flor de Cuba
Flor de Farach
Flor de Filipinas
Flor de Florez Cabinet Selection
Flor de Gonzalez
Flor de Honduras
Franco
Free Cuba
Garcia y Vega
Garo
Gilberto Oliva
Gispert
Grand Nica
H. Upmann Chairman's Reserve
Habana Gold Sterling Vintage
Hamiltons
Hamiltons Reserve
Harriel's Dream
Havana
Havana Cool
Havana Sunrise
Hugo Cassar Diamond Mystique
Hugo Cassar Diamond Mystique
Hugo Cassar Private Collection
Hugo Cassar Private Collection
Hugo Signature Series
Imperio Cubano
Indian
Island Amaretto
J. Cortes
Jose Marti
Jose Marti Vitola Series

Joya de Honduras
Juan y Ramon
La Diva
La Gianna
La Habanera
La Herencia Cubana
La Maximiliana
La Pantera Diamond Collection
La Pantera Sapphire Collection
La Primera
La Real
La Regional
La Tradicion Cubana
Legend • Ario
Leon
Lew's Smokers
Madrigal Habana
Maxius
Milano Santana
Montes de Oca
Morro Castle
Napa
Napa Reserve
Nat Sherman LSN Selection
Nat Sherman Metropolitan
Selection
Nestor 747 Series II
Opus X
Oro Negro
Orosi
Papayo
Petrus Etiquette Rouge
Pheasant
Pinnacle
Playboy by Don Diego
Por Matamor
Porfirio
Private Selection
Profesor Sila
Regalos
Ricos Dominicanos
Robali
Romanticos

Rosa Cuba
Royal Barbados
Royal Honduras
Rubirosa
Sabana
Sabor Habano
Saint Luis Rey
San Marcos
Siglo 21
Signet
660 Red
Sol y Mar
St. Tropez
Suave
Tabacos San Jose
Tabacos Universo

Tabantillas
Tamboril
Todo El Mundo
Tooth of the Dog
Topper Grande
Torcedor
V.M. Santana Collection
Vargas
Victor Sinclair
Victory Spirit
Villar y Villar
Villega Reales
West Indies Vanilla
Yumuri
Yumuri 1492

Mass-market (4):
Balmoral
Garcia Grande

La Paz
Travis Club Premium

The following brands have either been discontinued or are
not currently in production for national sale:

Handmade (39):
American Eagle
Caramba
Casa Mayan
Caz-Bar
CCI Gold Silk
Cibao
Cienfuego
Competere
Connisseur Silver Label
Craftman's Bench
Cuban Twist
Czar
Dominican Republic
Don Pishu
Don Rex
Don Rubio
El Beso

Executor
Flor del Caribe
Flor de Orlando
Habanos Hatuey
Hoja de Regal
Honduran Import Maduro
Jamaican Kings
Jamaican Supreme
J.P.B. Crown
Julia Marlowe
La Cohoba
La Corona Vintage
H.A. Ladrillo
La Llorona
Mocha Supreme
Nat Cicco's Supremos
 Dominicanos

Oro
Oro de Cuba
Peñamil

Topper's Handmade
Torquino
Voyager

Mass market (4):
Brazil
Celestino Vega

Sam Houston Special
San Christobal

2.02 BRAND FACTS

Here are some entertaining facts about cigar brands and where they are produced:

Ancient brands:
Some brands have been with us since the early part of the 19th Century, originating primarily in Cuba. Some of the older brand names still being produced for the U.S. market, with their original country of origin, include:

1810 Cabanas (Cuba)
1834 Por Larranaga (Cuba)
1837 Ramon Allones (Cuba)
1840 Bances (Cuba)
1840 Marsh Wheeling (USA)
1840 Punch (Cuba)
1844 H. Upmann (Cuba)
1845 La Corona (Cuba)
1845 Partagas (Cuba)
1848 El Rey del Mundo (Cuba)
1850 Romeo y Julieta (Cuba)
1867 Hoyo de Monterrey (Cuba)
1868 Bauza (Cuba)
1868 Macanudo (Jamaica)
1871 Baccarat (USA)
1873 Dannemann (Brazil)
1876 Temple Hall (Jamaica)
1881 Calixto Lopez (Cuba)
1882 Garcia y Vega (USA)

1884 Cuesta-Rey (USA)
1884 Judge's Cave (USA)
1887 White Owl (USA)
1888 Villiger (Germany)
1891 Fonseca (Cuba)
1896 Topper (USA)
1901 Bolivar (Cuba)
1903 Leon Jimenes (Dom. Rep.)
1903 Topstone (USA)
1905 Bering (USA)
1912 Arturo Fuente (USA)
1912 Muniemaker (USA)
1916 El Producto (USA)
1928 Rafael Gonzalez (Cuba)
1935 Montecristo (Cuba)
1946 Davidoff Chateau series
        of Hoyo de Monterrey
        (Cuba)
1959 Montecruz (Canary Islands)

Bands on brands:
It is well established that in 1850, Gustave Bock of the

Netherlands put bands on cigars for the first time, as a method of distinguishing his firm's Cuban-made cigars.

Brand production:
The Dominican Republic and Honduras dominate the production origin statistics of the 493 handmade brands profiled, but production is up everywhere.

Some 33.7 percent of the handmades come from the Dominican Republic, with another 31.6 percent from Honduras. But in comparison with statistics in the 1996 edition, the number of Dominican-produced brands increased from 113½ to 166 (46% increase!), while Honduran brands increased from 105 to 155⅔ (up 48%!).

A revival of cigar-making interest in the United States places the USA into third place with 44½ brands (nine percent), a stunning 102% increase in brand production.

A similar, remarkable increase is also noted for Nicaragua, up to nearly 43 brands from 17½ last year and for the Canary Islands, up to 16 now vs. eight last year.

In classifying the origin of each brand, fractional attributions were made for cigars that are produced in more than one country (example: Padron cigars are made in both Honduras and Nicaragua). The statistics by group and country:

Country	Handmade Cigars	Mass-market	Small Cigars	Total
Barbados	1			1
Belgium		1	3	4
Brazil	4	⅓	2	6⅓

Country	Handmade Cigars	Mass-market	Small Cigars	Total
Costa Rica	5			5
Denmark			2½	2½
Dominican Republic	166	1		167
Germany	1	3	6	10
Great Britain			1	1
Guatemala	1			1
Honduras	155⅔			155⅔
Indonesia	2		1	3
Ireland			1	1
Jamaica	14½			14½
Mexico	22½			22½
Netherlands		6⅓	3½	9 $\frac{5}{6}$
Nicaragua	42 $\frac{5}{6}$			42 $\frac{5}{6}$
Panama	4			4
Philippines	8			8
Spain:			1	1
. Canary Islands	16		1	17
Switzerland		⅓	2	2⅓
United States	44½	94	25	163½
. Puerto Rico	1	9	2	12
Venezuela	4			4

2.03   CIGARS: LARGE AND SMALL

Length:
The longest cigars? Here are the longest shapes:

18 inches	(x 66 ring)	Cuba Aliados General
18	(x 66)	Puros Indios Chief
14¼	(x 60)	Tabacalera Gigantes

13¾	(x 49)	Mexican Emperador
13	(x 50)	Juan Clemente Gargantua
10 inches		Cigars of this length are offered by Carbonell, Casa Blanca, Cuba Aliados, Dominican Original, King, Puros Indios, Royal Jamaica and Tabantillas.

The shortest? Cigarillos of just under three inches in length are offered by:

2¾	Al-Capone		2⅞	Dannemann
2¾	Villiger		2⅞	Henri Winterman
2⅞	Agio		2⅞	Panter

Ring gauge:
The fattest of the fat? Remembering that ring gauge is measured in 64ths of the inch, there are 17 in-production cigars of an inch (64/64) or more in diameter:

68 ring	(x 8 inches)	Carbonell Piramide Gigante
66	(x 18)	Cuba Aliados General
66	(x 18)	Puros Indios Chief
66	(x 10)	Casa Blanca Jeroboam
66	(x 10)	Dominican Original Fat Tub
66	(x 10)	King No. 9
66	(x 7¼)	Don Tito Piramides
66	(x 5)	Casa Blanca Half Jeroboam
66	(x 5)	Dominican Original Gorilla
66	(x 5)	King No. 13
64	(x 9½)	Ornelas 250 mm
64	(x 9)	Royal Jamaica Goliath
64	(x 7½)	Carbonell Piramide
64	(x 7½)	Charles Fairmorn Belmore Piramide
64	(x 7½)	Don Tonioli Epicure Super Torpedo
64	(x 7¼)	Moore & Bode Full Brass
64	(x 7)	Sosa Piramide No. 2

The thinnest? There are a number of brands of small cigars which match the ring gauge of cigarettes, at 20 ring.

Shapes:

The leading brands by the number of shapes offered under one brand name:

47	Nat Sherman	27	Punch
35	Don Alberto	27	Rosalones
31	H. Upmann	25	Te-Amo
31	Partagas	24	Arturo Fuente
29	El Rey del Mundo	23	Montecruz
28	Honduras Cuban Tobaccos	23	Ornelas
27	Flor de Nicaragua		

2.04 CIGARS: SPECIAL MODELS

Two new fashions in cigars today are flavored cigars and special double-wrapped cigars which emulate barber poles. A census of these brands:

Handmade brands with flavored shapes:	*Flavoring*
Arango Statesman	Vanilla
Baccarat Havana	Sugar cap
Camorra Limited Reserve	Sugar cap
Creston Prestige Cuvee	Sugar cap
Don Pablo Cigar Co.	Brandy, Cognac, Rum or Sweet
El Incomparable	Scotch
El Sublimado	Cognac
Famous Rum Runner	Rum
Island Amaretto	Amaretto
John T's	Amaretto, Cherry Cream, Capuccino or Cafe Ole
La Diva	Cognac
Las Favoritas	Vanilla
Las Vegas Cigar Co.	Rum or Sweet
Lew's Smokers	Sugar cap
Ornelas LTD al Cognac	Cognac
Ornelas Matinee Vanilla	Vanilla
Ornelas Vanilla	Vanilla
Suerdieck (cigarillos)	Cherry, Clove
West Indies Vanilla	Vanilla

Machine-made brands with flavored shapes:	*Flavoring*
Arango Sportsman	Vanilla
Garcia y Vega Whiffs	Pipe tobacco
Hav-A-Tampa	Menthol, Pipe tobacco, Sweet

Muriel	Cherry, Menthol, Pipe Aroma, Pipe tobacco, Sweet
Nat Cicco's	Almond Liquer, Cuban Cafe, Plaza Aromatic
Phillies	Sweet
Ruy Lopez Vanilla Surprise	Vanilla
Sierra Sweet	Sweet
Swisher Sweets	Sweet
Tampa Nugget	Sweet
Tampa Resagos	Sweet
White Owl	Sweet
William Penn	Sweet
Wolf Bros.	Rum, Vanilla

Three brands – Black & Mild, Cherry Blend and Gold & Mild – are dedicated to the use of pipe tobacco fillers.

Please note that many brands of small cigars have one or more models which have flavoring of one type or another:

Agio	Omega
Alamo	Pedroni
Al-Capone	Prince Albert
Alternativos	Rustlers
Avanti	St. Regis
Backwoods	Super Value
Captain Black	Supre Sweets
Charles Fairmorn	Tijuana Smalls
Dannemann	Tiparillo
Dutch Treats	The Tobacconist Choice
Erik	Winchester Little Cigars

Brands with "barber pole"-wrapped models include:

Brand	Model
AZ	Bolero
Don Alberto Royal Series	4 models
Hugo Cassar Diamond Dominican Mystique	5 models
Hugo Cassar Diamond Honduran Mystique	4 models
Oliveros	Dos Perez
Santa Clara	Fiesta

2.05   OUR FAVORITE BRANDS

Here are some of our favorite brands, primarily from the marketing perspective of interesting names of brands and shapes.

Themed brands:
The production of cigars is a serious business, but some manufacturers take a light-hearted - or at least a themed - approach to naming their shapes:

Brand	Theme
Black Label	9 Mexican cities
Cacique	7 American Indian tribes
Camorra Limited Reserve	7 Italian cities
Charles the Great	6 Spanish cities
Chevere	5 Jamaican cities
Double Happiness	5 states of high happiness
El Triunfo	7 American Indian tribes
Famous Rum Runner	3 pirate characters
Jamaica Gold	7 court characters
La Fontana	8 Italian artists and scientists
Las Cabrillas	9 New World explorers
Match Play	6 famous golf courses
Nat Sherman Landmarks	5 famous New York landmarks
Nat Sherman Manhattan	5 famous New York neighborhoods
Nat Sherman VIPs	6 famous New Yorkers
New York, New York	6 famous New York streets/sites
Pleiades	12 constellations and planets
Romanticos	6 great lovers and love-gods
Royal Honduras	8 royal court characters
Tiburon	3 types of sharks

Fun shape names:
Check out these names in the brand listings, compiled alphabetically for your amusement by our Associate Editor, Bruce Tenen:

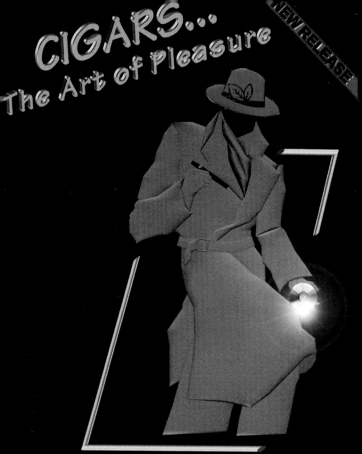

CIGARS...
The Art of Pleasure

NEW RELEASE

An Interactive CD-ROM Plus Experience

Complete With

Perelman's Cyclopedia of Cigars
Including Havanos

Call us at 1-800-265-1812

Shape name	(Translation)	Brand
Besos	("kisses")	Astral
Black Magic		Rigoletto
Bolero		AZ
Buccaneers		Mario Palomino
Capo		Don Vito
Capuccino		John T's
Charlemagne		La Gloria Cubana
Ecstacy		Double Happiness
Farouk Gigante		Creston Prestige Cuvee
Fancytale		Special Jamaicans
Fat Tub		Dominican Original
Goliath		Royal Jamaica
Insurrectos		La Flor Dominicana
Jeroboam		Casa Blanca
John McKay Super Rothschilds		Bustillo
King Kong		Dominican Original
Luchadore	("the wrestler")	Danlys
Monalisa		Da Vinci
No. 10 Downing Street		Royal Jamaica
Playboy		Rubirosa
Pythagoras		Credo
Rocket		El Valle
Rooster Arturo		Fighting Cock
Rough Rider		Rico Havana
Smokin' Lulu		Fighting Cock
Teepee		Indian
Tiger Shark		Tiburon
Victor No. 1		La Plata
Yumbo		Tesoros de Copan
Zorro		Hamiltons Reserve

2.06   THE CIGAR BOWL

Of course there was a college football bowl game named for cigars! The Cigar Bowl was played in the hotbed of U.S. cigar-making: Tampa, Florida, from 1947-54, between college-division teams. The scores:

I	1947	(Jan. 1)	Delaware 21, Rollins 7	(attendance 7,500)
II	1948	(Jan. 1)	Missouri Valley 26, West Chester 7	(10,000)
III	1949	(Jan. 1)	Missouri Valley 13, St. Thomas (Mn) 13	(11,000)
IV	1950	(Jan. 2)	Florida State 19, Wofford 6	(14,000)

V	1951	(Jan. 1)	Wisconsin-La Crosse 47, Valparaiso 14	(12,000)
VI	1951	(Dec. 29)	Brooke Army Medical 20, Camp LeJeune Marines 0	(7,500)
VII	1952	(Dec. 13)	Tampa 21, Lenoir-Rhyne 12	(7,500)
VIII	1954	(Jan. 1)	Missouri Valley 12, Wisconsin-LaCrosse 12	(5,000)
IX	1954	(Dec.)	Tampa 21, Morris Harvey 0	(unknown)

How about a bowl game in Havana? Absolutely! On January 1, 1937, Auburn and Villanova played to a 7-7 tie in the first and only "Bacardi Bowl," held before 12,000 spectators as a part of the Cuban National Sports Festival.

College football has also celebrated the leaf with the Smoke Bowl in 1941 (Norfolk All-Stars 16, Richmond All-Stars 2 at Richmond, Virginia) and the Tobacco Bowl in 1946 (Muhlenberg 26, St. Bonaventure 25 at Lexington, Kentucky).

JUAN
CLEMENTE

Cigar Legends: Juan Clemente

"Tobacco is my passion," smiles Jean Clement, who is better known in the cigar world as Juan Clemente.

A successful career in the merchandising of spirits and jewelry led Clement to the Dominican Republic in 1975. There he saw the La Aurora factory and fell in love with the idea of cigars as a way to express his own desires for quality in a field, which, outside of Cuba, was enjoying too little passion at the time.

In addition to his jewelry trade, he also began distributing cigars in the Caribbean area. But within a year, he began to dream of his own line, which would meet his own standards for consistency and taste.

By 1981, he had dropped his other interests and worked exclusively on creating the blend for a Juan Clemente cigar, which debuted in 1982 with distribution in France and Switzerland. Why the "Spanish-ization" of his name? The practical reply: "It's more reliable for cigars to have a Spanish-sounding name."

By 1986, the success of the brand resulted in the establishment of his own factory in Villa Gonzales, Dominican Republic. Now, he was free to set his own standards for excellence – and meet them. "I'm never satisfied completely, but we have reached a consistent level of quality," he notes with pride.

Even his trademark band on the foot of the cigar is about perfection: "We protect the fragile end, so that even when buying a single cigar, the wrapper does not split." Whether it is a Juan Clemente Classic cigar, or a model from the Club Selection which debuted in 1992, you know that it will be the best that passion can bring.

Big cigars:
Double Coronas and Giants

These are very large cigars, in fact, some of the largest available. The dimensions of these shapes include:

- Double Corona   6¾-7¾ inches long; 49-54 ring.

- Giant   8 inches and more; 50 ring and more.

Pictured opposite are:

▸ King No. 9	10 x 66	Giant
▸ Padron Magnum	9 x 50	Giant
▸ Don Tomas Gigantes	8½ x 52	Giant
▸ Punch Presidents	8½ x 52	Giant

The King No. 9's ring gauge of 66 is the largest you can buy in a regular-production, straight-sided cigar which is marketed in the United States. Also worth noting are the marvelous Maduro-shade wrappers on the Padron, Don Tomas and Punch cigars.

3.
HANDMADE CIGARS:
INDEX

Here are 493 handmade brands in a compact index to country of origin, body and shapes.

For each brand, a two-letter code designates the country of manufacture and a one-digit code indicates the strength of the brand:

Country of Origin
Ba Barbados
Be Belgium
Br Brazil
CI Canary Islands
CR Costa Rica
DR Dominican Republic
Ge Germany
Gu Guatemala
Ho Honduras
In Indonesia
Ja Jamaica
Mx Mexico
Ni Nicaragua
Pa Panama
Ph Philippines
US United States
Ve Venezuela

Strength
1 Mild
2 Mild to medium
3 Medium
4 Medium to full
5 Full

In addition, each line lists the shape "groups" in which the brand is produced. The 19 standard shapes listed in section 1.03 are broken into ten groups, including:

HANDMADE CIGARS: INDEX

The widest range? Only six brands had models in *all* ten shape groups:

- Davidoff   (Dominican Republic)
- El Rey del Mundo   (Honduras)
- Hoyo de Monterrey   (Honduras)
- La Gloria Cubana   (United States)
- Macanudo   (Jamaica & Dominican Republic)
- Punch   (Honduras)

Additional, detailed information about each of these brands is available in the following section, offering brand listings.

HANDMADE CIGARS: INDEX

Brand	Made in	Strength	Cigarillo	Panatela	Corona	Lonsdale	Grand Corona	Figurado	Robusto-Toro	Churchill	Double Corona	Giant
Abreu Anillo de Oro	DR	3	●	●		●	●		●			●
Adante	DR	1		●	●	●						
Aguila	DR	3			●	●	●		●		●	
Al-Capone	Ni	5			●				●			
Alhambra	Ph	1		●	●				●			●
Alta Gracia	US	4			●			●	●		●	
Alvaro	CI	1		●	●							
Andujar	DR	5	●	●		●			●		●	●
Anillo de Oro	DR	2		●	●	●	●					●
Antelo	US	1-5	●	●	●	●	●			●	●	
Arango Statesman	Ho	3			●					●		
Aromas de San Andres	Mx	3			●	●			●		●	
Arturo Fuente	DR	3-5		●		●	●		●	●	●	●
Ashton	DR	2		●	●	●	●	●	●	●	●	●
Astral	Ho	3				●			●	●	●	
Avo	DR	1		●	●	●	●	●	●	●	●	
AZ	Mx	5		●	●				●		●	
Babalu	US	2	●	●	●				●	●		●
Baccarat Havana	Ho	1		●	●	●		●	●		●	
Bahia	CR	4			●		●		●	●		●
Balboa	Pa	5		●	●	●				●		●

Brand	Made in	Strength	Cigarillo	Panatela	Corona	Lonsdale	Grand Corona	Figurado	Robusto-Toro	Churchill	Double Corona	Giant
Ballena Suprema	Ho Mx	3 4				● ●		●	● ●	● ●	 ●	●
Bances	Ho	4		●	●	●				●		●
Bauza	DR	4		●	●	●			●	●	●	
Belinda	Ho	4		●	●		●		●	●	●	
Bering	Ho	5		●	●	●	●	●	●			●
Beverly Hills-VIP	Ho	1		●	●				●		●	●
Big Butt	Ni	4							●		●	
Black Label	Mx	5	●	●			●		●		●	●
Blair	Ho	5				●			●	●		●
Blue Label	Ho	2	●	●	●				●	●	●	●
Blue Ribbon	Ni	3			●	●			●		●	
Boquilla	US	4	●	●	●			●	●	●	●	●
Bustillo	US	3,5							●			
Butera Royal Vint.	DR	3	●	●	●				●	●		
Caballeros	DR	2			●				●	●	●	
Cabanas	DR	1			●	●	●		●			
Cacique	DR	1	●	●	●				●	●	●	
Calixto Lopez	Ph	1	●	●	●	●			●			●
Calle Ocho	US	1	●			●		●	●	●	●	●
Camacho	Ho	5	●	●					●	●	●	●
Cammarata	US	3,5			●		●	●	●	●		
Camorra Imported Limited Reserve	Ho	3	●	●	●			●	●	●		

HANDMADE CIGARS: INDEX

Brand	Made in	Strength	Cigarillo	Panatela	Corona	Lonsdale	Grand Corona	Figurado	Robusto-Toro	Churchill	Double Corona	Giant
Canaria d'Oro	DR	4		●	●	●			●			
Canonero	Br	1		●	●	●			●	●	●	
C.A.O.	Ho	3			●	●		●	●			●
C.A.O. Gold	Ho	2			●				●	●	●	
Caoba	DR	2		●	●					●	●	
Caonabo	DR	2		●	●				●			
Capote	Cl	3		●		●			●		●	
Cara Mia	Cl	3		●				●	●		●	
Carbonell	DR	1	●	●	●			●	●	●	●	●
Carlin	DR	5		●					●	●		●
Carlos Torano	DR	1		●	●	●	●		●	●	●	
Carmen	Ho	3		●					●	●	●	
Carrington	DR	2		●	●			●	●	●	●	
Casa Blanca	DR	1		●	●	●			●		●	●
Casa Blanca Reserve	DR	1			●	●			●		●	
Casa Buena	Cl	3				●			●		●	
Casa de Nicaragua	Ni	4		●	●	●			●		●	●
Casa Martin	Cl	2			●	●			●	●		
Casanova	Cl	3			●	●		●	●	●	●	
Casillas	US	4	●	●			●	●	●	●	●	●
CCI Royal Satin	Ho	3			●			●	●	●	●	
Cedar Joe	Ho	2				●		●	●	●		●

HANDMADE CIGARS: INDEX

Brand	Made in	Strength	Cigarillo	Panatela	Corona	Lonsdale	Grand Corona	Figurado	Robusto-Toro	Churchill	Double Corona	Giant
Cedros	DR	1			●				●	●		
Celestino Vega	In	1	●	●	●	●		●	●	●	●	
Cerdan	DR	2	●	●	●	●			●		●	
Cervantes	Ho	3			●	●	●					
Chairman's Choice	Ho	3			●			●	●	●	●	
Charles Fairmorn	Ho	4		●	●						●	
Charles Fairmorn Belmore	DR	3		●		●		●	●	●	●	
Charles the Great	Ho	3			●		●		●		●	
Chavelo	US	3		●		●			●	●	●	
Chevere	Ja	2			●	●	●				●	●
Cifuentes	DR	3		●		●		●	●		●	
Clementine	Ho	5		●	●	●			●		●	●
Cleopatra	DR	2						●				
Cohiba	DR	5				●			●		●	
Cojimar	US	3		●		●		●	●			●
Coloniales	Ho	3			●	●	●		●		●	
Colorado	Ho	3				●		●	●		●	
Condal	CI	1		●	●	●			●	●	●	
Connisseur Gold	Ho	3		●	●	●			●	●	●	●
Conucos	DR	1			●				●			
Costa Dorada	DR	3			●	●			●	●		●
Credo	DR	3		●	●				●	●	●	

HANDMADE CIGARS: INDEX

Brand	Made in	Strength	Cigarillo	Panatela	Corona	Lonsdale	Grand Corona	Figurado	Robusto-Toro	Churchill	Double Corona	Giant
Creston Prestige Cuvee	Ho	3,4		●	●	●		●	●	●		●
Crispin Patiño	Ve	1	●	●		●						
Cristal de Leon	Ho	2,3			●							
Cruz Real	Mx	2		●	●	●			●		●	●
Cuba Aliados	Ho	3		●	●	●	●	●	●	●	●	●
Cubana La Tradicion	US	3		●	●			●	●		●	
Cuban Cigar Factory	US	1,4		●	●	●	●	●	●		●	
Cubita	DR	4		●	●	●			●		●	
Cuesta-Rey	DR	2,3		●	●	●			●	●	●	●
Cusano Hermanos	DR	5							●	●		
Cusano Romani	DR	5						●				
D. Marshall Signature	DR	4							●	●		
D. Marshall Signature	Ho	4		●					●		●	
Danlys	Ho	4		●	●	●			●		●	
Davidoff	DR	1,3	●	●	●	●	●	●	●	●	●	●
Da Vinci	Ho	2			●				●	●	●	●
Defiant	Ho	4		●				●	●		●	
Diamond Crown	DR	1							●		●	●
Diana Silvius	DR	3				●			●	●	●	
Domingold	DR	3			●				●		●	

HANDMADE CIGARS: INDEX

Brand	Made in	Strength	Cigarillo	Panatela	Corona	Lonsdale	Grand Corona	Figurado	Robusto-Toro	Churchill	Double Corona	Giant
Dominican Original	DR	3		•	•	•		•	•	•	•	•
Dominicana Superba	DR	1			•	•			•		•	•
Dominican Estates	DR	1			•	•			•		•	
Dominican Specials	DR	1			•	•			•		•	
Dominico	DR	2			•	•		•	•	•		•
Dominique	DR	1			•	•	•		•		•	•
Domino Park	US	3				•			•		•	•
Doña Elba	Ni	5							•	•		
Don Alberto	DR	2,3		•	•	•	•	•	•			•
Don Antonio	Ge	2,3	•	•								
Don Armando	Ho	3			•		•		•		•	•
Don Asa	Ho	4			•	•	•		•		•	
Don Barco	DR	3							•	•	•	
Don Diego	DR	1	•	•	•	•			•	•		
Don Esteban	DR	3			•	•			•		•	•
Don Fife	Ho	2		•	•				•	•		
Don Jose	Ho	3			•				•		•	•
Don Juan	Ni	3		•	•	•			•		•	•
Don Julio	DR	1			•	•			•			•
Don Leo	DR	2			•	•			•		•	
Don Lino	Ho	2		•	•	•	•	•	•		•	•
Don Manolo Coll.	DR	2,3			•		•	•	•		•	

HANDMADE CIGARS: INDEX

Brand	Made in	Strength	Cigarillo	Panatela	Corona	Lonsdale	Grand Corona	Figurado	Robusto-Toro	Churchill	Double Corona	Giant
Don Marcos	DR	2		•	•	•		•	•	•		
Don Mariano	DR	3		•	•	•			•	•	•	
Don Mateo	Ho	3		•	•	•			•	•	•	•
Don Melo	Ho	4			•		•		•		•	•
Don Melo Centenario	Ho	3			•				•		•	
Don Pablo	US	2		•	•	•		•	•	•	•	•
Don Pepe	Br	1		•	•				•	•	•	
Don Quijote	Ve	3		•	•		•					
Don Rene de Cuba	US	5		•	•	•		•	•		•	•
Don Salvador	Ni	4		•	•				•		•	•
Don Tito	US	5		•		•	•	•	•		•	
Don Tomas	Ho	4			•	•	•		•		•	
Don Tomas Int'l	Ho	5		•	•	•			•			
Don Tomas Special Edition	Ho	3		•		•	•		•		•	
Don Tonioli Epicure Selection	CR	3					•	•	•	•		
Don Tuto Habanos	CR	4			•			•	•			
Don Vito	DR	1		•	•	•			•			•
Don Xavier	Cl	1	•	•	•	•	•	•	•	•	•	
Don Yanes	Ve	5			•							
Double Happiness	Ph	1							•	•	•	

HANDMADE CIGARS: INDEX

Brand	Made in	Strength	Cigarillo	Panatela	Corona	Lonsdale	Grand Corona	Figurado	Robusto-Toro	Churchill	Double Corona	Giant
Dunhill	CI	2		●	●	●			●			
Dunhill	DR	2		●	●	●			●	●	●	
898 Collection	Ja	1			●	●			●		●	
1881	Ph	3			●	●			●			●
El Canelo	US	2		●	●	●			●	●		●
El Credito	US	3		●	●	●	●		●	●	●	●
Elegante	Ho	3		●	●	●			●	●		
El Incomparable	Ho	3			●			●	●	●		
El Paraiso	Ho	1		●	●				●	●	●	●
El Rey del Mundo	Ho	1,4	●	●	●	●	●	●	●	●	●	●
El Rico Habano	US	5		●	●	●			●	●	●	
El Sabinar	DR	5			●	●			●			
El Sublimado	DR	2			●			●	●			●
El Tigre	Ho	5			●			●	●		●	●
El Triunfo	Mx	3			●	●	●		●		●	
El Unicornio	Gu	5				●						●
El Valle	DR	2	●	●	●			●	●		●	
Encanto	Ho	4			●	●			●		●	●
Escudo Cubano	Ni	1		●		●		●	●		●	●
Espada de Oro	Ho	3		●	●				●		●	●
Espanola	DR	1,5		●	●	●		●	●	●	●	●
Estrella Fina	Ni	3							●		●	●
Evelio	Ho	5			●	●		●	●	●		

HANDMADE CIGARS: INDEX

Brand	Made in	Strength	Cigarillo	Panatela	Corona	Lonsdale	Grand Corona	Figurado	Robusto-Toro	Churchill	Double Corona	Giant
Excalibur	Ho	4	●	●	●		●		●	●	●	
Excelsior	Mx	3			●	●			●	●		●
Famous Rum Runner	US	1		●	●					●		
Fat Cat	DR	5						●	●		●	
F.D. Grave	Ho	5			●				●		●	
Felipe Gregorio	Ho	5			●			●	●	●	●	
Fighting Cock	Ph	3						●	●	●		
First Priming	Ho	3									●	●
Flor Cubana	Ho	2	●	●	●				●	●	●	
Flor de A. Allones	Ho	4	●						●			●
Flor de Consuegra	Ho	5	●	●	●	●			●	●		●
Flor de Cuba	PR	5		●						●		
Flor de Farach	Ni	4						●	●			
Flor de Filipinas	Ph	3	●	●	●					●		
Flor de Gonzalez	US	3			●	●		●	●		●	
Flor de Honduras	Ho	3			●	●			●		●	●
Flor de Jalapa	Ni	2			●				●	●		●
Flor del Caribe	Ho	4			●						●	●
Flor de Florez	Ho	2			●	●			●		●	
Flor de Florez Cabinet Selection	Ni	4			●		●	●	●	●	●	
Flor de Manila	Ph	2	●	●	●			●		●		
Flor de Mexico	Mx	5	●	●	●				●		●	

- 42 -

HANDMADE CIGARS: INDEX

Brand	Made in	Strength	Cigarillo	Panatela	Corona	Lonsdale	Grand Corona	Figurado	Robusto-Toro	Churchill	Double Corona	Giant
Flor de Nicaragua	Ni	1		●	●	●	●		●	●	●	●
Flor de Palicio	Ho	3			●	●				●		
Fonseca	DR	3			●		●	●	●		●	
Franco	DR	2		●	●	●			●		●	
Free Cuba	US	3		●		●		●	●	●	●	
Fundadore Jamaica	Ja	1		●	●	●	●		●		●	●
Galiano	DR	2		●	●				●	●	●	
Garo	DR	2		●	●	●		●	●	●	●	
Garcia y Vega	Ja	3		●		●				●		
Gilberto Oliva	Ni	3			●		●		●		●	
Gioconda	Ho	2					●		●	●	●	
Gispert	Ho	2				●			●		●	
Grand Nica	Ni	4				●		●	●		●	●
The Griffin's	DR	2		●	●	●			●			●
Guaranteed Jamaica	Ja	1		●	●	●	●		●		●	●
Habana Gold	Ho	3			●			●	●	●	●	●
Habana Gold Sterling Vintage	Ho	5			●			●	●	●	●	●
Habanica	Ni	3		●			●		●	●		
Hamiltons	DR	1	●	●	●	●			●	●		
Hamiltons Reserve	DR	3	●	●	●			●	●	●	●	●
Harriel's Dream	Ho	1		●		●			●	●		●

HANDMADE CIGARS: INDEX

Brand	Made in	Strength	Cigarillo	Panatela	Corona	Lonsdale	Grand Corona	Figurado	Robusto-Toro	Churchill	Double Corona	Giant
Hasa Rey	Ho	5		●	●	●			●		●	
Havana	US	4		●	●	●		●	●	●	●	●
Havana Classico	US	5			●	●		●	●	●	●	●
Havana Cool	Ni	4		●	●				●	●		
Havana Reserve	Ho	1		●		●	●	●	●		●	
Havana Sunrise	US	4	●	●	●			●	●	●	●	●
Henry Clay	DR	3		●			●			●		
Hidalgo	Pa	3		●	●					●		●
Hoja de Honduras	Ho	4		●	●	●			●		●	●
Hoja de Mexicali	Mx	5		●	●				●		●	●
Hoja de Nicaragua	Ni	5		●		●			●		●	●
Hoja de Oro	Mx	3			●	●			●		●	
Honduran Gold	Ho	1		●	●	●			●		●	●
Honduran Cuban Tobaccos	Ho	1-5		●	●	●		●	●	●	●	●
Honduras Special	Ho	3		●	●	●			●	●	●	●
Hoyo de Honduras	Ho	5		●	●	●			●		●	
Hoyo de Monterrey	Ho	4	●	●	●	●	●	●	●	●	●	●
Hugo Cassar	Ho	3			●	●			●	●	●	●
Hugo Cassar	Mx	5		●	●				●		●	●
Hugo Cassar Diamond Dominican	DR	1			●	●	●			●		●

HANDMADE CIGARS: INDEX

Brand	Made in	Strength	Cigarillo	Panatela	Corona	Lonsdale	Grand Corona	Figurado	Robusto-Toro	Churchill	Double Corona	Giant
Hugo Cassar Diamond Mystique	DR	1				●		●	●	●		●
Hugo Cassar Diamond Honduran	Ho	3			●		●	●	●		●	
Hugo Cassar Diamond Mystique	Ho	3			●			●	●	●		
Hugo Cassar Honduran Collection	Ho	3			●	●		●	●	●		
Hugo Cassar Private Collection	DR	1			●			●	●		●	
Hugo Cassar Private Collection	Ho	4			●	●			●		●	
Hugo Cassar Private Collection	Mx	5			●				●		●	
Hugo Signature Series	Ni	5			●	●			●	●		●
Imperio Cubano	US	3			●	●		●	●	●		
Indian	Ho	2	●	●				●	●		●	
Indian Head	Ho	2	●	●	●			●	●	●	●	●
Infiesta	US	1-3		●	●	●			●	●		●
Iracema	Br	3	●		●	●						
Island Amaretto	US	5		●						●		
Jamaica Bay	Ja	1		●	●	●			●		●	
Jamaica Gem	Ja	4		●	●	●	●				●	●

HANDMADE CIGARS: INDEX

Brand	Made in	Strength	Cigarillo	Panatela	Corona	Lonsdale	Grand Corona	Figurado	Robusto-Toro	Churchill	Double Corona	Giant
Jamaica Gold	Ja	3		●	●	●		●	●		●	
Jamaica Heritage	Ja	1			●	●	●		●		●	●
J. Cortes	DR	1		●	●				●			
John Aylesbury	Ho	3		●	●	●			●			
John Aylesbury Premium	DR	1		●	●	●			●	●		
John T's	DR	1		●			●					
Jose Benito	DR	3	●	●	●	●			●		●	●
Jose Llopis	Pa	3		●	●	●			●	●	●	●
Jose Llopis Gold	Pa	1		●	●	●			●	●		●
Jose Marti	DR	1		●	●	●			●	●		
Jose Marti	Ni	5		●	●	●		●	●		●	●
Jose Marti Vitola Series	Ho	5				●						●
Joya de Honduras	Ho	3		●	●			●	●		●	●
Joya del Rey	Ho	4		●	●	●			●		●	●
Joya de Nicaragua	Ni	1,5		●	●	●			●	●	●	●
Juan y Ramon	DR	3		●	●			●	●		●	
J-R Ultimate	Ho	5		●	●	●	●		●	●	●	●
Juan Clemente	DR	3	●	●	●	●	●	●	●	●		●
Juan Lopez	Ho	4			●	●			●		●	●
King	DR	1		●	●	●			●		●	●
Kingston	Mx	5		●	●	●			●		●	●
Kiskeya	DR	1		●	●	●			●	●	●	●

HANDMADE CIGARS: INDEX

Brand	Made in	Strength	Cigarillo	Panatela	Corona	Lonsdale	Grand Corona	Figurado	Robusto-Toro	Churchill	Double Corona	Giant
La Aurora	DR	3		●	●			●	●		●	
La Bala	Ho	5								●		
La Diligencia	Ho	2			●				●	●		●
La Diva	DR	3			●			●	●			●
La Eminencia	Ho	2		●	●		●		●	●		●
La Fabuloso	Ho	2		●	●	●			●		●	
La Fama	CI	1			●							
La Favoritas	Ho	1		●	●							
La Flor de Armando Mendez	US	3							●			
La Fontana Vintage	Ho	1		●	●	●		●	●	●	●	
La Finca	Ni	5		●	●	●			●		●	●
La Flor Dominicana	DR	2,4			●	●		●	●	●	●	
La Gianna Havana	Ho	5			●			●	●		●	
La Gloria Cubana	US DR	3	●	●	●	●	●	●	●	●	●	●
La Habanera	DR	1		●	●	●			●	●	●	
La Herencia Cubana	US	4	●	●	●	●	●	●	●		●	●
La Hoja Selecta	US	1		●	●	●			●	●	●	
La Isla	US	4		●	●	●			●	●		●
La Maximiliana	Ho	3			●	●			●			
Lambs Club	DR	3			●				●		●	

- 47 -

HANDMADE CIGARS: INDEX

Brand	Made in	Strength	Cigarillo	Panatela	Corona	Lonsdale	Grand Corona	Figurado	Robusto-Toro	Churchill	Double Corona	Giant
La Native	Ho	3			•				•	•		
La Pantera Diamond Coll.	Ho	2	•	•				•	•		•	•
La Pantera Sapphire Coll.	Ho	4	•	•				•	•		•	•
La Plata	US	1-5		•	•	•		•	•	•	•	•
La Primadora	Ho	1		•	•	•			•			•
La Primera	DR	5			•	•			•		•	•
La Real	Ni	5							•		•	
La Regional	CI	5		•	•	•			•	•	•	
Las Cabrillas	Ho	3		•	•	•			•		•	•
La Tradicion Cubana	US	4		•	•			•	•		•	
La Unica	DR	1			•	•			•		•	•
La Venga	Ho	4			•		•		•	•	•	•
Las Vegas Cigar	US	1-5	•		•	•		•	•		•	•
Legacy	Ho	3			•	•			•	•	•	•
Legend•Ario	Ho	3			•	•			•	•		
Lempira	Ho	3		•	•				•	•	•	
Leon	US	3		•		•			•	•	•	•
Leon	Ni	2		•		•		•	•		•	•
Leon Jimenes	DR	5		•	•	•		•	•	•	•	
Lew's Smokers	Ho	2		•						•		
Licenciados	DR	3		•	•	•		•	•		•	•

HANDMADE CIGARS: INDEX

Brand	Made in	Strength	Cigarillo	Panatela	Corona	Lonsdale	Grand Corona	Figurado	Robusto-Toro	Churchill	Double Corona	Giant
Los Reyes	DR	2		●	●		●		●			●
Macabi	DR	3			●	●		●	●		●	
Macanudo	Ja	2	●	●	●	●	●	●	●	●	●	●
Madrigal Habana	Mx	1			●	●			●		●	●
Maria Mancini	Ho	5		●	●	●			●		●	
Mario Palomino	Ja	5		●	●	●	●				●	
Matacan	Mx	3		●	●	●	●		●		●	●
MATASA Seconds	DR	1		●	●							
Match Play	DR	3			●			●	●	●	●	
Maxius	DR	2,4		●	●				●	●	●	
Maya	Ho	2		●	●	●		●	●	●	●	●
Medal of Honor	Ho	3				●					●	●
Mexican Emperador	Mx	3										●
MiCubano	Ni	5			●	●			●	●		●
Milano Santana	DR	3		●	●	●		●	●	●	●	●
Mocambo	Mx	5		●	●	●			●		●	●
Montague	In	3			●	●	●		●		●	
Monte Canario	Cl	1		●	●	●						
Montecassino	Ho	2		●		●						●
Montecristo	DR	4			●	●	●	●	●	●		
Montecruz	DR	2,4	●	●	●	●	●		●	●		●
Montero	DR	2			●			●	●	●	●	

Brand	Made in	Strength	Cigarillo	Panatela	Corona	Lonsdale	Grand Corona	Figurado	Robusto-Toro	Churchill	Double Corona	Giant
Montes de Oca	CR	5			●					●		
Montesino	DR	3			●	●				●		
Montoya	Ho	1			●	●			●		●	●
Moore & Bode	US	2,4	●	●		●	●	●		●		
Moreno Maduro	DR	2		●	●	●			●	●	●	●
Morro Castle	US	3		●		●		●	●	●	●	
Napa	DR	5			●			●	●	●		●
	Ho	4			●				●	●		
	Ni	2			●				●	●		
Napa Reserve	CI	3			●	●			●		●	
National Brand	Ho	2		●	●	●			●	●	●	●
Nat Sherman	DR	1-4	●	●	●	●	●	●	●		●	
	Ho	3		●	●	●	●	●	●		●	
Nestor 747	Ho	5								●		
Nester 747 Series II	Ho	5							●	●		
New York, New York	Mx	3			●	●	●		●	●		
Nicaragua Especial	Ni	3		●	●				●		●	●
Nording	DR	3			●	●			●		●	
Ocho Rios	Ja	1			●	●			●		●	●
Off Colors	Ho	3	●	●	●	●	●		●	●	●	●
Oh Que Bueno	CI	3			●	●						
Oliveros	DR	2,5			●	●			●		●	●

HANDMADE CIGARS: INDEX

Brand	Made in	Strength	Cigarillo	Panatela	Corona	Lonsdale	Grand Corona	Figurado	Robusto-Toro	Churchill	Double Corona	Giant
Olor	DR	3		●	●	●			●	●	●	
Onyx	DR	1			●		●		●		●	●
Opus X	DR	5		●	●	●	●		●	●	●	●
Orient Express	Ho	1		●	●	●			●		●	
Ornelas	Mx	1-2		●	●	●	●		●		●	●
Oro Negro	Ho	3			●		●	●	●		●	
Orosi	Ni	3			●				●		●	
Oscar	DR	4	●	●	●	●		●	●			●
Padron	Ho Ni	5		●	●	●	●	●	●	●	●	●
Pantera	DR	1		●	●		●		●			
Papayo	DR	1		●	●				●	●		
Partagas	DR	4	●	●	●	●	●	●	●		●	
Particulares	Ho	1		●	●	●			●	●	●	●
Paul Garmirian	DR	4		●	●	●	●	●	●	●	●	●
Peterson Hallmark	DR	2		●	●				●	●	●	
Peter Stokkebye	DR	1		●	●						●	
Petrus	Ho	2		●	●		●	●	●		●	
Petrus Etiquette Rouge	Ho	3			●			●	●	●		
Pheasant	Ho	3				●			●		●	
Phillips & King Guardsmen	DR	1		●	●				●	●	●	●
Pinnacle	DR	3							●	●		

HANDMADE CIGARS: INDEX

Brand	Made in	Strength	Cigarillo	Panatela	Corona	Lonsdale	Grand Corona	Figurado	Robusto-Toro	Churchill	Double Corona	Giant
Playboy	DR	3				●			●	●	●	
Pleiades	DR	1-5	●	●	●	●			●	●		●
Porfirio	DR	1			●	●			●		●	●
Por Larrañaga	DR	1		●	●	●		●	●		●	
Por Matamor	DR	3			●				●		●	
Porto Bello	DR	1		●	●	●		●	●	●	●	●
Pride of Copan	Ho	4	●	●	●						●	
Pride of Jamaica	Ja	1		●	●	●	●		●		●	●
Primera de Nicaragua	Ni	2			●				●		●	●
Primo del Cristo	Ho	4		●	●	●			●			●
Primo del Rey	DR	1	●	●	●	●			●		●	●
Primo del Rey Club Selection	DR	1			●					●	●	●
Primo del Rey Gift Pack	DR	1				●	●				●	●
Private Selection	Ho	3			●				●		●	●
Private Stock	DR	2	●	●	●		●		●		●	
Profesor Sila	CI	2		●			●		●			●
Punch	Ho	4	●	●	●	●	●	●	●	●	●	●
Puro Nicaragua	Ni	5		●	●	●			●		●	●
Puros Indios	Ho	3		●	●	●	●	●	●	●	●	●
Ramar	US	2		●	●	●	●	●	●	●	●	●
Ramon Allones	DR	4		●	●	●			●		●	

HANDMADE CIGARS: INDEX

Brand	Made in	Strength	Cigarillo	Panatela	Corona	Lonsdale	Grand Corona	Figurado	Robusto-Toro	Churchill	Double Corona	Giant
Regalos	Ho	5			•			•	•	•	•	•
Repeater	Ho	3			•	•					•	
Republica Dominicana	DR	1		•	•	•			•	•	•	•
Riata	Ho	1		•	•	•			•	•	•	•
Rico Havana	Ho	3			•	•			•	•		•
Ricos Dominicanos	DR	2			•	•			•		•	
Rigoletto	DR	3				•			•	•		
Robali	CR	3			•	•			•	•		•
Rodriguez & Menendez	US	3		•		•	•		•	•	•	
Rolando	DR	2			•	•		•	•	•		
Roller's Choice	DR	1			•		•	•	•		•	
Romanticos	DR	2		•	•			•	•		•	•
Romeo y Julieta	DR	3		•	•	•		•	•		•	•
Romeo y Julieta Vintage	DR	1			•		•	•	•	•	•	
Rosa Cuba	Ni	4			•	•	•		•	•	•	•
Rosalones	Ni	1		•	•	•	•		•	•	•	•
Royal Barbados	Ba	1		•	•		•					
Royal Court	Ho	1		•	•						•	•
Royal Dominicana	DR	2		•	•	•	•				•	
Royales	DR	1		•	•	•			•		•	•

HANDMADE CIGARS: INDEX

Brand	Made in	Strength	Cigarillo	Panatela	Corona	Lonsdale	Grand Corona	Figurado	Robusto-Toro	Churchill	Double Corona	Giant
Royal Honduras	Ho	2			●	●		●	●	●		●
Royal Jamaica	DR Ja	3	●	●	●	●	●		●		●	●
Royal Manna	Ho	3		●	●	●			●		●	
Royal Nicaraguan	Ni	3		●	●	●			●		●	●
Rubirosa	DR	1			●				●	●		●
Sabana	Ve	2	●	●	●		●					
Sabor Habano	Ni	3			●				●		●	●
Sabroso	Ni	5			●				●	●		●
Saint Luis Rey	Ho	5				●		●	●		●	
San Fernando	Ho	5			●				●	●		
San Luis	Ho	4		●	●	●			●		●	
San Marcos	Ho	5			●				●	●		●
San Vicente	Ni	3	●		●	●			●	●	●	●
Santa Clara 1830	Mx	3	●	●	●				●		●	
Santa Damiana	DR	3				●	●		●	●	●	
Santa Rosa	Ho	1		●	●	●	●	●	●		●	●
Santiago	DR	1		●	●		●			●		
Savinelli ELR	DR	3			●		●		●	●		
Segovia	Ni	5			●		●		●		●	
Siglo 21	DR	3				●			●	●		●
Signature Collection	US	3		●	●	●		●	●	●	●	
Signet	DR	1			●				●	●		

HANDMADE CIGARS: INDEX

Brand	Made in	Strength	Cigarillo	Panatela	Corona	Lonsdale	Grand Corona	Figurado	Robusto-Toro	Churchill	Double Corona	Giant
Sillem's Las Terenas	DR	1			●	●			●		●	
660 Red	US	5							●			
Sol y Mar	Ho	3						●	●		●	
Solo Aroma	Ho	2	●	●	●				●	●	●	●
Sosa	DR	3	●	●	●			●	●	●	●	
Sosa Family Selection	DR	4	●	●	●				●	●	●	
Spanish Honduran Red Label	Ho	3	●	●	●				●	●	●	●
Special Jamaican	DR	1	●	●	●			●	●		●	●
St. Tropez	Ho	1			●	●						
Suave	DR	3			●				●		●	
Suerdieck	Br	3	●	●	●		●					
Tabacalera	Ph	3		●	●	●		●	●			●
Tabacos San Jose	US	2			●	●		●	●	●	●	●
Tabacos Universo	Ho	3		●	●				●		●	●
Tabaquero	DR	2		●	●			●	●	●		●
Tabantillas	DR	5		●	●		●		●			●
Tamboril	DR	4		●	●			●	●	●		●
Te-Amo	Mx	3	●	●	●	●	●	●	●		●	●
Te-Amo Segundo	Mx	3		●	●	●	●		●		●	
Temple Hall	Ja	3		●	●	●		●	●		●	
Tena y Vega	Ho	4			●	●			●		●	

HANDMADE CIGARS: INDEX

Brand	Made in	Strength	Cigarillo	Panatela	Corona	Lonsdale	Grand Corona	Figurado	Robusto-Toro	Churchill	Double Corona	Giant
Tesoros de Copan	Ho	2		●	●		●		●		●	
Thomas Hinds Honduran Sel.	Ho	4			●	●		●	●		●	●
Thomas Hinds Nicaraguan Sel.	Ni	2			●	●		●	●		●	
Tia Martia	DR	2		●	●	●			●		●	
Tiburon	Ho	3		●	●					●		●
Todo El Mundo	DR	2			●	●			●	●	●	
Tooth of the Dog	Ni	3			●				●		●	
Topper Centennial	DR	3				●		●	●		●	
Topper Grande	Ni	4			●	●			●		●	
Torcedor	Ni	1				●			●		●	●
Tresado	DR	5			●	●	●			●		●
Troya	DR	3,4		●	●	●		●	●	●	●	
Tulas	Ho	1			●	●			●	●		●
H. Upmann	DR	3	●	●	●	●	●			●	●	
H. Upmann Cabinet Selection	DR	3							●			●
H. Upmann Chairman's Reserve	DR	3		●				●	●	●	●	
V Centennial	Ho	3		●	●	●		●	●	●		●
V.M. Santana	DR	1			●			●	●		●	
Vargas	Cl	1		●	●		●		●	●	●	
Veracruz	Mx	1		●	●	●				●		

HANDMADE CIGARS: INDEX

Brand	Made in	Strength	Cigarillo	Panatela	Corona	Lonsdale	Grand Corona	Figurado	Robusto-Toro	Churchill	Double Corona	Giant
Victor Sinclair	DR	2			●			●	●		●	
Victory Spirit	Ni	1			●				●	●		
Villar y Villar	Ni	3		●	●	●	●	●	●	●	●	●
Villega Reales	DR	3			●	●			●	●		
Vintage Honduran	Ho	4		●	●	●	●		●		●	●
Virtuoso Toraño	Ho	2			●	●			●			●
Vueltabajo	DR	2			●	●		●	●	●		●
W & D Bundles	Ho	1		●	●	●			●		●	●
West Indies Vanilla	US	5		●							●	
Yago	Ho	3			●	●					●	
Yumuri	DR	1			●	●			●	●		
Yumuri 1492	DR	2			●	●		●	●	●		
Zino	Ho	1	●	●	●	●	●		●		●	

Churchills and Double Coronas

These larger shapes are much loved for the full flavor they can deliver. The dimensions of these shapes include:

- Churchill   6¾-7⅞ inches long; 46-48 ring.

- Double Corona   6¾-7¾ inches long; 49-54 ring.

Pictured opposite, from left to right, are:

▶ Troya No. 72 Executive	7¾ x 50	Double Corona
▶ Evelio Double Corona	7⅝ x 47	Double Corona
▶ Cruz Real No. 14	7½ x 50	Double Corona
▶ Leon Jimenes No. 1	7½ x 50	Double Corona
▶ Cubita No. 2000	7 x 50	Double Corona
▶ Davidoff Anniversario No. 2	7 x 48	Churchill
▶ Felipe Gregorio Suntuoso	7 x 48	Churchill

These cigars illustrate the full range of wrapper shades from the light Claro-shade Davidoff to the dark Maduro-type Felipe Gregorio.

4.
HANDMADE CIGARS:
LISTINGS BY BRAND

This section provides the details on 493 brands of cigars marketed nationally in the United States, a net increase of 178 brands from the 1996 edition! Each brand listing includes notes on country of manufacture, the origin of the tobaccos used, shapes, names, lengths, ring gauges, wrapper color and a brief description *as supplied by the manufacturers and/or distributors of these brands.* Ring gauges for some brands of cigarillos were not available.

Please note that while a cigar may be manufactured in one country, it may contain tobaccos from many nations. The designation "handmade" indicates the use of long-filler tobacco unless otherwise noted.

Although manufacturers have recognized more than 70 shades of wrapper color, six major color groupings are used here. Their abbreviations include:

- ► DC = Double Claro: green, also known as American Market Selection or "AMS."
- ► Cl = Claro: a very light tan color.
- ► CC = Colorado Claro: a medium brown common to many cigars on this list.
- ► Co = Colorado: reddish-brown.
- ► CM = Colorado Maduro: dark brown.
- ► Ma = Maduro: very dark brown or black (also known as "double Maduro" or "Oscuro.")

Many manufacturers call their wrapper colors "Natural" or "English Market Selection." These colors cover a wide range of browns and we have generally grouped them in the "CC" range. Darker wrappers such as those from Cameroon show up most often in the "CM" category.

Shape designations are based on our shape chart in section 1.03. Careful readers will note the freedom with which manufacturers attach names of shapes to cigars which do not resemble that shape at all! For easier comparison, all lengths were rounded to the shortest eighth of an inch, although some manufacturers list sizes in 16ths or even 32nds of an inch.

Although hundreds of brands are listed, house brands of mail-order houses or individual tobacco stores do not appear. In general, all of these brands are available to retailers through wholesale distribution channels.

Readers who would like to see their favorite brand listed in the 1998 edition can call or write the compilers as noted after the Table of Contents.

ABREU ANILLO DE ORO
Handmade in Tamboril, Dominican Republic.

Wrapper: USA/Connecticut   *Binder: Dom. Rep.*   *Filler: Dom. Rep.*

Shape	Name	Lgth	Ring	Wrapper
Grand Corona	Churchill	6½	46	CC
Lonsdale	Corona	7	44	CC
Cigarillo	Especiales	5	26	CC
Long Panatela	Panatela	7½	38	CC
Giant	Presidente	8	50	CC
Robusto	Torito	5	50	CC

This is a new brand for 1996, made in the new factory in Tamboril, Dominican Republic. It's a medium-bodied smoke and offered in boxes of 25.

HANDMADE CIGARS: BRAND LISTINGS

ADANTE
Handmade, with short filler, in the Dominican Republic.

Wrapper: Mexico   Binder: Dom. Rep.   Filler: Dom. Rep.

Shape	Name	Lgth	Ring	Wrapper
Petit Corona	No. 405 Petit Corona	4½	42	CC
Corona	No. 504 Corona	5½	42	CC
Slim Panatela	No. 603 Palma Fina	6¼	34	CC
Long Corona	No. 702 Cetro	6	42	CC
Lonsdale	No. 801 Elegante	6⅝	43	CC

An excellent-quality cigar that is inexpensive, but still handmade from an excellent blend of Dominican and Havana-seed tobaccos. Adantes are mild and offered in packs of 3, 10 or 25 cigars each.

AGUILA
Handmade in Santiago, Dominican Republic.

Wrapper: USA/Connecticut   Binder: Dom. Rep.   Filler: Dom. Rep.

Shape	Name	Lgth	Ring	Wrapper
Corona	Coronita	5½	40	CC
Lonsdale	Brevas 44	7½	44	CC
Grand Corona	Brevas 46	6½	46	CC
Double Corona	Brevas 50	7½	50	CC
Robusto	Petit Gordo	4¾	50	CC

Created in 1989, this is a mild-to-medium-bodied cigar, which is hand-made in Santiago de los Caballeros, Dominican Republic. The Connecticut wrappers are aged for 5-7 years before production.

AL-CAPONE
Handmade in Esteli, Nicaragua.

Wrapper: Brazil   Binder: Nicaragua   Filler: Nicaragua

Shape	Name	Lgth	Ring	Wrapper
Robusto	Robusto	4¾	50	CM

HANDMADE CIGARS: BRAND LISTINGS

Lonsdale	Corona Grande	6¾	43	CM
Toro	Toro	6	50	CM

This is a 1996 extension of the long-time cigarillo brand produced in Germany. Named for the corpulent Chicago-based gangster of the 1920s, the brand is not surprising in its full-bodied flavor, but it also exhibits a slightly sweet taste. It is offered in boxes of 25.

ALHAMBRA
Handmade in Manila, the Philippines.

Wrapper: Indonesia/Java   *Binder: Philippines*   *Filler: Philippines*

Shape	*Name*	*Lgth*	*Ring*	*Wrapper*
Corona	Corona	5	42	CM
Giant	Corona Grande	8¼	47	CM
Giant	Double Corona	8½	50	CM
Lonsdale	Duque	6½	42	CM
Toro	Especiale	6½	50	CM

Introduced in 1970, Alhambra cigars are handmade in the well-respected factories of the Philippine islands and are packed in bundles of 25 cigars each. A well-made, mild-bodied cigar, it is modestly priced.

ALTA GRACIA
Handmade in Miami, Florida, USA.

Wrapper: Ecuador   *Binder: Dom. Rep.*   *Filler: Mexico, Nicaragua*

Shape	*Name*	*Lgth*	*Ring*	*Wrapper*
Robusto	Robusto	4¾	50	CC
Long Corona	Corona	6	44	CC
Toro	Toro	6	50	CC
Double Corona	Presidente	7½	52	CC
Torpedo	Torpedo	6¼	52	CC

Introduced in 1996, this Miami-based brand offers a medium-to-full taste in a slightly sweet blend, presented in boxes of 25.

HANDMADE CIGARS: BRAND LISTINGS

ALVARO
Handmade in Las Palmas, the Canary Islands of Spain.
Wrapper: USA/Connecticut   *Binder: Mexico*   *Filler: Brazil, Dom. Rep.*

Shape	Name	Lgth	Ring	Wrapper
Corona	Brevas	5¼	41	CC
Short Panatela	Saudos	4¾	39	CC
Corona	Cedros	5¼	41	CC
Short Panatela	Regalos	5	39	CC

Alvaro cigars are handmade in the historic Canary Islands, where the tradition of cigar making goes back for hundreds of years. This brand is very mild in body and is offered in boxes of 25.

ANDUJAR
Handmade in Santiago, Dominican Republic.
Wrapper: USA/Connecticut   *Binder: Dom. Rep.*   *Filler: Dom. Rep.*

Shape	Name	Lgth	Ring	Wrapper
Cigarillo	Romana	5	25	CC
Double Corona	Santiago	7½	50	CC
Giant	Azua	9	46	CC
Lonsdale	Macorix	6½	44	CC
Panatela	Samana	6	38	CC
Robusto	Vega	5	50	CC

Introduced in 1994, this line is the special favorite of Oscar Rodriguez, who developed the much-loved Oscar brand. Full-bodied, this line has a clean, gustatory flavor enhanced by each and every draw. The captivating aroma and exciting after-taste make this the perfect cigar for the most special moments. Andujar cigars are offered uncellophaned in all-cedar cabinets for only the truly serious smoker.

ANILLO DE ORO
Handmade in Tamboril, Dominican Republic.
Wrapper: Ecuador   *Binder: Dom. Rep.*   *Filler: Dom. Rep.*

HANDMADE CIGARS: BRAND LISTINGS

Shape	Name	Lgth	Ring	Wrapper
Grand Corona	Churchill	6½	46	CC
Giant	President	8	50	CC
Long Corona	Corona	6	44	CC
Lonsdale	Coronita	6½	44	CC
Robusto	Torito	5	50	CC
Long Panatela	Panatela	7½	38	CC

This is a new cigar for 1996, with a mild to medium-bodied taste. It features a Connecticut-seed wrapper grown in Ecuador and binder and Corojo filler tobaccos from the Dominican Republic.

ANTELO
Handmade in Miami, Florida, USA.
Wrapper: USA/Connecticut *Binder: Mexico* *Filler: Dom. Rep.*

Shape	Name	Lgth	Ring	Wrapper
Double Corona	Presidente	7⅝	50	Cl-Ma
Churchill	Churchill	7	46	Cl-Ma
Lonsdale	No. 1	6¾	42	Cl-Ma
Corona	Cetros	5¾	42	Cl-Ma
Cigarillo	Senoritas	4⅝	28	Cl-Ma
Panatela	Panatela	6⅞	36	Cl-Ma
Corona Extra	Wavell	5⅛	46	Cl-Ma
Giant Corona	Double Corona	7½	42	Cl-Ma
Churchill	Super Cazadore	7½	46	Cl-Ma

These cigars are made by hand in a small factory in Miami, using imported leaf. The taste ranges from mild (Senoritas and Panatelas) to medium (No. 1 and Cetros) to heavy (all other shapes).

ARANGO STATESMAN
Handmade in Danli and San Pedro Sula, Honduras.
Wrapper: Ecuador *Binder: Dom. Rep.* *Filler: Dom. Rep., Honduras*

HANDMADE CIGARS: BRAND LISTINGS

Shape	Name		Lgth	Ring	Wrapper
Churchill	Barrister		7½	46	CC-Ma
Corona	Counselor		5	40	CC-Ma
Petit Corona	Executor		6	43	CC-Ma

Introduced in 1988, these are medium-bodied, handmade cigars, which should not be confused with its sister brand, the Arango Sportsman, which is a flavored machine-made cigar. The Statesman is quite aromatic, with just a hint of vanilla flavor to charm the smoker.

AROMAS DE SAN ANDRES
Handmade in San Andres Tuxtula, Mexico.

Wrapper: Mexico   Binder: Mexico   Filler: Mexico

Shape	Name		Lgth	Ring	Wrapper
Lonsdale	Gourmet	(tubed)	6⅛	42	CM
Toro	Afficiando		6	50	CM
Double Corona	Maximillian		7½	52	CM
Robusto	Robusto		5	50	CM
Double Corona	Imperial	(tubed)	7	50	CM
Grand Corona	Crowns		6½	47	CM
Long Corona	Sceptors		6	44	CM

Produced by Tabacos San Andres S.A. de C.V., this line is composed of all-Mexican tobacco of interesting origins. Although all grown in the famous San Andres Valley, the filler and binder are native seed, while the wrapper leaf is Sumatran-type tobacco which is also grown in the S.A. Valley.

ARTURO FUENTE
Handmade in Santiago, Dominican Republic.

(The owners of this brand preferred not to provide information on the origins of the tobaccos in their cigars. Other sources have reported the tobaccos to come from:
Wrapper: USA/Connecticut and Cameroon
Binder: Dominican Republic   Filler: Dominican Republic)

HANDMADE CIGARS: BRAND LISTINGS

Shape	Name	Lgth	Ring	Wrapper
Corona	Brevas Royale /medium filler/	5½	42	CC-Ma
Giant	Canones	8½	52	CC-Ma
Robusto	Chateau Fuente	4½	50	CC-Ma
Churchill	Churchill	7¼	48	CC-Ma
Grand Corona	Corona Imperial	6½	46	CC-Ma
Corona Extra	Cuban Corona	5¼	45	CC-Ma
Lonsdale	Curly Head /medium filler/	6½	43	CC-Ma
Lonsdale	Curly Head Deluxe /medium filler/	6½	43	CC-Ma
Toro	Double Chateau Fuente	6¾	50	CC-Ma
Lonsdale	Fumas	7	44	CC-Ma
Long Panatela	Panatela Fina	7	38	CC-Ma
Short Panatela	Petit Corona	5	38	CC-Ma
Lonsdale	Seleccion Privada No. 1	6¾	44	CM-Ma
Robusto	Rothschild	4½	50	CC-Ma
Double Corona	Chateau Fuente Royal Salute	7⅝	54	CC-Ma
Lonsdale	Spanish Lonsdale	6½	42	CM-Ma
Grand Corona	Flor Fina 8-5-8	6	47	CM-Ma
	Don Carlos line:			
Robusto	Robusto	5	50	CC
	Hemingway Series:			*(perfecto tips)*
Robusto	Hemingway Short Story	4	48	CM
Robusto	Hemingway Between the Lines	5	54	CM
Double Corona	Hemingway Untold Story	7½	53	Ma
Churchill	Hemingway Classic	7	48	CM

| Grand Corona | Hemingway Signature | 6 | 47 | CM |
| Giant | Hemingway Masterpiece | 9 | 52 | CM |

Arturo Fuente learned the art of growing and processing tobacco and the making of premium, handmade cigars in Cuba at the end of the 19th century, producing his own line in 1912. Today, his son Carlos and grandson, Carlos, Jr. oversee the more than 500 rollers who manufacture more than 24 million cigars every year. Their line offers a medium-to-full-bodied taste, with the celebrated Hemingway series a little mellower, thanks to an additional 140 days of aging. Until recently, most of the natural-wrapped cigars featured Cameroon leaves, with Connecticut leaf used for maduros; more Connecticut leaf is now in use due to production difficulties in the Cameroons.

ASHTON
Handmade in Santiago, Dominican Republic.
Wrapper: USA/Connecticut   Binder: Dom. Rep.   Filler: Dom. Rep.

Shape	Name	Lgth	Ring	Wrapper
Double Corona	Churchill	7½	52	CC
Churchill	Prime Minister	6⅞	48	CC
Lonsdale	8-9-8	6½	44	CC
Panatela	Panatela	6	36	CC
Corona	Corona	5¼	44	CC
Slim Panatela	Cordial	5	30	CC
Toro	Double Magnum	6	50	CC
Robusto	Magnum	5	50	CC
Panatela	Elegante	6½	35	CC
	Aged Cabinet Selection:			
Perfecto	No. 1	9	52	CC
Perfecto	No. 2	7	46	CC
Perfecto	No. 3	6	46	CC
Robusto	No. 6	5½	52	CC
Toro	No. 7	6¼	52	CC
Double Corona	No. 8	7	49	CC

HANDMADE CIGARS: BRAND LISTINGS

Double Corona	No. 10	7½	52	CC
	Maduro:			
Double Corona	No. 60	7½	52	Ma
Churchill	No. 50	7	48	Ma
Toro	No. 40	6	50	Ma
Lonsdale	No. 30	6¾	44	Ma
Corona	No. 20	5½	44	Ma
Robusto	No. 10	5	50	Ma

Robert Levin of Holt's Tobacconist of Philadelphia, Pennsylvania set out to create a great cigar in 1985 . . . and he succeeded. Ashton cigars are manufactured without compromise, blending six tobaccos: Dominican filler and Dominican-grown, Cuban-seed binder leaves with perfect shade-grown wrapper leaves from the Connecticut Valley. The maduro wrappers are longer-aged Connecticut Broadleaf. The unique range of sizes includes three large perfecto-shaped cigars – tapered at both ends – in the Cabinet Selection series.

ASTRAL
Handmade in Danli, Honduras.

Wrapper: Ecuador   Binder: Ecuador   Filler: Honduras, Nicaragua

Shape	Name	Lgth	Ring	Wrapper
Lonsdale	Lujos	6½	44	CM
Double Corona	Maestro	7½	52	CM
Robusto	Besos	5	52	CM
Churchill	Favorito	7	48	CM
Churchill	Perfeccion	7	48	CM

More than three years of planning went into the production of this new brand, introduced in 1995 and made in Danli, Honduras. Mild in body, the Connecticut-seed wrappers give this line an elegant appearance, with silky expresso and cream flavors. Astral cigars are presented in stunning Mahogany boxes which underscore the total commitment to quality in the manufacturing process.

Robustos and Toros

These are very popular sizes as enthusiasts look for the flavor of a larger ring gauge of a Churchill or Double Corona combined with shorter lengths for a shorter smoke. The dimensions of these shapes include:

▸ Robusto   4½-5½ inches long; 48-54 ring.

▸ Toro   5⅝-6⅝ inches long; 48-54 ring.

Pictured opposite are:

▸ Joya de Nicaragua
  Toro   6 x 50   Toro

▸ MiCubano No. 650   6 x 50   Toro

▸ Gispert Robusto   5 x 52   Robusto

▸ La Aurora Robusto   5 x 50   Robusto

▸ Milano Santana Gold   5 x 50   Robusto
  Robusto

The term "Robusto" as a shape designation is fairly new. Previously, this size was known as "Royal Corona" or "Rothschild." Currently, some manufacturers split the size, naming 5 to 5½-inch shapes "Robustos" while retaining the Rothschild tag for 4½-4¾-inch long models of the same ring gauge.

HANDMADE CIGARS: BRAND LISTINGS

Avo
Handmade in Santiago, Dominican Republic.

Wrapper: USA/Connecticut   *Binder: Dom. Rep.*   *Filler: Dom. Rep.*

Shape	Name	Lgth	Ring	Wrapper
Lonsdale	Avo No. 1	6¾	42	Co
Toro	Avo No. 2	6	50	Co
Double Corona	Avo No. 3	7½	52	Co
Long Panatela	Avo No. 4	7	38	Co
Grand Corona	Avo No. 5	6¾	46	Co
Panatela	Avo No. 6	6½	36	Co
Long Corona	Avo No. 7	6	44	Co
Corona	Avo No. 8	5½	40	Co
Robusto	Avo No. 9	4¾	48	Co
Pyramid	Pyramid	7	54	Co
Torpedo	Belicoso	6	50	Co
Torpedo	Petit Belicoso	4¾	50	Co
	XO Series:			
Churchill	Maestoso	7	48	CC
Robusto	Intermezzo	5½	50	CC
Long Corona	Preludio	6	40	CC

The perfectly-balanced marraige of five different tobaccos, mostly from the
Cibao Valley of the Dominican Republic, gives the Avo line – introduced in
1987 – a rich flavor in a mild-bodied cigar. The newer XO Series offers a richer
blend of six tobaccos, using a Dominican-grown, Havana-seed binder with the
Connecticut Shade wrapper.

AZ
Handmade in San Andres Tuxtula, Mexico.

Wrapper: Mexico   *Binder: Mexico*   *Filler: Mexico*

Shape	Name	Lgth	Ring	Wrapper
Small Panatela	Cordial	4⅛	30	CM

HANDMADE CIGARS: BRAND LISTINGS

Petit Corona	Petit Corona	5	44	CM
Long Corona	Corona	6	43	CM
Robusto	Robusto	5	50	CM
Toro	Toro	6	48	CM
Double Corona	Churchill	7	50	CM
Long Corona	Bolero	6	40	CM
Double Corona	Phenom	7½	52	CM

Here's a well-known brand in other countries, but a new brand in the U.S. for 1996, featuring all-Mexican tobaccos and a full-bodied taste. All of the shapes use a natural wrapper, except for the Bolero, which offers a double-wrapped "barber pole" style. Maduro-wrapped versions of these shapes will likely debut in 1997.

BABALU
Handmade in Miami, Florida, USA.

Wrapper: Honduras   *Binder: Dom. Rep.*   *Filler: Dom. Rep., Honduras*

Shape	Name	Lgth	Ring	Wrapper
Short Panatela	Petite Palm	5	36	CM
Robusto	Robusto	5	48	CM
Corona	Corona	5½	40	CM
Churchill	Churchill	7¼	48	CM
Cigarillo	Bocaditos	3½	26	CM
Giant	Imperial	8¼	54	CM

Where's Ricky Ricardo? Although the name may remind you of "I Love Lucy," these cigars are no joke, but good reason for a smile. Made in Miami of all long-filler tobaccos, the brand was created in 1994 and is available nation-wide in 1996. Babalu has a mild-to-medium body and is offered in boxes of 25.

BACCARAT HAVANA SELECTION
Handmade in Danli, Honduras.

Wrapper: Honduras   *Binder: Mexico*   *Filler: Honduras*

HANDMADE CIGARS: BRAND LISTINGS

Shape	Name	Lgth	Ring	Wrapper
Small Panatela	Bonitas	4½	30	CC
Double Corona	Churchill	7	50	CC-Ma
Long Corona	Luchadore	6	43	CC
Lonsdale	No. 1	7	44	CC
Panatela	Panatela	6	38	CC
Corona	Petit Corona	5½	42	CC
Small Panatela	Platinum	4⅞	32	CC
Pyramid	Polo	7	52	CC
Robusto	Rothschild	5	50	CC-Ma

This fine cigar series was formally introduced in 1978, but actually dates back as far as 1871 when it was supervised by Carl Upmann. The mild body produced by the blending of the Havana-seed fillers, Mexican binder and Connecticut-seed wrapper are sweetened by the use of a special sealing gum in the cigar's cap.

BAHIA
Handmade in San Jose, Costa Rica.

Wrapper: Ecuador   Binder: Nicaragua   Filler: Nicaragua

Shape	Name	Lgth	Ring	Wrapper
Giant	Double Corona	8	50	CC
Churchill	Churchill	6⅞	48	CC-Ma
Toro	Esplendido	6	50	CC-Ma
Robusto	Robusto	5	50	CC-Ma
Grand Corona	No. 3	6	46	CC-Ma
Corona	No. 4	5½	42	CC

Tony Borhani introduced this brand in December 1994, and now offers his 1990 crop vintage selection. Rolled in September 1995, the entire production of only 280,000 cigars was aged until June 1996, when it was released. Packed uncellophaned in slide-top cabinets, Bahia is a limited production cigar of the highest quality and medium-to-full body in taste.

HANDMADE CIGARS: BRAND LISTINGS

BALBOA
Handmade in Colon, Panama.

Wrapper: Honduras   *Binder: Mexico*
Filler: Dominican Republic, Honduras, Panama

Shape	Name	Lgth	Ring	Wrapper
Giant	Viajante	8½	52	CC-Ma
Churchill	Churchill	7	48	CC-Ma
Lonsdale	No. 1	7	43	CC-Ma
Lonsdale	No. 2	6½	43	CC-Ma
Corona	No. 4	5½	43	CC-Ma
Long Panatela	Palma Extra	7	36	CC-Ma

This cigar is offered in bundles of 25 cigars each and is a full-bodied, even heavy, smoke.

BALLENA SUPREMA
Handmade in Danli, Honduras and San Andres Tuxtula, Mexico.

DANLI COLLECTION:
Wrapper: USA/Connecticut   *Binder: Mexico*   *Filler: Dom. Rep., Mexico*

SAN ANDRES COLLECTION:
Wrapper: USA/Connecticut   *Binder: Mexico*   *Filler: Mexico*

Shape	Name	Lgth	Ring	Wrapper
	Danli Collection, handmade in Honduras:			
Robusto	Consuelo	5	50	CC
Churchill	Alma	7	47	CC
Lonsdale	Ventaja	6⅞	44	CC
Giant	Encanto	8	50	CC
Pyramid	Capitan	7	54	CC
	San Andres Collection, handmade in Mexico:			
Robusto	Cordura	5	52	CC
Churchill	Concordia	7	48	CC

Lonsdale	Cortes	7	42	CC
Double Corona	Esperanza	7	50	CC
Toro	Patron	6½	52	CC

These "Great Whale" cigars are the product of the McClelland Tobacco Company, justly famous for pipe tobaccos for many years. Both lines are new for 1996 and are meticulously crafted, with the Honduran blend offering a medium-bodied taste and the Mexican style a medium-to-full bodied flavor. Both styles are presented in individual cellophane sleeves packed in elegant cedar boxes.

BANCES
Handmade in Cofradia, Honduras.
Wrapper: Ecuador and Indonesia   *Binder: Honduras*
Filler: Dominican Republic, Honduras and Nicaragua

Shape	Name	Lgth	Ring	Wrapper
Corona	Brevas	5½	43	CM-Ma
Lonsdale	Cazadores	6¼	44	Co-Ma
Churchill	Corona Immensas	6¾	48	CM-Ma
Panatela	El Prados	6¼	36	CM-Ma
Giant	Presidents	8½	52	CM-Ma
Panatela	Uniques	5½	38	CM-Ma

Bances cigars are now, for the most part, handmade in Honduras under the same supervision as the famous Hoyo de Monterrey and Punch lines. This is a true value cigar, with the same great smoking qualities of its more famous sister lines.

BAUZA
Handmade in Santiago, Dominican Republic.
Wrapper: Cameroon   *Binder: Dom. Rep.*   *Filler: Dom. Rep.*

Shape	Name	Lgth	Ring	Wrapper
Churchill	Casa Grande	6¾	48	CM
Double Corona	Fabuloso	7½	50	CM
Panatela	Florete	6⅞	35	CM

Corona	Grecos	5½	42	CM
Lonsdale	Jaguar	6½	42	CM
Lonsdale	Medalla d'Oro No. 1	6⅞	44	CM
Short Panatela	Petit Corona	5	38	CM
Double Corona	Presidente /combination filler/	7½	50	CM
Robusto	Robusto	5½	50	CM

Introduced in 1980, these medium-to-full-bodied cigars are high in quality and high in value. Enveloped in rare Cameroon wrappers, nine sizes are offered, eight of which are in elegant wooden boxes and one in a bundle of 25 cigars with combination filler.

BELINDA
Handmade in Honduras.
Wrapper: Ecuador, Honduras and USA/Connecticut
Binder: Honduras   Filler: Dominican Republic and Honduras

Shape	Name	Lgth	Ring	Wrapper
Panatela	Belinda	6½	36	CM
Corona	Breva Conserva	5½	43	CM
Corona Extra	Cabinet	5⅝	45	CM
Long Corona	Corona Grande	6¼	44	CM
Churchill	Ramon	7¼	47	CM
Toro	Excellente	6	50	CM-Ma
Double Corona	Prime Minister	7½	50	CM-Ma
Robusto	Medaglia D'Oro	4½	50	CC
Robusto	Robusto	4½	50	CM-Ma
Grand Corona	Vintage Corona	6¼	45	CM
Long Corona	Humidores	6	43	CC

This old Cuban brand has been successfully re-introduced in 1994 as a medium-to-heavy bodied cigar wrapped in Ecuadorian, Honduran or USA/Connecticut leaves, depending on the shade. It is expertly made and presented in all-cedar boxes that continue the aging process. Of note is the new Humidores model, presented in a glass humidor containing 20 cigars, and the Vintage Corona, presented in an ammunition crate of 105 cigars!

BERING
Handmade in Cofradia and Danli, Honduras.

Wrapper: Honduras & USA/Connecticut   *Binder: Honduras*
Filler: Dominican Republic, Honduras, Mexico, Nicaragua

Shape	Name		Lgth	Ring	Wrapper
Giant	Grande		8½	52	CC
Lonsdale	Barons		7¼	42	CC-Ma
Lonsdale	Casinos	*(tubed)*	7⅛	42	DC-CC
Grand Corona	Cazadores		6¼	45	CC
Grand Corona	Corona Grande		6¼	46	DC-CC
Long Corona	Corona Royale	*(tubed)*	6	41	CC
Corona Extra	Coronados		5⅛	45	DC-CC
Small Panatela	No. 8		4¼	32	CC
Slim Panatela	Gold No. 1		6¼	33	CC
Toro	Hispanos		6	50	CC-Ma
Corona	Imperials	*(tubed)*	5½	42	CC
Lonsdale	Inmensas		7⅛	45	CC-Ma
Long Corona	Plazas		6	43	DC-CC
Pyramid	Torpedo		7	54	CC
Robusto	Robusto		4¾	50	CC

Bering is a premium handmade cigar imported from Honduras. This blend of specially selected Cuban-seed, long-leaf tobaccos is the reason for the incredibly smooth draw, spicy aroma and full, rich taste. Berings are available in 15 shapes and a variety of wrappers and in a variety of packaging: 3s, 4s, 5s, 15s, 25s and 50s.

NEW BERING GRANDE.
PURE SMOKING PLEASURE.

BERING GRANDE®

FINE HANDMADE, FULL-SIZED (8½" X 52) CIGARS FROM
HONDURAS. EACH IS CAREFULLY ROLLED USING ONLY
LONG FILLER TOBACCOS, A NATURAL LEAF BINDER AND
CONNECTICUT WRAPPER. THE RESULT IS AN EASY DRAW AND
ROBUST TASTE. THEY COME IN A HINGED, FIFTEEN-COUNT
WOODEN BOX. BERINGS-NOW IN THIRTEEN POPULAR SHAPES.

IMPORTED BY SWISHER INTERNATIONAL, INC.

HANDMADE CIGARS: BRAND LISTINGS

BEVERLY HILLS - VIP
Handmade in Honduras.
*(The distributor provided only limited information on the origins
of the tobaccos used in this brand; see below.)*

Shape	Name	Lgth	Ring	Wrapper
Short Panatela	No. 535	5	35	CC
Long Panatela	No. 736	7	36	CC
Long Corona	No. 644	6	44	CC
Double Corona	No. 749	7	49	CC
Robusto	No. 550	5	50	CC
Giant	No. 854	8	54	CC

This is a handmade cigar with a Connecticut wrapper and tobaccos of five
different nations in the filler blend and binder. The brand offers a smooth draw
and mild body, and is offered in all-cedar boxes of 25.

BIG BUTT
Handmade in Esteli, Nicaragua.

Wrapper: Indonesia   *Binder: Nicaragua*   *Filler: Nicaragua*

Shape	Name	Lgth	Ring	Wrapper
Double Corona	El Jefe	7½	54	CM
Toro	Don Gordo	6	54	CM
Robusto	Gordito	4¾	54	CM

This new brand honors the memory of Don Carlos Santiago, better known as
"Don Gordo," a master roller who produced cigars in Cuba until the time of
nationalization, and who died in 1994. These big-ring cigars offer a medium-to-
full body and are packed in elegant cedar cases in individual cellophane
sleeves, and accompany a wide line of clothing and fashion accessories.

BLACK LABEL
Handmade in San Andres Tuxtula, Mexico.

Wrapper: Mexico   *Binder: Honduras*   *Filler: Mexico*

Shape	Name	Lgth	Ring	Wrapper
Long Corona	Acapulco	6	42	CC-Ma

HANDMADE CIGARS: BRAND LISTINGS

Giant	Cancun	8	52	CC-Ma
Panatela	Guadalajara	6⅝	35	CC-Ma
Double Corona	Jalisco	6⅞	54	CC-Ma
Double Corona	Monterrey	7½	50	CC-Ma
Robusto	Robusto	4¾	50	CC-Ma
Slim Panatela	Tijuana	5	32	CC-Ma
Toro	Toro	6	50	CC-Ma
Grand Corona	Veracruz	6⅝	46	CC-Ma

This bundle brand is a medium-bodied cigar, using primarily Mexican tobaccos in both natural and maduro wrapper colors. An excellent value, these long-filler cigars are available in bundles of 10 or 25 cigars.

BLAIR
Handmade in Danli, Honduras.

Wrapper: Ecuador   *Binder: Honduras*   *Filler: Honduras*

Shape	Name	Lgth	Ring	Wrapper
Giant	Presidente	8½	52	CC
Churchill	Churchill	7	48	CC
Toro	Robusto	6	50	CC
Robusto	Rothschild	4¾	50	CC
Lonsdale	Lonsdale	6½	44	CC

This is a new brand in 1996, offered in five handmade sizes, featuring an Ecuadorian-grown, Connecticut-seed wrapper. The taste is considered to be full-bodied and is presented in individual cellophane sleeves and packed in boxes of 25.

BLUE LABEL
Handmade in Danli, Honduras.

Wrapper: Ecuador   *Binder: Dom. Rep.*   *Filler: Honduras*

Shape	Name	Lgth	Ring	Wrapper
Toro	Bulvon	6⅝	54	CC-Ma

HANDMADE CIGARS: BRAND LISTINGS

Churchill	Churchill	6⅞	48	CC
Slim Panatela	Finos	7	30	CC
Giant	Imperial	8	52	CC-Ma
Lonsdale	No. 1	6⅝	44	CC
Long Corona	No. 2	6	42	CC
Panatela	Palma	6⅞	35	CC
Double Corona	Presidente	7½	50	CC-Ma
Robusto	Rothschild	4¾	50	CC-Ma
Toro	Toro	6¼	50	CC-Ma

These high-quality cigars are made by hand from leaves of three nations: the Dominican Republic, Honduras and Ecuador. Mild-to-medium-bodied in taste, they are attractively packaged in bundles of 10 or 25 cigars.

BLUE RIBBON
Handmade in Ocotal, Nicaragua.

Wrapper: Ecuador   *Binder: Nicaragua*   *Filler: Nicaragua*

Shape	Name	Lgth	Ring	Wrapper
Double Corona	No. 500	7½	52	CC
Toro	No. 501	6	50	CC
Robusto	No. 502	4¾	50	CC
Lonsdale	No. 503	6½	44	CC
Corona	No. 504	5½	42	CC

This cigar debuted in 1994. Its medium body comes from the Cuban-seed binder and filler and a Connecticut-seed wrapper grown in Ecuador. These cigars are offered in bundles of 25 cigars each at modest price, accessible to all smokers.

BOQUILLA
Handmade in Union City, New Jersey, USA.
Wrapper: Dominican Republic, Mexico, USA/Connecticut
Binder: Mexico   *Filler: Dominican Republic*

HANDMADE CIGARS: BRAND LISTINGS

Shape	Name	Lgth	Ring	Wrapper
Giant	Churchill	8	50	CC-Ma
Double Corona	Silverano	7	50	CC-Ma
Toro	Torito	6½	50	CC-Ma
Churchill	Imperiale	7½	46	CC-Ma
Lonsdale	Presidente	6½	44	CC-Ma
Long Corona	Senadore	6	44	CC-Ma
Long Panatela	Ninfa	7	36	CC-Ma
Lonsdale	Fuma	7	44	CC-Ma
Torpedo	Torpedo	6	54	CC-Ma
Pyramid	Pyramid	5½	46	CC-Ma
Robusto	Robusto	5	50	CC-Ma

This cigar is made by a small factory of the same name. These are medium-to-full bodied cigars, with an increased number of sizes and wrappers available for 1997.

BUSTILLO
Handmade in Tampa, Florida, USA.

Wrapper: Honduras   Binder: Honduras   Filler: Honduras

Shape	Name	Lgth	Ring	Wrapper
Robusto	John McKay Super Rothschilds	4½	49	CM
Robusto	Coppola Cafe Robusto	4½	49	Ma

Here is a zesty blend of seven-year-aged Cuban-seed Honduran wrappers, offering a medium body in the John McKay Super Rothschilds and a full-bodied taste in the Coppola Cafe Robusto shape.

BUTERA ROYAL VINTAGE
Handmade in La Romana, Dominican Republic.

Wrapper: USA/Connecticut   Binder: Proprietary   Filler: Dom. Rep.

HANDMADE CIGARS: BRAND LISTINGS

Shape	Name	Lgth	Ring	Wrapper
Robusto	Bravo Corto	4½	50	CC
Lonsdale	Cedro Fino	6½	44	CC
Toro	Dorado 652	6	52	CC
Churchill	Capo Grande	7½	48	CC
Corona	Fumo Dolce	5½	44	CC
Panatela	Mira Bella	6¾	38	CC
Toro	Cornetta No. 1	6	52	CC

Introduced in 1993, Butera Royal Vintage are true-blended, premium cigars handmade in the Dominican Republic by "first-row" cigar makers. Six distinctive whole-leaf tobaccos from three different countries are blended, including four specific types of long-filler leaves from the rarest Dominican crops. Every cigar is well-aged to maturity in cabinets of fine Spanish cedar and packaged in beautiful Mahogany chests. The spicy, flavorful blend is considered medium in body.

C.A.O.
Handmade in Danli, Honduras.
Wrapper: Costa Rica, USA/Connecticut

Binder: Honduras   *Filler: Mexico, Nicaragua*

Shape	Name	Lgth	Ring	Wrapper
Petit Corona	Petit Corona	5	40	CC
Long Corona	Corona	6	42	CC-Ma
Lonsdale	Lonsdale	7	44	CC
Robusto	Robusto	4½	50	CC-Ma
Toro	Corona Gorda	6	50	CC-Ma
Giant	Churchill	8	50	CC-Ma
Pyramid	Triangulare	7½	54	CC-Ma

Introduced in 1995, this medium-bodied cigar line can be enjoyed at any time of the day, with its blend of Cuban-seed tobaccos in the filler and binder and a Connecticut shade wrapper. The maduro-wrapped cigars utilize Connecticut Broadleaf-seed tobaccos grown in Costa Rica.

HANDMADE CIGARS: BRAND LISTINGS

C.A.O. GOLD
Handmade in Esteli, Nicaragua.

Wrapper: Ecuador *Binder: Nicaragua* *Filler: Nicaragua*

Shape	Name	Lgth	Ring	Wrapper
Corona	Corona	5½	42	Co
Robusto	Robusto	5	50	Co
Toro	Corona Gorda	6½	50	Co
Churchill	Churchill	7	48	Co
Double Corona	Double Corona	7½	54	Co

This is a new brand for 1996, featuring a Connecticut Shade-seed wrapper and a mild-to-medium taste. Box-pressed, these cigars are offered in elegant boxes of 25.

C.C.I. ROYAL SATIN SELECTION
Handmade in Danli, Honduras.

Wrapper: Ecuador *Binder: Dom. Rep.* *Filler: Honduras, Nicaragua*

Shape	Name	Lgth	Ring	Wrapper
Double Corona	No. 1	7½	50	CM
Churchill	No. 2	7	48	CM
Toro	No. 3	6	50	CM
Long Corona	No. 4	6¼	44	CM
Robusto	No. 5	5	50	CM
Torpedo	No. 6	7	54	CM
Double Corona	No. 7	7¾	50	CM

This line of small-batch cigars from Cigar Club International was introduced in 1995 and has a medium body and features Havana-seed filler tobaccos from Honduras and Nicaragua. It offers a vibrant aroma and its even burn generates a solid grey-white ash. A Dominican blend and a new maduro-wrapped lineare due in 1997.

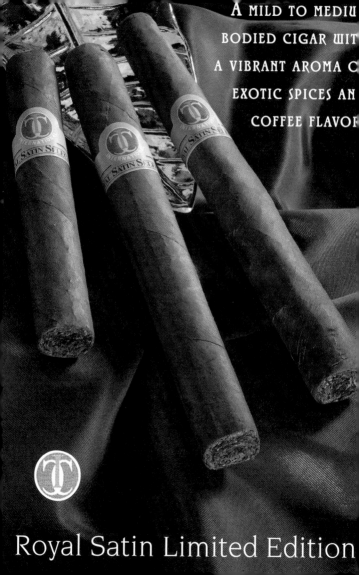

HANDMADE CIGARS: BRAND LISTINGS

CABALLEROS
Handmade in Santiago, Dominican Republic.
Wrapper: USA/Connecticut　　　*Binder: Dom. Rep.*　　　*Filler: Dom. Rep.*

Shape	Name	Lgth	Ring	Wrapper
Double Corona	Churchill	7	50	CC
Robusto	Rothschild	5	50	CC
Churchill	Double Corona	6¾	48	CC
Corona	Corona	5¾	43	CC
Corona	Petit Corona	5½	42	CC

Introduced in 1993, these are mild-to-medium bodied cigars with much flavor, produced with long filler and made completely by hand. Imported from the Dominican Republic, Caballeros cigars are offered in individual cellophane sleeves inside cedarwood boxes of 25.

CABANAS
Handmade in La Romana, Dominican Republic.
Wrapper: USA/Connecticut　　　*Binder: Dom. Rep.*　　　*Filler: Dom. Rep.*

Shape	Name	Lgth	Ring	Wrapper
Corona	Coronas	5½	42	Ma
Toro	Exquisitos	6½	48	Ma
Lonsdale	Premiers	6⅝	42	Ma
Grand Corona	Royales	5⅝	46	Ma

Fans of the darkest wrapper shades will not be disappointed by Cabanas, one of the oldest names in cigars; the flavorful Connecticut wrappers are essentially black. But the blend offers a mild and pleasant taste and is presented in boxes of 25.

CACIQUE
Handmade in Santiago, Dominican Republic.
Wrapper: USA/Connecticut　　　*Binder: Dom. Rep.*　　　*Filler: Dom. Rep.*

Shape	Name	Lgth	Ring	Wrapper
Panatela	No. 3 Jaraqua	6¾	36	CC

Long Corona	No. 2 Tainos	6	42	CC
Lonsdale	No. 1 Siboneyes	6¾	43	CC
Churchill	No. 7 Caribes	6⅞	46	CC
Double Corona	No. 8 Incas	7½	50	CC
Robusto	Azteca	4¾	50	CC-Ma
Toro	Apaches	6	50	CC-Ma

The Cacique is handmade in the Dominican Republic. It is blended with Dominican Havana-seed "ligero" and "seco" filler. It has a Havana-seed binder and is topped off with authentic Connecticut Shade wrapper. This combination of fine tobacco gives Cacique a full tobacco flavor, yet it is mild in strength.

CALIXTO LOPEZ
Handmade in Manila, the Philippines.

Wrapper: Indonesia/Java   *Binder: Philippines*   *Filler: Philippines*

Shape	Name	Lgth	Ring	Wrapper
Corona	Corona Exquisito	5⅝	43	CM
Giant Corona	Czar	8	45	CM
Giant	Gigante	8½	50	CM
Lonsdale	Lonsdale Suprema	6¾	42	CM
Grand Corona	Corona No. 1	6⅝	45	CM
Toro	Nobles Extra Fino	6½	50	CM
Long Panatela	Palma Royales	7¼	36	CM

Created in 1980 and offering a mild-bodied smoke, the Calixto Lopez line utilizes the best in Southeast Asian tobacco. The main element is home-grown Philippine tobacco from the highly-respected Isabela Valley on the northernmost Philippine island of Luzon.

CALLE OCHO
Handmade in Miami, Florida, USA.

Wrapper: Ecuador   *Binder: Ecuador*
Filler: Dominican Republic, Honduras, Mexico, Nicaragua

HANDMADE CIGARS: BRAND LISTINGS

Shape	Name	Lgth	Ring	Wrapper
Torpedo	Festivale	5	38	Cl
Robusto	Gordito	5	50	Cl
Toro	Gordito Largo	6	50	Cl
Lonsdale	Perfect Corona	6½	42	Cl
Long Panatela	Laguito	7½	38	Cl
Churchill	Doble	7½	46	Cl
Double Corona	Churchill	7¼	50	DC-Cl
Double Corona	Immenso	7½	54	Cl
Torpedo	Torpedo	6½	54	Cl
Pyramid	Pyramide	7¼	54	Cl
Giant	Embajador	9	60	Cl

Created in 1994, this is a mild-bodied blend of leaves from five nations! Named for the epicenter of the Cuban population in Miami – 8th Street or *Calle Ocho* in Spanish – this brand is offered in cedar boxes of 25.

CAMACHO
Handmade in Danli, Honduras.
Wrapper: Honduras and USA/Connecticut

Binder: Honduras   Filler: Honduras

Shape	Name	Lgth	Ring	Wrapper
Giant	El Cesar	8½	52	Cl-CC-Ma
Double Corona	Executives	7¾	50	Cl-CC-Ma
Churchill	Churchill	7	48	Cl-CC-Ma
Lonsdale	No. 1	7	44	Cl-CC-Ma
Robusto	Monarca	5	50	Cl-CC-Ma
Lonsdale	Cetros	6½	44	Cl-CC-Ma
Long Panatela	Pan Especial	7	36	Cl-CC-Ma
Panatela	Elegantes	6⅛	38	Cl-CC-Ma
Long Corona	Palmas	6	43	Cl-CC-Ma

HANDMADE CIGARS: BRAND LISTINGS

Corona	Nacionales	5½	44	Cl-CC-Ma
Lonsdale	Cazadores	6½	44	Cl-CC-Ma
Slim Panatela	Conchitas	5½	32	Cl-CC-Ma

This outstanding full-bodied brand was originated in the 1960s and first produced in Nicaragua before moving production to Honduras. It offers connoisseurs a wide range of sizes and features tobaccos primarily from the Jamastran Valley of Honduras. Connecticut wrappers are used for the "claro" series when available and maduro wrappers are often in short supply for this brand.

CAMMARATA
Handmade in Tampa, Florida, USA.
See tobacco blending notes for each group.

Shape	Name	Lgth	Ring	Wrapper
I: Wrapper: Honduras Binder: Dom. Rep.				*Filler: Dom. Rep.*
Robusto	Rothschild	5¾	50	CM
Churchill	Lonsdale	7	46	CM
Double Corona	Churchill	6¾	50	CM
Long Panatela	St. Julien Panatella	7	36	CM
II: Wrapper: Honduras Binder: Honduras				*Filler: Honduras*
Robusto	Rothschild Maduro	4	50	Ma
III: Wrapper: USA/Conn. Binder: Honduras				*Filler: Honduras*
Toro	Varsalona No. 4	6	50	CC
Double Corona	JFK	7½	49	CC
Churchill	Special Series No. 2	6¾	46	CC
Petit Corona	Special Series No. 1	5	44	CC
IV: Wrapper: Honduras Binder: Honduras				*Filler: Honduras*
Robusto	Havana 5x52	5	52	CM
Double Corona	Havava 7½x52	7½	52	CM
V: Wrapper: USA/Conn. Binder: Honduras				*Filler: Honduras*
Pyramid	Havana Pyramid	5	57	CC

VI:	Wrapper: Honduras	Binder: Honduras			Filler: Honduras
Toro	Cuban Robusto Maduro	6	54	Ma
VII:	Wrapper: USA/Conn.	Binder: Honduras			Filler: Honduras
Double Corona	Cuban Double Corona	7½	54	CC

Carmela Cammarata Varsalona is one of the few cigar rollers left from Ybor City, a West Tampa neighborhood that once hosted 300 cigar factories and 30,000 workers in the 1920s and '30s. She now rolls up to 300 cigars per day, with blends based on Cuban-seed tobaccos from the Dominican Republic, Honduras and the USA. The all-Honduras blends are full-bodied, while the multi-nation blends offer a medium strength.

CAMORRA IMPORTED LIMITED RESERVE
Handmade in Danli, Honduras.

Wrapper: Ecuador		Binder: Honduras			Filler: Honduras
Shape	Name		Lgth	Ring	Wrapper
Slim Panatela	Capri		5½	32	CM
Pyramid	Padova		5	44	CM
Panatela	Napoli		6⅛	38	CM
Robusto	Roma		5	50	CM
Corona	Genova		5½	44	CM
Lonsdale	Venizia		6½	44	CM
Churchill	San Remo		7	48	CM

Camorra Imported Limited Reserve cigars debuted in 1995 as one of the finest super-premium cigars made in Honduras. This unique blend of the finest available Honduran tobacco is blended with a smooth and oily Ecuadorian wrapper for a medium-bodied taste. Note the sweet initial taste, produced by the addition of sugar added to the vegetable gum used to seal the cap.

CANARIA D'ORO
Handmade in Santiago, Dominican Republic.

Wrapper: Mexico		Binder: Mexico		Filler: Dom. Rep., Mexico	
Shape	Name		Lgth	Ring	Wrapper
Small Panatela	Babies		4⅛	32	CC

HANDMADE CIGARS: BRAND LISTINGS

Slim Panatela	Finos	6	31	CC
Robusto	Rothschild	4½	50	Ma
Corona	Coronas	5½	43	CC
Lonsdale	Lonsdales	6½	43	CC
Robusto	Inmensos	5½	49	CC
Lonsdale	Supremos	7	45	CC

Made by hand in the Dominican Republic, this line has a creamy, medium-to-full-bodied taste with lots of aroma. Mexican tobaccos dominate the blend, combined with Dominican leaf in the filler blend.

CANONERO
Handmade in Saõ Gocalo, Brazil.
Wrapper: Ecuador　　　*Binder: Brazil*　　　　　*Filler: Brazil*

Shape	Name	Lgth	Ring	Wrapper
Double Corona	No. 1: Double Corona	7½	50	CC
Robusto	No. 2: Rothschild	5½	50	CC
Robusto	No. 3: Robusto	5	52	CC
Churchill	No. 4: Churchill	7	46	CC
Lonsdale	No. 10: Lonsdale	6½	42	CC
Petit Corona	No. 20: Corona	5½	42	CC
Short Panatela	No. 30: Potra	4¼	38	CC

This line began in 1995 and under the supervision of master blender Arthur Toraño offers a unique combination of Connecticut Shade-seed wrapper tobaccos with all-Brazilian binder and fillers. The result is a mild-bodied taste of excellent quality, offered in boxes of 10 (no. 30), 20 (nos. 1, 2 and 3) or 25 cigars (nos. 4, 10 and 20). Special 20-cigar gift boxes are now available for the Lonsdale and Robusto sizes as well.

CAOBA
Handmade in Santiago, Dominican Republic.
Wrapper: USA/Connecticut　　*Binder: Dom. Rep.*　　　*Filler: Dom. Rep.*

HANDMADE CIGARS: BRAND LISTINGS

Shape	Name	Lgth	Ring	Wrapper
Long Panatela	No. 1P Pantela	7½	36	CC
Corona	No. 2 Corona	5½	42	CC
Long Corona	No. 3 Lonsdale	6¼	44	CC
Churchill	No. 4 Churchill	7	46	CC
Double Corona	No. 5 Chairman	7	50	CC

This brand was started under a different name in 1993, but still offers the same mild-to-medium body. Caoba cigars are presented in individual cellophane sleeves and packed in all-cedar cabinets.

CAONABO
Handmade in Villa Gonzales, Dominican Republic.
Wrapper: USA/Connecticut   Binder: Dom. Rep.   Filler: Dom. Rep.

Shape	Name	Lgth	Ring	Wrapper
Small Panatela	Helenas	5	30	CC
Long Panatela	Caciques	7½	38	CC
Corona	Naborias	5	42	CC
Short Panatela	Nitainos	5	36	CC
Long Corona	Guanines	6	44	CC
Robusto	Petit Premier	4½	50	CC
Double Corona	Grand Premier	7½	50	CC

This is a new brand for 1996, named for the chief of the Taino tribe who resisted Spanish settlement on La Española island in 1493 and 1495. It offers a mild-to-medium body and exquisite construction and is offered in cedar boxes of 25. Coming later in 1997 will be a mild Dominican-made blend and a series of maduro-wrapped shapes.

CAPOTE
Handmade in Tenerife, the Canary Islands of Spain.
Wrapper: USA/Connecticut   Binder: Honduras   Filler: Dom. Rep.

Shape	Name	Lgth	Ring	Wrapper
Double Corona	No. 1	7	50	CC

HANDMADE CIGARS: BRAND LISTINGS

Toro	No. 2	6	50	CC
Lonsdale	No. 3	6½	43	CC
Panatela	No. 4	5½	39	CC

This is a new brand in 1996, offering medium body with a Connecticut Shade wrapper in boxes of 25.

CARA MIA
Handmade in Las Palmas, the Canary Islands of Spain.
Wrapper: Ecuador   *Binder: Canary Islands*   *Filler: Canary Islands*

Shape	Name	Lgth	Ring	Wrapper
Pyramid	Pyramid	7	52	Co
Double Corona	Churchill	7	50	Co
Toro	Toro	6	50	Co
Lonsdale	Lonsdale	6½	42	Co
Corona	Corona	5½	42	Co

Cara Mia was introduced in late 1995 as a new brand from the Canary Islands of Spain, one of the world's celebrated cigar-making regions. This is a medium-bodied cigar with excellent construction, featuring a Connecticut-seed wrapper grown in Ecuador and cured to a rich Colorado shade. Cara Mia cigars are packed uncellophaned in all-cedarwood boxes of 25.

CARBONELL
Handmade in Santiago, Dominican Republic.
Wrapper: Ecuador   *Binder: Dom. Rep.*   *Filler: Dom. Rep.*

Shape	Name	Lgth	Ring	Wrapper
Cigarillo	Palmaritos	4	28	CC
Small Panatela	Demi Tasse	5	30	CC
Slim Panatela	Panatella Thins	7	32	CC
Panatela	Panatella	6	36	CC
Long Panatela	Panatella Grande	7½	38	CC
Corona	Palma Short	5½	42	CC

HANDMADE CIGARS: BRAND LISTINGS

Lonsdale	Palma	6½	42	CC
Lonsdale	Palma Extra	7	42	CC
Lonsdale	Corona	6½	44	CC
Churchill	Churchill	6⅞	46	CC
Double Corona	Presidente	7½	49	CC
Robusto	Toro	5½	50	CC
Giant	Soberano	8½	52	CC
Giant	Gigante	10	56	CC
Pyramid	Piramide Breve	5½	56	CC
Pyramid	Piramide	7½	64	CC
Pyramid	Piramide Gigante	8	68	CC

Here is the largest-selling brand in the Dominican Republic, widely available in the United States in 1996. Created in 1907, it is produced in Santiago and features an Connecticut-seed, Ecuadorian-grown wrapper. Carbonell cigars are mild with exquisite flavor, devoid of any bitterness.

CARLIN
Handmade in Esteli, Nicaragua.

Wrapper: Nicaragua 　　　*Binder: Nicaragua* 　　　*Filler: Nicaragua*

Shape	*Name*	*Lgth*	*Ring*	*Wrapper*
Giant	Gigante	8	52	CM
Churchill	Churchill	7	48	CM
Toro	Toro	6	50	CM
Corona	Corona	5½	43	CM
Robusto	Robusto	4¾	52	CM

Introduced as a Dominican-made cigar in 1995, this brand is now made in Nicaragua and incorporates only Nicaraguan leaves. The full, robust flavor comes from the blending of three choice filler tobaccos, coddled by a beautiful Jalapa wrapper. Carlins are easily enjoyed, thanks to their outstanding construction.

HANDMADE CIGARS: BRAND LISTINGS

CARLOS TORAÑO
Handmade in Santiago, Dominican Republic.

Wrapper: USA/Connecticut   *Binder: Mexico*   *Filler: Dom. Rep.*

Shape	Name	Lgth	Ring	Wrapper
Toro	Carlos I	6	50	CM
Lonsdale	Carlos II	6¾	43	CM
Double Corona	Carlos III	7½	52	CM
Corona	Carlos IV	5¾	43	CM
Grand Corona	Carlos V	6	46	CM
Churchill	Carlos VI	7	48	CM
Robusto	Carlos VII	4¾	52	CM
Panatela	Carlos VIII	6½	36	CM

More than two years in the making, Carlos Toraño cigars debuted in 1995. They are mild in body and are distributed in France, Germany, Great Britain and the Netherlands in addition to the United States.

CARMEN
Handmade in Danli, Honduras.

Wrapper: USA/Connecticut   *Binder: Indonesia*
Filler: Dominican Republic, Honduras, Nicaragua

Shape	Name	Lgth	Ring	Wrapper
Churchill	Churchill	7	48	CM
Corona	Corona	5½	42	CM
Double Corona	Presidente	7¾	50	CM
Robusto	Robusto	5	50	CM
Toro	Toro	6	50	CM

Here's a familiar name to opera fans . . . and cigar fans. This is a medium-bodied blend made by hand in Honduras and attractively boxed in elegant all-cedar boxes of 25.

HANDMADE CIGARS: BRAND LISTINGS

CARRINGTON
Handmade in Santo Domingo, Dominican Republic.
Wrapper: USA/Connecticut   *Binder: Dom. Rep.*   *Filler: Dom. Rep.*

Shape	Name	Lgth	Ring	Wrapper
Double Corona	No. 1	7½	50	CI
Long Corona	No. 2	6	42	CI
Long Panatela	No. 3	7	36	CI
Corona	No. 4	5½	40	CI
Churchill	No. 5	6⅞	46	CI
Robusto	No. 6	4½	50	CI
Toro	No. 7	6	50	CI
Pyramid	No. 8	6⅞	60	CI

Introduced in 1984, Carrington cigars offer a mild to medium taste, with a solid core of spice and a nice, toasty flavor. The wrapper is Connecticut Shade tobacco, with Dominican filler and binders. Check out the No. 8, a pyramid-shape with one of the largest ring gauges (60) of any cigar available.

CASA BLANCA
Handmade in Santiago, Dominican Republic.
Wrapper: USA/Connecticut   *Binder: Mexico*   *Filler: Dom. Rep.*

Shape	Name	Lgth	Ring	Wrapper
Short Panatela	Bonita	4	36	CC
Corona	Corona	5½	42	CC
Toro	DeLuxe	6	50	CC-Ma
Robusto	Half Jeroboam	5	66	CC-Ma
Giant	Jeroboam	10	66	CC-Ma
Lonsdale	Lonsdale	6½	42	CC-Ma
Double Corona	Magnum	7	60	CC-Ma
Panatela	Panatela	6	35	CC
Double Corona	Presidente	7½	50	CC-Ma

HANDMADE CIGARS: BRAND LISTINGS

This line, which means "White House" in English, offers an extremely mild taste in a variety of sizes. Particularly noteworthy are the giant 66-ring Half Jeroboam and Jeroboam, the thickest straight-sided cigars offered on the U.S. market.

CASA BLANCA RESERVE
Handmade in Santiago, Dominican Republic.

Wrapper: Ecuador   *Binder: Mexico*   *Filler: Dom. Rep.*

Shape	Name	Lgth	Ring	Wrapper
Double Corona	No. 1	7½	50	CC
Toro	No. 2	6	50	CC
Lonsdale	No. 3	6½	42	CC
Corona	No. 4	5½	43	CC

"The best of the best" is the idea behind this upgraded selection of Casa Blanca, the Reserve Collection. Introduced in 1996, this elegant, mild line is offered in all-cedar cabinets of 25 cigars each.

CASA BUENA
Handmade in Las Palmas, the Canary Islands of Spain.

Wrapper: USA/Connecticut   *Binder: Mexico*   *Filler: Brazil, Dom. Rep.*

Shape	Name	Lgth	Ring	Wrapper
Double Corona	Especiales No. 1	7½	50	CC
Toro	Especiales No. 2	6	50	CC
Lonsdale	Especiales No. 3	6½	43	CC
Robusto	Especiales No. 4	4¾	50	CC

A 1996 introduction: a new blend from the Canary Islands that offers a medium-bodied smoke, thanks to its combination of slightly spicy interior tobaccos with a Connecticut wrapper, offered in boxes of 25.

CASA DE NICARAGUA
Handmade in Nicaragua.

Wrapper: Nicaragua   *Binder: Nicaragua*   *Filler: Nicaragua*

Shape	Name	Lgth	Ring	Wrapper
Robusto	Rothchild	5	50	CC

HANDMADE CIGARS: BRAND LISTINGS

Corona	Petit Corona	5½	42	CC
Long Corona	Corona	6	43	CC
Toro	Toro	6	50	CC-Ma
Long Panatela	Panatela Extra	7	36	CC
Lonsdale	Double Corona	7	44	CC-Ma
Double Corona	Churchill	7	49	CC
Double Corona	Presidente	7½	52	CC
Giant	Gigante	8	54	CC-Ma
Giant	Viajante	8½	52	CC

This brand uses all-Cuban seed tobaccos grown in Nicaragua, resulting in a medium-to-heavy-bodied smoke. These are well-constructed cigars, offered in all-cedar boxes of 25.

CASA MARTIN
Handmade in Las Palmas, the Canary Islands of Spain.
Wrapper: Indonesia   *Binder: Dom. Rep.*   *Filler: Dom. Rep.*

Shape	Name	Lgth	Ring	Wrapper
Corona	Corona	5½	42	CC
Robusto	Robusto	4¾	48	CC
Lonsdale	Numero Uno	6⅝	43	CC
Toro	Governor	6	48	CC
Churchill	Churchill	7	46	CC
Churchill	Double Corona	7½	48	CC

Formerly made in the Dominican Republic, this brand is virtually new for 1996. These cigars are mild to medium in strength, with a Ecuador-grown, Connecticut-seed wrapper and Dominican binder and filler tobaccos. The Casa Martin line is offered in bundles of 25 cigars each.

CASANOVA
Handmade in Las Palmas, the Canary Islands of Spain.
Wrapper: USA/Connecticut   *Binder: Dom. Rep.*   *Filler: Dom. Rep.*

HANDMADE CIGARS: BRAND LISTINGS

Shape	Name	Lgth	Ring	Wrapper
Corona	Consules	5½	42	CC
Lonsdale	Robusto	4¾	50	CC
Lonsdale	Sublimes	6⅝	42	CC
Toro	Matador	6	50	CC
Churchill	Churchill	7	46	CC
Double Corona	Imperiales	7½	50	CC
Torpedo	Torpedo	7	52	CC

The Casanova line is the latest in the distinguished history of the cigar makers of the Canary Islands. Offered in elegant cedar boxes of ten cigars each, this medium-bodied line was completely revamped in 1994.

CASILLAS
Handmade in Sacramento, California, and Reno, Nevada, USA.
Wrapper: Ecuador or USA/Connecticut (natural); Mexico (maduro)
Binder: Ecuador or Mexico
Filler: Dominican Republic, Honduras, Mexico, Nicaragua

Shape	Name	Lgth	Ring	Wrapper
Double Corona	Cuban Round	7½	54	CM-Ma
Double Corona	Churchill	7½	50	CM-Ma
Torpedo	Torpedo	6	50	CM-Ma
Toro	Casillas No. 1	6½	56	CM-Ma
Toro	Double Corona	6½	50	CM-Ma
Slim Panatela	Cubanito	6	34	CM-Ma
Long Corona	Corona Long	6	44	CM-Ma
Panatela	Panatela	6	36	CM-Ma
Toro	Toro	6½	52	CM-Ma
Corona Extra	Rothschild	5	46	CM-Ma
Long Corona	Petit Cetros	6	42	CM-Ma
Panatela	Pencil	5½	36	CM-Ma

HANDMADE CIGARS: BRAND LISTINGS

Giant	Jacaranda	8½	56	CM-Ma
Churchill	Presidente	7	46	CM-Ma
Robusto	Robusto	5¼	52	CM-Ma
Giant	Excalibur	8½	52	CM-Ma
Torpedo	Torpedito	6	50	CM-Ma
	Made with short filler:			
Churchill	Super Cazadores	7½	46	CM-Ma
Churchill	Cazadores	7½	46	CM-Ma
Long Corona	Fuma	6	44	CM-Ma

This blend of long-filler tobaccos is assembled under the direction of Macario Casillas, a Cuban native who began rolling cigars at age 13. He supervises three other ex-Cuban nationals who share his passion for quality and the medium-to-full bodied taste and smooth finish that characterizes the Casillas brand.

CEDAR JOE
Handmade in Danli, Honduras.

Wrapper: Honduras   *Binder: Honduras*   *Filler: Honduras*

Shape	Name	Lgth	Ring	Wrapper
Robusto	Rothchild	4½	50	CM
Lonsdale	Corona Gorda	6½	44	CM
Double Corona	Aristo	7½	52	CM
Torpedo	Mega Torpedo	7½	64	CM
Pyramid	Club Pyramid	5½	52	CM

A 1994 creation, the Cedar Joe line offers a mild-to-medium-bodied smoke in a fine value line. The three straight-sided shapes and the two shaped styles are each offered in boxes of 10.

CEDROS
Handmade in Santiago, Dominican Republic.

Wrapper: USA/Connecticut   *Binder: Dom. Rep.*   *Filler: Dom. Rep.*

HANDMADE CIGARS: BRAND LISTINGS

Shape	Name	Lgth	Ring	Wrapper
Toro	No. 1	6½	50	CC
Churchill	No. 2	6⅞	46	CC
Corona	No. 3	5½	42	CC

Created by Jim and Kathi Brown-Martin in 1994, this is a mild blend of Dominican leaves with a Connecticut Shade wrapper, offered in individual cellophane sleeves presented in cedar cabinets of 25.

CELESTINO VEGA
Handmade in Indonesia.

Wrapper: Indonesia   Binder: Indonesia
Filler: Dom. Rep., Indonesia and USA/Connecticut and Pennsylvania

Shape	Name	Lgth	Ring	Wrapper
Cigarillo	Tesorito	3⅝	20	CM
Petit Corona	Petit Corona	4¾	40	CM
Small Panatela	Senoritas	4⅛	32	CM
Robusto	Senator	3½	48	CM
Robusto	Rothchild	5	50	CM
Toro	Super Rothchild	6	50	CM
Cigarillo	Cuban Panatela	7	28	CM
Lonsdale	Cuban Corona	6½	42	CM
Perfecto	Cuban Perfecto	6	48	CM
Double Corona	Churchill	7	50	CM

These handmade, long-filler cigars feature Indonesian tobaccos grown on the islands of Java and Sumatra. Javan wrappers are used on all models except the Tesorito and Cuban Panatela, which have Sumatran leaves as wrappers. These cigars offer a full, flavorful taste and are uniquely packaged not only in boxes of 25 or 50, but triangular boxes of 21 or 45!

CERDAN
Handmade in Santiago, Dominican Republic.

Wrapper: USA/Connecticut   Binder: Dom. Rep.   Filler: Dom. Rep.

HANDMADE CIGARS: BRAND LISTINGS

Shape	Name	Lgth	Ring	Wrapper
Long Panatela	Juan Carlos	7	35	CC
Panatela	Executive	5½	38	CC
Long Panatela	Gables	7½	38	CC
Corona	Napoleon	5½	40	CC
Lonsdale	Welles	6¾	40	CC
Long Corona	Chamberlain	6	43	CC
Lonsdale	Churchill	7	45	CC
Double Corona	Don Juan	7½	50	CC
Slim Panatela	Gemma	6	30	CC
Giant Corona	Don Jose	7½	44	CC
Double Corona	Don Ramon	7½	50	CC
Toro	Don Julio	6½	54	CC
Cigarillo	Pettit Jenny's	4	23	CC

Wildly popular in Europe since its introduction in 1980, Cerdan cigars debuted in the United States in 1996. This brand, the creation of Juan Cerdan Soto, offers a mild-to-medium body in boxes of 25.

CERVANTES
Handmade in Danli, Honduras.

Wrapper: Honduras   Binder: Honduras   Filler: Honduras

Shape	Name	Lgth	Ring	Wrapper
Lonsdale	Churchill	7¼	45	Cl-CC
Grand Corona	Corona	6¼	46	CC
Long Corona	Senadores	6	42	CC

Cervantes are handmade cigars of excellent quality, made in Honduras of all-Honduran tobacco. They are medium in taste, and presented in boxes of 25.

Figurados:
Perfectos, Pyramids and Torpedos

These shapes are the most distinctive of all, with flared ends and/or conical heads. Although the dimensions vary, the definitions remain constant:

- Perfectos: A cigar with a conical-shaped head and foot.

- Pyramids: A cigar whose ring gauge increases continuously from head to foot. Also known as "triangulars" or "trumpets."

- Torpedos: A cigar with a shaped head that flares out to straight sides. Also known as "belicoso."

Pictured opposite are:

- The Famous Rum Runner Churchill
  Pirate   7 x 46   (note pigtail head)

- Don Tonioli
  Super Torpedo   7½ x 64   Torpedo

- Match Play Troon   7 x 54   Pyramid

- Saint Luis Rey
  Torpedo   6 x 54   Pyramid

- Calle Ocho Torpedo 6½ x 54   Torpedo

- Rosedale Perfecto   4⅞ x 46   Perfecto

HANDMADE CIGARS: BRAND LISTINGS

CHAIRMAN'S CHOICE
Handmade in Danli, Honduras.

Wrapper: Ecuador   Binder: Honduras   Filler: Honduras

Shape	Name	Lgth	Ring	Wrapper
Corona	V.P.	5½	42	CC
Robusto	Director	5	50	CC
Toro	Treasurer	6	50	CC
Churchill	President	6⅞	46	CC
Double Corona	CEO	7¾	50	CC
Torpedo	Chairman	7	54	CC

Here is a medium-bodied brand introduced in 1996. The names of the shapes are common enough in big corporations, but is it proper to offer the Chairman a torpedo?

CHARLES FAIRMORN
Handmade in Danli, Honduras.

Wrapper: Honduras   Binder: Honduras   Filler: Honduras

Shape	Name	Lgth	Ring	Wrapper
Double Corona	Churchill	6⅞	49	CM
Long Corona	Coronas	6¼	44	CM
Panatela	Elegante	6¾	38	CM
Small Panatela	Super Fino	4½	32	CM

Sought after since their introduction in 1979, the Charles Fairmorn line from Honduras is a medium-to-full-bodied cigar which is available in four sizes. It is made by hand from selected Cuban-seed leaves and offered in boxes of 25.

CHARLES FAIRMORN BELMORE
Handmade in Santiago, Dominican Republic.

Wrapper: USA/Connecticut   Binder: Dom. Rep.   Filler: Dom. Rep.

Shape	Name	Lgth	Ring	Wrapper
Panatela	Petit Corona	5⅝	38	CC
Long Panatela	Panatela	7	36	CC

HANDMADE CIGARS: BRAND LISTINGS

Robusto	Robusto	4¾	50	CC
Lonsdale	Elegante	7	43	CC
Churchill	Churchill	6⅞	46	CC
Toro	Matador	6	50	CC
Double Corona	Presidente	7½	50	CC
Torpedo	Piramide	7½	64	CC

This series, introduced in 1991, is produced in Santiago de los Caballeros in the Dominican Republic and uses only the smoothest Connecticut wrappers. These cigars are of medium body and are offered in boxes of 25.

CHARLES THE GREAT
Handmade in Santa Rosa de Copan, Honduras.
Wrapper: USA/Connecticut   Binder: Honduras   Filler: Honduras

Shape	Name	Lgth	Ring	Wrapper
Double Corona	Madrid	7½	50	CC
Toro	Barcelona	6	50	CC
Grand Corona	Valencia	6¾	46	CC
Robusto	Granada	5	50	CC
Long Corona	Toledo	6	42	CC
Petit Corona	Cordoba	5⅛	42	CC

This very old brand, produced decades ago as a clear Havana, has been resurrected by the Finck Cigar Company of San Antonio, Texas. It utilizes the brand's original box and label art and presents these medium-bodied cigars in all-wooden boxes of 25.

CHAVELO
Handmade in Miami, Florida, USA.
Wrapper: Ecuador   Binder: Mexico   Filler: Dom. Rep.

Shape	Name	Lgth	Ring	Wrapper
Double Corona	Presidente	7⅜	50	CC
Churchill	Churchill	6⅞	48	CC

HANDMADE CIGARS: BRAND LISTINGS

Panatela	Panatela	6⅝	36	CC
Lonsdale	No. 1	6⅞	44	CC
Lonsdale	No. 2	6⅞	44	CC
Toro	Toro	6	50	CC
Robusto	Robusto	5	50	CC

This is a handmade cigar from all-long filler tobacco and is medium in body.
They are offered either in boxes or bundles, in quantities of 25 cigars each.

CHEVERE
Handmade in Kingston, Jamaica.
Wrapper: USA/Connecticut   *Binder: Dom. Rep.*   *Filler: Dom. Rep.*

Shape	Name	Lgth	Ring	Wrapper
Double Corona	Kingston	7	49	CC
Grand Corona	Montego	6½	45	CC
Giant	Ocho Rios	8	49	CC
Corona	Port Antonio	5½	43	CC
Lonsdale	Spanish Town	6½	42	CC

Chevere cigars are quality, hand-made products of Jamaica, offering good
construction and a mild-to-medium body. Introduced in 1990, the brand's
shapes offer a natural wrapper, in bundles of 12 or 25 cigars each.

CIFUENTES
Handmade in Santiago, Dominican Republic.
Wrapper: USA/Connecticut   *Binder: Cameroon*
Filler: Dominican Republic, Jamaica, Mexico

Shape	Name	Lgth	Ring	Wrapper
Short Panatela	Petit Corona	5	38	CC
Lonsdale	Lonsdale	6½	42	CC
Torpedo	Pyramid	6½	50	CC
Double Corona	Churchill	7½	49	CC
Robusto	Corona Gorda	5½	49	CC

HANDMADE CIGARS: BRAND LISTINGS

The famous name – and face – of Ramon Cifuentes, who took over the Partagas brand in 1889 after the death of its founder, adorn this 1996-introduced brand of highly limited availability. Cigars under this brand name were produced in Havana until nationalization; today's version is medium-bodied and beautifully constructed.

CLEMENTINE
Handmade in Danli, Honduras.

Wrapper: Honduras   *Binder: Honduras*   *Filler: Honduras, Nicaragua*

Shape	Name	Lgth	Ring	Wrapper
Long Corona	Cetros	6¼	44	CM
Double Corona	Churchills	7	50	CM
Giant	Inmensas	8	54	CM
Lonsdale	No. 1	7	44	CM
Corona	No. 4	5½	44	CM
Long Panatela	Panatelas	7	36	CM
Double Corona	Presidente	7¾	50	CM
Robusto	Rothschild	5	50	CM
Toro	Toro	6	50	CM
Giant	Viajante	8½	52	CM

This is a long-filler, bundle cigar which was introduced in 1991 and offers a full-bodied taste. The name of the brand supposedly came from the favorite song of the buyers who were looking for tobacco on the backroads of Central America when the brand was introduced. Please . . .

CLEOPATRA
Handmade in La Romana, Dominican Republic.

Wrapper: Indonesia   *Binder: Dom. Rep.*   *Filler: Brazil, Dom. Rep.*

Shape	Name	Lgth	Ring	Wrapper
Perfecto	630	5½	48	CC
Perfecto	580	5	42	CC

This new brand from Consolidated Cigar Corporation celebrates one of history's most famous women - Cleopatra - with a cigar aimed at women who enjoy outstanding cigars. The taste of this 1997 introduction is expected to be mild-to-medium in body with both shapes tapered at both ends in a classic perfecto shape.

COHIBA
Handmade in Santiago, Dominican Republic.

Wrapper: USA/Connecticut   Binder: Mexico
Filler: Dominican Republic, Jamaica, Mexico

Shape	Name	Lgth	Ring	Wrapper
Robusto	Robusto	5½	50	CI
Lonsdale	Corona Especiale	6½	42	CI
Double Corona	Esplendido	7	49	CI

The Dominican Cohiba is made exclusively for the humidors of Alfred Dunhill. A robust and full-bodied blend of tobaccos is surrounded by a light-colored wrapper of Connecticut leaf. Once created, these cigars continue to age in cedar cabinet boxes.

COJIMAR
Handmade in Miami, Florida, USA.

Wrapper: Ecuador   Binder & Filler: Proprietary

Shape	Name	Lgth	Ring	Wrapper
Torpedo	Torpedo	6	54	CC
Giant	Presidente	8	50	CC
Lonsdale	Coronitas	6¾	44	CC
Panatela	Laguitos	6¾	38	CC
Panatela	Cortaditos	6¾	38	CC
Robusto	Toro	5½	50	CC
Small Panatela	Senoritas	5	30	CC

This is a new cigar in 1996, offering a range of popular sizes in a medium-bodied style.

HANDMADE CIGARS: BRAND LISTINGS

COLONIALES
Handmade, with short filler, in Danli, Honduras.

Wrapper: Honduras   *Binder: Honduras*   *Filler: Honduras*

Shape	Name	Lgth	Ring	Wrapper
Robusto	Robusto	5	50	CM
Toro	Toro	6	50	CM
Double Corona	Churchill	7	50	CM
Lonsdale	Cetro	6¾	44	CM
Corona	Corona Extra	5½	44	CM
Grand Corona	Corona Gorda	6	46	CM

New for 1996, this brand is made of all-Honduran, short-filler tobaccos and offers a medium-bodied taste with excellent construction.

COLORADO
Handmade in Danli, Honduras.

Wrapper: USA/Connecticut   *Binder: Honduras*   *Filler: Honduras, Nicaragua*

Shape	Name	Lgth	Ring	Wrapper
Lonsdale	Lonsdale	6½	44	Co
Robusto	Robusto	5½	50	Co
Torpedo	Torpedo	7	48	Co
Double Corona	Presidente	7½	50	Co

Colorado is a medium-bodied, premium cigar created in 1994 which has Honduran and Nicaraguan filler. This unique blend is wrapped with a rare, reddish-shaded Connecticut leaf which bestows a taste that defines excellence in cigar making.

CONDAL
Handmade in Las Palmas, the Canary Islands of Spain.

Wrapper: USA/Connecticut   *Binder: Mexico*   *Filler: Brazil, Dom. Rep.*

Shape	Name	Lgth	Ring	Wrapper
Lonsdale	No. 1	6⅝	42	CI
Corona	No. 3	5⅝	42	CI

HANDMADE CIGARS: BRAND LISTINGS

Corona	No. 4	5¼	42	Cl
Panatela	No. 6	6¼	35	Cl
Lonsdale	Inmenso	7¼	42	Cl
Churchill	No. 10	7	46	Cl
Robusto	Robusto	5½	50	Cl
Double Corona	Churchill	7½	50	Cl

Condal cigars are all handmade and are extremely mild; they are offered in boxes of 25.

CONNISSEUR GOLD LABEL
Handmade in Honduras.
(The distributor provided only limited information on the origins of the tobaccos used in this brand; see below.)

Shape	Name	Lgth	Ring	Wrapper
Giant	Viajante	8½	52	CC-Ma
Giant	Gigante	8	54	CC-Ma
Double Corona	Imperial	7½	50	CC-Ma
Churchill	Churchill	7	49	Cl-CC
Lonsdale	No. 1	7	43	CC-Ma
Panatela	No. 3	7	36	CC
Toro	Toro	6	50	CC-Ma
Long Corona	Corona	6	44	CC
Corona	No. 4	5½	43	CC
Robusto	Rothchild	4½	50	CC-Ma

This is a value-priced brand, with a Honduran-grown wrapper that gives these cigars a medium-bodied flavor; it is offered in bundles of 25.

CONUCOS
Handmade in Santiago, Dominican Republic.
Wrapper: USA/Connecticut   Binder: Dom. Rep.   Filler: Dom. Rep., Honduras

HANDMADE CIGARS: BRAND LISTINGS

Shape	Name	Lgth	Ring	Wrapper
Long Corona	Panatelas	5⅞	40	CC
Corona	Coronas	5¼	42	CC
Robusto	Robustos	5	50	CC
Long Corona	Celebracion	6¼	44	CC

New for 1996, this brand offers a smooth, mild body thanks to the blending of a genuine Connecticut wrapper with a Dominican binder and Dominican and Honduran filler leaves.

COSTA DORADA
Handmade in La Romana, Dominican Republic.
Wrapper: Ecuador   *Binder: Dom. Rep.*   *Filler: Dom. Rep.*

Shape	Name	Lgth	Ring	Wrapper
Churchill	Consul	7	48	CC
Giant	Director	8½	52	CC
Lonsdale	Elegante	6½	44	CC
Toro	Grand Corona	6	50	CC
Corona	Nobles	5½	42	CC

Introduced in 1994, this is a medium-bodied brand, newly blended with a Connecticut-seed wrapper and Dominican Republic-grown tobaccos inside and offered in bundles of 20 cigars each.

CREDO
Handmade in Santiago, Dominican Republic.
Wrapper: USA/Connecticut   Binder: Dom. Rep., Mexico   *Filler: Dom. Rep.*

Shape	Name	Lgth	Ring	Wrapper
Slim Panatela	Jubilante	5	34	CC
Corona	Anthanor	5¾	42	CC
Churchill	Magnificat	6⅞	46	CC
Robusto	Arcane	5	50	CC
Double Corona	Pythagoras	7	50	CC

HANDMADE CIGARS: BRAND LISTINGS

The Credo cigar line has been designed by the famous Belaubre family with a French flair. Their recipe produces a medium-strength smoke that is very smooth. Only the finest ingredients are used after being meticulously cured. The Magnificat, Arcane and Pythagoras models utilize a Dominican binder, while the Jubilate and Anthanor include a Mexican binder. The finished product, created in 1993, is offered in beautiful boxes imported from France.

CRESTON PRESTIGE CUVEE
Handmade in San Pedro Sula, Honduras.

Wrapper: Ecuador   Binder: Honduras   Filler: Honduras

Shape	Name	Lgth	Ring	Wrapper
	Ultra Premium with Habana Sweet Cap:			
Slim Panatela	Lady Creston	5½	32	CC
Panatela	Squire Creston	6⅛	38	CC
Robusto	Sir Creston	5	50	CC
Corona	Baron Creston	5½	44	CC
Lonsdale	Duke of Creston	6½	44	CC
Churchill	Lord Creston	7	48	CC
	Limited Reserve Old Habana style:		*(Honduran puro)*	
Robusto	Caballero	5	50	CM
Long Corona	Senor	6	43	CM
Toro	El Rey	6	50	CM
	Special:			
Pyramid	Pyramide Especial	6½	54	CC
Giant	Farouk Gigante	9	60	CC

This is a new cigar which offers a treat for smokers upon lighting: a sweet burst from a special sugar solution introduced into the vegetable gum used to seal the cap. This unique taste is only the beginning of a smooth and elegant smoke. The Prestige Cuvee is medium in body, while the Limited Reserve is medium-to-full in body, using all Honduran tobaccos. The Special cigars are very limited in supply and provide the enthusiast with pleasures of two hours or more at a sitting.

HANDMADE CIGARS: BRAND LISTINGS

CRISPIN PATIÑO
Handmade in Cumana, Venezuela.

Wrapper: Venezuela *Binder: Venezuela* *Filler: Venezuela*

Shape	Name	Lgth	Ring	Wrapper
Grand Corona	No. 3	6⅛	46	CM
Corona Extra	No. 2	5½	46	CM
Petit Corona	No. 1	4¾	42	CM
Slim Panatela	Purito	5	32	CM

Introduced to the U.S. market in 1996, this has been a popular Venezuelan brand since 1928. Mild in body and made of all Venezuelan tobaccos, it is produced with pride by the Patiño family, which started making cigars in 1900.

CRISTAL DE LEON
Handmade in Danli, Honduras.
Wrapper: Honduras or USA/Connecticut

Binder: Honduras *Filler: Dominican Republic, Honduras*

Shape	Name		Lgth	Ring	Wrapper
Corona	Cristals	*(tubed)*	5½	43	CC

Introduced in 1996, this is a handmade, all long-filler cigar from Honduras, featuring either a Sumatra-seed wrapper grown in Honduras for a medium-bodied taste or a Connecticut wrapper, which gives a mild-to-medium bodied flavor. The packaging is absolutely unique: each cigar is presented in an air-tight glass tube, topped by a Honduran penny!

CRUZ REAL
Handmade in Vera Cruz, Mexico.

Wrapper: Mexico *Binder: Mexico* *Filler: Mexico*

Shape	Name	Lgth	Ring	Wrapper
Lonsdale	No. 1	6⅝	42	CC-Ma
Long Corona	No. 2	6	42	CC-Ma
Panatela	No. 3	6⅝	35	CC-Ma
Double Corona	No. 14	7½	50	CC-Ma
Toro	No. 19	6	50	CC-Ma

Robusto	No. 24	4½	50	CC-Ma
Robusto	No. 25	5½	52	CC-Ma
Giant	No. 28	8½	54	CC-Ma

Cruz Real is a true "puro," using wrapper, binder and filler from Mexico. The fine combination of Mexican-grown Sumatra-seed wrappers (Cuban-seed for maduro) and San Andres binder and fillers are the perfect union for this lightly spicy, mild-to-medium-bodied cigar, which was introduced in 1994.

CUBA ALIADOS
Handmade in Danli, Honduras.

Wrapper: Ecuador   *Binder: Ecuador*   *Filler: Brazil, Dom. Rep.*

Shape	Name	Lgth	Ring	Wrapper
Lonsdale	Cazadore	7	45	CM
Double Corona	Churchill	7⅛	54	CC-CM
Grand Corona	Corona Deluxe	6½	45	CC-CM
Pyramid	Diademas	7½	60	CC-CM
Pyramid	Figurin	10	60	CM
Grand Corona	Fuma	6½	45	CM
Giant	General	18	66	CM
Lonsdale	Lonsdale	6½	42	CC-CM
Corona Extra	No. 4	5½	45	CC-CM
Long Panatela	Palma	7	36	CC-CM
Short Panatela	Petit Cetro	5	36	CC-CM
Pyramid	Piramides	7½	60	CC-CM
Corona	Remedios	5½	42	CC-CM
Robusto	Rothschild	5	51	CC-CM
Toro	Toro	6	54	CC-CM
Churchill	Valentino	7	48	CC-CM

Developed by master blender Rolando Reyes, these Honduran-made cigars offer a medium body with a distinct nutty flavor and beautiful Sumatran-seed

HANDMADE CIGARS: BRAND LISTINGS

Ecuadorian wrappers in a light or medium shade. Note the gigantic "General" shape, at 18 inches the longest regular-production cigar on the U.S. market.

CUBAN CIGAR FACTORY
Handmade in San Diego, California, USA.

Wrapper: Ecuador or USA/Connecticut (natural); Ecuador (maduro)
Binder: Ecuador   *Filler: Honduras, Mexico*

Shape	Name	Lgth	Ring	Wrapper
Panatela	Panatela	6¾	36	Cl
Corona	Corona	5¾	42	Cl
Lonsdale	El Cubano	6¾	44	Cl
Grand Corona	Havana	6	46	Cl
Robusto	Robusto	5	50	Cl
Robusto	Monterico	5½	52	Cl
Double Corona	C.R. Largo	7¼	50	Cl
Double Corona	Presidente	7¾	52	Cl
Torpedo	Torpedo	7	56	Cl
	Maestro series:			
Toro	No. 1	6	54	Ma
Toro	No. 2	6½	50	Ma
Robusto	No. 3	4¾	52	Ma

California, here I come! This brand is made by hand in a small factory/shop in the Gaslamp District of San Diego. The cigars are rolled by experienced hands, primarily from Cuba, now settled in California. The regular series began in 1994 and is mild in body, while the Maestro series began in 1995, and is medium-to-full in body.

CUBANA LA TRADICION CABINET SELECTION
Handmade in Miami, Florida, USA.

Wrapper: Ecuador   *Binder: Dominican Republic*
Filler: Dominican Republic, Honduras, Nicaragua

Shape	Name	Lgth	Ring	Wrapper
Long Panatela	Lanceros	7½	38	CC-CM-Ma

Long Corona	Coronas	6	44	CC-CM-Ma
Robusto	Robustos	5	50	CC-CM-Ma
Double Corona	Churchills	7	49	CC-CM-Ma
Double Corona	Double Coronas	7⅝	50	CC-CM-Ma
Torpedo	Torpedoes	6½	54	CC-CM-Ma

Introduced in 1996, this is a medium-bodied cigar from a small factory which is determined to achieve the highest quality possible in the manufacture of exquisite cigars of every shape and size.

CUBITA
Handmade in Santiago, Dominican Republic.
Wrapper: USA/Connecticut   *Binder: Dom. Rep.*   *Filler: Dom. Rep.*

Shape	Name	Lgth	Ring	Wrapper
Double Corona	No. 2000	7	50	CC
Corona	No. 500	5½	43	CC
Lonsdale	No. 8-9-8	6¾	43	CC
Panatela	No. 2	6¼	38	CC
Toro	No. 700	6	50	CC
Small Panatela	Delicias	5⅛	30	CC

Introduced in 1986, this is a medium-to-heavy bodied cigar, with excellent construction. The six-shape brand uses only aged tobaccos and offers these cigars in beautiful cedar cases of 25 cigars each.

CUESTA-REY
Handmade in Santiago, Dominican Republic.
Wrapper: Cameroon and USA/Connecticut   *Binder: Dom. Rep.*
Filler: Dominican Republic

Shape	Name	Lgth	Ring	Wrapper
	Cabinet Selection:			
Giant	No. 1	8½	52	CC-Ma
Long Panatela	No. 2	7	36	CC-Ma

HANDMADE CIGARS: BRAND LISTINGS

Lonsdale	No. 95	6¼	42	CC-Ma
Double Corona	No. 898	7	49	CC-Ma
Lonsdale	No. 1884	6¾	44	CC-Ma
	Centennial Collection:			
Giant	Dominican No. 1	8½	52	CC-Ma
Churchill	Dominican No. 2	7¼	48	CC-Ma
Long Panatela	Dominican No. 3	7	36	CC-Ma
Lonsdale	Dominican No. 4	6½	42	CC-Ma
Corona	Dominican No. 5	5½	43	CC-Ma
Robusto	Dominican No. 7	4½	50	CC-Ma
Toro	Dominican No. 60	6	50	CC-Ma
Churchill	Aristocrat *(tubed)*	7¼	48	CC
Long Corona	Captiva *(tubed)*	6⅛	42	CC
Long Panatela	Rivera *(tubed)*	7	36	CC
Small Panatela	Cameo	4¼	32	CC
Robusto	Robusto No. 7	4½	50	CC-Ma
Giant	Individual *(boxed)*	8½	52	CC

With more than a century of experience in the manufacture of handmade cigars since 1884, the Cuesta-Rey selection offers both mild-to-medium (Cabinet) and medium-bodied (Centennial) cigars. Connecticut Shade wrappers are used for all models except Cabinet Selection No. 95, which uses a Cameroon wrapper. Connecticut Broadleaf tobacco is used for all of the maduro wrappers.

CUSANO HERMANOS
Handmade in Santiago, Dominican Republic.
Wrapper: USA/Connecticut or Dominican Republic
Binder: Dom. Rep.   *Filler: Dom. Rep.*

Shape	*Name*	*Lgth*	*Ring*	*Wrapper*
Robusto	Bullet	4	50	CC-Ma
Robusto	Robusto	5	50	CC-Ma
Churchill	Churchill	6⅞	46	CC-Ma

HANDMADE CIGARS: BRAND LISTINGS

Robusto	Bellabusto	5	52	CC-Ma

This is a new brand for 1996, with a full-bodied taste and a smooth draw based on a blend of five tobaccos. The Dominican-grown maduro wrapper adds a spicy finish compared to the Connecticut Shade-wrapped models.

CUSANO ROMANI
Handmade in Santiago, Dominican Republic.
Wrapper: USA/Connecticut   Binder: Dom. Rep.   Filler: Dom. Rep.

Shape	Name	Lgth	Ring	Wrapper
Pyramid	Pyramid	6	54	CC

A single roller is specially appointed to create this pyramid shape, introduced in 1996. Five tobaccos – two Dominican-seed and two Cuban-seed – are combined with the elegant Connecticut Shade wrappers to create a smooth smoke with full body and a pleasant aroma.

DANIEL MARSHALL SIGNATURE/DOMINICAN RESERVE
Handmade in Santiago, Dominican Republic.
Wrapper: USA/Connecticut   Binder: Mexico   Filler: Dom. Rep.

Shape	Name	Lgth	Ring	Wrapper
Robusto	Robusto	5	50	CC
Churchill	Churchill	7	48	CC

A perfect complement to the famous D.Marshall humidors, this new brand was developed to Mr. Marshall's personal standards. It offers a medium-to-full body and consists entirely of three to four-year-old tobaccos.

DANIEL MARSHALL SIGNATURE/HONDURAN RESERVE
Handmade in Danli, Honduras.
Wrapper: USA/Connecticut   Binder: Honduras   Filler: Honduras, Nicaragua

Shape	Name	Lgth	Ring	Wrapper
Robusto	Robusto	5	50	CC
Long Corona	Corona	6	44	CC
Double Corona	Churchill	7	50	CC

HANDMADE CIGARS: BRAND LISTINGS

Created in 1996, this cigar exhibits none of the harshness which sometimes accompanies Honduran-made cigars. It boasts a Connecticut Shade wrapper and has a medium-to-full body; it is presented in all-cedar boxes of 25.

DANLYS
Handmade in Danli, Honduras.

Wrapper: Honduras   *Binder: Mexico*   *Filler: Honduras, Mexico*

Shape	Name	Lgth	Ring	Wrapper
Double Corona	Churchill	7	50	CM-Ma
Long Corona	Luchadore	6	42	CM-Ma
Panatela	Panatella	6	38	CM-Ma
Toro	Toro	6	50	CM-Ma
Lonsdale	No. 1	7	42	CM-Ma
Petit Corona	No. 4	5	42	CM-Ma

This is a fairly old brand, dating from 1972. It is medium-to-full in body and is offered in both natural and maduro wrapper shades, in economical bundles of 25.

DAVIDOFF
Handmade in Santiago, Dominican Republic.

Wrapper: USA/Connecticut   *Binder: Dom. Rep.*   *Filler: Dom. Rep.*

Shape	Name	Lgth	Ring	Wrapper
Long Panatela	No. 1	7½	38	CC
Panatela	No. 2	6	38	CC
Short Panatela	No. 3	5⅛	38	CC
Panatela	Tubos	6	38	CC
Cigarillo	Ambassadrice	4⅝	26	CC
	Aniversario Series:			
Giant	Aniversario No. 1	8⅔	48	CC
Churchill	Aniversario No. 2	7	48	CC
	Grand Cru Series:			
Lonsdale	Grand Cru No. 1	6⅛	42	CC

Corona	Grand Cru No. 2	5⅝	42	CC
Petit Corona	Grand Cru No. 3	5	42	CC
Petit Corona	Grand Cru No. 4	4⅝	40	CC
Petit Corona	Grand Cru No. 5	4	40	CC
	Special Series:			
Double Corona	Double "R"	7½	50	CC
Robusto	Special "R"	5	50	CC
Pyramid	Special "T"	6	52	CC
	Thousand Series:			
Small Panatela	1000	4⅝	34	CC
Petit Corona	2000	5	42	CC
Slim Panatela	3000	7	33	CC
Long Corona	4000	6⅛	42	CC
Grand Corona	5000	5⅝	46	CC

A carefully controlled series of events leads to the production of a Davidoff cigar. This celebrated brand, first created in Cuba in 1946, requires tobaccos which have been aged up to four years and only the finest leaves are used in a factory which is solely dedicated to the creation of this brand. Four different blends are used to create the five different series: the large-sized, but mild and light Anniversarios; the mild, delicate and aromatic Nos. 1-2-3, Tubos and Ambassadrice; the fuller-bodied, but still mild "Thousand" series; and the fullest-bodied Grand Cru and Special ranges, which share the same blend.

DA VINCI
Handmade in Danli, Honduras.

Wrapper: Ecuador   *Binder: Dominican Republic*
Filler: Dominican Republic, Honduras, Nicaragua

Shape	Name	Lgth	Ring	Wrapper
Double Corona	Renaissance	7	54	CC
Giant	Leonardo	8½	52	CC
Churchill	Ginerva de Benci	7	48	CC
Toro	Monalisa	6	50	CC

HANDMADE CIGARS: BRAND LISTINGS

| Long Corona | Cecilia Gallerani | 6 | 43 | CC |
| Robusto | Madonna | 5 | 50 | CC |

These masterpieces seek to reach the level of achievement of its namesake, the brilliant Italian artist and scientist who lived from 1452-1519. A full line of personal and smoking accessories is topped by the Connecticut Shade-seed wrapped cigar line, each of which offers a mild-to-medium body. The all-cedar boxes each feature a different da Vinci painting (except for the Renaissance model), including a notebook self-portrait for the Leonardo model.

DEFIANT
Handmade in Danli, Honduras.

Wrapper: Ecuador *Binder: Nicaragua* *Filler: Honduras, Nicaragua*

Shape	Name	Lgth	Ring	Wrapper
Robusto	Robusto	4¾	50	CC
Long Corona	Corona	6	44	CC
Toro	Toro	6	50	CC
Double Corona	Presidente	7½	52	CC
Pyramid	Pyramid	6½	52	CC

This brand was introduced in 1996 and offers a smooth, medium-to-full taste, presented in boxes of 25 cigars each.

DIAMOND CROWN
Handmade in Santiago, Dominican Republic.

Wrapper: USA/Connecticut *Binder: Dom. Rep.* *Filler: Dom. Rep.*

Shape	Name	Lgth	Ring	Wrapper
	Robusto series:			
Giant	No. 1	8½	54	CC
Double Corona	No. 2	7½	54	CC
Toro	No. 3	6½	54	CC
Robusto	No. 4	5½	54	CC
Robusto	No. 5	4½	54	CC

HANDMADE CIGARS: BRAND LISTINGS

This mild-bodied, all-54 ring series is a new, but impossible-to-find product of the Tabacalera A. Fuente y Cia., made for the M&N Cigar Manufacturers, Inc. of Tampa, Florida.

DIANA SILVIUS
Handmade in Santiago, Dominican Republic.

Wrapper: USA/Connecticut   Binder: Dom. Rep.   Filler: Dom. Rep.

Shape	Name	Lgth	Ring	Wrapper
Double Corona	Diana Churchill	7	50	CC
Robusto	Diana Robusto	4⅞	52	CC
Churchill	Diana 2000	6¾	46	CC
Lonsdale	Diana Corona	6½	42	CC

Introduced in 1990, this is a superb smoke which is medium in body and rich in flavor. Diana Silvius cigars strike a subtle balance between taste and aroma. The blend of four filler tobaccos, predominantly Cuban-seed leaves grown in the Dominican Republic, produces a smooth finish that leaves a hint of sweetness on the palate. Every one of these cigars is handmade by the master rollers of Tabacalera A. Fuente y Cia.

DOMINGOLD
Handmade in Santiago, Dominican Republic.

Wrapper: Cameroon   Binder: USA/Connecticut   Filler: Brazil, Dom. Rep.

Shape	Name	Lgth	Ring	Wrapper
Toro	Toro	6	50	CC
Long Corona	Lonsdale	6¼	42	CC
Robusto	Robusto	5	50	CC
Corona	Corona	5½	42	CC
Double Corona	Churchill	7	50	CC

These bundles of 20 cigars are seconds of one of the finest cigar factories in the Dominican Republic. You'll be hard-pressed to tell the difference between these medium-strength cigars and their more-famous siblings.

HANDMADE CIGARS: BRAND LISTINGS

DOMINICAN ESTATES
Handmade in the Dominican Republic.

Wrapper: USA/Connecticut   Binder: Mexico   Filler: Dom. Rep.

Shape	Name	Lgth	Ring	Wrapper
Toro	Corona Gorda	6	50	CC
Double Corona	Double Corona	7	50	CC
Corona	Full Corona	5½	43	CC
Lonsdale	Lonsdale	6½	43	CC
Robusto	Robusto	4½	50	CC

These cigars are mild to the taste, thanks to their Connecticut wrappers, and very well constructed for an easy draw.

DOMINICAN ORIGINAL
Handmade in Santiago, Dominican Republic.

Wrapper: USA/Connecticut   Binder: Dom. Rep.   Filler: Dom. Rep.

Shape	Name	Lgth	Ring	Wrapper
Long Corona	Cetros	6	44	CC
Churchill	Churchill	6⅞	46	CC-Ma
Giant	Fat Tub	10	66	CC-Ma
Robusto	Gorilla	5	66	CC-Ma
Giant	King Kong	8½	52	CC-Ma
Small Panatela	Miniatures	4¼	32	CC
Double Corona	Monster	7	60	CC-Ma
Lonsdale	No. 1	6¾	43	CC-Ma
Corona	No. 2	5¾	43	CC-Ma
Long Panatela	Palma Fina	7	37	CC-Ma
Pyramid	Piramide	6½	56	CC-Ma
Double Corona	Presidente	7½	50	CC-Ma
Robusto	Robusto	4½	50	CC-Ma
Torpedo	Torpedo	7	50	CC-Ma

HANDMADE CIGARS: BRAND LISTINGS

Talk about sizes! Here is the brand for the lover of unusual, especially large sizes. The Connecticut wrapper and Dominican filler give these cigars a mild taste, and they are offered in bundle packs.

DOMINICAN SPECIALS
Handmade, with mixed filler, in Santiago, Dominican Republic.

Wrapper: USA/Connecticut   Binder: Dom. Rep.   Filler: Dom. Rep.

Shape	Name	Lgth	Ring	Wrapper
Double Corona	Churchill	7	50	CC-Ma
Toro	Toro	6	50	CC-Ma
Lonsdale	Fuma	6⅞	43	CC-Ma
Corona	Breva	5½	43	CC-Ma

Here is a modestly-priced, high-quality bundled cigar from the Dominican Republic. New for 1996, it offers a mild taste with a Connecticut Broadleaf wrapper. The filler is a sandwich of long-filler leaves surrounding a short-filler core.

DOMINICANA SUPERBA
Handmade in Santiago, Dominican Republic.

Wrapper: Dom. Rep.   Binder: Dom. Rep.   Filler: Dom. Rep.

Shape	Name	Lgth	Ring	Wrapper
Giant	No. 1	8½	52	CC-Ma
Double Corona	No. 2	7	49	CC-Ma
Lonsdale	No. 3	6¾	44	CC-Ma
Robusto	No. 4	4½	50	CC-Ma
Corona	No. 5	5½	43	CC-Ma
Double Corona	No. 6	7½	50	CC-Ma

Introduced in 1989, these are mild cigars of very high quality, offered in conveniently-packaged (and priced) bundles of 20 cigars each.

HANDMADE CIGARS: BRAND LISTINGS

DOMINICO
Handmade in Santiago, Dominican Republic.

Wrapper: Indonesia   *Binder: Dom. Rep.*   *Filler: Dom. Rep.*

Shape	Name	Lgth	Ring	Wrapper
Pyramid	No. 700	7½	60	CC
Giant	No. 701	8½	52	CC
Churchill	No. 702	7	48	CC
Toro	No. 703	6	50	CC
Lonsdale	No. 704 -	7	43	CC
Corona	No. 705	5½	43	CC
Robusto	No. 706	4¾	52	CC

These high-quality bundled cigars debuted in 1994 and now feature an Indonesian-grown wrapper with a Dominican Olor binder and a Cuban-seed, Dominican-grown filler. They offer a mild to medium body and an excellent value.

DOMINIQUE
Handmade in Santiago, Dominican Republic.

Wrapper: USA/Connecticut   *Binder: Dom. Rep.*   *Filler: Dom. Rep.*

Shape	Name	Lgth	Ring	Wrapper
Giant	No. 52	8½	52	Cl-CC-Ma
Lonsdale	No. 74	7	43	Cl-CC-Ma
Grand Corona	Madison	6	46	Cl-CC-Ma
Corona	Nacionales	5½	42	CC
Double Corona	Pierce	6⅞	49	Cl-CC-Ma
Robusto	Toro	4½	50	CC-Ma

These bundles are of high quality and moderate pricing, offering a mild flavor in packages of 25 cigars each.

HANDMADE CIGARS: BRAND LISTINGS

DOMINO PARK
Handmade in Miami, Florida, USA.

Wrapper: Ecuador　　　　*Binder: Ecuador*　　*Filler: Dom. Rep., Nicaragua*

Shape	Name	Lgth	Ring	Wrapper
Robusto	Robusto	5	50	CC
Toro	Robusto Largo	6	50	CC
Lonsdale	Corona	6½	42	CC
Double Corona	Churchill	7	50	CC
Giant	Presidente	8	52	CC

Introduced in 1995 by the Caribbean Cigar Company, this is a medium-bodied cigar which salutes Domino Park, a traditional meeting place in Miami's "Little Havana" district, and are offered in boxes of 25.

DON ALBERTO
Handmade in Santiago, Dominican Republic.
Wrapper: USA/Connecticut, Dominican Republic, Indonesia
Binder: Dom. Rep.　　　　　　　　　　　　　　*Filler: Dom. Rep.*

Shape	Name	Lgth	Ring	Wrapper
	Superior Habana series:			
Pyramid	Piramid	6½	53	CC-Ma
Robusto	Robusto	5	50	CC-Ma
Giant	Churchill	8	48	CC-Ma
Grand Corona	Double Corona	6½	46	CC-Ma
Lonsdale	Corona	7	44	CC-Ma
Long Panatela	Panatela	7½	38	CC-Ma
Small Panatela	Reina	5	30	CC-Ma
	Oro de Habana series:			
Pyramid	Piramid	6½	53	CC
Robusto	Robusto	5	50	CC
Giant	Churchill	8	48	CC
Grand Corona	Double Corona	6½	46	CC

HANDMADE CIGARS: BRAND LISTINGS

Lonsdale	Corona	7	44	CC
	Santiago series:			
Giant	Presidente	8	50	CI
Grand Corona	Double Corona	6½	46	CI
Robusto	Robusto	5	50	CI
Lonsdale	Corona	7	44	CI
	Classico Dominican series:			
Toro	Piramid	6½	53	Ma
Robusto	Robusto	5	50	Ma
Giant	Churchill	8	48	Ma
Grand Corona	Double Corona	6½	46	Ma
Lonsdale	Corona	7	44	Ma
Long Panatela	Panatela	7½	38	Ma
Small Panatela	Reina	5	30	Ma
	Royal series:			
Pyramid	Piramid	6½	53	CC/Ma
Giant	Presidential	8	48	CC/Ma
Lonsdale	Corona	7	44	CC/Ma
Robusto	Robusto	5	50	CC/Ma
	Grand Cru series:			
Giant	Presidente	8	50	Ma
Lonsdale	Corona	7	44	Ma
Pyramid	Piramid	6½	53	Ma
Robusto	Robusto	5	50	Ma
	Licey series:			
Giant	Churchill	8	48	Ma
Lonsdale	Corona	7	44	Ma
Pyramid	Piramid	6½	53	Ma

HANDMADE CIGARS: BRAND LISTINGS

Robusto	Robusto	5	50	Ma

Created in 1996, here is a series of cigars offering different blends and tastes, all within the mild-to-medium range, with the Grand Cru series rating a medium-bodied classification. All feature binder and filler tobaccos grown in the Dominican Republic, with genuine Connecticut wrappers used on the Oro de Havana, Superior Habana and Santiago series. The Royal series offers the "barber pole" double wrapper style, utilizing intertwined Connecticut and Dominican leaves. The Classico Dominican, Superior Habana and Licey series use Dominican-grown leaves for the maduro wrapper, while the Grand Cru shapes use an Indonesian maduro wrapper.

DON ANTONIO
Handmade in Dingelstadt, Germany.
Wrapper: Brazil, Indonesia   Binder: Indonesia
Filler: Brazil, Dominican Republic, Honduras, Indonesia

Shape	Name	Lgth	Ring	Wrapper
Cigarillo	El Gusto	6⅛	25	CC-CM
Short Panatela	El Toro	4⅜	38	CC-CM

Here is a rarity: a handmade, dry-cure cigar from Germany. Other shapes in the Don Antonio line are machine-produced, but these are made by hand and offered a mild to medium flavor depending on your choice of wrapper: mild Indonesian leaf grown in Sumatra, or the strong Brazilian leaf from the Bahia region. Both sizes are offered in packs of 5 or 20 and also in aluminum tubes.

DON ARMANDO
Handmade in Santa Rosa de Copan, Honduras.
Wrapper: Honduras   Binder: Honduras   Filler: Honduras

Shape	Name	Lgth	Ring	Wrapper
Giant	Viajante	8½	50	CM
Double Corona	Embajadores	7¾	50	CM
Long Corona	Corona	6¼	44	CM
Toro	Toro	6	50	CM
Corona Extra	Corona Extra	5½	46	CM
Corona	Bonitas	5½	42	CM

| Robusto | Rothschild | 4½ | 50 | CM |

This brand was introduced in 1996 and is produced at the La Flor de Copan factory in Santa Rosa de Copan. It offers a medium body and is presented in boxes of 20 cigars each.

DON ASA
Handmade in Danli, Honduras.

Wrapper: Honduras   *Binder: Mexico*   *Filler: Honduras, Nicaragua*

Shape	Name	Lgth	Ring	Wrapper
Petit Corona	Blunts	5	42	CC
Lonsdale	Cetros	6½	44	CC
Robusto	Coronas	5½	50	CC
Giant Corona	Imperials	8	44	CC
Double Corona	President	7½	50	CC
Robusto	Rothschild	4½	50	CC
Corona Extra	Toros	5½	46	CC

This brand debuted in 1963, with a medium-to-full-bodied taste. Made with all long-filler tobaccos of three nations, Don Asa cigars are presented in all-wooden boxes of 25.

DON BARCO
Handmade in Santiago, Dominican Republic.

Wrapper: Indonesia   *Binder: Dom. Rep.*   *Filler: Dom. Rep.*

Shape	Name	Lgth	Ring	Wrapper
Double Corona	Galeon	7¾	50	CC
Toro	Admiral	6	50	CC
Robusto	Capitan	5	50	CC
Churchill	Marinero	6¾	46	CC

Introduced in 1996, this is a medium-bodied cigar from the Dominican Republic, offered in boxes of 20 cigars each.

HANDMADE CIGARS: BRAND LISTINGS

DON DIEGO
Handmade in La Romana, Dominican Republic.

Wrapper: USA/Connecticut   Binder: Dom. Rep.   Filler: Brazil, Dom. Rep.

Shape	Name		Lgth	Ring	Wrapper
Small Panatela	Babies		5	33	CM
Toro	Coronas Bravas		6½	48	CC
Petit Corona	Coronas Major	*(tubed)*	5	42	CC
Corona	Coronas		5⅝	42	DC-CC
Panatela	Grecos		6½	38	CC
Lonsdale	Lonsdales		6⅝	42	DC-CC
Churchill	Monarchs	*(tubed)*	7¼	46	CC
Petit Corona	Petit Coronas		5⅛	42	DC-CC
Panatela	Royal Palmas	*(tubed)*	6⅛	36	CC
	Machine-made, with short filler:				
Cigarillo	Preludes		4	28	CC

Well-known for its mild taste, Don Diego cigars have earned a wide following, thanks to their consistency of construction, accessible strength and excellent value for the money. Fans of rarely-seen Candela wrappers on handmade cigars will find three major shapes available. This brand was originated in 1964 in the Canary Islands, but production was moved to the Dominican Republic in 1982.

DON ESTEBAN
Handmade in Santiago, Dominican Republic.

Wrapper: Ecuador, Dom. Rep.   Binder: Dom. Rep.   Filler: Dom. Rep.

Shape	Name	Lgth	Ring	Wrapper
Giant	Viajante	8	50	CC-Ma
Double Corona	Presidente	7½	49	CC-Ma
Toro	Emperador	6	50	CC-Ma
Robusto	Robusto	5	50	CC-Ma
Lonsdale	Elegante	6½	44	CC-Ma

Corona	Puritano	5½	42	CC-Ma

Re-blended for 1996, this medium-bodied cigar offers a Ecuadorian-grown wrapper in the natural shade and a Dominican-grown wrapper for the maduro shade.

DON FIFE
Handmade in Danli, Honduras.
Wrapper: Ecuador or USA/Connecticut

Binder: Honduras   Filler: Honduras

Shape	Name	Lgth	Ring	Wrapper
Churchill	Churchill	7	48	CM
Lonsdale	Numero 1	7	43	CM
Lonsdale	Double Corona	6½	44	CM
Toro	Corona Gorda	6	50	CM
Corona	Petit Cetro	5½	43	CM
Small Panatela	Petit	4½	30	CM

This brand is mild-to-medium in body and was introduced in 1996. Made by hand in Danli, Honduras, Don Fife cigars are offered in six favorite sizes and presented in elegant cedar boxes of 25.

DON JOSE
Handmade in Danli, Honduras.

Wrapper: Honduras   Binder: Honduras   Filler: Honduras

Shape	Name	Lgth	Ring	Wrapper
Giant	El Grandee	8½	52	CC-Ma
Double Corona	San Marco	7	50	CC-Ma
Toro	Turbo	6	50	CC-Ma
Long Corona	Granada	6	43	CC-Ma
Robusto	Valrico	4½	50	CC-Ma

These Honduran handmades provide a rich taste in both a natural and maduro wrapper. The tobaccos are all grown in Honduras of Cuban-seed origin and are offered in bundles of 20 cigars each.

HANDMADE CIGARS: BRAND LISTINGS

DON JUAN
Handmade in Ocotal, Nicaragua.

Wrapper: Ecuador   Binder: Nicaragua   Filler: Dom. Rep., Nicaragua

Shape	Name	Lgth	Ring	Wrapper
Panatela	Lindas	5½	38	CM
Long Corona	Cetros	6	43	CM
Panatela	Palma Fina	6⅞	36	CM
Robusto	Robusto	5	50	CM
Lonsdale	No. 1	6⅝	44	CM
Toro	Matador	6	50	CM
Double Corona	Churchill	7	49	CM
Giant	Presidente	8½	50	CM

Introduced in 1992, Don Juan is a handmade cigar from Nicaragua. The filler is Nicaraguan, with a Dominican Havana-seed binder and a Connecticut Shade wrapper. Cigar connoisseurs consider this a medium-strength cigar.

DON JULIO
Handmade in Santiago, Domincan Republic.

Wrapper: USA/Connecticut   Binder: Dom. Rep.   Filler: Dom. Rep.

Shape	Name	Lgth	Ring	Wrapper
Lonsdale	Corona Deluxe	7	44	CC
Toro	Fabulosos	6	50	CC
Corona	Miramar	5¾	43	CC
Robusto	Private Stock No. 1	4½	50	CC
Giant	Supremos	8½	52	CC

Don Julio cigars are handmade, bundled cigars produced in the Dominican Republic. These cigars are mild-bodied, easy to draw, yet exceptionally flavorful. The composition of select Cuban-seed tobaccos took several months to develop, giving Don Julio its delicate taste.

HANDMADE CIGARS: BRAND LISTINGS

DON LEO
Handmade in Santiago, Dominican Republic.

Wrapper: Dom. Rep.   Binder: Mexico   Filler: Dom. Rep., Mexico

Shape	Name	Lgth	Ring	Wrapper
Double Corona	Churchill	7½	50	CM
Lonsdale	Corona	6½	44	CM
Corona	Petite Corona	5½	42	CM
Toro	Robusto	6	50	CM
Robusto	Rothschild	4½	50	CM

Don Leo is a handmade, long-filler cigar from the recently established Puros de Villa Gonzales factory near Santiago. The blend of leaves from the Dominican and Mexico provide a mild-to-medium body.

DON LINO
Handmade in Danli, Honduras.
Wrapper: Ecuador and USA/Connecticut

Binder: Honduras   Filler: Honduras

Shape	Name		Lgth	Ring	Wrapper
Torpedo	Torpedo		7	48	CC
Double Corona	Churchill		7½	50	CC
Long Panatela	Panetelas		7	36	CC
Lonsdale	No. 1		6½	44	CC
Long Corona	No. 5		6¼	44	CC
Corona Extra	Toros		5½	46	CC
Robusto	Corona		5½	50	CC
Lonsdale	Tubos	(tubed)	6½	44	CC
Petit Corona	No. 4		5	42	CC
Robusto	Robusto		5½	50	CC
Robusto	Rothchild		4½	50	CC
Small Panatela	Epicure		4½	32	CC
Giant	Supremos		8½	52	CC

	Don Lino Oro:			
Lonsdale	No. 1	6½	44	CM
Long Panatela	Panatela	7	36	CM
Corona Extra	Toros	5½	46	CM
Double Corona	Churchill	7½	50	CM

Don Lino are premium, hand-rolled cigars from Honduras, first introduced in 1990. The brand is known for its mild-to-medium-bodied taste and consistent smooth flavors, thanks to a Connecticut wrapper and Honduran-grown fillers and binders. The Don Lino Oro series debuted in 1991 and benefits from Ecuadorian-grown, Cameroon-seed wrappers, which give these cigars a more robust, full-bodied taste.

DON MANOLO COLLECTION
Handmade in Santiago, Dominican Republic.
Wrapper: Cameroon or Dominican Republic

Binder: Dom. Rep.

Filler: Dom. Rep.

Shape	Name	Lgth	Ring	Wrapper
	Maduro:			
Robusto	Robusto	5½	50	Ma
Grand Corona	Corona Grande	6¾	46	Ma
Double Corona	Churchill	7	50	Ma
	Samatra:			
Robusto	Robusto	5½	50	CM
Long Corona	Corona	6	44	CM
Double Corona	Churchill	7	50	CM
Pyramid	Pyramid	6	54	CM

This brand made its debut in 1996, with a mild-to-medium bodied maduro group and a medium-bodied, Cameroon-wrapped Samatra group. Both are available as bundles of 25 or in all-cedar boxes of 25.

HANDMADE CIGARS: BRAND LISTINGS

DON MARCOS
Handmade in La Romana, Dominican Republic.
Wrapper: USA/Connecticut   *Binder: Dom. Rep.*   *Filler: Dom. Rep.*

Shape	Name		Lgth	Ring	Wrapper
Corona	Coronas		5½	42	CC
Toro	Toros		6	50	CC
Torpedo	Torpedos		6	50	CC
Panatela	Naturals	(tubed)	6	38	CC
Lonsdale	Cetros		6½	42	CC
Toro	Double Corona		6½	48	CC
Churchill	Monarchs		7	46	CC

This brand was one of the best-sellers in the western U.S. during the 1960s and 1970s and was re-introduced in a big way in 1995. Well made and easy to smoke, the Don Marcos line has a mild to medium body and an inviting Connecticut Shade wrapper.

DON MARIANO
Handmade in Santiago, Dominican Republic.
Wrapper: USA/Connecticut   *Binder: Dom. Rep.*   *Filler: Dom. Rep.*

Shape	Name	Lgth	Ring	Wrapper
Corona	Indios	5½	40	CC
Robusto	Gran Corona	5½	48	CC
Corona	Pandukas	5¾	42	CC
Lonsdale	Pelas Corona	6½	44	CC
Lonsdale	Nobles	6¾	42	CC
Panatela	Panatelas	6¾	36	CC
Churchill	X&T Churchills	7	46	CC
Double Corona	Conquistadores	7½	50	CC
Long Panatela	No. 1	7½	38	CC
Churchill	Connoisseur	8¼	48	CC

HANDMADE CIGARS: BRAND LISTINGS

A product of the cigar artisans of the Dominican Republic, Don Mariano cigars are created only in limited quantities. The blend of aged tobaccos, led by the Connecticut Shade wrappers, offer a smooth smoke with subtle aromas and medium body. This brand, introduced in 1985, is offered in stunning all-mahogany boxes, interleaved with cedar to provide the finest care for a fine, premium cigar.

DON MATEO
Handmade in Danli, Honduras.

Wrapper: Mexico   *Binder: Mexico*   *Filler: Nicaragua*

Shape	Name	Lgth	Ring	Wrapper
Slim Panatela	No. 1	7	30	CC
Panatela	No. 2	6⅞	35	CC
Long Corona	No. 3	6	42	CC
Corona	No. 4	5½	44	CC
Lonsdale	No. 5	6⅝	44	CC
Churchill	No. 6	6⅞	48	CC
Robusto	No. 7	4¾	50	CC-Ma
Toro	No. 8	6¼	50	CC-Ma
Double Corona	No. 9	7½	50	CC-Ma
Giant	No. 10	8	52	CC-Ma
Toro	No. 11	6⅝	54	CC-Ma

A medium-bodied taste in a banded, bundled cigar is the promise of the well-made and modestly-priced Don Mateo line. The Mexican wrapper is available in both natural and maduro wrappers for most sizes.

DON MELO
Handmade in Santa Rosa de Copan, Honduras.

Wrapper: Honduras   *Binder: Honduras*   *Filler: Honduras*

Shape	Name	Lgth	Ring	Wrapper
Giant	Presidente	8½	50	Ma
Double Corona	Churchill	7	49	Ma
Long Corona	Corona Gorda	6¼	44	Ma

Long Corona	No. 2	6	42	Ma
Corona Extra	Corona Extra	5½	46	Ma
Corona	Petit Corona	5½	42	Ma
Robusto	Nom Plus	4¾	50	Ma
Petit Corona	Cremas	4½	42	Ma

This line honors the father of the Honduran cigar trade, who was the first Honduran national to open a cigar factory in that country in 1896. From humble origins in 1789, the cigar trade has grown considerably in the town of Santa Rosa de Copan and this medium-to-full-bodied smoke, wrapped in all-black leaf, salutes that success.

DON MELO CENTENARIO
Handmade in Santa Rosa de Copan, Honduras.
Wrapper: Honduras   *Binder: Honduras*   *Filler: Honduras*

Shape	Name	Lgth	Ring	Wrapper
Churchill	Liga A	7	48	CM
Toro	Liga B	6	55	CM
Long Corona	Liga C	6	44	CM
Robusto	Liga D	5	52	CM

Here is a limited edition, centennial salute to the man (Don Melo Bueso) who help found the modern Honduran cigar industry. Only 2,000 boxes of each size will be made of this medium-bodied smoke. Even the boxes will be special: hand-crafted in Caoba wood with a removable tray of Spanish cedarwood.

DON PABLO
Handmade in Las Vegas, Nevada, USA.
Wrapper: USA/Connecticut   *Binder: Dominican Republic*
Filler: Brazil, Dominican Republic, Ecuador, Mexico

Shape	Name	Lgth	Ring	Wrapper
Slim Panatela	Pencil	7	32	CC
Slim Panatela	Panatela	7	34	CC
Lonsdale	Panatela Especial	7	40	CC-Ma

Corona	Corona	5¾	42	CC
Toro	Monterico	5¾	52	CC-Ma
Toro	Cuban Round	6	48	CC-Ma
Churchill	Imperial	6¾	46	CC-Ma
Double Corona	Cuban Round Largo	7½	50	CC-Ma
Giant	El Cubano	8½	52	CC
Torpedo	Torpedo	6¾	58	CC-Ma
Double Corona	Largo Cognac	7½	50	CC
Toro	Monterico Cognac	5¾	52	CC
Double Corona	Corona Grande	7½	50	CC
Churchill	Emperador	7	46	CC

These are mild to medium-bodied cigars of good quality, handmade in a storefront on the Las Vegas strip. Fully in keeping with its location, this small factory offers some gaudy specialties, including the Largo and Monterico sizes made with five-year-aged tobaccos cured with 20-year-old Cognac. You can also order your cigars cured with rum or brandy or sweetened for a modest additional charge!

DON PEPE
Handmade in Cruz des Almas, Brazil.

Wrapper: Brazil   *Binder: Brazil*   *Filler: Brazil*

Shape	Name	Lgth	Ring	Wrapper
Double Corona	Double Corona	7½	50	CM
Robusto	Robusto	5	50	CM
Short Panatela	Half Corona	4⅜	35	CM
Slim Panatela	Slim Panatela	5⅛	30	CM
Long Corona	Petit Lonsdale	6	40	CM
Churchill	Churchill	7	47	CM

Introduced in 1994, this brand is produced by the famed Suerdieck factory in Brazil. The wrapper is a Sumatran-seed tobacco, with native Brazilian leaves used for the binder and filler to blend into a mild-bodied cigar.

HANDMADE CIGARS: BRAND LISTINGS

DON QUIJOTE
Handmade, with short filler, in Cumana, Venezuela.

Wrapper: Honduras   *Binder: Venezula*   *Filler: Venezuela*

Shape	Name	Lgth	Ring	Wrapper
Grand Corona	Churchill	6⅝	46	CC
Corona	No. 5	5½	42	CC
Panatela	Carolinas	6½	38	CC

New for 1996 is this unique brand from Venezuela, made under the supervision of master cigar maker Vladimir Perez and offered in boxes of 25.

DON RENE DE CUBA
Handmade in Miami, Florida, USA.

Wrapper: Ecuador   *Binder & Filler: Proprietary*

Shape	Name	Lgth	Ring	Wrapper
Torpedo	Torpedo	6½	54	CC-Ma
Giant	Presidente	8½	50	CC
Double Corona	Churchill	7¼	50	CC
Lonsdale	Corona	6½	44	CC
Corona	Coronita	5½	42	CC-Ma
Robusto	Robusto	5½	50	CC-Ma
Long Panatela	Lancero	7	38	CC
Small Panatela	Senoritas	5	30	CC

Here is a new brand for 1996, made by master craftsmen, offering a full-bodied taste and presented in boxes of 25.

DON SALVADOR
Handmade in Esteli, Nicaragua.

Wrapper: Nicaragua   *Binder: Nicaragua*   *Filler: Nicaragua*

Shape	Name	Lgth	Ring	Wrapper
Panatela	Elegante	6½	38	CM
Corona	Seleccion	5½	42	CM

Long Corona	Cazador	6¼	44	CM
Robusto	Consul	5	52	CM
Giant	Presidente	8	54	CM
Double Corona	Churchill	7	49	CM
Toro	Toro	6	50	CM

Here is a new brand for 1996, featuring all-Nicaraguan tobacco in a medium-to-full-bodied smoke, and offered in boxes of 25.

DON TITO
Handmade in Miami, Florida, USA.
Wrapper: Ecuador　　　　　　　　　　　　　　　*Binder: Nicaragua*
Filler: Dominican Republic, Honduras, Nicaragua

Shape	Name	Lgth	Ring	Wrapper
Double Corona	Churchill	7	50	CC
Double Corona	Double Corona	7¾	49	CC
Lonsdale	No. 1	6¾	43	CC
Lonsdale	No. 2	6½	43	CC
Long Panatela	Panatela	7	38	CC
Pyramid	Piramides	7¼	66	CC
Robusto	Robusto	5	50	CC
Grand Corona	Taino	6¼	46	CC
Torpedo	Torpedo	6½	60	CC

Don Tito is a new brand in 1996, from the "Little Havana" area of Miami, sporting a balanced blend that provides a rich, full-bodied taste. The brand has some of the largest sizes you can find anywhere and is presented in boxes of 25.

DON TOMAS
Handmade in Danli, Honduras.
Wrapper: Ecuador and USA/Connecticut
Binder: Honduras　　　　　　　　　　　　　　*Filler: Dom. Rep., Honduras*

HANDMADE CIGARS: BRAND LISTINGS

Shape	Name	Lgth	Ring	Wrapper
Double Corona	Presidentes	7½	50	CM-Ma
Lonsdale	Corona Grandes (tubed)	6½	44	CM
Lonsdale	Cetros No. 2	6½	44	CM-Ma
Robusto	Coronas	5½	50	CM-Ma
Corona Extra	Toros	5½	46	CM
Petit Corona	Blunts	5	42	CM
Robusto	Rothschild	4½	50	CM-Ma

Don Tomas cigars are justly famous for their medium-to-full-bodied taste and silky construction. Havana-seed tobaccos are nurtured in the fertile valleys of Honduras and then collected and aged, eventually ending as the top-quality cigars which are so well known to smokers worldwide. The natural wrappers utilize Ecuadorian-grown Connecticut-seed leaves and all-Honduran filler, while the maduro wrappers are Connecticut Broadleaf and the blend include some Dominican-grown leaf in the filler.

DON TOMAS INTERNATIONAL SELECTION
Handmade in Danli, Honduras.

Wrapper: Honduras   Binder: Honduras   Filler: Honduras

Shape	Name	Lgth	Ring	Wrapper
Lonsdale	No. 1	6½	44	CM
Robusto	No. 2	5½	50	CM
Corona	No. 3	5½	42	CM
Long Panatela	No. 4	7	36	CM

The Special Edition features the finest leaves from farms in Talanga, Honduras, using Connecticut, Cuban and Dominican seeds, blended to offer an effortless draw filled with rich coffee and mocha flavors for a full-bodied smoke.

DON TOMAS SPECIAL EDITION
Handmade in Danli, Honduras.

Wrapper: Ecuador   Binder: Honduras   Filler: Dom. Rep., Honduras

HANDMADE CIGARS: BRAND LISTINGS

Shape	Name	Lgth	Ring	Wrapper
Double Corona	No. 100	7½	50	CC
Lonsdale	No. 200	6½	44	CC
Robusto	No. 300	5	50	CC
Long Panatela	No. 400	7	36	CC
Corona Extra	No. 500	5½	46	CC

Distinctive in the all-red wood box is the Don Tomas Special Edition. This is a medium-bodied but slightly spicy cigar, offered in boxes of 25.

DON TONIOLI EPICURE SELECTION
Handmade in San Jose, Costa Rica.

Wrapper: Ecuador   *Binder: Nicaragua*   *Filler: Nicaragua*

Shape	Name	Lgth	Ring	Wrapper
Pyramid	Piramides	6	52	CC
Torpedo	Torpedo	6	52	CC
Torpedo	Super Torpedo	7½	64	CC
Churchill	Churchills	7	47	CC
Grand Corona	Corona Extras	5¾	46	CC
Robusto	Robustos	5	50	CC

Now this is a cigar! One look at the massive Piramides, which tapers from 26 at the tip to a 52 ring, or either of the two Torpedo shapes, and it is obvious that this is not a brand for the feint of heart. This new brand was created in 1995 and made in Danli, Honduras. In 1996, production was shifted to the Tabacalera Tambor in San Jose, where the cigars are wrapped in an exquisite Sumatra-seed leaf grown in Ecuador and aged for 11 months after rolling to provide a medium-bodied taste.

DON TUTO HABANOS
Handmade in San Jose, Costa Rica.
Wrapper: Ecuador, Indonesia, Nicaragua

Binder: Nicaragua   *Filler: Nicaragua*

HANDMADE CIGARS: BRAND LISTINGS

Shape	Name	Lgth	Ring	Wrapper
Petit Corona	Petit Corona /Nicaraguan wrapper/	4½	42	Cl
Long Corona	Coronas /Indonesian wrapper/	6	43	Cl
Robusto	Robusto /Ecuadorian wrapper/	5	50	CC
Pyramid	Piramides /Indonesian wrapper/	7	48	Cl
Toro	Toro Maduro /Nicaraguan wrapper/	6	50	Ma

Introduced in 1996, this namesake brand of the family-owned Factory Don Tuto in Costa Rica offers a medium-to-full-bodied taste. Each cedar box of 25 is painted by hand, with each cigar individually packed in a cellophane sleeve.

DON VITO
Handmade in Santiago, Dominican Republic.

Wrapper: USA/Connecticut   Binder: Dom. Rep.   Filler: Dom. Rep.

Shape	Name	Lgth	Ring	Wrapper
Giant	Troncos	8	50	CC
Robusto	Alfonso	5	50	CC
Small Panatela	Alfonsitos	5	30	CC
Long Corona	Virginianos	6	44	CC
Corona	Caobas	5½	42	CC
Long Panatela	Padrinos	7½	38	CC
Lonsdale	Capo	6¾	44	CC

This is a mild blend of leaves from Connecticut and the Dominican Republic, for a brand which has been in and out of the U.S. market since the 1950s. Introduced in its current form in 1996, Don Vito shapes are offered in boxes of 5 or 25 cigars.

HANDMADE CIGARS: BRAND LISTINGS

DON XAVIER
Handmade in Las Palmas, the Canary Islands of Spain.
Wrapper: USA/Connecticut   *Binder: Canary Islands*
Filler: Brazil, Canary Islands, Dominican Republic

Shape	Name	Lgth	Ring	Wrapper
Long Panatela	Panatela	7½	39	CC
Panatela	Petit Panatela	5⅝	39	CC
Lonsdale	Lonsdale	6⅝	42	CC
Corona	Petit Lonsdale	5⅝	42	CC
Churchill	Gran Corona	7	46	CC
Corona Extra	Corona	5⅝	46	CC
Double Corona	Churchill	7½	50	CC
Robusto	Robusto	4⅝	50	CC
Pyramid	Pyramid	7	52	CC
Cigarillo	Petit	4	29	CC

The flagship of the Marcos Miguel line, this is a mild blend of tobaccos of four nations in a variety of shapes. Introduced in the current range in 1996, Don Xavier cigars are offered in boxes of 5, 10 and 25 cigars each.

DON YÀNES
Handmade in Cumana, Venezuela.
Wrapper: USA/Connecticut   *Binder: Venezuela*   *Filler: Venezuela*

Shape	Name	Lgth	Ring	Wrapper
Long Corona	No. 1	6¼	42	CI

Here is an old Venezuelan standard, introduced to the U.S. market in 1996. This is an all long-filler cigar which is made by hand and is considered full-bodied.

DOÑA ELBA
Handmade in Esteli, Nicaragua.
Wrapper: Nicaragua   *Binder: Nicaragua*   *Filler: Nicaragua*

HANDMADE CIGARS: BRAND LISTINGS

Shape	Name	Lgth	Ring	Wrapper
Churchill	Revolver	7	48	CC-CM
Toro	Toro	6	50	CC-CM
Robusto	Robusto	4⅞	50	CC-CM

Here is a high quality, hard-to-find brand from Nicaragua, where the full-bodied flavor comes through in either of two wrapper shades.

DOUBLE HAPPINESS
Handmade in Manila, the Philippines.

Wrapper: USA/Connecticut   Binder: Philippines   Filler: Philippines

Shape	Name	Lgth	Ring	Wrapper
Pyramid	Nirvana	6	52	CC
Toro	Euphoria	6½	50	CC
Robusto	Bliss	5¼	48	CC
Perfecto	Rapture	5	50	CC
Churchill	Ecstacy	7	47	CC

This brand is debuted in 1995 and handmade in Manila, the Philippines, with a Connecticut Shade-grown wrapper and an Isabela binder and filler, grown in the Philippines. Each shape is presented in a magnificent varnished Narra wood box of 26 (really!), including a hand-sewn crushed velvet liner!

DUNHILL
Handmade in Las Palmas, the Canary Islands of Spain.

Wrapper: USA/Connecticut   Binder: Dom. Rep.   Filler: Dom. Rep.

Shape	Name	Lgth	Ring	Wrapper
Robusto	Coronas Extra	5½	50	CC
Lonsdale	Corona Grandes	6½	43	CC
Corona	Coronas	5½	43	CC
Lonsdale	Lonsdale Grandes	7½	42	CC
Slim Panatela	Panatelas	6	30	CC

This year, the Philippines will import 24 billion dollars worth of goods, and export a handful of these. We'd call that a fair trade.

THE SPLENDID SEED TOBACCO COMPANY
FINE CIGARS FROM A RATHER EXOTIC PLACE.

HANDMADE CIGARS: BRAND LISTINGS

This hand-rolled cigar debuted in 1986 and is mild enough for the casual smoker, yet its distinctive taste will satisfy the connoisseur. The tobacco blend and binder and are both grown in the Canary Islands and the cigar is completed with a rich tasting Cameroon wrapper.

DUNHILL
Handmade in La Romana, Dominican Republic.

Wrapper: USA/Connecticut   *Binder: Dom. Rep.*   *Filler: Brazil, Dom. Rep.*

Shape	Name		Lgth	Ring	Wrapper
Double Corona	Peravias		7	50	CI
Toro	Condados		6	48	CI
Lonsdale	Diamantes		6⅝	42	CI
Panatela	Samanas		6½	38	CI
Corona	Valverdes		5½	42	CI
Robusto	Altamiras	(tubed)	5	48	CI
Churchill	Cabreras	(tubed)	7	48	CI
Giant	Esplendido		8½	52	CI
Petit Corona	Caleta		4	42	CI

Introduced in 1989, Dunhill's master cigar makers roll a special selection of Piloto Cubano and Olor tobaccos from the Cibao Valley of the Dominican Republic. Wrapping the blend in a Dominican binder, the bunch is then finished with the finest quality Connecticut shade-grown leaf from the Windsor Valley. Prior to final packaging, these cigars are aged in cedar-lined rooms to provide the final mellowing of their mild-to-medium-bodied flavor.

898 COLLECTION
Handmade in Kingston, Jamaica.

Wrapper: USA/Connecticut   *Binder: Dom. Rep.*   *Filler: Dom. Rep.*

Shape	Name	Lgth	Ring	Wrapper
Double Corona	Churchill	7½	49	CC
Corona	Corona	5½	42	CC
Lonsdale	Lonsdale	6½	42	CC
Lonsdale	Monarch	6¾	45	CC

HANDMADE CIGARS: BRAND LISTINGS

Robusto	Robusto	5½	49	CC

Introduced in 1991 and made completely by hand in Kingston, Jamaica, the 898 Collection is uncompromising in its commitment to quality of construction and ease in smoking. These are mild-bodied cigars, offered in boxes of 25 cigars each.

1881
Handmade in Manila, the Philippines.
Wrapper: Indonesia/Java   Binder: Philippines   Filler: Dom.Rep., Philippines

Shape	Name	Lgth	Ring	Wrapper
Corona	Corona	5½	44	CM
Robusto	Robusto	5	50	CM
Giant Corona	Centennial	7½	42	CM
Giant	Double Corona	8½	50	CM

The Philippine cigar industry is hundreds of years old and La Flor de la Isabella was formally incorporated in 1881 – hence the name of this brand. It offers excellent craftsmanship and a medium-bodied taste.

EL CANELO
Handmade in Miami, Florida, USA.
Origin of wrapper, binder and filler leaves varies, depending on availability.

Shape	Name	Lgth	Ring	Wrapper
Giant	Viajantes	8½	52	CC-Ma
Giant	Embajadores	8	50	CC
Giant	Soberano	8	50	CC
Churchill	Sargentos	7½	46	CC
Churchill	Olympic	7½	46	CC
Churchill	Presidentes	7½	46	CC-Ma
Churchill	Churchills	7½	48	CC-Ma
Long Corona	Smokers	7	43	CC-Ma
Toro	Toros	6	50	CC

Robusto	Nom-Plus	4¾	50	CC-Ma
Lonsdale	Infiesta No. 1	7	43	CC-Ma
Long Corona	San Marcos	6	44	CC-Ma
Long Panatela	Elegante	7	36	CC
Corona	Fumas	5½	43	CC-Ma
Slim Panatela	Panatela Rabito	7	30	CC-Ma
Slim Panatela	St. Georges	7	30	CC-Ma
Slim Panatela	St. Augustine	5½	30	CC-Ma
Corona	Corona	5½	42	CC-Ma
Small Panatela	Princess	4½	30	CC

These are mild-to-medium cigars with Connecticut wrappers, made in a small factory in the Little Havana section of Miami.

EL CREDITO
Handmade in Miami, Florida, USA.

Wrapper: Ecuador   Binder: Nicaragua   Filler: Dom. Rep., Nicaragua

Shape	Name	Lgth	Ring	Wrapper
Giant	Gigantes	9	49	CC-Ma
Giant	Senadores	8	52	CC-Ma
Double Corona	Monarchs	7¼	54	CC-Ma
Double Corona	Imperiales	7¾	49	CC-Ma
Double Corona	Churchill	7	50	CC-Ma
Churchill	Supremos	7½	48	CC-Ma
Toro	Small Churchill	6	52	CC-Ma
Robusto	Rothchild	5	50	CC-Ma
Grand Corona	Corona Extra	6¼	46	CC-Ma
Giant Corona	Corona Grande	7¾	44	CC-Ma
Lonsdale	No. 1	6¾	43	CC-Ma
Long Corona	Cetros	6¼	43	CC-Ma

HANDMADE CIGARS: BRAND LISTINGS

Corona	Nacionales	5½	43	CC-Ma
Small Panatela	Small Corona	4½	40	CC-Ma
Long Panatela	Panetelas	7	37	CC-Ma
	Made with short filler:			
Churchill	Super Habanero	7½	46	CC-Ma
Lonsdale	Fumas	6¾	44	CC-Ma

This is a medium-bodied smoke, made in the famous El Credito factory in Miami and offered in bundles of 25 cigars each.

ELEGANTE
Handmade in Danli, Honduras.

Wrapper: Ecuador   *Binder: Honduras*   *Filler: Dom. Rep., Honduras*

Shape	*Name*	*Lgth*	*Ring*	*Wrapper*
Churchill	Grande	8	48	CC
Churchill	Especial	7	48	CC
Lonsdale	Centimo	7	44	CC
Long Panatela	Panatela Larga	7	36	CC
Long Corona	Petit Cetro	6	42	CC
Robusto	Queen	4¾	50	CC

Originally made in Tampa beginning in 1985 and now made in Honduras, this is a medium-bodied combination of Cuban seed, Dominican long fller, wrapped in a light Ecuadorian-grown leaf, and offered in boxes of 25.

EL INCOMPARABLE
Handmade in Danli, Honduras.

Wrapper: Ecuador   *Binder: Dom. Rep.*   *Filler: Mexico, Nicaragua*

Shape	*Name*	*Lgth*	*Ring*	*Wrapper*
Long Corona	Corona	6	44	CC
Robusto	Robusto	4½	50	CC
Churchill	Churchill	8	48	CC

Torpedo	Torpedo	7	56	CC

This is a new brand, introduced in 1996, which is unique for its process that imbues the tobacco with 25-year-old Springbank Single Malt Scotch Whisky. These striking cigars are offered in equally stunning packaging: either in a five-pack of aluminum tubes or in a three-pack in an elegant wooden box.

EL PARAISO
Handmade in Danli, Honduras.

Wrapper: USA/Connecticut *Binder: Mexico* *Filler: Dom. Rep., Jamaica*

Shape	Name	Lgth	Ring	Wrapper
Giant	Grande	8½	52	CC-Ma
Double Corona	Presidente	7½	50	CC
Torpedo	Torpedo	7	54	CC-Ma
Churchill	Double Corona	7	46	CC
Panatela	Panatelas	6½	36	CC
Toro	Toro	6	50	CC-Ma
Corona	Corona	5¾	43	CC
Robusto	Robustos	4¾	52	CC-Ma
Slim Panatela	Pequenos	5	30	CC

Tobaccos from four nations go into the creation of El Paraiso, which results in a mild-bodied blend and excellent construction. Packed in cedar boxes of 18, 25 or 50 – depending on size – this brand is also modestly priced.

EL REY DEL MUNDO
Handmade in Cofradia, Honduras.
Wrapper: Ecuador, USA/Connecticut

Binder: Honduras *Filler: Dominican Republic, Honduras*

Shape	Name	Lgth	Ring	Wrapper
Robusto	Robusto	5	54	Ma
Toro	Robusto Larga	6	54	Ma
Double Corona	Robusto Suprema	7¼	54	Ma
Robusto	Robusto Zavalla	5	54	CM

HANDMADE CIGARS: BRAND LISTINGS

Robusto	Rothschilde	5	50	CM
Grand Corona	Rectangulares	5⅝	45	CM
Panatela	Tino	5½	38	CM
Lonsdale	Cedars	7	43	CM
Toro	Choix Supreme	6⅛	49	CM
Grand Corona	Classic Corona	5⅝	45	CM
Grand Corona	Corona	5⅝	45	CM
Giant	Coronation	8½	52	CM
Double Corona	Double Corona	7	49	CM
Torpedo	Flor de Llaneza	6½	54	CM
Pyramid	Flor de LaVonda	6½	52	CM
Double Corona	Flor del Mundo	7¼	54	CM
Petit Corona	Petit Lonsdale	4⅝	43	CM
Churchill	Principale	8	47	CM
Churchill	Individuale	7½	47	CM
Churchill	Corona Inmensa	7¼	47	CM-Ma
	Deluxe Edition Diamonds series:			
Corona	Habana Club *(tubed)*	5⅝	42	CM
Grand Corona	Originales *(tubed)*	5⅝	45	CM
Toro	Montecarlo *(tubed)*	6⅛	48	CM
Double Corona	Imperiale *(tubed)*	7¼	52	CM
	Lights series:			
Slim Panatela	Plantations	6½	30	CC
Cigarillo	Elegantes	5⅜	29	CC
Short Panatela	Reynitas	5	38	CC
Small Panatela	Cafe au Lait	4½	35	CC
Petit Corona	Tres Petit Corona	4¾	43	CC

HANDMADE CIGARS: BRAND LISTINGS

This name means "The King of the World" in Spanish and it lives up to its name with its excellent construction and strong flavor from the Honduran filler and binder and Sumatran-seed Ecuadorian wrapper. Launched in its current form in 1994, a total of 47 sizes are planned, of which 29 are currently in production. The "Lights" group is mild in strength, with a Connecticut wrapper, Honduran binder and filler tobacco from the Dominican Republic.

EL RICO HABANO
Handmade in Miami, Florida, USA and
Villa Gonzales, Dominican Republic.

Wrapper: Ecuador   *Binder: Nicaragua*   *Filler: Honduras, Nicaragua*

Shape	Name	Lgth	Ring	Wrapper
Double Corona	Gran Habanero Deluxe	7¾	50	CM
Churchill	Double Coronas	7	47	CM
Corona Extra	Gran Coronas	5¾	46	CM
Long Corona	Lonsdale Extra	6¼	44	CM
Corona	Coronas	5¾	42	CM
Petit Corona	Petit Habanos	5	40	CM
Robusto	Habano Club	5	48	CM
Long Panatela	No. 1	7½	38	CM

This is a heavy-bodied cigar produced with imported Havana-seed tobaccos and made by hand in Ernesto Carrillo's famous El Credito cigar factory in Miami and the new El Credito facility in Villa Gonzales, Dominican Republic. They are the most robust of the family of brands which includes La Hoja Selecta (mild) and La Gloria Cubana (medium-bodied).

EL SABINAR
Handmade in Santiago, Dominican Republic.

Wrapper: Ecuador   *Binder: Dom. Rep.*   *Filler: Dom. Rep.*

Shape	Name	Lgth	Ring	Wrapper
Toro	No. 2	6	50	CC
Robusto	No. 3	4½	52	CC
Corona	No. 4	5¼	42	CC

Corona Extra	No. 5	5½	46	CC

This is a new brand for 1996, offering a full-bodied blend. The wrapper is a glorious Sumatra-seed leaf grown in Ecuador. El Sabinar cigars are offered in all-cedar cabinets of 25.

EL SUBLIMADO
Handmade in Danli, Honduras.

Wrapper: Ecuador   *Binder: Dom. Rep.*   *Filler: Dom. Rep.*

Shape	Name	Lgth	Ring	Wrapper
Long Corona	Corona	6	44	CC
Robusto	Regordete	4½	50	CC
Torpedo	Torpedo	7	56	CC
Giant	Churchill	8	48	CC

With its mild-to-medium body and totally unique flavor, El Sublimado cigars have earned a place in the hearts of discriminating smokers. Three-year-old leaves from the Cibao Valley of the Dominican Republic are mellowed with 50-year-old Noces d'Or cognac following a secret (and patented) method which enhances the flavor and combined with Connecticut-seed wrappers grown in Ecuador. The unusual packaging of this 1993 brand offers these cigars in boxes of five aluminum tubes, or three cigars in an elegant wooden case.

EL TIGRE
Handmade in Danli, Honduras.

Wrapper: Ecuador   *Binder: Nicaragua*   *Filler: Honduras, Mexico*

Shape	Name	Lgth	Ring	Wrapper
Long Corona	Lonsdale	6	42	CM
Robusto	Robusto	5	50	CM
Double Corona	Churchill	7	49	CM
Giant	Double Corona	8½	52	CM
Torpedo	Pyramid	5½	52	CM

"The Tiger" is a new brand for 1996, full-bodied and featuring a Sumatra-seed wrapper grown in Ecuador. El Tigre is offered in boxes of 25 cigars each.

HANDMADE CIGARS: BRAND LISTINGS

EL TRIUNFO
Handmade in San Andres Tuxtula, Mexico.

Wrapper: Mexico   Binder: Mexico   Filler: Mexico, Nicaragua

Shape	Name	Lgth	Ring	Wrapper
Double Corona	No. 1 Mayans	7½	50	CM
Toro	No. 2 Aztecs	6⅝	50	CM
Toro	No. 3 Toltecs	6	50	CM
Grand Corona	No. 4 Tulas	6⅝	46	CM
Grand Corona	No. 5 Palenques	6	46	CM
Lonsdale	No. 6 Mitlas	6⅝	42	CM
Long Corona	No. 7 Pueblas	6	42	CM

These are made-by-hand, all long filler cigars from Mexico, with a medium-bodied taste. Offered in packs of 25 cigars each, El Triunfo cigars are well made and modestly priced.

EL UNICORNIO
Handmade in Guatemala.

Shape	Name	Lgth	Ring	Wrapper
Lonsdale	Corona	6½	44	CM
Giant	Presidente	8½	52	CM

Here is "the Unicorn," an all-long filler, handmade cigar from Guatemala, offering a full-bodied taste in boxes of 25.

EL VALLE
Handmade in Santiago, Dominican Republic.

Wrapper: Indonesia/Sumatra   Binder: Dom. Rep.   Filler: Dom. Rep.

Shape	Name	Lgth	Ring	Wrapper
Robusto	No. 1	4½	50	CC
Long Corona	No. 2	6	44	CC
Long Panatela	No. 3	7	36	CC
Double Corona	No. 4	7	50	CC

HANDMADE CIGARS: BRAND LISTINGS

Cigarillo	No. 5	8	28	CC
Perfecto	Rocket	6	54	CC

Created for introduction in 1997, this product of the Tabaquera Rubirosa offers a mild-to-medium bodied, flavorful blend of leaves in six shapes, including the odd-shaped "Rocket" with tapered ends and a bulge in the middle!

ENCANTO
Handmade in Santa Rosa de Copan, Honduras.
Wrapper: Honduras　　　　　*Binder: Honduras*　　　　　*Filler: Honduras*

Shape	Name	Lgth	Ring	Wrapper
Giant	Grandioso	7	60	CM
Giant	Viajante	8½	50	CM
Double Corona	Churchill	7	49	CM-Ma
Lonsdale	Elegante	7⅛	43	CM
Toro	Toro	6	50	CM-Ma
Lonsdale	Corona Larga	6¼	44	CM
Long Corona	Cetro	6	42	CM-Ma
Robusto	Rothschild	4¾	50	CM-Ma
Corona	Numero 4	5½	42	CM
Corona	Petit Corona	5⅛	42	CM

This is a very well made cigar, introduced in 1977, offering a medium-to-heavy bodied taste in a variety of sizes and wrappers.

ESCUDO CUBANO
Handmade in Esteli, Nicaragua.
Wrapper: Ecuador　　　　　*Binder: Nicaragua*　　　　　*Filler: Nicaragua*

Shape	Name	Lgth	Ring	Wrapper
Giant	Presidente	8½	52	CC
Double Corona	Churchill	7	50	CC
Lonsdale	No. 1	6½	44	CC
Torpedo	Torpedo	7½	54	CC

HANDMADE CIGARS: BRAND LISTINGS

Pyramid	Piramide	7	50	CC
Long Panatela	Lancero	7	38	CC
Robusto	Robusto	5	50	CC

Introduced in 1996, this is a mild blend of tobaccos, including a Connecticut-seed wrapper grown in Ecuador. These cigars are presented in unique cedar boxes of 25, topped with a plexiglass top!

ESPADA DE ORO
Handmade in Danli, Honduras.
Wrapper: Honduras   Binder: Honduras   Filler: Honduras

Shape	Name	Lgth	Ring	Wrapper
Giant	Viajantes	8½	52	Ma
Giant	Presidente	8½	50	Ma
Double Corona	Executive	7¾	50	Ma
Double Corona	Torpedo	7	54	Ma
Double Corona	Monarch	7	52	Ma
Long Corona	Corona Gorda	6¼	44	Ma
Panatela	Palma Fina	6⅞	36	Ma
Robusto	Rothschild	5	50	Ma

Created in 1992, this is a Honduran "puro" that offers a medium-bodied taste, thanks to a specially-selected blend of Cuban-seed tobaccos grown in Honduras. It is offered in specially-constructed boxes of 10 and 20 cigars each.

ESPANOLA
Handmade in Santiago, Dominican Republic.
Wrapper: USA/Connecticut   Binder: Dom. Rep.   Filler: Dom. Rep.

Shape	Name	Lgth	Ring	Wrapper
Panatela	Torito	6	36	CC
Corona	Corona	5½	42	CC
Churchill	Excellente	6⅞	46	CC
Robusto	Robusto	5	50	CC

HANDMADE CIGARS: BRAND LISTINGS

Toro	Sassoun	6	50	CC
Double Corona	Churchill	6¾	50	CC
Double Corona	Presidente	7	50	CC
	Reserve series:			
Short Panatela	Demi Tasse	4½	36	CC
Petit Corona	Petit Corona	5	42	CC
Lonsdale	Excellente	6½	42	CC
Long Corona	Corona Grande	6	44	CC
Churchill	Churchill	7	48	CC
Robusto	Robusto	5	50	CC
Toro	Toro	6	50	CC
Double Corona	Double Corona	7½	50	CC
Torpedo	Belicoso	5½	52	CC
Giant	Fabuloso	8	52	CC

Silky smooth Connecticut shade-grown wrappers encase this mild blend from the Dominican Republic. New for 1996, the seven shapes of standard Espanola series, as well as the Reserve series, are presented without cellophane in cedar cabinets of 25 cigars. The Reserve series is a full-bodied blend, also new for 1996, available in a wider variety of shapes.

ESTRELLA FINA
Handmade in Esteli, Nicaragua.

Wrapper: Ecuador *Binder: Nicaragua* *Filler: Nicaragua*

Shape	Name	Lgth	Ring	Wrapper
Giant	Double Corona	8	50	CC
Double Corona	Churchill	7	50	CC
Robusto	Robusto	5	50	CC
Toro	Corona	6	50	CC

Here is a new, all 50-ring brand from Nicaragua, offering excellent construction and silky Connecticut-seed wrappers grown in Ecuador. Introduced in 1996, the brand is in limited distribution and is considered medium in body.

ESPAÑOLA

ESPAÑOLA

HANDMADE CIGARS: BRAND LISTINGS

EVELIO
Handmade in Danli, Honduras.

Wrapper: Ecuador   *Binder: Nicaragua*

Filler: Honduras, Mexico, Nicaragua

Shape	Name	Lgth	Ring	Wrapper
Corona	Corona	5¾	42	CC
Churchill	Double Corona	7⅝	47	CC
Lonsdale	No. 1	7	44	CC
Robusto	Robusto	4¾	54	CC
Toro	Robusto Larga	6	54	CC
Pyramid	Torpedo	7	54	CC

The lifetime of expertise which resides in master roller Evelio Oviedo is the secret behind this brand, introduced in 1996. This is a full-bodied but smooth smoke in six of the most popular sizes, prepared in the same all-by-hand method that Oviedo knew from his days in Cuba at the H. Upmann factory in Havana. Evelio cigars are presented in all-cedar boxes of 25.

EXCALIBUR
BY HOYO DE MONTERREY
Handmade in Cofradia, Honduras.

Wrapper: USA/Connecticut   *Binder: Honduras*

Filler: Dominican Republic, Honduras and Nicaragua

Shape	Name		Lgth	Ring	Wrapper
Double Corona	No. I		7¼	54	CC-Ma
Churchill	No. II		6¾	47	CC-Ma
Toro	No. III		6⅛	48	CC-Ma
Grand Corona	No. IV		5⅝	46	CC-Ma
Grand Corona	No. V		6¼	45	CC-Ma
Panatela	No. VI		5½	38	CC-Ma
Petit Corona	No. VII		5	43	CC-Ma
Churchill	Banquets	(tubed)	6¾	48	CC
Cigarillo	Miniatures		3	22	CC

HANDMADE CIGARS: BRAND LISTINGS

Excalibur cigars are handmade in Honduras and are the choicest cigars picked from the famous Hoyo de Monterrey line of fine cigars. A new shape, the Miniature, joins the initial eight shapes, and all are wrapped in beautiful Connecticut Shade wrappers, which gives each and every Excalibur cigar a robust, but exquisitely smooth taste.

EXCELSIOR
Handmade in San Andres Tuxtula, Mexico.

Wrapper: USA/Connecticut   *Binder: Mexico*   *Filler: Dom. Rep., Mexico*

Shape	Name	Lgth	Ring	Wrapper
Long Corona	No. 1	6¼	42	CC
Lonsdale	No. 2	6¾	44	CC
Robusto	No. 3	5½	52	CC
Churchill	No. 4	7	48	CC
Giant	No. 5	8	50	CC
Giant	Individuale	8½	52	CC

This is a new brand for 1996, offering a blend of tobaccos and a medium-bodied flavor in boxes of 25 cigars each, except for the Individuale, which is offered in boxes of 10.

F.D. GRAVE
Handmade in Danli, Honduras.

Wrapper: USA/Connecticut   *Binder: USA/Connecticut*   *Filler: Honduras, Indonesia*

Shape	Name	Lgth	Ring	Wrapper
Double Corona	Churchill	7¾	50	CM
Double Corona	Corona Grande	7	52	CM
Long Corona	Lonsdale	6¼	44	CM
Robusto	Robusto	5	50	CM

One of the most respected names in U.S. cigar history is back with an all-handmade line of exceptional quality, made in Honduras. Introduced in late 1995, the four-shape line is full-bodied in taste and offers a Connecticut Broadleaf wrapper and filler, to complement the Honduran and Indonesian fillers. The F.D. Grave series are presented in individual cellophane sleeves inside an all-wood cabinet box.

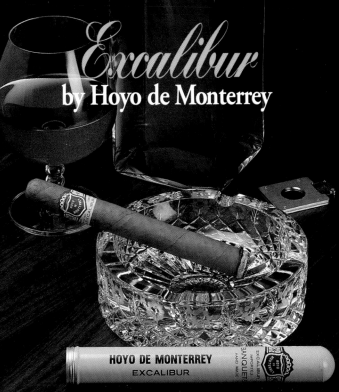

Excalibur
by Hoyo de Monterrey

HOYO DE MONTERREY
EXCALIBUR

Finest of Their Kind In the Best of Taste

Since 1845 our master cigar-makers developed a technique to marry the full-bodied flavor of the English market wrapper with the supreme mildness of the Claro into a world-class, hand-made cigar like Excalibur.

Our craftsmen make sure that every precious long-filler leaf, binder and wrapper that goes into each Excalibur is hand-bunched in the traditional, time-honored way, then packed in a Spanish cedar Boite Nature Box to enhance the seasoning and taste to guarantee a classic smoke that is truly the finest of its kind.

Available at Fine Tobacconists Everywhere. There are eight sizes and shapes available in English Claro and Rich Maduro to satisfy the most discriminating smoker.

Imported by Danby-Palacio Division
VILLAZON & CO., INC.

HANDMADE CIGARS: BRAND LISTINGS

THE FAMOUS RUM RUNNER
Handmade, with medium filler, in Miami, Florida, USA.

Wrapper: Brazil   Binder: Brazil

Filler: Dominican Republic, Ecuador, Honduras, Nicaragua

Shape	Name	Lgth	Ring	Wrapper
Short Panatela	Wench	5	38	CM
Corona	Bucaneer	5½	44	CM
Churchill	Pirate	7	46	CM

This is a flavored cigar produced by the Caribbean Cigar Company and introduced in 1994. Made by hand, it uses medium filler and offers a mild and sweet flavor. Not surprisingly, the black and gold band features the skull-and-crossbones emblem of pirate ships of yore!

FAT CAT
Handmade in Tamboril, Dominican Republic.

Wrapper: Indonesia/Sumatra   Binder: Dom. Rep.   Filler: Dom. Rep.

Shape	Name	Lgth	Ring	Wrapper
Robusto	Robusto	5	52	CC
Double Corona	Churchill	7	50	CC
Torpedo	Torpedo	6½	52	CC

These are "fat" cigars indeed, each with a ring gauge of 50 or more. Offered in "Fat Pacs" of five cigars each, or trays of 75 cigars (25 of each of the three shapes), this is a full-bodied brand with silky wrappers of Sumatra seed, grown in Indonesia.

FELIPE GREGORIO
Handmade in Danli, Honduras.

Wrapper: Honduras   Binder: Honduras   Filler: Honduras

Shape	Name	Lgth	Ring	Wrapper
Double Corona	Glorioso	7¾	50	CM
Churchill	Suntuoso	7	48	CM
Torpedo	Belicoso	6	54	CM
Corona	Sereno	5¾	42	CM

HANDMADE CIGARS: BRAND LISTINGS

| Robusto | Robusto | 5 | 52 | CM |
| Petit Corona | Nino | 4¼ | 44 | CM |

Introduced in 1992, this brand shows off the efforts of a single plantation in Honduras – Jamastram – in the famous valley of the same name. Their Havana-seed tobaccos offer full-bodied, but mellow flavor with an elegant, sweet aroma.

FIGHTING COCK
Handmade in Manila, the Philippines.

Wrapper: Indonesia/Java   Binder: Philippines   Filler: Philippines

Shape	Name	Lgth	Ring	Wrapper
Pyramid	Sidewinder	6	52	CM
Toro	Texas Red	6½	50	CM
Robusto	Smokin' Lulu	5¼	48	CM
Perfecto	Rooster Arturo	5	50	CM
Churchill	C.O.D.	7	47	CM

Introduced in 1995, these hand-made, Manila-manufactured cigars offer a medium-bodied taste, combining a Javan sun-grown wrapper with Philippine Isabela binder and filler. The brand is presented in stunning varnished wooden boxes of 25, each equipped with a hand-sewn, crushed velvet liner. The shapes are named after actual champion roosters!

FIRST PRIMING
Handmade in Danli, Honduras.

Wrapper: Honduras   Binder: Honduras   Filler: Honduras

Shape	Name	Lgth	Ring	Wrapper
Giant	Grandees	8½	52	CC-Ma
Double Corona	Largos	7½	50	CC-Ma

This is a medium-bodied cigar, made of all Honduran tobacco. An excellent value, it is offered in modestly-priced bundles of 25.

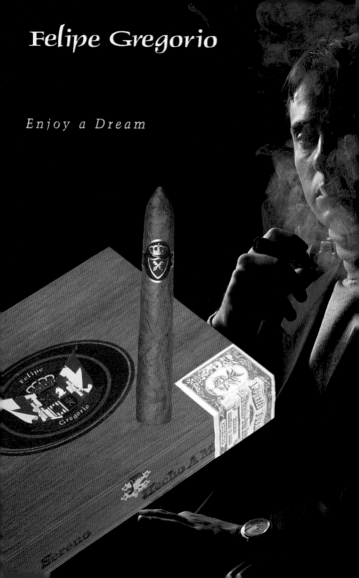

HANDMADE CIGARS: BRAND LISTINGS

FLOR CUBANA
Handmade in Danli, Honduras.

Wrapper: Cameroon   *Binder: Indonesia*   *Filler: Dom. Rep., Nicaragua*

Shape	Name	Lgth	Ring	Wrapper
Double Corona	Presidente	7½	50	CC
Churchill	Churchill	7	48	CC
Lonsdale	Lonsdale	7	44	CC
Corona	Corona	5½	44	CC
Robusto	Robusto	5	50	CC
Long Panatela	Panatela	7½	38	CC

This is a mild to medium-bodied smoke featuring a natural wrapper and leaves from four nations, presented in individual cellophane sleeves in boxes of 25.

FLOR DE A. ALLONES
Handmade in Cofradia, Honduras.

Wrapper: Ecuador and Indonesia   *Binder: Honduras*
Filler: Dominican Republic, Honduras and Nicaragua

Shape	Name	Lgth	Ring	Wrapper
Toro	No. 50	6¼	50	CM-Ma
Robusto	No. 100	4½	50	CM-Ma
Giant	No. 110	8	47	CM-Ma
Panatela	No. 150	5½	38	CM-Ma

This is an ancient Cuban brand, now made in small, very high quality lots in Honduras. Hard to find, Flor de A. Allones has a medium-to-heavy body and is offered in elegant slide-top, all-cedar boxes of 25.

FLOR DE CONSUEGRA
Handmade in Cofradia, Honduras.

Wrapper: Honduras   *Binder: Honduras*   *Filler: Honduras*

Shape	Name	Lgth	Ring	Wrapper
Corona	Corona	5½	42	CM
Churchill	Corona Inmensa	7¼	47	CM

HANDMADE CIGARS: BRAND LISTINGS

Grand Corona	Cuban Corona	5⅝	45	CM
Lonsdale	Lonsdale	6½	42	CM
Short Panatela	Panatela	5⅝	38	CM
Giant	President	8½	49	CM
Robusto	Robusto	4½	50	CM
Grand Corona	Corona Grande	6¼	45	CM
Long Corona	Corona Extra	6	42	CM

This looks like a heavy-bodied cigar, and it is. It is marked by a rich, deep-brown colored, Havana-seed wrapper. Not for the timid!

FLOR DE CUBA
Handmade in Mayaguez, Puerto Rico.

Wrapper: Cameroon   *Binder: Puerto Rico*   *Filler: Puerto Rico*

Shape	Name	Lgth	Ring	Wrapper
Churchill	Selectos	7	46	CM-Ma
Long Corona	Embajadores	6	44	CM-Ma
Long Corona	Cazadores	6	44	CM-Ma
Churchill	Especiales	7	46	CM-Ma

The origins of this brand date back to 1916. Cigar-making in Puerto Rico has a longstanding tradition and this brand delivers a full-bodied taste in boxes of 25 (Selectos, Embajadores) or in bundles of 25 (Cazadores, Especiales).

FLOR DE FARACH
Handmade in Esteli, Nicaragua.

Wrapper: Ecuador   *Binder: Honduran*
Filler: Dominican Republic, Honduras, Nicaragua

Shape	Name	Lgth	Ring	Wrapper
Torpedo	Momotombo	6¾	54	CC
Torpedo	Momotomito	7	52	CC
Pyramid	Pyramid	7	48	CC
Toro	Regios	6½	54	.CC

HANDMADE CIGARS: BRAND LISTINGS

Here is the revival of an ancient Cuban brand which dates from 1903, much appreciated until it disappeared in 1960. Now, in 1996, a Nicaraguan version of the Flor de Farach is a medium-to-full-bodied cigar, with a beautiful Sumatra-seed wrapper grown in Ecuador and a rich flavor.

FLOR DE FILIPINAS
Handmade in Manila, the Philippines.

Wrapper: Philippines   *Binder: Philippines*   *Filler: Philippines*

Shape	Name	Lgth	Ring	Wrapper
Churchill	Churchill	6¾	47	CC
Lonsdale	Coronas Largas	6¾	44	CC
Corona	Coronas	5½	44	CC
Panatela	Cetros	5⅞	39	CC
Short Panatela	Half Corona	4	39	CC
Short Panatela	Panatellas	4⅞	35	CC

Introduced in 1996, this is an inexpensive, medium-bodied but handmade brand from the Philippines. Made from Philippine Isabela tobacco in the binder and filler, it is covered in a Philippine Cagayan Valley wrapper and offered in boxes of 25.

FLOR DE GONZALEZ
Handmade in Miami, Florida, USA.

Wrapper: Ecuador   *Binder: Honduras*   *Filler: Dom. Rep., Honduras*

Shape	Name	Lgth	Ring	Wrapper
Double Corona	Churchill	7	50	CC-Ma
Toro	Corona Extra	6	50	CC-Ma
Double Corona	Magnum	7¼	62	CC-Ma
Lonsdale	No. 1	6¾	44	CC-Ma
Corona	No. 4	5½	44	CC-Ma
Pyramid	Piramide	7	62	CC-Ma
Double Corona	President	7½	50	CC-Ma
Torpedo	Torpedo	6¼	52	CC-Ma

Robusto	Wavell	4¾	50	CC-Ma

This is a new brand for 1996, made in the Miami area and offering a wide range, including some really, really big ring gauges. Available in both natural and maduro wrappers, the body is medium and all shapes are offered in boxes of 25.

FLOR DE HONDURAS
Handmade in Danli, Honduras.
(The distributor declined to provide any information about the origins of the tobaccos used in this brand.)

Shape	Name	Lgth	Ring	Wrapper
Giant	Viajantes	8½	52	CM
Double Corona	Churchill	7	49	CM
Lonsdale	No. 1	7	43	CM
Toro	Toro	6	50	CM
Long Corona	Corona	6¼	43	CM
Robusto	Robustos	5	50	CM

This is a new brand for 1996, offered a medium-bodied taste and attractively packaged in all-cedar, book-style boxes of 25.

FLOR DE JALAPA
Handmade in Esteli, Nicaragua.

Wrapper: Ecuador   *Binder: Nicaragua*   *Filler: Nicaragua*

Shape	Name	Lgth	Ring	Wrapper
Giant	Presidente	8½	52	CM
Toro	Toro	6	50	CM
Long Corona	Grand Corona	6	44	CM
Churchill	Churchill	7	48	CM
Robusto	Robusto	4¾	50	CM

This brand was introduced in January 1996. It is light to medium in strength and uses a Havana-seed wrapper, grown in Ecuador. These cigars are offered in boxes of 25.

A BREAK FOR SMOKERS OF HANDMADE/IMPORTED CIGARS.

INTRODUCING SIGLO 21, FLOR DE JALAPA AND LA DILIGENCIA CIGARS.

These exquisite handmade, long-filler cigars are all imported. Each cigar features carefully selected tobaccos for a satisfying taste and aroma.

They come from three of the finest tobacco growing regions of the world - Siglo 21s from the Dominican Republic, Flor de Jalapas from the Jalapa Valley of Nicaragua and La Diligencias from Honduras.

Imported by
Swisher International, Inc.

HANDMADE CIGARS: BRAND LISTINGS

FLOR DE FLOREZ
Handmade in Danli, Honduras.

Wrapper: Honduras *Binder: Honduras* *Filler: Honduras*

Shape	Name	Lgth	Ring	Wrapper
Double Corona	Presidente	7	49	CM
Lonsdale	Cetros No. 2	6½	44	CM
Toro	Corona	6	49	CM
Robusto	Rothchild	4⅞	47	CM
Long Corona	Blunt	6	42	CM

Essentially a family secret, American smokers discovered Flor de Florez in 1995. Now produced in Honduras, these cigars are mild to medium in body, using an all-Honduran blend, including a Connecticut Shade-seed wrapper.

FLOR DE FLOREZ CABINET SELECTION
Handmade in Managua, Nicaragua.

Wrapper: Nicaragua *Binder: Nicaragua* *Filler: Nicaragua*

Shape	Name	Lgth	Ring	Wrapper
Double Corona	Gigantes	7½	49	CM
Churchill	Sir Winston	7	47	CM
Torpedo	Belicoso	6½	52	CM
Corona Extra	Florez-Florez	5½	46	CM
Robusto	Robusto	5	50	CM
Petit Corona	Coronita	5	42	CM

This is the new line from Flor de Florez, introduced in 1996. This is an all-Nicaraguan cigar, offering a medium-to-full-bodied flavor with rich spices in the taste, offered in boxes of 25.

FLOR DE MANILA
Handmade in Manila, the Philippines.

Wrapper: Philippines *Binder: Philippines* *Filler: Philippines*

Shape	Name	Lgth	Ring	Wrapper
Churchill	Churchill	7	47	CC

HANDMADE CIGARS: BRAND LISTINGS

Lonsdale	Coronas Largas	7	44	CC
Corona	Coronas	5½	44	CC
Long Panatela	Cetros Largos	7½	39	CC
Panatela	Cetros	6	39	CC
Corona	Londres	5¾	44	CC
Panatela	Panatela	5¾	35	CC
Torpedo	Cortado	5	50	CC

This is a mild to medium-bodied cigar in very limited distribution, which blends Cuban-seed tobaccos grown in the Philippines for a pleasant, unique taste.

FLOR DE MEXICO
Handmade in San Andres Tuxtula, Mexico.

Wrapper: Mexico   *Binder: Mexico*   *Filler: Mexico*

Shape	Name	Lgth	Ring	Wrapper
Double Corona	Churchill	7½	50	CM
Toro	Toro	6	50	CM
Lonsdale	No. 1	6⅝	42	CM
Long Corona	No. 2	6	42	CM
Panatela	No. 3	6⅝	35	CM
Petit Corona	No. 4	5	42	CM

Created in 1979, this is a full-bodied cigar made in Mexico and offered in bundles of 25 cigars each.

FLOR DE NICARAGUA
Handmade in Esteli, Nicaragua.

Wrapper: Nicaragua   *Binder: Nicaragua*   *Filler: Nicaragua*

Shape	Name	Lgth	Ring	Wrapper
Giant	Presidente	8	54	CC-Ma
Giant	Viajante	8½	52	CC-Ma
Double Corona	Presidente Corto	7¼	54	CC-Ma

HANDMADE CIGARS: BRAND LISTINGS

Double Corona	Viajante Corto	7	52	CC-Ma
Double Corona	Emperador	7¾	50	CC-Ma
Double Corona	Emperador Corto	7½	50	CC-Ma
Churchill	Churchill	6⅞	48	CC-Ma
Churchill	No. 11	7½	46	CC-Ma
Toro	Duke	6	50	CC-Ma
Long Panatela	No. 9	8	38	CC-Ma
Long Panatela	No. 9 Corto	7	38	CC-Ma
Corona Extra	Corona Extra	5½	46	CC-Ma
Robusto	Consul	4½	52	CC-Ma
Lonsdale	No. 1	6⅝	44	CC-Ma
Lonsdale	No. 10	6½	43	CC-Ma
Long Corona	No. 3	6	44	CC-Ma
Corona	Nacional	5½	44	CC-Ma
Panatela	No. 5	6⅞	35	CC-Ma
Long Corona	No. 6	6	41	CC-Ma
Corona	Seleccion B	5½	42	CC-Ma
Slim Panatela	No. 7	7	30	CC-Ma
Panatela	Elegante	6½	38	CC-Ma
Petit Corona	No. 2	4½	42	CC-Ma
Short Panatela	Petits	5½	38	CC-Ma
Slim Panatela	Senoritas	5½	34	CC-Ma
Small Panatela	Piccolino	4⅛	30	CC-Ma
Toro	Corona	5⅝	48	CC-Ma

Introduced in 1995, the 27-shape Flor de Nicaragua range is a Nicaraguan puro. These mild-bodied cigars use filler and binder leaf from the Jalapa Valley of Nicaragua, combined with Nicaraguan wrappers.

HANDMADE CIGARS: BRAND LISTINGS

FLOR DE PALICIO
Handmade in Cofradia, Honduras.

Wrapper: Ecuador and Indonesia   *Binder: Honduras*
Filler: Dominican Republic, Honduras and Nicaragua

Shape	Name	Lgth	Ring	Wrapper
Lonsdale	No. 1	7	40	CM
Long Corona	No. 2	6	42	CM
Churchill	Corona	6¾	48	CM

This is a handmade, medium-bodied cigar, created under the supervision of the master cigar makers who manufacture Hoyo de Monterrey and Punch. This elegant brand is offered in equally elegant boxes of 25 each.

FLOR DEL CARIBE
Handmade in Danli, Honduras.

Wrapper: Ecuador and Indonesia   *Binder: Honduras*
Filler: Dominican Republic, Honduras and Nicaragua

Shape	Name	Lgth	Ring	Wrapper
Corona	Duques	5½	42	CM-Ma
Churchill	Super Cetro	7	46	CM-Ma
Double Corona	Sovereign	7	52	CM-Ma

This brand is offered in elegant boxes of 25 cigars each. The medium-to-full-bodied range has been reduced from six to three sizes for 1996, with a maduro wrapper now available for all sizes.

FONSECA
Handmade in Santiago, Dominican Republic.

Wrapper: USA/Connecticut   *Binder: Mexico*   *Filler: Dom. Rep.*

Shape	Name	Lgth	Ring	Wrapper
Long Corona	8-9-8	6	43	Co
Grand Corona	7-9-9	6½	46	Co-Ma
Double Corona	10-10	7	50	Co-Ma
Robusto	5-50	5	50	Co-Ma

HANDMADE CIGARS: BRAND LISTINGS

| Petit Corona | 2-2 | 4¼ | 40 | Co-Ma |
| Pyramid | Triangular | 5½ | 56 | Co |

One of the world's most famous names in Port is also a respected name in cigars. Medium in body, this refined, cabinet-selection brand debuted in 1962 and was re-introduced in its current blend in 1991. It is blended from the choicest tobaccos grown in the Cibao Valley of the Dominican Republic. The wrapper is outstanding Connecticut Shade (natural) or Connecticut Broadleaf (maduro) leaf. The Triangular shape is one of the hardest to make and offers a rich flavor, concentrated by its conical shape.

FRANCO
Handmade in Santiago, Dominican Republic.
Wrapper: USA/Connecticut   Binder: Dom. Rep.   Filler: Dom. Rep.

Shape	Name	Lgth	Ring	Wrapper
Lonsdale	Condado	6½	44	CC
Corona	Eminente	5½	42	CC
Long Panatela	Gourmet	7	38	CC
Double Corona	Magnum	7½	50	CC
Robusto	Regio	5½	50	CC

Here is a mild-to-medium bodied brand which is new for 1996, which features five popular shapes in boxes of 25 cigars each.

FREE CUBA
Handmade in Miami, Florida, USA.
Wrapper: Indonesia/Java   Binder: Nicaragua   Filler: Dom. Rep.

Shape	Name	Lgth	Ring	Wrapper
Short Panatela	Miniature	5	36	CM
Robusto	Robusto	5	50	CM
Toro	Robusto Largo	6	50	CM
Lonsdale	Corona	6½	42	CM
Churchill	Double Corona	7½	46	CM
Double Corona	Churchill	7¼	50	CM

HANDMADE CIGARS: BRAND LISTINGS

Torpedo	Torpedo	6½	54	CM
Perfecto	Perfecto	6½	48	CM

This brand was introduced in 1996 by the Caribbean Cigar Company, which is headquartered in Miami, Florida. Despite the presence of Havana seed binders and fillers, Free Cuba belies its fiery name with a medium-bodied flavor, offered in carefully-crafted boxes of 25.

FUNDADORE JAMAICA
Handmade in Kingston, Jamaica.

Wrapper: USA/Connecticut   *Binder: Mexico*
               Filler: Dominican Republic, Jamaica, Mexico

Shape	Name	Lgth	Ring	Wrapper
Double Corona	Churchill	7½	49	CC-Ma
Giant	King Ferdinand	8	50	CC-Ma
Toro	Ultra	6	50	CC-Ma
Grand Corona	Bristol	6	45	CC-Ma
Lonsdale	Rothschild	6½	42	CC-Ma
Corona	Corona	5½	42	CC-Ma
Panatela	Cetro	6¾	38	CC-Ma

This brand is produced by the Combined Tobacco Co. of Kingston, Jamaica and offers mild, rich flavors. Offered in boxes of 25, Connecticut Shade wrappers are offered in both a natural and maduro style.

GALIANO
Handmade in Santiago, Dominican Republic.

Wrapper: USA/Connecticut   *Binder: Dom. Rep.*   *Filler: Dom. Rep.*

Shape	Name	Lgth	Ring	Wrapper
Double Corona	Presidente	7½	50	CC
Slim Panatela	Panatela	7	32	CC
Corona	Corona	5¾	43	CC
Churchill	Churchill	7	48	CC
Robusto	Robusto	4¾	52	CC

HANDMADE CIGARS: BRAND LISTINGS

| Toro | Toro | 6 | 50 | CC |
| Small Panatela | Chicos | 4¾ | 30 | CC |

Originally introduced in 1994, this is a mild-to-medium-bodied brand which is in national distribution in the U.S. for the first time in 1996. Very well constructed, it features a genuine Connecticut Shade wrapper.

GARO
Handmade in Santiago, Dominican Republic.
Wrapper: USA/Connecticut   *Binder: Dom. Rep.*   *Filler: Dom. Rep.*

Shape	Name	Lgth	Ring	Wrapper
Double Corona	Presidente	7½	50	CC
Churchill	Churchill	7	48	CC
Toro	Opus	6	50	CC
Lonsdale	Numero Uno	7	43	CC
Robusto	Robusto	4¾	52	CC
Pyramid	Pyramide	6½	56	CC
Corona	Corona	5¾	43	CC
Long Panatela	Panatela	7	36	CC

New for 1996, the Garo line is made by hand in the Dominican Republic, offering a mild-to-medium body. It uses only Cuban-seed long filler, combined with a Dominican Olor binder and genuine Connecticut Shade-grown wrapper leaves. Even the band is elegant, employing the famous "Fleur de Lis" design.

GARCIA Y VEGA
Handmade in Kingston, Jamaica.
Wrapper: USA/Connecticut   *Binder: Mexico*   *Filler: Dom. Rep., Mexico*

Shape	Name	Lgth	Ring	Wrapper
Churchill	Churchill	7	45	CC
Lonsdale	Lonsdale	6½	42	CC
Panatela	Corona	5½	38	CC

HANDMADE CIGARS: BRAND LISTINGS

Garcia y Vega has been a famous name in cigars since it was introduced in 1882. In 1996, a new handmade series appears to complement the existing machine-made line with a Connecticut Shade wrapper and offering a medium body.

GILBERTO OLIVA
Handmade in Esteli, Nicaragua.

Wrapper: Ecuador   *Binder: Dom. Rep.*   *Filler: Dom. Rep., Nicaragua*

Shape	Name	Lgth	Ring	Wrapper
Lonsdale	No. 1	6½	44	CC
Robusto	Robusto	5½	50	CC-Ma
Double Corona	Churchill	7	50	CC-Ma
Toro	Viajante	6	52	CC
Torpedo	Torpedo	6	52	CC

Although this brand is new for 1996, it comes from the experienced hands of Gilberto Oliva. Here is a medium-bodied, richly flavored cigar in both a natural and maduro-shade wrapper in the most popular sizes. The line is complemented by the elegant, all-cedar boxes in which 25 cigars are held.

GIOCONDA
Handmade in Danli, Honduras.

Wrapper: USA/Connecticut   *Binder: Honduras*
Filler: Dominican Republic, Honduras, Nicaragua

Shape	Name	Lgth	Ring	Wrapper
Double Corona	President	7¼	54	CC-Ma
Grand Corona	Lonsdale	6¼	45	CC-Ma
Churchill	Churchill	6¾	48	CC-Ma
Robusto	Robusto	4½	50	CC-Ma

New life was given to this brand by Vincent & Tampa Cigar Co.'s Mario Garrido, which is now made in Honduras. It offers a mild-to-medium blend and is presented in boxes of 25.

HANDMADE CIGARS: BRAND LISTINGS

GISPERT
Handmade in Danli, Honduras.

Wrapper: Ecuador   *Binder: Dom. Rep.*
Filler: Dominican Republic, Honduras, Nicaragua

Shape	Name	Lgth	Ring	Wrapper
Double Corona	Churchill	7½	50	CM
Toro	Toro	6	50	CM
Robusto	Robusto	5	52	CM
Lonsdale	Lonsdale	6½	44	CM

New for 1996, this is a Honduran version of an old Cuban brand, with excellent construction and a mild-to-medium-bodied taste. The wrapper is Connecticut-seed grown in Ecuador and each box of 25 is packed in cedar. The brand is only available in limited distribution to the members of the Tobacconists' Association of America (TAA).

GRAND NICA
Handmade in Esteli, Nicaragua.

Wrapper: Nicaragua   *Binder: Nicaragua*   *Filler: Nicaragua*

Shape	Name	Lgth	Ring	Wrapper
Toro	Toro	6	50	CM
Lonsdale	Lonsdale	6½	44	CM
Double Corona	Churchill	7	52	CM
Robusto	Robusto	5	52	CM
Giant	Gigante	8	54	CM
Torpedo	Torpedo	6½	54	CM

New for 1996, this all-Nicaraguan line features all-Cuban seed tobaccos and offers a medium-to-full-bodied taste.

THE GRIFFIN'S
Handmade in Santiago, Dominican Republic.

Wrapper: USA/Connecticut   *Binder: Dom. Rep.*   *Filler: Dom. Rep.*

HANDMADE CIGARS: BRAND LISTINGS

Shape	Name	Lgth	Ring	Wrapper
Long Panatela	No. 100	7	38	CC
Lonsdale	No. 200	7	43	CC
Long Corona	No. 300	6¼	43	CC
Panatela	No. 400	6	38	CC
Corona	No. 500	5	43	CC
Slim Panatela	Privilege	5	32	CC
Giant	Prestige	7½	50	CC
Robusto	Robusto	5	50	CC

While the mythical character of the Griffin gives this brand its name, the effort which gives the cigars their high quality is very real. The filler includes three different Cibao Valley tobaccos, combined with a Dominican binder and Connecticut wrapper to give it a mildly spicy, flavorful taste.

GUARANTEED JAMAICA
Handmade in Kingston, Jamaica.

Wrapper: Ecuador   Binder: Mexico
Filler: Dominican Republic, Jamaica, Mexico

Shape	Name	Lgth	Ring	Wrapper
Double Corona	No. 1000	7½	49	CC
Giant	No. 1002	8	50	CC
Toro	No. 600	6	50	CC
Grand Corona	No. 900	6	45	CC
Lonsdale	No. 100	6½	42	CC
Corona	No. 200	5½	42	CC
Panatela	No. 300	6¾	38	CC

These cigars are familiar sights on discount shelves and in mail-order catalogs. They are well-made, quality cigars from the Combined Tobacco Co. factory in Kingston, Jamaica. The Ecuadorian wrapper helps to give this brand a mild, rich taste. Guaranteed Jamaica cigars are offered in bundles of 25.

HANDMADE CIGARS: BRAND LISTINGS

HABANA GOLD
Handmade in Danli, Honduras.
Wrappers: Black Label: Indonesia; White Label: Nicaragua
Binder: Nicaragua   Filler: Nicaragua

Shape	Name	Lgth	Ring	Wrapper
Petit Corona	Petite Corona	5	42	CC-CM
Long Corona	Corona	6	44	CC-CM
Robusto	Robusto	5	50	CC-CM
Pyramid	Torpedo	6	52	CC-CM
Double Corona	Churchill	7	52	CC-CM
Churchill	Double Corona	7½	46	CC-CM
Giant	Presidente	8½	52	CC-CM
Torpedo	No. 2	6⅛	52	CC-CM

Cuban-seed tobaccos are married with wrappers from Nicaragua (White Label)
or Sumatra-grown leaves (Black Label) to create a distinctive new brand:
Habana Gold. Medium in body, these cigars continue to age, as they are
offered in cellophane sleeves inside beautiful cedar boxes.

HABANA GOLD STERLING VINTAGE
Handmade in Danli, Honduras.
Wrapper: Ecuador   Binder: Ecuador   Filler: Nicaragua

Shape	Name	Lgth	Ring	Wrapper
Petit Corona	Petite Corona	5	42	CM
Long Corona	Corona	6	44	CM
Robusto	Robusto	5	50	CM
Pyramid	Torpedo	6	52	CM
Double Corona	Churchill	7	52	CM
Churchill	Double Corona	7½	46	CM
Giant	Presidente	8½	52	CM
Torpedo	No. 2	6⅛	52	CM

HANDMADE CIGARS: BRAND LISTINGS

This new blend includes an Ecuador-grown wrapper and binder, offering dark, full flavor, thanks to the specially aged wrapper leaf. The taste is nothing less than "sterling."

HABANICA
Handmade in Condega, Nicaragua.

Wrapper: Nicaragua   Binder: Nicaragua   Filler: Nicaragua

Shape	Name	Lgth	Ring	Wrapper
Churchill	Serie 747	7	47	CM
Grand Corona	Serie 646	6	46	CM
Panatela	Serie 638	6	38	CM
Corona Extra	Serie 546	5¼	46	CM
Robusto	Serie 550	5	50	CM

Created in 1995, this is a medium-bodied smoke that is smooth and non-acidic. Made in Condega, Nicaragua, it combines choice Havana-seed tobaccos grown in nearby Jalapa to create a pleasant, rich taste.

HAMILTONS
Handmade in La Romana, Dominican Republic.

Wrapper: Indonesia   Binder: Dom. Rep.   Filler: Dom. Rep.

Shape	Name	Lgth	Ring	Wrapper
Churchill	George I	7½	48	CC
Robusto	George II	5	50	CC
Toro	George III	6	50	CC
Lonsdale	George IV	6½	44	CC
Corona	George V	5½	42	CC
Long Panatela	George VI	7½	38	CC
Cigarillo	George VII	4½	28	CC
Panatela	George VIII	6¾	38	CC

Here is a new brand for 1996, established by the noted actor and celebrity George Hamilton, a man who is never without his trademark tan. These eight sizes are made in the Consolidated Cigar Company factory in the Dominican

HANDMADE CIGARS: BRAND LISTINGS

Republic, and differ from the separate series produced by Tabacos Dominicanos. This is a fairly mild blend and is available only at selected retailers.

HAMILTONS RESERVE
Handmade in Santiago, Dominican Republic.

Wrapper: USA/Connecticut *Binder: Dom. Rep.* *Filler: Dom. Rep.*

Shape	Name	Lgth	Ring	Wrapper
Cigarillo	Lady H	5	26	CC
Slim Panatela	Ashley	5½	31	CC
Long Panatela	Zorro	7½	38	CC
Corona	Corona	5½	42	CC
Churchill	Don Jorge	7	48	CC
Robusto	Robusto	5	50	CC
Double Corona	King George	7½	50	CC
Giant	Lord H	9¼	50	CC
Torpedo	Torpedo	6⅛	52	CC

A 1996 companion brand to the Hamiltons brand above, this nine-shape line is produced at the Tabadom factory in Santiago. This is a medium-bodied blend, with a smooth Connecticut wrapper.

HARRIEL'S DREAM
Handmade in Danli, Honduras.

Wrapper: Ecuador *Binder: USA/Connecticut* *Filler: Dom. Rep.*

Shape	Name	Lgth	Ring	Wrapper
Lonsdale	Elegante	7	43	CC
Long Panatela	Palma	7	38	CC
Churchill	Churchill	7	48	CC
Giant	Grandioso	8	52	CC
Robusto	Rothschild	5	50	CC

HANDMADE CIGARS: BRAND LISTINGS

The Ecuadorian-grown, Connecticut-seed wrappers, combined with Connecticut binder and Dominican filler, offer a mild, rich taste. Available only in limited distribution, this brand is presented in all-cedar boxes of 25.

HASA REY
Handmade in Danli, Honduras.

Wrapper: Honduras　　　　*Binder: Honduras*　　　　*Filler: Honduras*

Shape	Name	Lgth	Ring	Wrapper
Long Corona	Cazadore	6	42	CM
Double Corona	Churchill	7	50	CM
Panatela	Panatella	6	38	CM
Robusto	Rothchild	5	50	CM
Toro	Toro	6	50	CM
Lonsdale	No. 1	7	42	CM
Petit Corona	No. 4	5	42	CM

The name is a phonetic version of the Yiddish word "chazarai," (pronounced HAAS-a-RYE) originally referring to junk or trash, but now in use as a general reference to goods or "stuff." This cigar stuff dates from 1969 and is a full-bodied bundle of 25 cigars, made from all-Honduran tobaccos. Stuff one in your mouth and light up!

HAVANA
Handmade in Union City, New Jersey, USA.
Wrapper: Dominican Republic, Mexico, USA/Connecticut
Binder: Mexico, USA/Connecticut　　　*Filler: Dominican Republic, Honduras*

Shape	Name	Lgth	Ring	Wrapper
Giant	Churchill	8	50	CC-Ma
Double Corona	Silverano	7	50	CC-Ma
Toro	Torito	6½	50	CC-Ma
Churchill	Imperiale	7½	46	CC-Ma
Lonsdale	Presidente	6½	44	CC-Ma
Long Corona	Senadore	6	44	CC-Ma
Long Panatela	Ninfa	7	36	CC-Ma

HANDMADE CIGARS: BRAND LISTINGS

Lonsdale	Fuma	7	44	CC-Ma
Torpedo	Torpedo	6	54	CC-Ma
Pyramid	Pyramid	5½	46	CC-Ma
Robusto	Robusto	5	50	CC-Ma

This cigar is made by the Boquilla cigar factory in Union City. These are medium-to-full bodied cigars – now banded – with an increased number of sizes and wrappers available for 1997.

HAVANA CLASSICO
Handmade in Miami, Florida, USA.

Wrapper: Ecuador   *Binder: Ecuador*
Filler: Dominican Republic, Indonesia, Mexico

Shape	Name	Lgth	Ring	Wrapper
Torpedo	Puntas	5	38	Ma
Corona	Varadero	5½	44	Ma
Robusto	Robusto	5	50	Ma
Toro	Robusto Largo	6	50	Ma
Lonsdale	Corona Classic	6½	42	Ma
Churchill	Double Corona	7½	46	Ma
Double Corona	Churchill	7¼	50	Ma
Double Corona	Presidente	7½	54	Ma
Torpedo	Torpedo	6½	54	Ma
Pyramid	Pyramide	7¼	54	Ma
Giant	Malecon	9	60	Ma

This brand was created in 1994 and is a featured maduro-wrapped brand of the Caribbean Cigar Company. This is a full-bodied brand with complex flavors offered in a wide variety of sizes.

HAVANA COOL
Handmade, with short filler, in Esteli, Nicaragua.
Wrapper: Nicaragua   *Binder: Nicaragua*   *Filler: Nicaragua*

HANDMADE CIGARS: BRAND LISTINGS

Shape	Name	Lgth	Ring	Wrapper
Long Corona	Alhambra	6	44	CM
Robusto	Granada	5	50	CM
Churchill	Riviera	7	48	CM
Short Panatela	Salamanca	4	38	CM

This is a medium-to-full bodied smoke, introduced in 1996 and made with all-Nicaraguan tobacco and offered in boxes of 25.

HAVANA RESERVE
BY DON LINO
Handmade in Danli, Honduras.

Wrapper: USA/Connecticut   *Binder: Honduras*   *Filler: Honduras*

Shape	Name		Lgth	Ring	Wrapper
Lonsdale	No. 1		6½	44	CC
Corona Extra	Toros		5½	46	CC
Long Panatela	Panatela		7	36	CC
Double Corona	Churchill		7½	50	CC
Torpedo	Torpedo		7	48	CC
Robusto	Rothchild		4½	50	CC
Lonsdale	Tubes	(tubed)	6½	44	CC
Robusto	Robustos		5½	50	CC

Introduced in 1993, Havana Reserve is a handmade cigar with Honduran long filler and binder that assures consistent, mild taste and burning qualities. The wrapper is selected from only the finest Connecticut leaf for the unique taste that is only found in Havana Reserve.

HAVANA SUNRISE
Handmade in Miami, Florida, USA.
Wrapper: Ecuador, USA/Connecticut

Binder: Honduras   *Filler: Dom. Rep.*

HANDMADE CIGARS: BRAND LISTINGS

Shape	Name	Lgth	Ring	Wrapper
Cigarillo	Panatela - Cache	5	28	Co
Robusto	Robusto	5	50	Co
Torpedo	Torpedo	6	54	Co
Long Corona	Corona	6	44	Co
Toro	Double Corona	6	48	Co
Toro	Emperador	6¼	54	Co
Churchill	Havana	6¾	46	Co
Torpedo	Pyramid	7	60	Co
Long Panatela	Lancero	7½	38	Co
Double Corona	Churchill	7½	50	Co
Giant	Presidente	8	52	Co

Created in the heart of "Little Havana" in Miami, Florida, Havana Sunrise cigars are new for 1996. Offering a medium-to-full-bodied flavor, they are presented in elegant cedar boxes of 25, where the cigars continue to age and obtain an even more elegant finish.

HENRY CLAY
Handmade in La Romana, Dominican Republic.
Wrapper: USA/Connecticut   Binder: Dom. Rep.   Filler: Dom. Rep.

Shape	Name	Lgth	Ring	Wrapper
Corona	Brevas	5½	42	Ma
Corona Extra	Brevas a la Conserva	5⅝	46	Ma
Churchill	Brevas Finas	6½	48	Ma

There aren't a lot of sizes in this brand, but don't tell that to its devoted followers, who are lovers of its medium-bodied taste and Connecticut Broadleaf maduro wrappers. Undoubtedly named for the famous American politician of the same name (U.S. senator from Kentucky 1806-07, 1810-11, 1831-42, 1849-52; U.S. representative and Speaker of the House 1811-14, 1815-21, 1823-25; U.S. secretary of state 1825-29), this brand originated in Cuba and the Henry Clay factory in Havana is still pictured on the brand's box.

HANDMADE CIGARS: BRAND LISTINGS

HIDALGO
Handmade, with mixed filler, in Colon, Panama.

Wrapper: Ecuador   *Binder: Mexico*
Filler: Dominican Republic, Honduras, Panama

Shape	Name	Lgth	Ring	Wrapper
Lonsdale	Cazadore	7	44	CC
Lonsdale	Fuma	7	44	Ma
Corona	Corona	5½	42	CC-Ma
Churchill	Double Corona	7	48	CC-Ma
Giant	Monarch	8½	52	CC-Ma

These medium-bodied cigars use mixed filler (long and short) and are offered in bundles of 20 cigars each.

HOJA DE HONDURAS
Handmade in Danli, Honduras.

Wrapper: Ecuador   *Binder: Honduras*   *Filler: Honduras*

Shape	Name	Lgth	Ring	Wrapper
Double Corona	Churchill	7	50	CC
Giant	General	8½	52	CC
Giant	Inmensas	8	54	CC
Lonsdale	Number 1	7	43	CC
Long Panatela	Palma Extra	7	36	CC
Corona	Reyes	5½	42	CC
Toro	Toro	6	50	CC

These are medium-to-full bodied cigars, well constructed and offered in boxes of 25.

HOJA DE MEXICALI
Handmade in San Andres Tuxtla, Mexico.

Wrapper: Mexico   *Binder: Mexico*   *Filler: Mexico*

HANDMADE CIGARS: BRAND LISTINGS

Shape	Name	Lgth	Ring	Wrapper
Lonsdale	Lonsdale	6⅝	42	CM
Long Corona	Royal Corona	6	42	CM
Double Corona	Soberano	7½	50	CM
Toro	Toro	6	50	CM-Ma
Giant	Viajante	8½	52	CM-Ma

This Mexican "puro" is a heavy-bodied cigar, created in 1985, with all-San Andres Valley tobacoos, offered in convenient bundles of 25 cigars each.

HOJA DE NICARAGUA
Handmade in Esteli, Nicaragua.

Wrapper: Nicaragua   Binder: Nicaragua   Filler: Nicaragua

Shape	Name	Lgth	Ring	Wrapper
Double Corona	Churchill	7	49	CM-Ma
Robusto	Consul	4½	52	CM-Ma
Grand Corona	Corona Nacio	5⅝	48	CM-Ma
Long Corona	Numero 3	6	44	CM-Ma
Long Corona	Numero 6	6	42	CM-Ma
Double Corona	Presidente	7½	50	CM-Ma
Giant	Viajante	8½	52	CM-Ma

Here is an all-Nicaraguan cigar offered in elegant boxes of 25, offering a spicy, full-bodied taste.

HOJA DE ORO
Handmade in San Andres Tuxtla, Mexico.

Wrapper: Mexico   Binder: Mexico   Filler: Mexico

Shape	Name	Lgth	Ring	Wrapper
Double Corona	No. 100	7	50	CC-Ma
Double Corona	No. 101	7½	50	CC-Ma
Toro	No. 103	6	50	CC-Ma

Lonsdale	No. 104	6¾	45	CC-Ma
Robusto	No. 105	4½	50	CC-Ma
Grand Corona	No. 106	6	45	CC-Ma
Corona Extra	No. 107	5	45	CC-Ma

Another product of the famous San Andres Valley in Mexico, the Hoja de Oro line utilizes all-Mexican tobacco, including filler tobacco from San Andres mixed with Cuban-seed leaf grown in the northern part of the Mexican state of Veracruz. The binder is San Andres-grown, while the wrapper is Sumatran-seed, also grown in the San Andres Valley.

HONDURAN GOLD
Handmade in Honduras.
(The distributor provided only limited information on the origins of the tobaccos used in this brand.)

Shape	Name	Lgth	Ring	Wrapper
Corona	Mayor	5½	42	CC
Long Panatela	Panatelas	7	36	CC
Lonsdale	Senator	7	43	CC
Toro	Governor	6	50	CC
Double Corona	General	7	49	CC
Giant	Presidente	8½	52	CC

This is a mild blend of long-filler tobaccos, influenced by a Ecuadorian-grown wrapper of Connecticut seed origin. This is a value-priced brand, offered in uniquely-shaped triangular bundles of 25 cigars each.

HONDURAS CUBAN TOBACCOS
Handmade in Danli, Honduras.
Wrappers: Costa Rica, Ecuador, Mexico, USA/Connecticut
Binders: Costa Rica, Dom. Rep., Honduras, Indonesia/Sumatra,
Mexico, Nicaragua, USA/Pennsylvania
Fillers: Brazil, Costa Rica, Dom. Rep., Ecuador, Honduras,
Indonesia/Sumatra, Mexico, Nicaragua, Puerto Rico, USA/Connecticut

HANDMADE CIGARS: BRAND LISTINGS

Shape	Name	Lgth	Ring	Wrapper
Torpedo	Torpedo: 1	7½	64	Varies
Torpedo	Torpedo: 2	7	64	Varies
Pyramid	Piramides: 1	6½	54	Varies
Pyramid	Piramides: 2	6	52	Varies
Pyramid	Piramides: 3	5½	52	Varies
Giant	Gigantes: 1	8	54	Varies
Giant	Gigantes: 2	11	50	Varies
Giant	Double Corona: 1	8½	52	Varies
Double Corona	Double Corona: 2	7½	52	Varies
Double Corona	Double Corona: 3	7	52	Varies
Double Corona	Churchill: 1	7¾	50	Varies
Double Corona	Churchill: 2	7	50	Varies
Double Corona	Churchill: 3	7	49	Varies
Double Corona	Churchill: 4	6⅞	49	Varies
Churchill	Churchill: 5	7	47	Varies
Toro	Toro: 1	6	54	Varies
Toro	Toro: 2	6	52	Varies
Robusto	Robusto: 1	5¼	52	Varies
Robusto	Robusto: 2	5	50	Varies
Robusto	Robusto: 3	4½	50	Varies
Lonsdale	Lonsdale: 1	6½	44	Varies
Lonsdale	Lonsdale: 2	6½	43	Varies
Corona	Corona: 1	6	43	Varies
Corona	Corona: 2	6	42	Varies
Corona	Corona: 3	5½	42	Varies
Long Panatela	Palmas: 1	7	38	Varies
Panatela	Palmas: 2	6⅞	36	Varies

HANDMADE CIGARS: BRAND LISTINGS

Slim Panatela	Petit	5½	34	Varies

The Honduras Cuban Tobaccos company in Danli, Honduras produces private label cigars from 15 different blends, using leaves from around the world. HCT also offers its clients a choice of brand names, if desired, including CONQUISTADOR, DON CHRISTOBAL, DON RAMON and SEÑORIAL. Whether in bundles or boxes of 5, 10 or 25 cigars, these brands are high in quality and are even occasionally offered for public sale under one or more of the afore-mentioned brand names.

HONDURAS SPECIAL
Handmade in Danli, Honduras.

Wrapper: Honduras *Binder: Honduras* *Filler: Honduras*

Shape	Name	Lgth	Ring	Wrapper
Giant	No. 201	8	52	CM
Short Panatela	No. 202	4½	37	CM
Double Corona	No. 203	7½	50	CM
Toro	No. 204	6¼	50	CM
Robusto	No. 205	4¾	50	CM
Lonsdale	No. 206	6⅝	44	CM
Long Corona	No. 207	6	42	CM
Panatela	No. 208	6⅞	35	CM
Churchill	No. 209	6⅞	48	CM

This hard-to-find brand is medium-bodied and sells quickly, thanks to its packaging in bundles of just 10 cigars, which keeps the modest price within reach of every smoker.

HOYO DE HONDURAS
Handmade in Danli, Honduras.

Wrapper: Honduras *Binder: Honduras* *Filler: Honduras*

Shape	Name	Lgth	Ring	Wrapper
Lonsdale	No. 1	7	42	CM-Ma
Petit Corona	No. 4	5	42	CM-Ma

Double Corona	Churchill	7	50	CM-Ma
Long Corona	Corona	6	42	CM-Ma
Panatela	Panatela	6	38	CM-Ma
Short Panatela	Petit	5	38	CM-Ma
Robusto	Rothschild	4½	50	CM-Ma
Toro	Toro	6	50	CM-Ma

Created in 1985, this is a all-Honduran, full-bodied cigar, offered in econonical bundles of 25.

HOYO DE MONTERREY
Handmade in Cofradia, Honduras.

Wrapper: Ecuador, Indonesia   *Binder: Honduras*
Filler: Dominican Republic, Honduras and Nicaragua

Shape	Name		Lgth	Ring	Wrapper
Giant	Presidents		8½	52	DC-CC-Ma
Double Corona	Sultans		7¼	54	DC-CC-Ma
Churchill	Double Coronas		6¾	48	DC-CC-Ma
Toro	Governors		6⅛	50	DC-CC-Ma
Corona	Cafe Royales	*(tubed)*	5⅝	43	DC-CC-Ma
Small Panatela	Petit		4¾	31	DC-CC-Ma
Grand Corona	Churchills		6¼	45	DC-CC-Ma
Lonsdale	No. 1		6½	43	DC-CC-Ma
Corona Extra	Coronas		5⅝	46	DC-CC-Ma
Robusto	Rothschilds		4½	50	DC-CC-Ma
Churchill	Cuban Largos		7¼	47	DC-CC-Ma
Grand Corona	Dreams		5¾	46	DC-CC-Ma
Corona	Super Hoyos		5½	44	DC-CC-Ma
Long Corona	Ambassadors		6¼	44	DC-CC-Ma
Slim Panatela	Largo Elegantes		7¼	34	DC-CC-Ma
Cigarillo	Margaritas		5¼	29	DC-CC-Ma

HANDMADE CIGARS: BRAND LISTINGS

Culebras	Culebras	6	35	DC-CC-Ma
Corona	No. 55	5¼	43	DC-CC-Ma
Panatela	Delights	6¼	37	DC-CC-Ma
Short Panatela	Demitasse	4	39	DC-CC-Ma
Petit Corona	Sabrosos	5	40	DC-CC-Ma

This ancient brand began in Cuba, but first appeared in a Honduran-manufactured blend in 1969. Hoyo de Monterrey cigars are medium-to-heavy in flavor. Handmade in Honduras, these are truly quality cigars with a large variety of sizes, to give exceptional satisfaction to the smoker. The tobaccos are blended from four nations, including the Cuban-seed Honduran binder and wrappers from Ecuador and Sumatra in Indonesia.

HUGO CASSAR
Handmade in Danli, Honduras.

Wrapper: USA/Connecticut *Binder: Honduras* *Filler: Honduras*

Shape	Name	Lgth	Ring	Wrapper
Robusto	No. 1	4¾	50	CC
Corona Extra	No. 2	5½	46	CC
Lonsdale	No. 3	6¾	44	CC
Churchill	No. 4	7	48	CC
Double Corona	No. 5	6¾	54	CC
Double Corona	No. 6	7½	50	CC
Giant	No. 7	8	52	CC

A careful blend and smooth draw is the mark of these cigars, which are expertly crafted, medium in body and packaged in bundles of 25 cigars. An excellent value.

HUGO CASSAR
Handmade in San Andres Tuxtula, Mexico.

Wrapper: Mexico *Binder: Mexico* *Filler: Mexico*

Shape	Name	Lgth	Ring	Wrapper
Robusto	Tulum	4¾	50	CC-Ma

HANDMADE CIGARS: BRAND LISTINGS

Long Corona	Monterey	6	42	CC-Ma
Panatela	Durango	6¾	36	CC-Ma
Double Corona	Veracruz	7	54	CC-Ma
Double Corona	Yucatan	7½	50	CC-Ma
Giant	Sierra Madre	8	52	CC-Ma

These cigars are Mexican puros, offered in both a natural and maduro wrapper. They offer a spicy, sweet flavor, with full body, and are packaged in bundles of 25 cigars each.

HUGO CASSAR DIAMOND DOMINICAN
Handmade in Santiago, Dominican Republic.

Wrapper: USA/Connecticut   *Binder: Dom. Rep.*   *Filler: Dom. Rep.*

Shape	Name	Lgth	Ring	Wrapper
Robusto	Robusto	4¾	50	CC
Corona	Corona	5½	42	CC
Grand Corona	Grand Corona	6	46	CC
Toro	Toro	6½	52	CC
Lonsdale	Lonsdale	7	44	CC
Giant	El Presidente	8	50	CC

This careful blend of aged tobaccos, introduced in 1996, produces a cigar which is filled with a rich spiciness, with cocoa flavors and a mild body, and offered in specially-constructed cedar boxes of 20 (except for El Presidente, available in 10s).

HUGO CASSAR DIAMOND DOMINICAN MYSTIQUE
Handmade in Santiago, Dominican Republic.
Wrapper: Dominican Republic, USA/Connecticut

Binder: Dom. Rep.   *Filler: Dom. Rep.*

Shape	Name	Lgth	Ring	Wrapper
Torpedo	Torpedo	6	53	CM
Toro	Toro	6¼	50	CM
Lonsdale	Lonsdale	7	44	CM

HANDMADE CIGARS: BRAND LISTINGS

| Churchill | Maestro | 7 | 48 | CM |
| Giant | Churchill | 8 | 50 | CM |

Talk about unique! Here is a ''barber pole'' of a cigar, with a double wrapper: Connecticut Shade and a Dominican brewleaf, surrounding Dominican binder and filler tobaccos, for a mild body. Introduced in 1996, there's no doubting the popularity of this new concept in cigar making, which are presented in all-cedar boxes.

HUGO CASSAR DIAMOND HONDURAN
Handmade in Danli, Honduras.

Wrapper: Ecuador   *Binder: Dom. Rep.*   *Filler: Nicaragua*

Shape	Name	Lgth	Ring	Wrapper
Robusto	Robusto	5	50	CC
Corona	Corona	5½	44	CC
Torpedo	Torpedo	6	53	CC
Toro	Double Corona	6¼	52	CC
Grand Corona	Lonsdale	6⅝	46	CC
Double Corona	Presidente	7	49	CC
Double Corona	Chairman	7¾	50	CC

A luxury cigar that has all of the characteristics of the finest cigars made today. The filler is a special blend of aged tobaccos, bonded with a special Dominican binder. The reddish-brown, Ecuadorian shade-grown wrappers create a cigar that offers a sweet, medium-bodied taste and is slightly aromatic.

HUGO CASSAR HONDURAN COLLECTION
Handmade in Danli, Honduras.

Wrapper: Indonesia   *Binder: Honduras*
Filler: Costa Rica, Honduras, Nicaragua

Shape	Name	Lgth	Ring	Wrapper
Robusto	Robusto	5	50	CC
Corona Extra	Corona	5½	46	CC
Lonsdale	Lonsdale	6½	44	CC

HANDMADE CIGARS: BRAND LISTINGS

| Churchill | Churchill | 7 | 48 | CC |
| Double Corona | Presidente | 7½ | 52 | CC |

Here is a 1996-introduced, high-value cigar which blends tobaccos from four nations for a medium-bodied taste, which is offered in bundles of 25.

HUGO CASSAR DIAMOND HONDURAN MYSTIQUE CLASSIC
Handmade in Danli, Honduras.
Wrapper: Costa Rica, Ecuador
Binder: Mexico   Filler: Dominican Republic, Nicaragua

Shape	Name	Lgth	Ring	Wrapper
Long Corona	Corona	6	44	CM
Toro	Toro	6½	52	CM
Torpedo	Torpedo	6	53	CM
Churchill	Churchill	7¾	47	CM

Introduced in 1996, this is a deeply-colored, beautifully-prepared "barber pole" cigar, this is a medium-bodied smoke with a double wrapper from Costa Rica (maduro shade) and Ecuador (natural shade). These cigars are elegantly presented in perfectly fitted all-cedar boxes of 20 cigars each.

HUGO CASSAR PRIVATE COLLECTION
Handmade in Santiago, Dominican Republic.
Wrapper: Dom. Rep.   Binder: Dom. Rep.   Filler: Dom. Rep.

Shape	Name	Lgth	Ring	Wrapper
Robusto	Robusto	5	50	CC
Long Corona	Corona	6	42	CC
Torpedo	Torpedo	6	53	CC
Toro	Toro	6½	52	CC
Double Corona	Presidente	7½	49	CC

Here is a mild cigar introduced in 1996. It features all Dominican tobacco, prepared elegantly and presented in stunning all-cedar boxes of 25 cigars (except for the Torpedo, which has 24 per box).

HANDMADE CIGARS: BRAND LISTINGS

HUGO CASSAR PRIVATE COLLECTION
Handmade in Danli, Honduras.

Wrapper: Ecuador   Binder: Dom. Rep.   Filler: Mexico, Nicaragua

Shape	Name	Lgth	Ring	Wrapper
Robusto	Robusto	4¾	52	CC
Long Corona	Corona	6	42	CC
Toro	Elegantes	6½	50	CC
Lonsdale	Imperial	7	44	CC
Double Corona	Emperador	7¾	47	CC

Beautifully finished, this is a medium-to-full-bodied smoke with tobaccos from four nations. The cigars are presented in precisely-finished cedar boxes of 25 cigars each.

HUGO CASSAR PRIVATE COLLECTION
Handmade in San Andres Tuxtula, Mexico.

Wrapper: Mexico   Binder: Mexico   Filler: Mexico

Shape	Name	Lgth	Ring	Wrapper
Robusto	Rothschild	4½	50	CC-Ma
Long Corona	Corona	6	42	CC-Ma
Toro	Toro	6½	50	CC-Ma
Robusto	Robusto	5½	52	CC-Ma
Double Corona	Churchill	7½	50	CC-Ma

From the fertile San Andres Valley comes the Hugo Cassar Private Collection. These are full-bodied cigars, with all-Mexican tobacco, packed in cedar boxes to maintain them at the peak of flavor. The natural-shade wrappers are Mexican-grown Sumatra-seed tobaccos, while the maduro wrappers are Mexican-grown, Cuban-seed leaves.

HUGO SIGNATURE SERIES
Handmade in Esteli, Nicaragua.

Wrapper: Indonesia   Binder: Nicaragua   Filler: Nicaragua

HANDMADE CIGARS: BRAND LISTINGS

Shape	Name	Lgth	Ring	Wrapper
Lonsdale	Lonsdale	6¾	44	CC
Corona	Corona	5½	42	CC
Toro	Toro	6	50	CC
Robusto	Robusto	4¾	52	CC
Churchill	Churchill	7	48	CC
Giant	Giant	8	54	CC

More Hugo! Just when you thought he's come up with every conceivable style of smoke from the Dominican Republic, Honduras and Mexico, here's a signature series from Nicaragua! It's a full-bodied smoke introduced in 1996, offered upright in honeycombed boxes of 25.

IMPERIO CUBANO
Handmade in Miami, Florida, USA.

Wrapper: Ecuador   *Binder: Mexico*   *Filler: Dom. Rep.*

Shape	Name	Lgth	Ring	Wrapper
Torpedo	Torpedo	6¼	54	CC
Churchill	Churchill	6¾	48	CC
Toro	Toro	6	50	CC
Robusto	Robusto	5	50	CC
Lonsdale	Lonsdale	6¾	43	CC
Corona	Corona	5½	43	CC

From Little Havana in Miami comes this new brand for 1996, available only in limited distribution and with limited production. Master cigar maker Juan Sosa offers a medium-bodied flavor in this brand, thanks in part to a Connecticut-seed wrapper grown in Ecuador.

INDIAN
Handmade in Danli, Honduras.
Wrapper: Ecuador, USA/Connecticut
Binder: USA/Connecticut, Mexico   *Filler: Honduras, Nicaragua*

HANDMADE CIGARS: BRAND LISTINGS

Shape	Name	Lgth	Ring	Wrapper
Double Corona	Chief	7½	52	CM
Long Corona	Warrior	6	42	CM
Robusto	Boxer	4½	50	CM
Torpedo	Teepee	5½	52	CM
Slim Panatela	Arrow	5½	34	CM

Here is a much-celebrated 1995 addition to the cigar scene, offering a mild-to-medium-bodied taste in an exquisitely-crafted cigar. The Chief and Warrior sizes feature a Connecticut wrapper and Mexican Morron binder, while the Boxer, Arrow and Teepee sizes use an Ecuador-grown, Sumatra-seed wrapper and a Connecticut Broadleaf binder.

INDIAN HEAD
Handmade in Danli, Honduras.

Wrapper: Ecuador   Binder: Honduras   Filler: Dom. Rep., Honduras

Shape	Name	Lgth	Ring	Wrapper
Small Panatela	Princesse	4½	30	CC
Slim Panatela	Petit Coronas	5½	34	CC
Panatela	Lindas	5½	38	CC
Corona	No. 4	5½	42	CC-Ma
Slim Panatela	Pinceles	7	30	CC
Long Corona	No. 2	6	43	CC-Ma
Panatela	Panatelas	6⅞	35	CC
Long Corona	Corona Gorda	6¼	44	CC-Ma
Robusto	Rothschild	5	50	CC-Ma
Lonsdale	No. 1	7	43	CC-Ma
Long Panatela	Palma de Mayorca	8	38	CC
Toro	Toros	6	50	CC-Ma
Churchill	Corona Grande	7½	46	CC
Double Corona	Churchills	6⅞	49	CC-Ma

HANDMADE CIGARS: BRAND LISTINGS

Double Corona	Monarch	7	52	CC-Ma
Double Corona	Soberanos	7¾	50	CC-Ma
Giant	Viajantes	8½	52	CC-Ma
Giant	Gigantes	8	54	CC-Ma
Torpedo	Torpedos	7	54	CC
	Mixed filler:			
Lonsdale	Fumas	7	44	CC
Long Corona	Cazadores	6¼	44	CC

Indian Head cigars are mild-to-medium in strength, using Honduran filler and binder tobaccos, combined with a Ecuador-grown, Connecticut-seed wrapper (natural and maduro). They are presented in bundles of 25 cigars each. The mixed-filler Fumas is noteworthy for its twisted head.

INFIESTA
Handmade in St. Augustine, Florida, USA.
Origin of wrapper, binder and filler leaves varies, depending on availability.

Shape	Name	Lgth	Ring	Wrapper
Giant	Soberanos	8	50	DC-CC-Ma
Small Panatela	Miniatures	4½	30	DC-CC-Ma
Churchill	Churchill	7	48	DC-CC-Ma
Toro	Governos	6	50	DC-CC-Ma
Lonsdale	Cetros No. 1	7	43	DC-CC-Ma
Lonsdale	Cetros No. 2	6½	42	DC-CC-Ma
Long Panatela	Panatelas No. 3	7	36	DC-CC-Ma
Slim Panatela	Panatelas Rabito	7	30	DC-CC-Ma
Long Corona	San Marcos	6	44	DC-CC-Ma
Lonsdale	Fumas	7	44	DC-CC-Ma
Churchill	Cazadores	7	46	DC-CC-Ma
Corona	No. 4	5½	42	DC-CC-Ma

HANDMADE CIGARS: BRAND LISTINGS

This all-long filler brand is made by hand under the supervision of the El Canelo factory of Miami, Florida.

IRACEMA
Handmade in Cruz des Almas, Brazil.

Wrapper: Brazil 　　　　　*Binder: Brazil* 　　　　　*Filler: Brazil*

Shape	Name	Lgth	Ring	Wrapper
Corona	Santana	5⅜	43	CM
Corona	Autentico-Fumas	5¼	44	CM
Lonsdale	Macumba	6½	42	CM
Corona	Mata Fina Especial	5¼	44	CM
Cigarillo	Santo Amaro	3½	25	CM
	Machine-made:			
Cigarillo	Cigarrilhas	3⅛	28	CM

Introduced about 1960, this cigar is a product of the famous Suerdieck Charutos e Cigarrilhas Ltda. factory in Brazil. The range offers a medium-bodied flavor in four shapes. The tobaccos are all Brazilian grown, including Mata Fina leaf for the wrappers of the Macumba and Mata Fina shapes, offering up a seductive, tropical aroma.

ISLAND AMARETTO
Handmade, with medium filler, in Miami, Florida, USA.

Wrapper: Brazil 　　　　　　　　　　　　　　*Binder: Brazil*
Filler: Dominican Republic, Ecuador, Honduras, Nicaragua

Shape	Name	Lgth	Ring	Wrapper
Short Panatela	Bellissima	5	38	CM
Churchill	Grand Bella	7	46	CM

This is a flavored cigar produced by the Caribbean Cigar Company and introduced in 1995. It is handmade using 100% tobacco, but with medium filler instead of long filler leaves. It has a full-bodied taste and is offered in boxes of 25 cigars each.

Lonsdales, Coronas Extra and Grand Coronas

Here are examples of three larger-sized cigars: the Lonsdale (named for the Earl of Lonsdale), the Corona Extra and the Grand Corona. The dimensions of these shapes include:

- ▸ Lonsdale   6½-7¼ inches long; 40-44 ring.

- ▸ Giant Corona   7½ inches and more; 42-45 ring.

- ▸ Corona Extra   4½-5½ inches long; 45-47 ring.

- ▸ Grand Corona   5⅝-6⅝ inches long; 45-47 ring.

Pictured opposite, from left to right, are:

- ▸ Oliveros Dos Perez   6¾ x 42   Lonsdale
- ▸ Romeo y Julieta
  Cetros   6½ x 44   Lonsdale
- ▸ V Centennial Cetros 6¼ x 44   Lonsdale
- ▸ Caonabo Guanines   6 x 44   Long Corona
- ▸ Don Asa Toros   5½ x 46   Corona Extra

The Oliveros shows off the new fashion in wrappers: a combination of both natural and maduro shade leaves that emulates a barber pole! The Romeo y Julieta, V Centennial, Caonabo and Don Asa brands all show off a "natural" colored wrapper which is usually graded anywhere from Colorado Claro to Colorado Maduro.

HANDMADE CIGARS: BRAND LISTINGS

JAMAICA BAY
Hand-rolled, with machine bunching, in Jamaica.

Wrapper: USA/Connecticut   Binder: Mexico   Filler: Dom. Rep., Mexico

Shape	Name	Lgth	Ring	Wrapper
Double Corona	No. 100	7½	49	CC
Toro	No. 200	6	50	CC
Lonsdale	No. 300	6¾	45	CC
Lonsdale	No. 400	6½	42	CC
Panatela	No. 500	6¾	38	CC
Corona	No. 600	5½	42	CC

These are mild cigars, machine-bunched and then hand-wrapped with Connecticut Shade leaves. They are offered only in limited distribution, in bundles of 20 cigars each.

JAMAICA GEM
Handmade in Kingston, Jamaica.

Wrapper: Mexico   Binder: Mexico   Filler: Jamaica, Mexico

Shape	Name	Lgth	Ring	Wrapper
Petit Corona	Petit Corona	5	40	CC
Slim Panatela	Palma	6¾	34	CC
Corona	Corona	5½	40	CC
Long Corona	Royal Corona	6	40	CC
Lonsdale	Corona Grande	6½	42	CC
Giant	Churchill	8	51	CC
Lonsdale	Double Corona	7	45	CC
Grand Corona	Magnum	6	47	CC
Double Corona	Giant Corona	7½	49	CC
Slim Panatela	Palmitas	6	30	CC

This cigar was created in 1983 and is made in Jamaica, but with a Mexican-grown, Connecticut-seed wrapper. It is medium to full in body and offered in bundles of 25 cigars each.

HANDMADE CIGARS: BRAND LISTINGS

JAMAICA GOLD
Handmade in Santa Rosa de Copan, Honduras.

Wrapper: Ecuador *Binder: Honduras* *Filler: Honduras*

Shape	Name	Lgth	Ring	Wrapper
Double Corona	Prince	7¾	50	CM
Panatela	Earl	6¾	38	CM
Lonsdale	Baron	6½	44	CM
Panatela	Count	5½	38	CM
Corona	Duke	5½	42	CM
Small Panatela	Dutchess	4½	30	CM
Toro	King	6	50	CM
Torpedo	Torpedo	7	50	CM

Created in 1982, this is a medium-bodied cigar, with a Connecticut-seed wrapper. The brand is offered in all-wooden boxes of 25 cigars, plus handy five-packs in the Baron, Duke and Earl shapes.

JAMAICA HERITAGE
Handmade in Kingston, Jamaica.

Wrapper: Ecuador *Binder: Mexico*
Filler: Dominican Republic, Jamaica, Mexico

Shape	Name	Lgth	Ring	Wrapper
Double Corona	No. 100	7½	49	CC-Ma
Giant	No. 102	8	50	CC-Ma
Toro	No. 200	6	50	CC-Ma
Grand Corona	No. 500	6	45	CC-Ma
Lonsdale	No. 400	6½	42	CC-Ma
Corona	No. 700	5½	42	CC-Ma

From one of the finest factories in Kingston, Jamaica comes Jamaica Heritage, a celebration of the famous Jamaican cigar industry. These cigars offer a mild, rich taste and are available in bundles of 25.

HANDMADE CIGARS: BRAND LISTINGS

J. CORTES
Handmade in the Dominican Republic.

Wrapper: USA/Connecticut   Binder: Dom. Rep.   Filler: Brazil, Dom. Rep.

Shape	Name	Lgth	Ring	Wrapper
Slim Panatela	No. 2	5	32	CC
Corona	No. 3	5½	40	CC
Toro	No. 6	6¼	48	CC

J. Cortes is an old Belgian brand, which started in 1926. The handmade, all-long-filler shapes are new for 1996 and offer a mild taste in boxes of 25.

JOHN AYLESBURY
Handmade in Danli, Honduras.

Wrapper: Honduras, Mexico   Binder: Honduras   Filler: Honduras

Shape	Name	Lgth	Ring	Wrapper
Toro	Churchill	6⅝	49	CC-Ma
Lonsdale	Pinceles	7	43	CC
Long Corona	Puritos	6	43	CC
Panatela	Morning	5½	39	CC
Panatela	Panatela Larga	6¾	36	CC
Small Panatela	Picos	4½	32	CC
Toro	Rothschild	6	50	CC-Ma

Introduced in 1978, the John Aylesbury Honduran series has a medium body and a subtle aroma. All seven sizes are offered with a Honduran-grown wrapper, while the maduro-wrapped shapes feature a Mexican leaf.

JOHN AYLESBURY PREMIUM
Handmade in La Romana, Dominican Republic.

Wrapper: USA/Connecticut   Binder: Dom. Rep.   Filler: Dom. Rep.

Shape	Name	Lgth	Ring	Wrapper
Slim Panatela	Panatela	6	32	CC
Lonsdale	Lonsdale	6⅝	42	CC

Corona	Corona	5½	42	CC
Panatela	Elegante	6¾	38	CC
Churchill	Churchill	7	46	CC
Robusto	Rothschild	4½	50	CC

The John Aylesbury Premium line offers a mild-bodied smoke in a beautifully-constructed cigar that debuted in 1991. These cigars are matured and then offered in graceful, solid mahogany boxes.

JOHN T'S
Handmade in the Dominican Republic.

Wrapper: USA/Connecticut   Binder: Dom. Rep.   Filler: Pipe tobaccos

Shape	Name		Lgth	Ring	Wrapper
Panatela	Brown Gold	(tubed)	5½	38	CC
Panatela	Cherry Cream	(tubed)	5½	38	CC
Panatela	Capuccino	(tubed)	5½	38	CC
Panatela	Cafe Ole	(tubed)	5½	38	CC
Panatela	Amaretto	(tubed)	5½	38	CC
Grand Corona	Magnum Amaretto		6½	46	CC
Grand Corona	Magnum Brown Gold		6½	46	CC
Grand Corona	Magnum Cherry Cream		6½	46	CC
Grand Corona	Magnum Capuccino		6½	46	CC

Nicknamed "The Crowdpleaser," this brand has been created to offer a more pleasant, sweeter aroma than most cigars. The result is a mild smoke with considerable flavor (take your pick!) in a panatela (packed in bundles of 20 tubes) or grand corona shape (packed in cedar boxes of 25). Unusual to say the least!

JOSE BENITO
Handmade in Santiago, Dominican Republic.

Wrapper: Indonesia   Binder: Dom. Rep.   Filler: Dom. Rep.

Shape	Name	Lgth	Ring	Wrapper
Double Corona	Presidente	7¾	50	CM

Double Corona	Churchill	7	50	CM
Lonsdale	Corona	6¾	43	CM
Panatela	Panatela	6¾	38	CM
Long Corona	Palma	6	43	CM
Panatela	Petite	5½	38	CM
Robusto	Rothschild	4¾	50	CM
Small Panatela	Chico	4¼	32	CM
Cigarillo	Havanitos	5	25	CM
Giant	Magnum	8¾	60	CM

Since its introduction in the 1970s, every Jose Benito cigar is the result of individually-chosen long-filler tobacco, blended from the finest Dominican farms and specially selected Indonesian wrapper leaves. They result in a medium-bodied smoke, upholding the family's tradition of excellence in tobacco which began in the mid-1800s.

JOSE LLOPIS
Handmade in Colon, Panama.

Wrapper: Ecuador   *Binder: Mexico*
Filler: Dominican Republic, Honduras, Panama

Shape	Name	Lgth	Ring	Wrapper
Giant	Viajante	8½	52	CC-Ma
Churchill	Churchill	7	48	CC-Ma
Lonsdale	No. 1	7	43	CC-Ma
Lonsdale	No. 2	6½	43	CC-Ma
Corona	No. 4	5½	43	CC-Ma
Long Panatela	Palma Extra	7	36	CC-Ma
Robusto	Rothschild	4¾	50	CC-Ma
Double Corona	Soberano	7¼	52	CC-Ma

Introduced in 1984, this cigar is offered in bundles of 20 and is medium in strength; it should not be confused with its milder sibling brand, Jose Llopis Gold.

HANDMADE CIGARS: BRAND LISTINGS

JOSE LLOPIS GOLD
Handmade in Colon, Panama.

Wrapper: USA/Connecticut   Binder: Mexico
Filler: Dominican Republic, Honduras, Panama

Shape	Name	Lgth	Ring	Wrapper
Giant	Viajante	8½	52	CC-Ma
Churchill	Churchill	7	48	CC-Ma
Lonsdale	No. 1	7	43	CC-Ma
Lonsdale	No. 2	6½	43	CC-Ma
Long Panatela	Palma Extra	7	36	CC-Ma
Corona	No. 4	5½	43	CC-Ma
Robusto	Rothschild	4½	50	CC-Ma

Created in 1989, this well-respected brand is all handmade and wrapped in
Connecticut shade-grown leaves (natural) or Connecticut Broadleaf (maduro).
All of its sizes are offered in cedar boxes. This mild-bodied cigar is distinctive
for its gold band.

JOSE MARTI
Handmade in Santiago, Dominican Republic.

Wrapper: USA/Connecticut   Binder: Dom. Rep.   Filler: Dom. Rep.

Shape	Name	Lgth	Ring	Wrapper
Slim Panatela	Creme	6	34	CC
Corona	Corona	5½	40	CC
Lonsdale	Palma	7	42	CC
Lonsdale	Maceo	6⅞	44	CC
Robusto	Robusto	5½	50	CC
Churchill	Jose Marti	7½	48	CC

Introduced in 1994, Jose Marti is a very mild, sweet cigar with a golden brown
Connecticut wrapper. It offers excellent draw, a silky, smooth taste and a
wonderful aroma.

HANDMADE CIGARS: BRAND LISTINGS

JOSE MARTI VITOLA SERIES
Handmade in Cofradia, Honduras.

Wrapper: Honduras   *Binder: Honduras*   *Filler: Honduras*

Shape	Name	Lgth	Ring	Wrapper
Lonsdale	Vitola 42	6½	42	CM
Giant Corona	Vitola 11	8⅛	42	CM
Giant	Vitola 27	8	47	CM

Introduced in late 1996, this blend offers a complex, but exceptionally smooth, full-bodied flavor in three longer sizes.

JOSE MARTI
Handmade in Esteli, Nicaragua.

Wrapper: Ecuador   *Binder: Honduras*
Filler: Dominican Republic, Honduras, Nicaragua

Shape	Name	Lgth	Ring	Wrapper
Lonsdale	Lonsdale	6½	44	CC
Double Corona	La Trinidad	7	50	CC
Torpedo	Masaya Figurado	6¾	54	CC
Pyramid	Piramide	7	48	CC
Short Panatela	Petite Lancero	4½	38	CC
Corona	Remedios	5½	44	CC
Robusto	Robusto	4½	52	CC
Giant	Rey del Rey	8½	52	CC
Toro	Robusto Extra	6½	52	CC

This is a new, 1996 blend for the Jose Marti brand, offering a spicy, full-bodied taste and showing off an Ecuadorian-grown, Sumatra-seed wrapper. The brand has an excellent array of shapes and sizes, including two shaped cigars.

JOYA DE HONDURAS
Handmade in Danli, Honduras.

Wrapper: Ecuador   *Binder: Nicaragua*   *Filler: Honduras*

HANDMADE CIGARS: BRAND LISTINGS

Shape	Name	Lgth	Ring	Wrapper
Corona	Cuatro	5½	42	CM
Corona	Cinco	5½	40	CM
Double Corona	Churchill	7	50	CM
Giant	Soberano	8½	54	CM
Long Panatela	Palma	7	38	CM
Pyramid	Pyramid	5½	52	CM
Robusto	Robusto	5	50	CM
Torpedo	Torpedo	6	52	CM

This is an old brand which has now been revived in an eight-shape range, offering a size of interest to almost every smoker. Made by hand in Honduras, these cigars are offered in all-wood boxes of 25.

JOYA DEL REY
Handmade in Honduras.

Wrapper: Ecuador		Binder: Honduras			Filler: Honduras

Shape	Name	Lgth	Ring	Wrapper
Long Panatela	No. 35	7	35	CC
Corona	No. 42	5½	42	CC
Lonsdale	No. 43	7	43	CC
Double Corona	No. 49	7	49	CC
Toro	No. 50	6	50	CC
Giant	No. 52	8½	52	CC

The translation of this brand name means "Gems of the King." This is a medium-to-heavy bodied brand, using Cuban-seed tobaccos for the binder and filler. Joya del Rey cigars are offered in all-cedar boxes of 25.

JOYA DE NICARAGUA
Handmade in Esteli, Nicaragua.
Wrapper: Ecuador (CC), Costa Rica (maduro)

Binder: Nicaragua   Filler: Nicaragua

HANDMADE CIGARS: BRAND LISTINGS

Shape	Name	Lgth	Ring	Wrapper
Giant	Viajante	8½	52	CC
Churchill	Churchill	6⅞	49	CC
Toro	Toro	6	50	CC
Slim Panatela	Senorita	5½	34	CC
Small Panatela	Piccolino	4½	30	CC
Panatela	Petit	5½	38	CC
Robusto	Consul	4½	52	CC
Lonsdale	No. 1	6⅝	44	CC
Panatela	No. 5	6⅞	35	CC
Long Corona	No. 6	6	42	CC
	Maduro Deluxe:			
Double Corona	Presidente	7½	50	Ma
Toro	Toro	6	50	Ma
Robusto	Robusto	4¾	52	Ma

Always popular since its introduction in the 1970s, this cigar is newly blended for 1996. The standard series now sports a mild taste, thanks to an Ecuadorian-grown, Connecticut-seed wrapper, while the Maduro line continues as a full-bodied smoke. These cigars are meticulously cured and skillfully rolled which makes them truly the "Jewel of Nicaragua."

JUAN Y RAMON
Handmade in Villa Gonzales, Dominican Republic.
Wrapper: Dominican Republic, USA/Connecticut
Binder: Dominican Republic   Filler: Dominican Republic

Shape	Name	Lgth	Ring	Wrapper
Toro	Short Churchill	6½	50	CC-Ma
Pyramid	Figurado	6¼	53	CC-Ma
Double Corona	Churchill	7½	50	CC
Corona	Corona	5½	42	CC
Long Corona	Grand Corona	6	44	CC

Panatela	Panatela	6	38	CC
Robusto	Rothschild	5	50	CC-Ma
Small Panatela	Fino	5	30	CC-Ma

Introduced in 1996, this is a medium-bodied blend of Piloto Cubano and Olor leaves in the filler, surrounded by a Connecticut Shade-grown wrapper (maduros are Dominican-grown). Elegantly packaged, Juan y Ramon cigars are available in all-cedar boxes of 20, except for the Figurado, offered in 24s.

J-R ULTIMATE
Handmade in Cofradia, Honduras.

Wrapper: Honduras   *Binder: Honduras*   *Filler: Honduras*

Shape	Name	Lgth	Ring	Wrapper
Lonsdale	Cetro	7	42	Cl-CC-Ma
Grand Corona	Corona	5⅝	45	Cl-CC-CM-Ma
Grand Corona	Corona Tubos *(tubed)*	5⅝	45	CC
Churchill	Double Corona	6¾	48	Cl-CC-CM-Ma
Giant	Estelo Individuel	8½	52	CM
Double Corona	No. 1	7¼	54	CC-CM-Ma
Long Corona	No. 5	6⅛	44	Cl-CC-CM-Ma
Toro	Padron	6	54	CC-Ma
Panatela	Palma Extra	6⅞	38	CC-CM-Ma
Panatela	Petit Cetro	5½	38	CC-CM-Ma
Petit Corona	Petit Corona	4⅝	43	CC-CM-Ma
Giant	President	8½	52	CC-CM-Ma
Robusto	Rothschild	4½	50	CC-CM-Ma
Panatela	Slims	6⅞	36	CC-CM-Ma
Giant Corona	Super Cetro	8¼	43	CC
Toro	Toro	6	50	Cl-CC-CM-Ma

This is a full-bodied cigar with Havana-seed wrappers in multiple shades. Made in Cofradia, Honduras, these cigars are carefully aged for at least one year and

HANDMADE CIGARS: BRAND LISTINGS

packed uncellophaned in thick cedar cases.

JUAN CLEMENTE
Handmade in Santiago, Dominican Republic.

Wrapper: USA/Connecticut   *Binder: Dom.Rep.*   *Filler: Dom.Rep.*

Shape	Name	Lgth	Ring	Wrapper
	Classic:			
Petit Corona	Corona	5	42	Co
Long Corona	Grand Corona	6	42	Co
Panatela	Panatela	6½	34	Co
Long Panatela	Especiale	7½	38	Co
Churchill	Churchill	6⅞	46	Co
Cigarillo	Demi Tasse	3⅝	34	Co
Small Panatela	"530"	5	30	Co
Petit Corona	Demi-Corona	4	40	Co
Robusto	Rothschild	4⅞	50	Co
Giant	Gigante	9	50	Co
Giant	Gargantua	13	50	Co
Cigarillo	Mini	4⅛	22	Co
Panatela	Especiale No. 2	6	38	Co
	Club Selection:			
Toro	No. 1	6	50	Co
Corona Extra	No. 2	4½	46	Co
Lonsdale	No. 3	7	44	Co
Corona	No. 4	5¾	42	Co
Torpedo	Obelisco	6	54	Co

Sought after since 1982, this is the product of a small cigar factory that has only one, ultra-demanding client, the Juan Clemente Classic line offers a full, round, medium-bodied smoke with complex flavors and spices. The vintage "Club Selection" line is a more robust blend, with four years of aging that creates a rich, smooth character for an exquisite cigar for the connoisseur.

HANDMADE CIGARS: BRAND LISTINGS

JUAN LOPEZ
Handmade in Danli, Honduras.

Wrapper: Ecuador   *Binder: Honduras*   *Filler: Honduras*

Shape	Name	Lgth	Ring	Wrapper
Giant	No. 300	8½	50	CM
Double Corona	No. 301	7½	50	CM
Toro	No. 302	6	50	CM
Lonsdale	No. 303	6½	42	CM
Corona	No. 304	5½	42	CM

Recognize the brand name? It's a famous old Havana brand, produced for the U.S. market since the mid-1980s as a bundle cigar of good quality. The all-handmade blend of Honduras tobaccos plus an Ecuadorian-grown, Connecticut-seed wrapper is offered in 25-cigar packs and has a medium-to-full body.

HANDMADE CIGARS: BRAND LISTINGS

KING
Handmade in Santiago, Dominican Republic.

Wrapper: USA/Connecticut Shade (both shades)   Binder: Dom. Rep.
Wrapper: Brazil, Dominican Republic

Shape	Name	Lgth	Ring	Wrapper
Lonsdale	No. 1	6½	42	CC-Ma
Corona	No. 2	5½	42	CC-Ma
Panatela	No. 3	6¾	38	CC
Panatela	No. 5	5½	38	CC
Robusto	No. 6	4¾	50	CC-Ma
Giant	No. 7	8½	52	CC-Ma
Double Corona	No. 8	7	60	CC-Ma
Giant	No. 9	10	66	CC-Ma
Double Corona	No. 10	7½	49	CC-Ma
Robusto	No. 13	5	66	CC-Ma

A full, yet deliciously mild cigar, introduced in 1989. The natural-wrappered version has a smooth herbal character, while the maduro wrapper offers a rich earthiness to the palate. These delicate flavors and the line's smooth draw are truly unique, as are its range in some of the largest available ring gauges.

KINGSTON
Handmade in San Andres Tuxtula, Mexico.

Wrapper: Mexico   Binder: Mexico   Filler: Mexico

Shape	Name	Lgth	Ring	Wrapper
Lonsdale	Corona Grande	6⅝	42	CC-Ma
Double Corona	Giant Corona	7½	50	CC-Ma
Panatela	Panatela	6½	35	CC-Ma
Long Corona	Royal Corona	6	42	CC-Ma
Toro	Toro	6	50	CC-Ma
Robusto	Rothschild	4½	50	CC-Ma
Giant	Viajante	8½	50	Ma

HANDMADE CIGARS: BRAND LISTINGS

All of the tobacco in this brand is grown in Mexico, with the wrapper grown from Sumatran seeds. It is full-bodied and offered in bundles of 25.

KISKEYA
Handmade in Santiago, Dominican Republic.

Wrapper: Ecuador   Binder: Dom. Rep.   Filler: Dom. Rep.

Shape	Name	Lgth	Ring	Wrapper
Corona	No. 4	5½	42	CC
Long Panatela	Palma Fina	7	36	CC
Corona	No. 2	5¾	42	CC
Robusto	Rothschild	4¾	50	CC-Ma
Long Corona	Cetros	6	44	CC
Lonsdale	No. 1	6¾	43	CC
Toro	Toros	6	50	CC-Ma
Churchill	Churchills	6⅞	46	CC
Double Corona	Presidentes	7½	50	CC
Giant	Viajantes	8½	52	CC

These cigars are handmade with long filler, with natural and maduro wrappers of Ecuador-grown, Connecticut-seed tobacco. Mild in body, they are packed in bundles of 25 cigars, in the classic 8-9-8 layered pattern.

LA AURORA
Handmade in Santiago, Dominican Republic.

Wrapper: Cameroon   Binder: Dom. Rep.   Filler: Dom. Rep.

Shape	Name	Lgth	Ring	Wrapper
Short Panatela	Petit Coronas	4½	37	CM
Corona	Aurora No. 4	5¼	43	CM
Short Panatela	Coronas	5	38	CM
Long Corona	Cetros	6⅜	41	CM
Toro	Bristol Especiales	6⅜	48	CM
Panatela	Palmas Extra	6¾	35	CM

HANDMADE CIGARS: BRAND LISTINGS

Short Panatela	Sublimes	(tubed)	5	38	CM
Robusto	Robusto		5	50	CM
Double Corona	Double Corona		7½	50	CM
Small Panatela	Finos		4	30	CM
Torpedo	Belicoso		6½	52	CM

Respected since its introduction in 1903, La Aurora is a medium-bodied cigar offering a unique blend of Dominican fillers and binder, completed with a rare Cameroon wrapper for a soft, accessible taste.

LA BALA
Handmade in Cofradia, Honduras.

Wrapper: Honduras *Binder: Honduras* *Filler: Honduras*

Shape	Name	Lgth	Ring	Wrapper
Churchill	Maduro	6¾	46	Ma

This cigar is not for the feint of heart – or taste! It is a heavy-bodied, all-Honduran cigar, offered in burlap-wrapped bundles of 25 cigars each.

LA DILIGENCIA
Handmade in Danli, Honduras.

Wrapper: USA/Connecticut *Binder: Dominican Republic*
Filler: Dominican Republic, Honduras, Nicaragua

Shape	Name	Lgth	Ring	Wrapper
Giant	Presidente	8½	52	CC
Toro	Toro	6	50	CC
Long Corona	Grand Corona	6	44	CC
Churchill	Churchill	7	48	CC
Robusto	Robusto	4¾	50	CC

This brand was introduced in 1996 and offers a light to medium body, thanks to a blend of tobaccos from four nations. La Diligencia offers lots of flavor and is packaged in boxes of 25 cigars each.

HANDMADE CIGARS: BRAND LISTINGS

LA DIVA
Handmade in Santiago, Dominican Republic.
Wrapper: USA/Connecticut   Binder: Dom. Rep.   Filler: Dom. Rep.

Shape	Name	Lgth	Ring	Wrapper
Long Corona	Corona	6	44	CC
Robusto	Robusto	4½	50	CC
Giant	Churchill	8	50	CC
Torpedo	Torpedo	7	54	CC

This cigar was introduced in 1996 and is unique for the process which imbues the leaves with the essence of the marvelous Cognac Pierre Ferrand. Combined with Conneciteut Shade wrappers and Dominican leaves in the interior of the cigar, the blend has a medium body and is offered in either glass tubes, elegant wooden boxes or individually cellophaned in bundles of 25.

LA EMINENCIA
Handmade in Danli, Honduras.
Wrapper: Ecuador   Binder: Honduras
Filler: Brazil, Dominican Republic, Honduras, Nicaragua

Shape	Name	Lgth	Ring	Wrapper
Giant	Supreme	8½	52	CC-Ma
Toro	After Dinner	6⅛	50	CC-Ma
Robusto	Rothschild	4½	50	CC-Ma
Churchill	Corona Inmensa	7¼	46	CC-Ma
Grand Corona	Fumas No. 1	6½	46	CC-Ma
Corona Extra	Robusto	5⅝	46	CC-Ma
Corona	Fancy Cubanitas	5½	44	CC-Ma
Long Panatela	Palmas	7	38	CC-Ma

Back in distribution after a short absence, La Eminencia is made by hand in Honduras and by machine in Tampa, Florida. The blend is mild to medium-bodied, with both natural and maduro wrappers available in all sizes.

HANDMADE CIGARS: BRAND LISTINGS

LA FABULOSO
Handmade in Danli, Honduras.

Wrapper: Honduras   *Binder: Honduras*   *Filler: Honduras*

Shape	Name	Lgth	Ring	Wrapper
Lonsdale	No. 1	7	42	CM-Ma
Petit Corona	No. 4	5	42	CM-Ma
Double Corona	Churchill	7	50	CM-Ma
Long Corona	Corona	6	42	CM-Ma
Panatela	Panatela	6	38	CM-Ma
Short Panatela	Petit	5	38	CM-Ma
Robusto	Rothschild	4½	50	CM-Ma
Toro	Toro	6	50	CM-Ma

Created in the early 1970s, this is a mild-to-medium-bodied cigar, offered in economical bundles of 25.

LA FAMA
Handmade in Las Palmas, the Canary Islands of Spain.

Wrapper: USA/Connecticut   *Binder: Mexico*   *Filler: Brazil, Dom. Rep.*

Shape	Name	Lgth	Ring	Wrapper
Corona	Gran Fama	6½	41	CC
Corona	Corona Fama Platas	6½	41	CC
Petit Corona	Fama Coronas	5⅛	40	CC

This brand is very mild in body and is made by hand in the Canary Islands. It is offered in elegant boxes of 25 cigars each.

LA FAVORITAS
Handmade in Danli, Honduras.

Wrapper: Ecuador   *Binder: Honduras*   *Filler: Nicaragua*

Shape	Name	Lgth	Ring	Wrapper
Long Corona	La Francesca	6	43	CC
Panatela	La Patricia	6	38	CC

HANDMADE CIGARS: BRAND LISTINGS

Slim Panatela	La Blanca	5½	32	CC

This brand dates from 1991, and offers a uniquely mild taste, with just a hint of vanilla scent. The flavored scent comes from the box in which the cigars are packed.

LA FLOR DE ARMANDO MENDEZ
Handmade in Tampa, Florida, USA.
Wrapper: USA/Connecticut   *Binder: Honduras*   *Filler: Honduras*

Shape	*Name*	*Lgth*	*Ring*	*Wrapper*
Toro	La Flor de A. Mendez	6	50	CM

This is a medium-bodied blend, offered in six-packs from the respected Cammarata Cigar Factory in the Ybor City section of Tampa, Florida.

LA FONTANA VINTAGE
Handmade in Danli, Honduras.
Wrapper: USA/Connecticut   *Binder: Mexico*   *Filler: Honduras*

Shape	*Name*	*Lgth*	*Ring*	*Wrapper*
Corona	Verdi	5½	44	CC
Robusto	Galileo	5	50	CC
Lonsdale	Puccini	6½	44	CC
Churchill	Da Vinci	6⅞	48	CC
Double Corona	Michelangelo	7½	52	CC
Slim Panatela	Rossini	5½	33	CC
Pyramid	Mona Lisa	4¾	46	CC
Torpedo	Belicoso	6	54	CC
Panatela	Dante	5½	38	CC

This is a mild blend which debuted in 1993. It is constructed of Honduran-grown tobaccos in the binder and a light Connecticut wrapper. This creation of master blender Tino Argudin includes two new, shaped sizes for 1997 and is offered in elegant 25-cigar boxes.

HANDMADE CIGARS: BRAND LISTINGS

LA FINCA
Handmade in Esteli, Nicaragua.

Wrapper: Nicaragua *Binder: Nicaragua* *Filler: Nicaragua*

Shape	Name	Lgth	Ring	Wrapper
Double Corona	Bolivare	7½	50	CM-Ma
Corona	Corona	5½	42	CM-Ma
Long Panatela	Flora	7	36	CM-Ma
Giant	Gran Finca	8½	52	CM-Ma
Toro	Joya	6	50	CM-Ma
Petit Corona	Petit Corona	4½	42	CM-Ma
Panatela	Pico	6	36	CM-Ma
Robusto	Robusto	4½	50	CM-Ma
Lonsdale	Romeo	6½	42	CM-Ma
churchill	Valentino	7	48	CM-Ma

This is a Nicaraguan "puro" featuring all Nicaraguan tobaccos from the Jamastran Valley. A heavy-bodied cigar, La Finca shapes are offered in boxes of 25 cigars each.

LA FLOR DOMINICANA
Handmade in Santiago, Dominican Republic.

Wrapper: USA/Connecticut *Binder: Dom. Rep.* *Filler: Dom. Rep.*

Shape	Name	Lgth	Ring	Wrapper
	Premium:			
Churchill	Mambises	6⅞	48	CC
Robusto	Maceo	5	48	CC
Lonsdale	Alcalde	6½	44	CC
Corona	Insurrectos	5½	42	CC
Petit Corona	Macheteros	4	40	CC
Torpedo	Figurados	6½	52	CC
Giant	Presidente	8	50	CC

HANDMADE CIGARS: BRAND LISTINGS

	Reserva Especial:			
Double Corona	Churchill	6⅞	49	CC
Robusto	Robusto	5	48	CC
Robusto	Belicoso	5½	52	CC

Introduced in 1994, Cuban-seed tobaccos from the Cibao Valley of the Dominican Republic are the stuff of which La Flor Dominicana cigars are founded. These leaves are wrapped with Connecticut Shade leaves to produce a mild-to-medium bodied cigar of ultimate quality from Santiago, in the Dominican Republic. The Reserva Especial line has a medium-to-full-bodied taste, with a creamy flavor and a touch of pepper.

LA GIANNA HAVANA
Handmade in Danli, Honduras.

Wrapper: Ecuador   *Binder: Nicaragua*   *Filler: Nicaragua*

Shape	Name	Lgth	Ring	Wrapper
Long Corona	No. 2	6¼	44	CM
Double Corona	Churchill	7	49	CM
Robusto	Rothchild	5	50	CM
Torpedo	Torpedo	6	54	CM

This is a new brand for 1996, offering a rich, full-bodied taste in four popular shapes. The aging process continues in the elegant cedar boxes in which La Gianna cigars are presented.

LA GLORIA CUBANA
Handmade in Miami, Florida, USA and
Villa Gonzales, Dominican Republic.

Wrapper: Ecuador   *Binder: Nicaragua*   *Filler: Dom.Rep., Nicaragua*

Shape	Name	Lgth	Ring	Wrapper
Giant	Crown Imperial	9	49	DC-CC-Ma
Giant	Soberano	8	52	DC-CC-Ma
Double Corona	Charlemagne	7¼	54	DC-CC-Ma
Double Corona	Double Corona	7¾	49	DC-CC-Ma

HANDMADE CIGARS: BRAND LISTINGS

Double Corona	Churchill	7	50	DC-CC-Ma
Churchill	Glorias Inmensas	7½	48	DC-CC-Ma
Toro	Corona Gorda	6	52	DC-CC-Ma
Robusto	Wavell	5	50	DC-CC-Ma
Grand Corona	Glorias Extra	6¼	46	DC-CC-Ma
Giant Corona	Coronas Extra Larga	7¾	44	DC-CC-Ma
Lonsdale	Medaille D'Or No. 1	6¾	43	DC-CC-Ma
Long Corona	Medaille D'Or No. 2	6¼	43	DC-CC-Ma
Corona	Glorias	5½	43	DC-CC-Ma
Small Panatela	Minutos	4½	40	DC-CC-Ma
Long Panatela	Panatela De'Luxe	7	37	DC-CC-Ma
Cigarillo	Medaille D'Or No. 3	7	28	DC-CC-Ma
Panatela	Medaille D'Or No. 4	6	32	DC-CC-Ma
Torpedo	Torpedo No. 1	6½	Tpr	DC-CC-Ma
Pyramid	Piramides	7¼	Tpr	DC-CC-Ma

This is a medium-bodied smoke, of absolutely exquisite quality, made in the El Credito factory in Miami, Florida and in a new facility in Villa Gonzales, Dominican Republic. All sizes are offered in boxes of 25, except for the Crown Imperial and the Piramides, which are offered in boxes of 10.

LA HABANERA
Handmade in Santiago, Dominican Republic.

Wrapper: USA/Connecticut   Binder: Dom. Rep.   Filler: Dom. Rep.

Shape	Name	Lgth	Ring	Wrapper
Churchill	Churchill	6⅞	46	CI
Long Corona	Diplomaticos	6	44	CI
Lonsdale	Elegante	6⅞	42	CI
Robusto·	Emperadores	5½	50	CI
Small Panatela	Especiale	5	30	CI
Double Corona	Presidente	7½	50	CI

| Corona | Puntanos | 5¾ | 42 | CI |
| Long Panatela | Selectos | 7 | 36 | CI |

New for 1996, this brand offers a genuine Connecticut wrapper with Dominican-grown binder and fillers for a mild, enjoyable taste. La Habanera is presented in all-cedar boxes of 25.

LA HERENCIA CUBANA
Handmade in Miami, Florida, USA.

Wrapper: Ecuador   *Binder: Cameroon*
Filler: Dominican Republic, Ecuador, Nicaragua

Shape	Name	Lgth	Ring	Wrapper
Giant	Gigante	8½	52	CI-CC-Ma
Double Corona	Churchill	7½	50	CI-CC-Ma
Cigarillo	Princesa	7	28	CI-CC-Ma
Torpedo	Torpedo	6½	54	CI-CC-Ma
Lonsdale	No. 1	6½	44	CI-CC-Ma
Panatela	Cubanita	6½	36	CI-CC-Ma
Lonsdale	Cojimar	6¾	42	CI-CC-Ma
Grand Corona	Gloria Habana	6¼	46	CI-CC-Ma
Corona	Corona	5¾	48	CI-CC-Ma
Corona Extra	Mojito	5½	46	CI-CC-Ma
Robusto	Robusto	5	50	CI-CC-Ma

"The Heritage of Cuba" is celebrated in this cigar, introduced in 1996. Master *torcedor* Roberto Ramirez of Santa Clara, Cuba arrived in the U.S. in 1994 and immediately found collaborators in a Miami-based factory. This is a medium-to-full-bodied brand, aged carefully in temperature-controlled cedar rooms for at least four months prior to release.

LA HOJA SELECTA
Handmade in Miami, Florida, USA.

Wrapper: USA/Connecticut   *Binder: Ecuador*   *Filler: Dom.Rep., Nicaragua*

HANDMADE CIGARS: BRAND LISTINGS

Shape	Name	Lgth	Ring	Wrapper
Double Corona	Chateau Sovereign	7½	52	CI
Churchill	Cosiac	7	48	CI
Toro	Choix Supreme	6	50	CI
Robusto	Palais Royals	4¾	50	CI
Lonsdale	Selectos No. 1	6½	42	CI
Corona	Cetros de Oro	5¾	43	CI
Panatela	Bel Aires	6¾	38	CI
Slim Panatela	Geneves	6½	32	CI

These are the mildest cigars produced by the El Credito factory in Miami, Florida, thanks to their Connecticut Shade wrappers and filler tobaccos from the Dominican Republic.

LA ISLA
Handmade in Union City, New Jersey, USA.

Wrapper: USA/Connecticut   *Binder: Dom. Rep.*
Filler: Costa Rica, Dominican Republic, Honduras, Mexico

Shape	Name	Lgth	Ring	Wrapper
Churchill	Torches	7¼	46	CC-Ma
Robusto	Silverano Corto	5½	50	CC-Ma
Giant	Presidente	8	50	CC-Ma
Churchill	Especiale	7	46	CC-Ma
Churchill	Corona	7¼	46	CC-Ma
Panatela	Panatela	6	36	CC-Ma
Long Panatela	Palmas	7	35	CC-Ma
Lonsdale	Fumas	7	44	CC-Ma
Lonsdale	No. 1	7¼	42	CC-Ma
Long Corona	No. 2	6¼	40	CC-Ma
Corona	No. 4	5½	40	CC-Ma

HANDMADE CIGARS: BRAND LISTINGS

These medium-to-full-bodied cigars are handmade in a small store in Union City, New Jersey. The wide variety of sizes – 11 in all – are enveloped in Connecticut-grown leaves, including Connecticut Broadleaf tobaccos for the maduro wrappers.

LA MAXIMILIANA
Handmade in Danli, Honduras.

Wrapper: Indonesia/Sumatra   *Binder: Honduras*   *Filler: Nicaragua*

Shape	Name	Lgth	Ring	Wrapper
Lonsdale	Fumas	7	44	CC
Toro	Optimus	6	48	CC
Long Corona	Luxus	6	43	CC
Corona	Dulcis	5½	42	CC

Here is a new, 1996 brand with a medium body and a spicy taste, thanks to its Sumatra-grown wrapper, combined with Honduran and Nicaraguan leaves inside. La Maximiliana cigars are presented in a traditional box-pressed format in individual cellophane sleeves.

LA NATIVE
Handmade in Danli, Honduras.

Wrapper: Nicaragua   *Binder: Honduras*   *Filler: Honduras, Nicaragua*

Shape	Name	Lgth	Ring	Wrapper
Churchill	Churchill	6⅞	49	CM
Robusto	Rothchild	5	50	CM
Toro	Toro	6	50	CM
Long Corona	Cetros	6	43	CM

These Honduran-made cigars were introduced in 1994 and offer a very smooth draw with a medium-bodied taste and excellent construction. La Native is offered in boxes of 10 and 20.

LA PANTERA DIAMOND COLLECTION
Handmade in Danli, Honduras.

Wrapper: Ecuador   *Binder: Nicaragua*   *Filler: Honduras*

La Native

Good taste

Made by hand
Cedar aged to
perfection

classic quality

La Native Premium Cigars

Visit your local tobacconist

Distributed by Hiland Trading Company

Photography by Larry Sammons

HANDMADE CIGARS: BRAND LISTINGS

Shape	Name	Lgth	Ring	Wrapper
Double Corona	Churchill	7	50	CM
Corona	Numero 4	5½	42	CM
Long Panatela	Palma Fina	7	38	CM
Pyramid	Pyramid	5½	52	CM
Robusto	Rothchild	5	50	CM
Torpedo	Torpedo	7	54	CM
Giant	Gigante	8½	54	CM

New for 1996, the La Pantera Diamond Collection is a mellow, mild-to-medium bodied cigar, thanks to its Sumatra-seed wrapper, offered in wooden boxes of 25.

LA PANTERA SAPPHIRE COLLECTION
Handmade in Danli, Honduras.

Wrapper: Honduras   Binder: Nicaragua   Filler: Honduras

Shape	Name	Lgth	Ring	Wrapper
Double Corona	Churchill	7	50	CM
Corona	Numero 4	5½	42	CM
Long Panatela	Palma Fina	7	38	CM
Pyramid	Pyramid	5½	52	CM
Robusto	Rothchild	5	50	CM
Torpedo	Torpedo	7	54	CM
Giant	Gigante	8½	54	CM

This is a stronger blend than its sister brand, the La Pantera Diamond Collection. Spicier and more robust, this is a medium-to-full-bodied cigar which features aged tobaccos.

LA PLATA
Handmade in Los Angeles, California, USA.

Wrapper: Ecuador, Mexico, USA/Connecticut   Binder: Ecuador
Filler: Dominican Republic, Ecuador, Honduras, Mexico

HANDMADE CIGARS: BRAND LISTINGS

Shape	Name	Lgth	Ring	Wrapper
Giant	Rockets	8	50	CC-Ma
Double Corona	Enterprise	7	52	CC-Ma
Lonsdale	Internationals	7	42	CC-Ma
Churchill	Victor No. 1	7	46	CC-Ma
Toro	Jr. Enterprise	6	52	CC-Ma
Lonsdale	Numero Dos	6½	42	CC-Ma
Long Panatela	Reinas	7	34	CC-Ma
Slim Panatela	Tito Specials	6	34	CC-Ma
Short Panatela	Dessert Specials	5	36	CC-Ma
Torpedo	Torpedo	6	54	CC-Ma
Robusto	Victor No. 2	5	50	CC-Ma
Long Panatela	Victor No. 3	7	38	CC-Ma
Petit Corona	Jr. Magnificos	5	42	CC-Ma
	Premium Selection:			
Giant	Prime Minister	8	50	Ma
Double Corona	Royal Wilshire	7	52	Ma
Robusto	Robusto Uno	4½	52	Ma
Long Corona	Magnificos	6	42	Ma
Robusto	Hercules	5½	54	CI
Double Corona	Pyramid Classic	7	50	CI
Panatela	Ashford Classic	6	34	CI
Long Corona	Grand Classic	6	42	CI
Double Corona	Enterprise Classic	7	52	CI

Founded in 1947, the La Plata factory is the last large-scale cigar manufacturing enterprise left in Los Angeles. But it's more vibrant then ever, with two major lines. The original series combines filler tobaccos from the Dominican Republic, Ecuador and Mexico with an Ecuadorian binder and wrappers from Ecuador (natural) or Mexico (maduro). The newer premium series offers smokers Ecuadorian and Dominican fillers (plus a Dominican leaf

HANDMADE CIGARS: BRAND LISTINGS

for maduro-wrapped cigars), an Ecuadorian binder and silky Connecticut Shade wrappers (natural) or Connecticut Broadleaf wrappers in maduro.

LA PRIMADORA
Handmade in Danli, Honduras.

Wrapper: Ecuador, Mexico   *Binder: Indonesia*   *Filler: Honduras, Nicaragua*

Shape	Name	Lgth	Ring	Wrapper
Giant	Emperor	8½	50	CC-Ma
Toro	Solitaire	6	50	CC-Ma
Robusto	Starbrite	4½	50	CC-Ma
Panatela	Falcon	6½	34	CC-Ma
Lonsdale	Excellentes	6½	42	CC-Ma
Corona	Petite Cetros	5½	42	CC-Ma

La Primadora is a mild-bodied cigar with a unique and slightly spicy blend of long-filler tobaccos. These imported cigars are well constructed, with a consistent finish and offered in bundles of 25 cigars each.

LA PRIMERA
Handmade in Santiago, Dominican Republic.

Wrapper: Ecuador   *Binder: Nicaragua*   *Filler: Dom.Rep., Nicaragua*

Shape	Name	Lgth	Ring	Wrapper
Giant	Presidente	8½	52	CC
Double Corona	Churchill	7	50	CC
Toro	Toro	6	50	CC
Lonsdale	Cetro Grande	6¾	44	CC
Robusto	Rothschild	5	50	CC
Corona	Petite Corona	5¾	43	CC

This is a new brand for 1996 from one of the most respected factories in the Dominican Republic. It offers a full-flavored blend with considerable smoothness and is offered in wooden boxes of 25.

HANDMADE CIGARS: BRAND LISTINGS

LA REAL
Handmade in Condega, Nicaragua.

Wrapper: Nicaragua   *Binder: Nicaragua*   *Filler: Nicaragua*

Shape	Name	Lgth	Ring	Wrapper
Double Corona	Imperiales	7	50	CM
Robusto	Baron	5	50	CM

This is a all-Nicaraguan, full-bodied smoke which debuted in 1995. It's for the serious smoker, though: packed without cellophane and in boxes of 50. Light 'em up!

LA REGIONAL
Handmade in Las Palmas, the Canary Islands of Spain.

Wrapper: Ecuador   *Binder: Mexico*   *Filler: Nicaragua*

Shape	Name	Lgth	Ring	Wrapper
Double Corona	Monarch	7¼	50	CC
Churchill	Churchill	6⅞	46	CC
Lonsdale	Lonsdale	6⅝	42	CC
Corona	Corona	5⅝	42	CC
Panatela	Delicioso	6⅝	36	CC
Slim Panatela	Palmas	5½	33	CC
Toro	Matador	6⅛	50	CC

Here is a full-bodied brand introduced in 1995 and produced in one of the world's historic cigar regions: the Canary Islands of Spain, blending Nicaraguan and Mexican tobaccos with a Connecticut Shade-seed wrapper grown in Ecuador.

LAS CABRILLAS
Handmade in Danli, Honduras.

Wrapper: USA/Connecticut   *Binder: Mexico*   *Filler: Nicaragua*

Shape	Name	Lgth	Ring	Wrapper
Small Panatela	Pizarro	5½	32	CC
Double Corona	Maximilian	7	56	CC-Ma

HANDMADE CIGARS: BRAND LISTINGS

Giant	Columbus	8¼	52	CC-Ma
Double Corona	Balboa	7½	54	CC-Ma
Double Corona	De Soto	6⅞	50	CC-Ma
Robusto	Cortez	4¾	50	CC-Ma
Lonsdale	Ponce de Leon	6¾	44	CC-Ma
Long Corona	Magellan	6	42	CC
Panatela	Coronado	6⅞	35	CC

The explorers of the "New World" are saluted in this brand, which debuted in 1993 and which offers a medium-bodied taste. New for 1997 is the Maximilian, a double corona, which will be offered in boxes of 20, while the rest of the brand – except Columbus (10s) and Pizarro (60s) – is available in boxes of 25.

LA TRADICION CUBANA
Handmade in Miami, Florida, USA.
Wrapper: Ecuador   Binder: Honduras   Filler: Dom.Rep., Honduras

Shape	Name	Lgth	Ring	Wrapper
Double Corona	Churchill	7	50	CC
Long Corona	Corona	6	44	CC
Double Corona	Double Corona	7¼	50	CC
Long Panatela	Lanceros	7	38	CC
Robusto	Robusto	5	50	CC
Torpedo	Torpedo	6½	52	CC

Introduced in 1996, this brand is made by a small factory which prizes quality above all else. Offered in boxes of 25, the blend has a medium-to-full body.

LA UNICA
Handmade in Santiago, Dominican Republic.
Wrapper: USA/Connecticut   Binder: Dom. Rep.   Filler: Dom. Rep.

Shape	Name	Lgth	Ring	Wrapper
Giant	No. 100	8½	52	Cl-Ma
Double Corona	No. 200	7	49	Cl-Ma

HANDMADE CIGARS: BRAND LISTINGS

Lonsdale	No. 300	6¾	44	Cl-Ma
Robusto	No. 400	4½	50	Cl-Ma
Corona	No. 500	5½	42	Cl-Ma

Introduced in 1986, this brand has a mild flavor and aroma in a well-constructed cigar, with a natural or maduro wrapper. An excellent value, these long-filler cigars are packaged in bundles of 20 cigars each.

LA VENGA
Handmade in Honduras.
Wrapper: Ecuador, Indonesia/Sumatra *Binder: Honduras*
Filler: Dominican Republic, Honduras and Nicaragua

Shape	Name	Lgth	Ring	Wrapper
Corona	No. 10	5½	43	CC
Robusto	No. 37	4½	50	CC-Ma
Double Corona	No. 59	7¼	54	CC-Ma
Long Corona	No. 60	6¼	44	CC-Ma
Toro	No. 61	6¼	50	CC-Ma
Corona Extra	No. 62	5½	47	CC-Ma
Churchill	No. 63	7¼	46	CC-Ma
Churchill	No. 70	6¾	48	CC-Ma
Giant	No. 80	8½	52	CC-Ma
	Short-filler tobacco:			
Corona	Fuma	5½	44	CC-Ma

The complex blend of this cigar provides a medium-to-full bodied taste and is offered in economically-priced bundles of 25.

LAMBS CLUB
Handmade in Santiago, Dominican Republic.
Wrapper: Ecuador *Binder: Honduras* *Filler: Brazil, Dom. Rep.*

Shape	Name	Lgth	Ring	Wrapper
Double Corona	Churchill	7	50	CC

HANDMADE CIGARS: BRAND LISTINGS

Long Corona	Corona Extra	6½	43	CC
Toro	Toro	6	50	CC
Robusto	Rothschild	4¾	50	CC
Petit Corona	Chico	4½	40	CC

Lambs Club is a super-premium Dominican cigar, handmade by one of the most respected manufacturers in that country. Its rich, flavorful character is derived from the finest Dominican Olor and Piloto tobaccos, which together with a smooth Ecuadorian wrapper, develops a spicy, medium-bodied taste.

LAS VEGAS CIGAR CO.
Handmade in Las Vegas, Nevada, USA.

Wrapper: Ecuador, Mexico   Binder: Dom. Rep.   Filler: Dom. Rep., Mexico

Shape	Name	Lgth	Ring	Wrapper
Long Panatela	Palma	7	38	Cl
Robusto	Rothchild	4½	50	Cl-Ma
Small Panatela	Nix	5	30	Cl
Corona	Corona	5¾	42	Cl-Ma
Corona	Montefino	5¾	52	Cl-Ma
Slim Panatela	Pencil	6¾	30	Cl
Toro	Punch	6½	52	Cl-Ma
Lonsdale	Corona Largo	6¾	44	Cl-Ma
Lonsdale	Fuma *(short filler)*	6¾	46	Cl
Panatela	Panatela	6¾	36	Cl
Double Corona	Churchill	7½	50	Cl-Ma
Churchill	Imperial	7	46	Cl-Ma
Giant	Excalibur	8¾	52	Cl-Ma
Giant	El Rey	9	60	Cl-Ma
Toro	El Rey Corto	5	62	Cl-Ma
Torpedo	Torpedo	7	60	Cl-Ma
Lonsdale	Rum	6¾	44	Cl-Ma

HANDMADE CIGARS: BRAND LISTINGS

You'll find this small factory in a storefront on the famous Las Vegas Strip. The body varies from mild (Corona, Corona Largo) to heavy (Excalibur, El Rey), with the majority of the sizes rated as medium. Note the large number of shapes with big ring gauges.

LEGACY
Handmade in Danli, Honduras.

Wrapper: Ecuador   *Binder: Honduras*   *Filler: Honduras*

Shape	Name	Lgth	Ring	Wrapper
Giant	No. 6 Napoleon	8½	52	CC-Ma
Double Corona	No. 5 Monarch	7	52	CC-Ma
Churchill	No. 4 Corona Grande	7½	46	CC
Lonsdale	No. 3 Elegante	7	43	CC
Robusto	No. 2 Rothchild	5	50	CC-Ma
Long Corona	No. 1 Super Cetro	6	43	CC

This is a premium, imported cigar, offered in unique, 18-pack bundles. Made entirely by hand with high-quality, long-filler tobaccos, the price is just as captivating as the medium-bodied taste.

LEGEND ● ARIO
Handmade in Danli, Honduras.

Wrapper: Ecuador   *Binder: Honduras*   *Filler: Honduras*

Shape	Name	Lgth	Ring	Wrapper
Churchill	Churchill	7	48	CC
Lonsdale	No. 1	6½	44	CC
Corona	No. 5	5½	44	CC
Toro	Super Rothschild	6	50	CC
Robusto	Rothschild	5	50	CC

This is a new brand for 1996, offering five classic shapes in a medium-bodied blend matching an Ecuadorian-grown wrapper with Honduran binder and filler leaves.

HANDMADE CIGARS: BRAND LISTINGS

LEMPIRA
Handmade in Danli, Honduras.

Wrapper: Ecuador   *Binder: Dom. Rep.*   *Filler: Honduras, Nicaragua*

Shape	Name	Lgth	Ring	Wrapper
Corona	Coronas	5½	42	Co
Robusto	Robusto	5	50	Co
Lonsdale	Lonsdale	6½	44	Co
Long Panatela	Lanceros	7½	38	Co
Toro	Toro	6	50	Co
Churchill	Churchills	7	48	Co
Double Corona	Presidents	7¾	50	Co

The Lempira is manufactured in Honduras using a blended filler from Honduras and Nicaragua, adding a binder from the Dominican Republic for extra flavor. The wrapper is Ecuadorian-grown, Connecticut Shade. This is a medium-strength cigar with lots of flavor.

LEON
Handmade in Los Angeles, California, USA.

Wrapper: Ecuador   *Binder & Filler: Central American blend*

Shape	Name	Lgth	Ring	Wrapper
Lonsdale	Cazadores	7	44	Ma
Lonsdale	Cetro	6½	44	CC
Churchill	Cubarro	7	46	CC
Lonsdale	Fuma	7	44	Ma
Long Panatela	Panetelas	7	36	CC
Double Corona	Presidentes	7½	50	CC-Ma
Lonsdale	Numero 4	6½	44	Ma
Toro	Tronquito	5¾	50	CC-Ma
Giant	Gigante	8	52	Ma

In a nondescript shop on 6th Street in midtown Los Angeles is Roberto Leon, putting together handmade, medium-bodied cigars that are favored by enthusiasts who appreciate quality and value. One common sight: motorcycle-mounted police lighting up a Presidentes for the road!

LEON
Handmade in Esteli, Nicaragua.

Wrapper: Ecuador   Binder: Nicaragua   Filler: Nicaragua

Shape	Name	Lgth	Ring	Wrapper
Giant	Presidente	8½	52	CC
Double Corona	Churchill	7	50	CC
Lonsdale	No. 1	6½	44	CC
Torpedo	Torpedo	7½	54	CC
Pyramid	Piramide	7	50	CC
Long Panatela	Lancero	7	38	CC
Robusto	Robusto	5	50	CC

This is a new brand for 1996, offering a mild-to-medium body with a Connecticut-seed wrapper grown in Ecuador. It is presented with unique packaging, as the cedar box is topped with plexiglass, giving a full view of the precious gems inside!

LEON JIMENES
Handmade in the Santiago, Dominican Republic.

Wrapper: USA/Connecticut   Binder: Dom. Rep.   Filler: Dom. Rep.

Shape	Name		Lgth	Ring	Wrapper
Double Corona	No. 1		7½	50	CM
Churchill	No. 2		7	47	CM
Lonsdale	No. 3		6½	42	CM
Corona	No. 4		5⅝	42	CM
Short Panatela	No. 5		5	38	CM
Robusto	Robusto		5½	50	CM
Pyramid	Torpedo		6	58	CM
Lonsdale	Tubos	(tubed)	6½	42	CM

HANDMADE CIGARS: BRAND LISTINGS

Introduced in the 1970s, Leon Jimenes is a hand-made, full-bodied cigar with Dominican fillers and binder, encased in a Connecticut wrapper that provides excellent balance and an exquisite aroma. The brand is presented in individual cellophane sleeves, packed in elegant all-cedar boxes of 10 or 25.

LEW'S SMOKERS
Handmade in Cofradia, Honduras.

Wrapper: Honduras   Binder: Mexico   *Filler: Honduras*

Shape	Name	Lgth	Ring	Wrapper
Churchill	Sunday Special	7	48	CM
Long Corona	Pop's Choice	6	44	CM

Here is a new for 1996 brand from the endlessly creative Lew Rothman, who puts his name on a mild to medium-bodied blend of Havana seed fillers, Mexican binder and Connecticut-seed wrappers grown in Honduras. The gimmick? A special sweetening of the gum used to seal the cap, to give a sweet taste upon lighting!

LICENCIADOS
Handmade in Santiago, Dominican Republic.

Wrapper: USA/Connecticut   Binder: Dom. Rep.   *Filler: Dom. Rep.*

Shape	Name	Lgth	Ring	Wrapper
Double Corona	Churchill	7	50	CM
Long Corona	Excellentes	6¾	43	CM
Small Panatela	Expreso	4½	35	CM
Torpedo	Figurado	6	56	CM
Corona	No. 4	5¾	43	CM
Long Panatela	Panatela Linda	7	38	CM
Giant	Presidentes	8	50	CM
Giant	Soberanos	8½	52	CM
Toro	Toro	6	50	CM
Robusto	Wavell	5	50	CC-Ma
Corona	No. 200	5¾	43	Ma
Lonsdale	No. 300	6¾	43	Ma

HANDMADE CIGARS: BRAND LISTINGS

Toro	No. 400	6	50	Ma
Giant	No. 500	8	50	Ma

Introduced in 1988, this handmade brand has earned a reputation for excellence, in taste, construction and value. The wide range of shapes and medium-bodied flavor makes it accessible to many smokers.

LOS REYES
Handmade in Santiago, Dominican Republic.

Wrapper: Dom. Rep.   *Binder: Dom. Rep.*   *Filler: Dom. Rep.*

Shape	Name	Lgth	Ring	Wrapper
Robusto	Santo Domingo	5	50	CC
Long Corona	Santiago	6	44	CC-CM-Ma
Grand Corona	Don Miguel	6⅞	46	CC
Long Panatela	Gitanos	7	36	CC
Small Panatela	Le Petit Chateau	5	30	CC
Giant	Los Reyes	8½	51	CC

Offered since 1952 in limited distribution, Los Reyes are now widely available and offer a mild-to-medium bodied smoke. The filler includes four different Dominican leaves, held together by a Dominican binder and a Connecticut Seed filler, also grown in the Dominican Republic. The Santiago shape is also available, if desired, with either a Cameroon or a maduro wrapper.

MACABI
Handmade in Santiago, Dominican Republic.

Wrapper: USA/Connecticut   *Binder: Mexico*   *Filler: Dom. Rep., Nicaragua*

Shape	Name	Lgth	Ring	Wrapper
Double Corona	Super Corona	7¾	52	Co
Double Corona	Double Corona	6⅞	49	Co
Lonsdale	No. 1	6¾	44	Co
Torpedo	Belicoso Fino	6¼	52	Co
Toro	Corona Extra	6	50	Co
Corona	Media Corona	5½	43	Co

Robusto	Royal Corona	5	50	Co

Introduced in 1995, this brand – launched as the "pride of Miami" – will be made in Santiago, Dominican Republic beginning in 1997. Handmade in the centuries-old tradition and under the watchful eye of master cigar maker Juan Sosa, Macabi brings a medium-bodied flavor to connoisseurs of fine cigars. Very smooth and slightly spicy, these gems are offered uncellophaned in slide-top cedar boxes.

MACANUDO
*Handmade in Santiago, Dominican Republic
and in Kingston, Jamaica.*

Wrapper: USA/Connecticut   Binder: Mexico   Filler: Dom. Rep., Mexico

Shape	Name		Lgth	Ring	Wrapper
	Handmade in Jamaica:				
Small Panatela	Ascot		4⅛	32	Cl
Short Panatela	Caviar		4	36	Cl⁄
Slim Panatela	Claybourne		6	31	DC-Cl
Short Panatela	Petit Corona		5	38	Cl
Corona	Duke of Devon		5½	42	DC-Cl-Ma
Long Panatela	Portofino	*(tubed)*	7	34	Cl
Corona	Hampton Court	*(tubed)*	5¾	43	Cl
Robusto	Hyde Park		5½	49	Cl-Ma
Lonsdale	Baron de Rothschild		6½	42	DC-Cl-Ma
Robusto	Crystal	*(tubed)*	5½	50	Cl
Torpedo	Duke of Windsor		6	50	Cl
Giant	Prince of Wales		8	52	Cl
Cigarillo	Miniature		3¾	24	Cl
	Handmade in the Dominican Republic:				
Double Corona	Prince Philip		7½	49	DC-Cl-Ma
	Vintage Cabinet Selection, handmade in Jamaica:				
Double Corona	I		7½	49	CM

Lonsdale	II		6½	43	CM
Corona	III		5½	43	CM
Corona Extra	IV		4½	47	CM
Robusto	V		5½	49	CM
Long Panatela	VII		7½	38	CM
Robusto	VIII	(tubed)	5½	50	CM
Churchill	XX		7	47	CM

An exceptionally consistent cigar, made with Connecticut Shade wrappers that have been aged for at least three years. The cigar has a silky feel to the hand and has a taste which is only found in a Macanudo. The most popular premium brand in America is supervised by master cigar-maker Benjamin Menendez. The Vintage Cabinet Selection cigars are each more than four years in the making and include filler leaves from the Dominican Republic, Jamaica and Mexico.

MADRIGAL HABANA
Handmade in San Andres Tuxtla, Mexico.

Wrapper: Mexico   *Binder: Mexico*   *Filler: Mexico*

Shape	Name	Lgth	Ring	Wrapper
Giant	Monarch	8	54	CC-Ma
Double Corona	Imperial	7½	52	CC-Ma
Robusto	Robusto	5	52	CC-Ma
Toro	Governor	6	50	CC-Ma
Lonsdale	Classic Corona	7	44	CC-Ma
Corona	Petit Corona	5½	42	CC-Ma

Re-introduced in 1996, this is an old Havana brand which had been kicked around by several cigar manufacturers since the 1970s and was produced primarily in Honduras. In 1985, Brick-Hanauer acquired the brand and found the right formula for a new, mild smoke featuring all-Mexican tobacco. The blend includes Connecticut Shade-seed tobacco for the natural wrappers and Jaltepec leaves for the maduro wrappers. Even the box speaks elegance: it is an exact copy of a 1927 box of Madrigal, made in Havana.

HANDMADE CIGARS: BRAND LISTINGS

MARIA MANCINI
Handmade in Cofradia, Honduras.

Wrapper: Honduras   *Binder: Honduras*   *Filler: Honduras*

Shape	Name	Lgth	Ring	Wrapper
Double Corona	Clemenceau	7	49	CC-CM
Corona	Corona Classico	5½	43	CC-CM
Long Corona	Corona Larga	6¼	43	CC-CM
Robusto	De Gaulle	5	50	CM
Lonsdale	Grandee	6¾	43	CC-CM
Panatela	Palma Delgado	7	39	CC-CM

This is a heavy-bodied, all-Honduran blend, featuring Cuban-seed tobaccos that produce a full-flavored taste with an easy draw.

MARIO PALOMINO
Handmade in Kingston, Jamaica.

Wrapper: USA/Connecticut   *Binder: Mexico*   *Filler: Jamaica*

Shape	Name	Lgth	Ring	Wrapper
Slim Panatela	Buccaneers	5½	32	CC
Petit Corona	Petit Corona	5	41	CC
Slim Panatela	Rapier	6	32	CC
Long Corona	Festivale	6	41	CC
Lonsdale	Cetro	6½	42	CC
Grand Corona	Corona Immensa	6	47	CC
Lonsdale	Caballero	7½	45	CC
Double Corona	Presidente	7½	49	CC

These cigars are manufactured by The Palomino Brothers Tobacco Co. in Jamaica. The blend features Jamaican filler and in combination with the Mexican binder and Connecticut Shade wrapper produce a heavy, full-bodied flavor.

HANDMADE CIGARS: BRAND LISTINGS

MATACAN
Handmade in San Andres Tuxtula, Mexico.

Wrapper: Mexico   Binder: Mexico   Filler: Mexico, Nicaragua

Shape	Name	Lgth	Ring	Wrapper
Double Corona	No. 1	7½	50	CC-Ma
Toro	No. 2	6	50	CC-Ma
Grand Corona	No. 3	6⅝	46	CC-Ma
Lonsdale	No. 4	6⅝	42	CC-Ma
Long Corona	No. 5	6	42	CC-Ma
Panatela	No. 6	6⅝	35	CC-Ma
Robusto	No. 7	4¾	50	CC-Ma
Giant	No. 8	8	52	CC-Ma
Small Panatela	No. 9	5	32	CC-Ma
Double Corona	No. 10	6⅞	54	CC-Ma

Good value, good quality and a medium-bodied taste led by San Andres Valley tobaccos is the promise of Matacan. These cigars are offered in bundles of 20.

MATASA SECONDS
Handmade in Santiago, Dominican Republic.

Wrapper: USA/Connecticut   Binder: Mexico   Filler: Dom. Rep.

Shape	Name	Lgth	Ring	Wrapper
Long Corona	Corona	6	43	CC
Lonsdale	No. 2	6½	43	CC-Ma
Corona	No. 4	5½	42	CC-Ma
Long Panatela	Palma Fina	7	36	CC
Short Panatela	Palmita	5	38	CC
Panatela	Super Fino	6	36	CC-Ma

"MATASA" is a highly-respected name in the cigar trade as it is the name of one of the Dominican Republic's finest cigar manufacturing groups. These seconds are overruns of some of the factory's "big name" cigars, and are very mild with a beautiful Connecticut wrapper.

HANDMADE CIGARS: BRAND LISTINGS

MATCH PLAY
Handmade in the Santiago, Dominican Republic.
Wrapper: Ecuador   *Binder: Dom. Rep.*   *Filler: Dom. Rep.*

Shape	Name	Lgth	Ring	Wrapper
Robusto	Cypress	4¾	50	CC
Long Corona	St. Andrews	6¼	44	CC
Toro	Turnberry	6	50	CC
Churchill	Prestwick	6⅞	46	CC
Double Corona	Olympic	7½	50	CC
Pyramid	Troon	7	54	CC

This brand was introduced in 1995; it is a handmade, medium-bodied cigar that is the product of a balanced blend from four distinctly different tobaccos. It is enhanced by a Connecticut Seed wrapper that has a unique growing cycle and final processing procedure.

MAXIUS
Handmade in Santiago, Dominican Republic.
Wrapper: Indonesia/Sumatra and Mexico

Binder: Dom. Rep.   *Filler: Dom. Rep.*

Shape	Name	Lgth	Ring	Wrapper
	Sumatra line:			
Corona	Corona	5¼	43	CC
Robusto	Robusto	5	50	CC
Panatela	Panatella	6½	39	CC
Churchill	Churchill	7	47	CC
Double Corona	Double Corona	7½	50	CC
	Maduro line:			
Long Corona	Corona	6	44	Ma
Robusto	Robusto	5	50	Ma
Slim Panatela	Panatella	7	32	Ma
Churchill	Churchill	6⅞	46	Ma

HANDMADE CIGARS: BRAND LISTINGS

This brand is new for 1996 and offers two different styles: the Sumatra line, which is medium-to-full in body and has a spicy finish, and the Maduro line, which is mild-to-medium in body and slightly sweet. Both are products of the finest manufacturing facilities in the Dominican Republic; a third line to feature a genuine Connecticut Shade wrapper is already planned.

MAYA
Handmade in Danli, Honduras.

Wrapper: Ecuador   *Binder: Honduras*   *Filler: Dom. Rep., Honduras*

Shape	Name	Lgth	Ring	Wrapper
Slim Panatela	Petit	5½	34	CI
Robusto	Robusto	5	50	CI-Ma
Torpedo	Torpedo	7	54	CI
Double Corona	Executives	7¾	50	CI-Ma
Churchill	Churchills	6⅞	49	CI-Ma
Lonsdale	Elegantes	7	43	CI
Long Corona	Corona	6¼	44	CI-Ma
Long Corona	Cetros	6	43	CI
Panatela	Palma Fina	6⅞	36	CI
Corona	Petit Coronas	5½	42	CI
Toro	Matador	6	50	CI-Ma
Giant	Viajantes	8½	52	CI

Introduced in the mid-1980s, the Maya brand is a Honduran, handmade, long-filler cigar with predominantly Honduran filler blended with Dominican Havana seed tobaccos. Maya's Havana-seed binder and Ecuadorian-grown, Connecticut-seed wrapper complete this mild-to-medium strength cigar.

MEDAL OF HONOR
Handmade in Danli, Honduras.

Wrapper: USA/Connecticut   *Binder: Honduras*   *Filler: Honduras*

Shape	Name	Lgth	Ring	Wrapper
Lonsdale	No. 300	6½	42	CC-Ma
Double Corona	No. 500	7½	50	CC-Ma

HANDMADE CIGARS: BRAND LISTINGS

Giant	No. 700	8½	52	CC-Ma

A new standard for value, this premium bundle was introduced in 1995 and is 100% handmade in Honduras, using excellent-quality, long-filler tobaccos and distinctive packaging. These cigars are available in a choice of a Connecticut Shade or maduro wrapper.

MEXICAN EMPERADOR
Handmade in San Andres Tuxtla, Mexico.

Wrapper: Mexico   Binder: Mexico   Filler: Mexico

Shape	Name	Lgth	Ring	Wrapper
Giant	Emperador	13¾	49	CC

The size says it all! This is a unique product of the famous San Andres Valley region of Mexico, the birthplace of many great brands. Despite its immense length, the 49-ring width makes it an accessible smoke, albeit a time-consuming one. The Emperador is individually packaged in an elegant, slide-top cedar box.

MILANO SANTANA
Handmade in Santiago, Dominican Republic.

Wrapper: Dom. Rep.   Binder: Dom. Rep.   Filler: Dom. Rep.

Shape	Name	Lgth	Ring	Wrapper
Giant	Presidente	8	52	CC-CM-Ma
Giant	Elegante	8	50	CC-CM-Ma
Double Corona	Churchill	7½	50	CC-CM-Ma
Churchill	Prime Ministro	7	48	CC-CM-Ma
Long Panatela	Conchita	7	36	CC-CM-Ma
Lonsdale	Grande	6½	44	CC-CM-Ma
Toro	Toro	6	52	CC-CM-Ma
Corona	Corona	5½	42	CC-CM-Ma
Robusto	Robusto	5½	50	CC-CM-Ma
Torpedo	Torpedo	7	44	CC-CM-Ma

HANDMADE CIGARS: BRAND LISTINGS

Take your pick of three beautiful wrappers: a Colorado Claro in the Bronze series, a Colorado Maduro in the Silver series or real Maduro in the Oro (gold) line. These are elegantly made, limited-distribution, medium-bodied cigars, offered in all-cedar boxes of 25.

MiCubano
Handmade in Esteli, Nicaragua.

Wrapper: Nicaragua　　　　*Binder: Nicaragua*　　　　*Filler: Nicaragua*

Shape	Name	Lgth	Ring	Wrapper
Robusto	No. 450	4¾	50	CM
Corona	No. 542	5½	42	CM
Toro	No. 650	6	50	CM
Lonsdale	No. 644	6½	44	CM
Churchill	No. 748	7	48	CM
Giant	No. 852	8½	52	CM

Here, at long last, is a cigar made up of 100 percent Cuban-seed tobacco, which debuted in 1995. Grown in Nicaragua, the filler, binder and wrapper combine for a rich, uninhibited, full-bodied taste that is offered uncellophaned in beautiful all-cedar boxes of 25 cigars each.

Mocambo
Handmade in San Andres Tuxtula, Mexico.

Wrapper: Mexico　　　　*Binder: Mexico*　　　　*Filler: Mexico*

Shape	Name	Lgth	Ring	Wrapper
Double Corona	Churchill	7	50	CC-Ma
Toro	Double Corona	6	51	CC-Ma
Panatela	Empire	6½	39	CC-Ma
Giant	Inmensa	8½	50	CC-Ma
Lonsdale	Premier	6⅝	43	CC-Ma
Long Corona	Royal Corona	6	42	CC-Ma

This is a heavy-bodied cigar, offered with a choice of a natural-colored wrapper or a sweeter, maduro-shade wrapper.

THE EMBARGO DOESN'T MATTER ANYMORE.
CUBAN TASTE IS HERE.

MiCubano

MiCubano

MiCubano

MiCubano

MiCubano **MiCubano** **MiCubano** **MiCubano**

MiCubano

MiCubano
~650~

100% Cuban Seed Tobacco

The first 100% Cuban seed tobacco cigar with true Cuban taste made outside of Cuba. MiCubano is produced in Nicaragua, but the difference ends there. The filler, binder and wrapper leaf are all grown from Cuban seed. All the tobacco is grown and cured in the Cuban tradition. All MiCubanos are hand made in a factory owned and supervised by a Cuban expatriate. And the packaging is uniquely Cuban. But what distinguishes the taste of MiCubano is the quality of its blend and its wrapper - the only wrapper ever grown outside of Cuba that rivals its Cuban counterpart. Many have tried, but all have failed ... until MiCubano. MiCubano and true Cuban taste are here.

HANDMADE CIGARS: BRAND LISTINGS

MONTAGUE
Handmade in Pandaan, Indonesia.

Wrapper: Brazil, Indonesia   *Binder: Indonesia*
Filler: Brazil, Indonesia

Shape	Name	Lgth	Ring	Wrapper
Double Corona	No. 1	7¼	50	Cl-Ma
Grand Corona	No. 2	6⅔	45	Cl-Ma
Long Corona	No. 3	6	40	Cl-Ma
Robusto	Robustos	5	50	Cl-Ma
Lonsdale	Lanceros	7½	40	Cl-Ma

Made by hand with a medium-bodied taste, this brand is made by hand in Indonesia. Two shades of wrapper are available: a light Claro of Indonesian Vorstenlanden tobacco and a deep maduro, of Brazilian Mata Fina, both which produce a sophisticated and unique taste.

MONTE CANARIO
Handmade in Las Palmas, the Canary Islands of Spain.

Wrapper: USA/Connecticut   *Binder: Dominican Republic*
Filler: Brazil, Canary Islands, Dominican Republic

Shape	Name	Lgth	Ring	Wrapper
Lonsdale	Nuncios	6¾	44	CC
Lonsdale	Imperiales	6½	42	CC
Corona	No. 3	5¾	42	CC
Panatela	Panatela	6	38	CC

Part of the long history of cigar-making in the Canary Islands, the Monte Canario brand has been around in one form or another since the 1920s. It's a mild smoke, featuring a Connecticut wrapper and a blend of leaves from three nations on the interior.

MONTECRUZ
Handmade in La Romana, Dominican Republic.

Wrapper: Indonesia/Java or USA/Connecticut
Binder: Dominican Republic   *Filler: Brazil, Dominican Republic*

HANDMADE CIGARS: BRAND LISTINGS

Shape	Name		Lgth	Ring	Wrapper
Churchill	No. 200		7¼	46	CI-CM
Grand Corona	No. 201		6¼	46	CM
Lonsdale	No. 205		7	42	CM
Lonsdale	No. 210		6½	42	DC-CI-CM
Corona	No. 220		5½	42	DC-CI-CM
Petit Corona	No. 230		5	42	CM
Panatela	No. 250		6½	38	CM
Long Panatela	No. 255		7	36	CI-CM
Panatela	No. 265		5½	38	CM
Short Panatela	No. 270		4¾	36	CM
Slim Panatela	No. 276		6	32	CM
Cigarillo	No. 280		7	28	CM
Cigarillo	No. 281		6	28	CM
Cigarillo	No. 282		5	28	CM
Petit Corona	Cedar Aged		5	42	CI-CM
Robusto	Robusto		4½	49	CM
Giant	Individuales		8	46	CM
Toro	Colossus		6½	50	CM
Long Corona	Tubos	(tubed)	6	42	CM
Panatela	Tubulares	(tubed)	6⅛	36	CI-CM
	Machine-made small cigars:				
Cigarillo	Chicos		4	28	CI-CM
Slim Panatela	Juniors		5¼	33	CI-CM
Panatela	Senores		5¾	35	CI-CM

Originated in 1959 in the Canary Islands of Spain, Montecruz Sun Grown cigars have been hand crafted in La Romana in the Dominican Republic since 1977. The filler is a blend of Dominican-grown Piloto Cubano, Olor and Brazilian tobaccos, while the binder is a Santo Domingo leaf. The cigar is then finished

HANDMADE CIGARS: BRAND LISTINGS

with a Java wrapper known for its silky feel and rich taste. The Natural Claro line, which debuted in 1988, delivers the rich flavor that Montecruz is famous for, but with a milder taste due to the use of a Connecticut Shade wrapper, from the famous Windsor Valley.

MONTECASSINO
Handmade in Danli, Honduras.

Wrapper: Honduras   *Binder: Honduras*   *Filler: Honduras*

Shape	Name	Lgth	Ring	Wrapper
Giant	Imperial	8½	52	CM
Lonsdale	Cazadores	6½	44	CM
Giant	Diamantes	8	50	CM
Lonsdale	No. 225	6½	44	CM
Long Panatela	Picadores	7	35	CM

These cigars are all made by hand and have a mild-to-medium body, despite their all-Honduran tobaccos. Montecassinos are offered in modestly-priced bundles of 25 cigars each.

MONTECRISTO
Handmade in La Romana, Dominican Republic.

Wrapper: USA/Connecticut   *Binder: Dom. Rep.*   *Filler: Dom. Rep.*

Shape	Name		Lgth	Ring	Wrapper
Churchill	Churchill		7	48	CC
Lonsdale	No. 1		6½	44	CC
Torpedo	No. 2		6	50	CC
Corona	No. 3		5½	44	CC
Robusto	Robustos		4¾	50	CC
Lonsdale	Tubos	(tubed)	6¼	42	CC
Toro	Double Corona		6¼	50	CC
Corona Extra	Corona Grande		5¾	46	CC

This famous name in cigars is relatively young, as the brand was originated in 1935 in Cuba. Today's Dominican version, introduced in 1995, offers outstanding craftsmanship and a slow-burning, medium-to-heavy-bodied smoke whose obvious quality is the lasting impression.

MONTERO
Handmade in Santiago, Dominican Republic.
Wrapper: USA/Connecticut   *Binder: Dom. Rep.*   *Filler: Dom. Rep.*

Shape	Name	Lgth	Ring	Wrapper
Torpedo	Torpedo	7	54	CI
Double Corona	Presidente	7½	50	CI
Churchill	Churchill	6⅞	46	CI
Toro	Toro	6	50	CI
Long Corona	Cetro	6	44	CI
Robusto	Robusto	5	50	CI

The Montero is a premium cigar from the Dominican Republic, introduced in 1995. It is hand made with the long filler and binder from the Dominican Republic and the wrapper from Connecticut. Available only in a natural wrapper, the Montero is a mild-to-medium-bodied cigar.

MONTES DE OCA
Handmade in San Jose, Costa Rica.
Wrapper: Nicaragua   *Binder: Costa Rica*   *Filler: Costa Rica*

Shape	Name	Lgth	Ring	Wrapper
Corona	No. 3	5½	42	CM
Long Corona	No. 2	6	44	CM
Churchill	Churchill	7¾	48	CM

New for 1996, this brand is only in limited distribution. If you can find it, you'll enjoy a rich, full-bodied taste, presented uncellophaned in all-cedar boxes of 25.

MONTESINO
Handmade in Santiago, Dominican Republic.
Wrapper: USA/Connecticut   *Binder: Dom. Rep.*   *Filler: Dom. Rep.*

HANDMADE CIGARS: BRAND LISTINGS

Shape	Name	Lgth	Ring	Wrapper
Churchill	Gran Corona	6¾	48	CM-Ma
Lonsdale	No. 1	6⅞	43	CM-Ma
Long Corona	No. 2	6¼	44	CM-Ma
Corona	Diplomatico	5½	42	CM-Ma
Churchill	Napoleon Grande	7	46	CM-Ma
Lonsdale	Fumas	6¾	44	CM

This well-known brand debuted in its current format in 1981 and is handmade in Santiago, Dominican Republic. Its quality of construction and taste, combined with its modest cost, make it an excellent value.

MONTOYA
Handmade in Danli, Honduras.
Wrapper: Honduras   *Binder: Dom. Rep.*   *Filler: Dom. Rep.*

Shape	Name	Lgth	Ring	Wrapper
Giant	Presidente	8½	52	CC
Double Corona	Churchill	7½	50	CC
Lonsdale	No. 1	6⅞	43	CC
Corona	Petit Corona	5½	43	CC
Robusto	Rothschild	5	50	CC

This is a high-quality cigar, offered in bundles of 25 cigars each. Montoya debuted in 1992 and is considered mild in body.

MOORE & BODE
Handmade in Miami, Florida, USA.
Wrapper: USA/Connecticut   *Binder and Filler: Central & South American*

Shape	Name	Lgth	Ring	Wrapper
	Miami blend:			
Corona	Bishop	5	41	CI
Grand Corona	Corona	6	46	CI
Lonsdale	Corona Largo	7	44	CI

HANDMADE CIGARS: BRAND LISTINGS

Slim Panatela	34's	6¾	34	Cl
Robusto	Salvadore	5	50	Cl
Toro	North Greenway	6¾	50	Cl
Double Corona	Number Ten	7½	50	Cl
Pyramid	Brass	5½	58	Cl
Pyramid	Full Brass	7¼	64	Cl
	Flamboyan blend:			
Corona	Bishop	5	41	Cl
Grand Corona	Corona	6	46	Cl
Lonsdale	Corona Largo	7	44	Cl
Slim Panatela	34's	6¾	34	Cl
Robusto	Salvadore	5	50	Cl
Toro	North Greenway	6¾	50	Cl
Double Corona	Number Ten	7½	50	Cl
Pyramid	Brass	5½	58	Cl
Pyramid	Full Brass	7¼	64	Cl

There are cigars, and there is the art of the cigar. Moore & Bode cigars are one of the foremost exposition of the roller's art, expressed in the highest possible quality of construction. Two series of identical shapes are made; the Miami Blend (introduced 1991) is a mild-to-medium bodied cigar, while the Flamboyan Blend (1995) is medium to heavy.

MORENO MADURO
Handmade in La Romana, Dominican Republic.

Wrapper: Mexico   *Binder: Dom. Rep.*   *Filler: Brazil, Dom. Rep.*

Shape	Name	Lgth	Ring	Wrapper
Corona	No. 445	5½	44	Ma
Slim Panatela	No. 326	6	32	Ma
Lonsdale	No. 426	6½	42	Ma
Churchill	No. 467	7¼	46	Ma

HANDMADE CIGARS: BRAND LISTINGS

Toro	No. 486	6	48	Ma
Double Corona	No. 507	7	50	Ma
Giant	No. 528	8½	52	Ma

These are mild to medium-bodied cigars, wrapped in dark maduro wrappers and featuring a pleasant blend of tobacco from three nations.

MORRO CASTLE
Handmade in Miami, Florida, USA.

Wrapper: Ecuador   *Binder: Nicaragua*   *Filler: Nicaragua*

Shape	Name	Lgth	Ring	Wrapper
Short Panatela	Miniature	5	36	CM
Robusto	Robusto	5	50	CM
Toro	Robusto Largo	6	50	CM
Lonsdale	Corona	6½	42	CM
Churchill	Double Corona	7½	46	CM
Double Corona	Churchill	7¼	50	CM
Torpedo	Torpedo	6½	54	CM
Perfecto	Perfecto	6½	48	CM

Named for the famous landmark which guards Havana's harbor, this is a medium-bodied blend of Nicaraguan-grown, Cuban-seed filler, Nicaraguan binder and Ecuadorian-grown wrapper. Introduced in 1996 and sporting an elegantly-designed band, Morro Castle cigars are offered in boxes of 25.

NAPA
Handmade in Santiago, Dominican Republic, Danli, Honduras and Esteli, Nicaragua.

DOMINICAN SELECTION:
Wrapper: Dom. Rep. • *Binder: Dom. Rep.* • *Filler: Dom. Rep.*

HONDURAN SELECTION:
Wrapper: Indonesia • *Binder: Dom. Rep.* • *Filler: Honduras*

HANDMADE CIGARS: BRAND LISTINGS

Shape	Name	Lgth	Ring	Wrapper
	Dominican Selection:			
Corona		5½	42	CC
Robusto		5	50	CC
Churchill		7½	48	CC
Giant		8	52	CC
Torpedo	Figurado	6¾	52	CC
	Honduran Selection:			
Corona		5½	43	CM
Robusto		5	50	CM
Toro		6	50	CM
Churchill		7½	48	CM
	Nicaraguan Selection:			
Petit Corona		5	42	CM
Corona		5½	44	CM
Robusto		4¾	50	CM
Toro		6	50	CM
Churchill		7½	48	CM

Here is a three-series brand introduced in the final months of 1996 which bears the name of the famous California valley in which some of the world's finest wines are produced. The cigars are equally well crafted, albeit unnamed, with the Dominican shapes offering a full-bodied blend marked by a purple band. The Honduran Selection is a medium-to-full-bodied smoke, identified by its orange-color band. The Nicaraguan series has a green band and is mild-to-medium in strength. All of the shapes are presented in all-cedar boxes.

NAPA RESERVE
Handmade in Las Palmas, the Canary Islands of Spain.
Wrapper: Indonesia/Sumatra   Binder: Canary Isl.   Filler: Canary Isl., Dom. Rep.

Shape	Name	Lgth	Ring	Wrapper
Corona		5¾	42	CC
Lonsdale		6¾	44	CC
Robusto		4¾	50	CC
Toro		6	50	CC
Double Corona		7½	50	CC

Scheduled to debut in early 1997, this is designed to be one of the finest, most delicately balanced cigars produced anywhere. The wrapper is grown in Sumatra and the cigars are presented in all-cedar boxes to help continue the mellowing of the tobaccos from the factory to the smoker's own living room.

NATIONAL BRAND
Handmade in Danli, Honduras.

Wrapper: Honduras   *Binder: Mexico*   *Filler: Honduras*

Shape	Name	Lgth	Ring	Wrapper
Giant	Imperial	8½	52	CC-Ma
Double Corona	Churchill	7½	50	CC-Ma
Lonsdale	Lonsdale	6½	42	CC-Ma
Corona	Corona	5½	42	CC
Toro	S. Rothschild	6	50	CC-Ma
Churchill	Soberanos	6⅞	46	CC
Panatela	Royal Palm	6⅞	37	CC

First offered in 1978, this is a Honduran-produced cigar with all Honduran-grown tobacco, including a Connecticut-seed wrapper, offered in bundles of 25 cigars each. It is considered mild-to-medium in strength.

NAT SHERMAN
Handmade in the Dominican Republic and Honduras.

EXCHANGE SELECTION:
Wrapper: USA/Connecticut • Binder: Mexico • Filler: Dom. Rep.

HANDMADE CIGARS: BRAND LISTINGS

LANDMARK SELECTION:
Wrapper: Cameroon • Binder: Mexico • Filler: Dom. Rep.

MANHATTAN SELECTION:
Wrapper: Mexico • Binder: Mexico • Filler: Dom. Rep.

GOTHAM SELECTION:
Wrapper: USA/Connecticut • Binder: Dom. Rep. • Filler: Dom. Rep.

VIP SELECTION:
Wrapper: USA/Connecticut • Binder: Dom. Rep. • Filler: Brazil, Dom. Rep.

CITY DESK SELECTION:
Wrapper: Mexico • Binder: Dom. Rep. • Filler: Dom. Rep., Mexico

HOST SELECTION:
Wrapper: Ecuador • Binder: Honduras • Filler: Honduras

METROPOLITAN SELECTION:
Wrapper: USA/Connecticut • Binder: Dom. Rep. • Filler: Dom. Rep.

LSN SELECTION:
Wrapper: USA/Connecticut • Binder: Mexico • Filler: Dom. Rep.

Shape	Name	Lgth	Ring	Wrapper
	Exchange Selection, made in the Dominican Republic:			
Small Panatela	Academy No. 2	5	31	CC
Panatela	Murray Hill No. 7	6	38	CC
Lonsdale	Butterfield No. 8	6½	42	CC
Grand Corona	Trafalgar No. 4	6	47	CC
Double Corona	Oxford No. 5	7	49	CC
Lonsdale	Carpe Diem	6¾	43	CC
	Landmark Selection, made in the Dominican Republic:			
Panatela	Metropole	6	34	CM
Corona	Hampshire	5½	42	CM
Lonsdale	Algonquin	6¾	43	CM
Grand Corona	Vanderbilt	6	47	CM

HANDMADE CIGARS: BRAND LISTINGS

Double Corona	Dakota	7½	49	CM
	Manhattan Selection, made in the Dominican Republic:			
Cigarillo	Beekman	5¼	28	CM
Slim Panatela	Tribeca	6	31	CM
Panatela	Chelsea	6½	38	CM
Lonsdale	Gramercy	6¾	43	CM
Robusto	Sutton	5½	49	CM
	Gotham Selection, made in the Dominican Republic:			
Slim Panatela	No. 65	6	32	CC
Long Corona	No. 1400	6¼	44	CC
Toro	No. 711	6	50	CC
Double Corona	No. 500	7	50	CC
	VIP Selection, made in the Dominican Republic:			
Panatela	Zigfeld "Fancytale"	6¾	38	CC
Corona	Barnum (tubed)	5½	42	CC
Lonsdale	Morgan	7	42	CC
Robusto	Astor	4½	50	CC
Toro	Carnegie	6	48	CC
	City Desk Selection, made in the Dominican Republic:			
Long Corona	Gazette	6	42	Ma
Grand Corona	Dispatch	6½	46	Ma
Toro	Telegraph	6	50	Ma
Double Corona	Tribune	7½	50	Ma
	Host Selection, made in Honduras:			
Small Panatela	Hudson	4⅝	32	CM
Corona	Hamilton	5½	42	CM
Lonsdale	Hunter	6	43	CM
Grand Corona	Harrington	6	46	CM

HANDMADE CIGARS: BRAND LISTINGS

Robusto	Hobart	5	50	CM
Double Corona	Hampton	7	50	CM
Giant Corona	Halstead	8	40	CM
Pyramid	Hanover	5½	56	CM
Pyramid	Huron	4½	44	CM
	Metropolitan Selection, made in the Dominican Republic:			
Corona	Anglers	5½	43	CC
Pyramid	Nautical	7	48	CC
Toro	University	6	50	CC
Pyramid	Explorers	5½	56	CC
Pyramid	Metropolitan	7	60	CC
	LSN Selection, made in the Dominican Republic:			
Slim Panatela	A2	5	31	CC
Lonsdale	A4	6¾	43	CC
Robusto	A6	5½	49	CC
Double Corona	A8	7½	49	CC

Nat Sherman, "tobacconist to the world" for more than six decades offers enough variety in its series to keep the serious smoker trying new sizes and blends for several months. The Exchange Selection provides a mild, smooth and polished flavor thanks to its Connecticut wrapper; the Landmark Selection is more intensely flavorful and full-bodied due to its Cameroon wrapper; the Manhattan Selection is a lean and racy blend of medium body and a nut-like flavor, finished with a soft, light-tasting Mexican wrapper; the Gotham Selection is the most delicate and mild of the group, finished in a mellow Connecticut wrapper; the VIP Selection offers a rich, crisp aroma along with buttery smoothness in the draw and mild taste; the City Desk Selection uses a dark maduro wrapper to give a full, hearty flavor, but without harshness; and the Host Selection matches a sweet Connecticut wrapper with Cuban-seed filler and binders to provide a solid flavor of medium strength, a rustic aroma and hints of woods and fruit.

New selections include the Metropolitan (introduced in 1995), which offers a medium-to-full-bodied smoke and three shaped sizes, and the LSN Selection (1996), which is also medium-to-full in body, but more spicy.

HANDMADE CIGARS: BRAND LISTINGS

NESTOR 747
Handmade in Danli, Honduras.

Wrapper: Honduras   *Binder: Nicaragua*   *Filler: Honduras, Nicaragua*

Shape	Name	Lgth	Ring	Wrapper
Churchill	747	7⅝	47	CM

This is a full-bodied cigar, developed in 1994, which salutes Nestor Plasencia, one of the world's most prolific cigar makers. His factories in Honduras produce dozens of outstanding brands, including this one, to which he put his name. The 747 is box-pressed, produced in limited quantities, and the plain cedar box understates the quality of the product it presents.

NESTOR 747 SERIES II
Handmade in Danli, Honduras.

Wrapper: Ecuador   *Binder: Honduras*   *Filler: Honduras, Nicaragua*

Shape	Name	Lgth	Ring	Wrapper
Robusto	454	4¾	54	CM-Ma
Toro	654	6	54	CM
Churchill	747	7⅝	47	CM

The second generation of the Nester 747 is the three-shape Series II line, also a full-bodied cigar. However, this group uses 1989-vintage leaves and is presented in its original rounded shape in cedar cabinets of 50 cigars each. Each completed bunch of 50, tied with a silk ribbon, is aged for nine months after rolling to ensure that the aromas and flavors of the bunch have penetrated each of the cigars.

NEW YORK, NEW YORK
BY TE-AMO
Handmade in San Andres Tuxtula, Mexico.

Wrapper: Mexico   *Binder: Mexico*   *Filler: Mexico*

Shape	Name	Lgth	Ring	Wrapper
Lonsdale	Park Avenue	6⅝	42	CC
Corona	Fifth Avenue	5½	44	CC
Grand Corona	7th Avenue	6½	46	CC

HANDMADE CIGARS: BRAND LISTINGS

Churchill	Broadway	7¼	48	CC
Toro	Wall Street	6	52	CC
Robusto	La Guardia	5	54	CC

A cigar salute to the Big Apple! Given the widespread popularity of Te-Amo in New York — just look at the number of "Te-Amo" signs above newsstands and tobacco shops — it's little wonder that this specially-blended and banded brand was introduced. Medium in body, these cigars are offered in boxes of 25.

NICARAGUA ESPECIAL
Handmade in Ocotal, Nicaragua.

Wrapper: Ecuador   *Binder: Nicaragua*   *Filler: Nicaragua*

Shape	Name	Lgth	Ring	Wrapper
Panatela	No. 1 Linda	5½	38	CC
Long Corona	No. 2 Super Cetro	6	44	CC
Toro	No. 3 Matador	6	50	CC
Double Corona	No. 4 Presidente	7⅜	50	CC
Giant	No. 5 Viajante	8½	52	CC

An excellent buy in a handmade, medium-bodied cigar, the Nicaragua Especial debuted in 1992 and offers high-quality construction in a bundle of 25 cigars, in which each cigar is individually wrapped for maximum protection and freshness.

NORDING
Handmade in Danli, Honduras.

Wrapper: USA/Connecticut   *Binder: Nicaragua*   *Filler: Dom. Rep., Nicaragua*

Shape	Name	Lgth	Ring	Wrapper
Toro	Corona Grande	6	50	CC
Double Corona	Presidente	7½	52	CC
Lonsdale	Lonsdale	6¾	43	CC
Corona	Corona	5½	43	CC
Robusto	Robusto	4¾	52	CC

HANDMADE CIGARS: BRAND LISTINGS

One of Denmark's most distinguished craftsmen, Erik Nording has created cigars of expert manufacture, using Cuban-seed Dominican and Nicaraguan filler, Nicaraguan binder and a Connecticut wrapper. The result is a medium-bodied smoke that was introduced in 1995, packed with a unique humidification system designed by Nording himself.

OCHO RIOS
Handmade in Kingston, Jamaica.

Wrapper: Ecuador	Binder: Dom. Rep.			Filler: Dom. Rep., Jamaica
Shape	Name	Lgth	Ring	Wrapper
Double Corona	President	7	50	CC
Toro	Toro	6	50	CC
Giant	Viajante	8¼	52	CC
Petit Corona	No. 4	5	42	CC
Lonsdale	No. 1	7	43	CC

Originated in 1955, this is a handmade Jamaican cigar of mild body and all long-filler tobaccos, offered in bundles of 25.

OFF COLORS
Handmade in Cofradia, Honduras.

Wrapper: Honduras	Binder: Honduras			Filler: Honduras
Shape	Name	Lgth	Ring	Wrapper
Lonsdale	No. 1	6½	43	CM
Corona	No. 10	5½	43	CM
Panatela	No. 15	5½	38	CM
Cigarillo	No. 32	5⅜	28	CM
Robusto	No. 37	4½	50	CM
Robusto	No. 37-L	5	50	CM
Corona	No. 38	5	43	CM
Giant Corona	No. 42	8¼	42	CM
Double Corona	No. 59	7¼	54	CM
Grand Corona	No. 60	6¼	45	CM

Toro	No. 61	6⅛	50	CM
Grand Corona	No. 62	5⅝	47	CM
Churchill	No. 63	7¼	46	CM
Panatela	No. 65	6⅞	36	CM
Panatela	No. 67	6⅞	39	CM
Lonsdale	No. 68	7	43	CM
Churchill	No. 70	6¾	48	CM
Corona	No. 75	5¼	44	CM
Giant	No. 80	8½	52	CM
Long Corona	No. 88	6	42	CM
Corona	Fuma Corta	5½	44	CM
Grand Corona	Fuma Larga	6½	45	CM

This a medium-bodied cigar, with limited availability. But they are all handmade, with long-filler tobacco, and priced to be an unbeatable value in bundles of 25.

OH QUE BUENO
Handmade in Las Palmas, the Canary Islands of Spain.
Wrapper: USA/Connecticut   Binder: Indonesia   Filler: Brazil, Dom.Rep.

Shape	Name	Lgth	Ring	Wrapper
Lonsdale	No. 1	7	41	CC
Corona	Corona	5¼	41	CC

Very well constructed, this brand blends tobaccos of four nations to produce a medium-bodied smoke, offered in boxes of 25 cigars each.

OLIVEROS
Handmade in Santiago, Dominican Republic.
Wrapper: Dominican Republic, Indonesia/Java, USA/Connecticut
Binder: Dom. Rep.   Filler: Dom. Rep.

Shape	Name	Lgth	Ring	Wrapper
Giant	Presidente	8	50	CC-Ma

HANDMADE CIGARS: BRAND LISTINGS

Toro	Maestro	6½	50	CC-Ma
Double Corona	Coronel	7	50	CC-Ma
Toro	Toro	5¾	50	CC-Ma
Lonsdale	Dos Perez	6¾	42	CC-Ma
Corona	Reyes	5½	42	CC-Ma

Oliveros cigars have been produced in one form or another since 1927. The current edition offers either a natural wrapper – using Connecticut or Javan leaves – or a maduro wrapper using Dominican tobacco. The natural-wrapped cigars are mild-to-medium in body, while the maduro wrapper offers a full-bodied taste.

OLOR
Handmade in Santiago, Dominican Republic.

Wrapper: USA/Connecticut   Binder: Dom. Rep.   Filler: Dom. Rep.

Shape	Name	Lgth	Ring	Wrapper
Double Corona	Cacique	7⅝	54	CC-Ma
Robusto	Rothschild	4½	50	CC-Ma
Corona	Momento	5½	43	CC-Ma
Toro	Paco	6	50	Cl-CC-Ma
Lonsdale	Lonsdale	6½	42	CC-Ma
Churchill	Colossus	7¼	48	CC-Ma
Short Panatela	Pronto	4	38	CC

This brand is now in national distribution and has won new friends among many cigar enthusiasts. Individually cellophaned and packed in slide-top cedar cabinets, these cigars are an excellent value and a smooth, medium-bodied smoke.

ONYX
Handmade in La Romana, Dominican Republic.

Wrapper: Mexico   Binder: Indonesia/Java   Filler: Dom. Rep., Mexico

Shape	Name	Lgth	Ring	Wrapper
Long Corona	No. 642	6	42	Ma

HANDMADE CIGARS: BRAND LISTINGS

Grand Corona	No. 646	6⅝	46	Ma
Toro	No. 650	6	50	Ma
Double Corona	No. 750	7½	50	Ma
Giant	No. 852	8	52	Ma

This all-maduro series debuted in 1992 and is hand crafted from the finest tobaccos to be the best in their class. The filler is a Dominican blend of Piloto Cubano and Olor, with some Mexican leaf. A Java leaf is used for the binder, then the cigar is finished with a dark Mexican maduro leaf. The taste is mild, with a pleasant spicy note.

OPUS X
Handmade in Santiago, Dominican Republic.
Wrapper: Dom. Rep.　　*Binder: Dom. Rep.*　　*Filler: Dom. Rep.*

Shape	Name	Lgth	Ring	Wrapper
Toro	Perfecxion No. 2	6⅛	52	CM
Double Corona	Double Corona	7⅝	49	CM
Grand Corona	Fuente Fuente	5⅝	46	CM
Churchill	Reserva d'Chateau	7	48	CM
Petit Corona	Perfecxion No. 8	4⅞	40	CM
Panatela	Petite Lancero	6¼	39	CM
Robusto	Robusto	5¼	50	CM
Lonsdale	No. 1	6½	42	CM
Giant	A	9¼	47	CM

This full-bodied brand was introduced in 1996 and is scarely available anywhere. A new project from the Tabacalera A. Fuente y Cia., this brand features all-Dominican tobacco, including the new wrapper leaf grown on the Fuente's own farm.

ORIENT EXPRESS
Handmade in Danli, Honduras.
Wrapper: Ecuador　　*Binder: Dom. Rep.*　　*Filler: Mexico, Nicaragua*

ONYX
The Gem of Maduro

The most precious

maduro cigars.

Handcrafted

in the Dominican

Republic from

the finest tobaccos

to be the best

in their class.

HANDMADE CIGARS: BRAND LISTINGS

Shape	Name	Lgth	Ring	Wrapper
Long Panatela	Le Twist 2	8	38	CM
Panatela	No. 2407	6⅞	36	CM
Lonsdale	No. 2418	6⅝	44	CM
Toro	Expresso	6	48	CM
Robusto	No. 2406	5	50	CM
Petit Corona	No. 2414	4	40	CM
Corona	No. 2415	5½	44	CM
Long Corona	Le Twist	6	40	CM
Double Corona	No. 2410	6⅞	49	CM
Double Corona	Le Club	7¾	50	CM

This brand debuted in 1994 and offers the exquisite pleasure of aged filler tobaccos in a mild, slightly aromatic cigar. Please note the unfinished, pigtail heads on the two Le Twist sizes. The quality of the construction extends to the boxes, which are made of cedar and offer 10 or 25 cigars each.

ORNELAS
Handmade in San Andres Tuxtula, Mexico.

Wrapper: Mexico   Binder: Mexico   Filler: Mexico

Shape	Name	Lgth	Ring	Wrapper
Long Corona	LTD al Cognac	6¼	42	Ma
Lonsdale	Ornelas No. 1	6¾	44	CC
Long Corona	Ornelas No. 2	6	44	CC
Long Panatela	Ornelas No. 3	7	38	CC
Petit Corona	Ornelas No. 4	5	44	CC
Panatela	Ornelas No. 5	6	38	CC
Short Panatela	Ornelas No. 6	5	38	CC
Double Corona	Churchill	7	49	CC-Ma
Robusto	Robusto	4¾	49	CC-Ma
Grand Corona	Cafetero Grande	6½	46	Ma

HANDMADE CIGARS: BRAND LISTINGS

Corona Extra	Cafetero Chico	5½	46	Ma
Slim Panatela	Matinee	6	30	CC
Small Panatela	Matinee Lights	4¾	30	CC
Slim Panatela	ABC Extra	7	30	CC
Giant	250 mm	9½	64	CC
Lonsdale	Ornelas No. 1 Vanilla	6¾	44	CC
Long Corona	Ornelas No. 2 Vanilla	6	44	CC
Long Panatela	Ornelas No. 3 Vanilla	7	38	CC
Petit Corona	Ornelas No. 4 Vanilla	5	44	CC
Panatela	Ornelas No. 5 Vanilla	6	38	CC
Short Panatela	Ornelas No. 6 Vanilla	5	38	CC
Slim Panatela	Matinee Vanilla	6	30	CC
Small Panatela	Matinee Lights Vanilla	4¾	30	CC

Re-introduced in 1995, the Ornelas line continues a 60-year tradition. Each of these handmade cigars is a mild Mexico "puro" with special shapes such as the LTD al Cognac line, featuring cognac-treated wrappers and the eight shapes of vanilla-treated cigars, plus the huge "250," one of the largest cigars available anywhere.

ORO NEGRO
Handmade in Santa Rosa de Copan, Honduras.
Wrapper: Honduras   *Binder: Honduras*   *Filler: Honduras*

Shape	Name	Lgth	Ring	Wrapper
Double Corona	Double Corona	7¾	50	Ma
Double Corona	Churchill	7	50	Ma
Long Corona	No. II	6¼	44	Ma
Corona Extra	Corona Sublime	5½	46	Ma
Torpedo	Antonius	5	54	Ma
Robusto	Rothschild	4¾	50	Ma

HANDMADE CIGARS: BRAND LISTINGS

Here is a new cigar for 1996, wrapped in a superb Honduran maduro wrapper, around a blend of all-Honduran-grown tobaccos. This is a medium-bodied smoke, available in all-cedar boxes of 25, with each cigar protected in an individual cellophane sleeve.

OROSI
Handmade in Condega, Nicaragua.

Wrapper: Nicaragua   Binder: Nicaragua   Filler: Nicaragua

Shape	Name	Lgth	Ring	Wrapper
Double Corona	Oro 700	7	49	CC
Long Corona	Oro 600	6¼	44	CC
Toro	Oro 650	6	50	CC
Corona	Oro 500	5½	42	CC
Robusto	Oro 550	5	50	CC

This brand debuted in 1996, offering a medium-bodied taste. The blend features a Connecticut-seed, Nicaraguan-grown wrapper and is offered in individual cellophane sleeves inside all-cedar boxes of 25.

OSCAR
Handmade in Santiago, Dominican Republic.

Wrapper: USA/Connecticut   Binder: Dom. Rep.   Filler: Dom. Rep.

Shape	Name	Lgth	Ring	Wrapper
Cigarillo	Oscarito	4	20	CC
Short Panatela	Prince	5	30	CC
Long Panatela	No. 100	7	38	CC
Lonsdale	No. 200	7	44	CC
Long Corona	No. 300	6¼	44	CC
Panatela	No. 400	6	38	CC
Robusto	No. 500	5½	50	CC
Robusto	No. 600	4½	50	CC
Pyramid	No. 700	7	54	CC
Petit Corona	No. 800	4	42	CC

HANDMADE CIGARS: BRAND LISTINGS

| Giant | Supreme | 8 | 48 | CC |
| Giant | Don Oscar | 9 | 46 | CC |

Introduced in October 1988, the Oscar is medium to full-bodied, offering a rich bouquet. The experience is mouth-filling with its smooth draw and the luxurious indulgence of the taste of the Dominican blend with a flawless Connecticut wrapper. Produced by only the most experienced artisans, Oscars are packed uncellophaned in cedar cabinets. A maduro-wrapped version is coming soon!

PADRON
Handmade in Danli, Honduras and Esteli, Nicaragua.
Wrapper: Nicaragua　　　*Binder: Nicaragua*　　　*Filler: Nicaragua*

Shape	Name	Lgth	Ring	Wrapper
Giant	Magnum	9	50	Cl-CM-Ma
Giant Corona	Grand Reserve	8	41	Cl-CM-Ma
Double Corona	Executive	7½	50	Cl-CM-Ma
Churchill	Churchill	6⅞	46	Cl-CM-Ma
Lonsdale	Ambassador	6⅞	42	Cl-CM-Ma
Panatela	Panatela	6⅞	36	Cl-CM-Ma
Long Corona	Palmas	6¼	42	Cl-CM-Ma
Corona	Londres	5½	42	Cl-CM-Ma
Panatela	Chicos	5½	36	Cl-CM-Ma
Corona Extra	Delicias	4⅞	46	Cl-CM-Ma
Robusto	2000	5	50	Cl-CM-Ma
Robusto	3000	5½	52	Cl-CM-Ma
	30th Anniversary Series:			
Double Corona	Diplomatico	7	50	CM
Pyramid	Pyramide	6⅞	52	CM
Robusto	Exclusivo	5½	50	CM
Grand Corona	Monarca	6½	46	CM
Lonsdale	Superior	6½	42	CM

Long Corona	Corona	6	42	CM

The Padron family began manufacturing cigars by hand in Miami in 1964, using the experience of their Cuban forefathers, who began making cigars in 1853. Only Cuban-seed tobaccos are used in the manufacture of this medium-to-full-bodied range from all Nicaraguan tobaccos in factories in Honduras and Nicaragua. The 30th Anniversary Series was introduced to considerable acclaim in 1994.

PANTERA
Handmade, with short filler, in Santiago, Dominican Republic.
Wrapper: Dom. Rep.   *Binder: Dom. Rep.*   *Filler: Dom. Rep.*

Shape	Name	Lgth	Ring	Wrapper
Robusto	No. 10	5½	50	CC
Corona Extra	No. 20	5½	46	CC
Corona	No. 30	5½	42	CC
Panatela	No. 40	5½	38	CC

This handmade brand is mild in taste and offered in economical bundles of 25 cigars each.

PAPAYO
Handmade in the Dominican Republic.
(The distributor declined to provide any information about the origins of the tobaccos used in this brand.)

Shape	Name	Lgth	Ring	Wrapper
Churchill	No. 1 Churchill	6¾	46	CC
Panatela	No. 3 Brevas	6	38	CC
Corona	No. 4 Corona	5½	42	CC
Toro	No. 5 Toro	6	50	CC

This is a new brand from the Dominican Republic. Expected to be mild in strength, it is offered in pine boxes of 25.

Presenting 20 Ways To Smoke a Cuban Cigar.

If you're looking for nirvana, you won't find it in Havana.

Once upon a time, you could. As a child growing up in the village of Pinar del Rio,
Jose Padron learned to cultivate, cure, smoke and hand roll cigars. It was his family's heritage.
Lovingly passed down from his father and grandfather – and now to his own children and grandchildren.

When he left Cuba in 1964, Jose brought his family, his traditions, his tobacco seed.
The mythical smoke of Havana is a fading memory. But not to the Padrons.

Any one of these Padron Cigars from Nicaragua will blow the old notion of Cuban superiority right out the window.
No wonder it's the premium cigar of choice among more Cubans living in Miami.

Once you've had a taste of Padron, you'll never dream of Cuba again.

HANDMADE CIGARS: BRAND LISTINGS

PARTAGAS
Handmade in Santiago, Dominican Republic.

Wrapper: Cameroon   Binder: Mexico   Filler: Dom. Rep., Mexico

Shape	Name		Lgth	Ring	Wrapper
Torpedo	Aristocrat		6	50	CM
Double Corona	Anniversario		7	52	CM
Long Panatela	No. 9		9	38	CM
Small Panatela	Puritos		4⅛	32	CM
Cigarillo	No. 5		5¼	28	CM
Panatela	No. 6		6	34	CM
Short Panatela	No. 4		5	38	CM
Corona	No. 3		5¼	43	CM
Robusto	Robusto		4½	49	CM
Corona	No. 2		5¾	43	CM
Robusto	Naturales		5½	50	CM
Grand Corona	Maduro		6¼	48	Ma
Lonsdale	No. 1		6¾	43	CM
Long Corona	Sabroso	*(tubed)*	5⅞	44	CM
Slim Panatela	Tubos	*(tubed)*	7	34	CM
Lonsdale	Humitube	*(tubed)*	6¾	43	CM
Grand Corona	Almirantes		6¼	47	CM
Lonsdale	8-9-8		6⅞	44	CM
Double Corona	No. 10		7½	49	CM
	Limited Reserve series:				
Lonsdale	Royale		6¾	43	CM
Grand Corona	Regale		6¼	47	CM
Robusto	Robusto		5½	49	CM
Short Panatela	Epicure		5	38	CM

HANDMADE CIGARS: BRAND LISTINGS

	150 Signature Series:			
Double Corona	AA	7½	49	CM
Lonsdale	A	6¾	43	CM
Grand Corona	B	6½	47	CM
Robusto	C	5½	49	CM
Short Panatela	D	5	38	CM
Toro	Figurado	6	50	CM
Robusto	Robusto	4½	49	CM
Double Corona	Don Ramon	7	52	CM

This famous brand, originated in 1845, continues to use only the highest quality Cameroon wrappers, which combined with tobaccos from the Dominican Republic, Jamaica and Mexico, gives it a spicy, full flavor. In a salute to the brand's 150th anniversary, the limited edition 150th Signature Series debuted in late 1995. Wrapped in specially-cured, 18-year-old Cameroon tobaccos, these cigars are aged an additional four months and presented in unique, vanished cedar boxes of 25, 50 or 100 cigars.

PARTICULARES
Handmade in Danli, Honduras.

Wrapper: Ecuador   Binder: Honduras   Filler: Dom. Rep., Honduras

Shape	Name	Lgth	Ring	Wrapper
Slim Panatela	Petit	5⅛	34	CC
Corona	No. 4	5½	42	CC
Panatela	Panatelas	6⅞	35	CC
Long Corona	Royal Coronas	6¼	43	CC
Robusto	Rothschild	5	50	CC-Ma
Lonsdale	Supremos	7	43	CC
Toro	Matador	6	50	CC-Ma
Churchill	Churchills	6⅞	49	CC
Double Corona	Presidentes	7¾	50	CC
Giant	Viajantes	8½	52	CC-Ma

HANDMADE CIGARS: BRAND LISTINGS

Giant	Executive	8½	52	CC

Introduced in the 1980s, the Particulares is made in Honduras, using a filler predominantly from Honduras blended with tobacco from the Dominican Republic. The binder is Havana-seed, grown in Honduras, and the wrapper is from Ecuador. This is considered a mild cigar in strength.

PAUL GARMIRIAN
Handmade in Santiago, Dominican Republic.

Wrapper: USA/Connecticut *Binder: Dom. Rep.* *Filler: Dom. Rep.*

Shape	Name	Lgth	Ring	Wrapper
Giant	P.G. Celebration	9	50	CC
Double Corona	P.G. Double Corona	7⅝	50	CC
Torpedo	P.G. Belicoso	6¼	52	CC
Churchill	P.G. Churchill	7	48	CC
Long Panatela	P.G. No. 1	7½	38	CC
Grand Corona	P.G. Corona Grande	6½	46	CC
Torpedo	P.G. Belicoso Fino	5½	52	CC
Lonsdale	P.G. Lonsdale	6½	42	CC
Toro	P.G. Connoisseur	6	50	CC
Robusto	P.G. Epicure	5½	50	CC
Robusto	P.G. Robusto	5	50	CC
Robusto	P.G. No. 2	4¾	48	CC
Corona	P.G. Corona	5½	42	CC
Petit Corona	P.G. Petit Corona	5	43	CC
Short Panatela	P.G. Petit Bouquet	4½	38	CC
Petit Corona	P.G. No. 5	4	40	CC
Petit Corona	P.G. Bombones	3½	43	CC
Panatela	P.G. Especial	5¾	38	CC

''Smooth, subtle, spicy and delicious.'' That's the response of many smokers who were delighted to enjoy a Dominican-produced cigar which has so many attributes of a high-quality Havana. The charcteristics of the P.G. line include a scarce and richly-flavored medium to dark reddish-brown Colorado-colored Connecticut Shade wrappers which are the favorite of many connoisseurs. The new Especial shape is specially configured to be of interest to women smokers.

PETER STOKKEBYE
Handmade in Santiago, Dominican Republic.

Wrapper: USA/Connecticut   *Binder: Proprietary*   *Filler: Dom. Rep.*

Shape	Name	Lgth	Ring	Wrapper
Double Corona	Santa Maria No. 1	7	50	CC
Panatela	Santa Maria No. 2	6¾	38	CC
Corona	Santa Maria No. 3	5½	43	CC

The famous Stokkebye family is now in its eighth generation in the tobacco trade. They were once one of the appointed cigar rollers to Winston Churchill! Their cigars, introduced in 1987, are blended with a delicate balance to simultaneously provide a mild and flavorful smoke.

PETERSON HALLMARK
Handmade in Santiago, Dominican Republic.

Wrapper: USA/Connecticut   *Binder: Ecuador*   *Filler: Dom. Rep.*

Shape	Name		Lgth	Ring	Wrapper
Double Corona	Presidente		7½	50	CI
Churchill	Churchill	(tubed)	7	48	CI
Toro	Toro	(tubed)	6	50	CI
Corona	Corona	(tubed)	5¾	43	CI
Petit Corona	Petite Corona	(tubed)	5	43	CI
Robusto	Robusto	(tubed)	4¾	50	CI
Short Panatela	Tres Petite Corona		4½	38	CI

Famous for pipes for more than 100 years, the Peterson Hallmark Collection brings a mild-to-medium-bodied taste to this range. The initial Peterson of Dublin range, introduced in 1995, includes seven shapes, made from specially-selected leaf in the Dominican Republic. Peterson has also introduced an exquisite line of cigar accessories to complement its cigars.

HANDMADE CIGARS: BRAND LISTINGS

PETRUS
Handmade in Santa Rosa de Copan, Honduras.

Wrapper: Ecuador   *Binder: Honduras*   *Filler: Honduras*

Shape	Name	Lgth	Ring	Wrapper
Double Corona	Double Corona	7¾	50	CC
Long Panatela	Lord Byron	8	38	CC
Double Corona	Churchill	7	50	CC
Long Corona	No. II	6¼	44	DC-CC
Toro	No. III	6	50	CC
Panatela	Palma Fina	6	38	CC
Panatela	No. IV	5⅝	38	CC
Corona Extra	Corona Sublime	5½	46	CC
Torpedo	Antonius	5	52	CC
Petit Corona	Gregorius	5	42	CC
Robusto	Rothschild	4¾	50	CC
Short Panatela	Chantaco	4¾	35	CC
Small Panatela	Duchess	4½	30	CC

This outstanding line, which debuted in 1989, adds a new panatela shape for 1997 and a double claro wrapper for the No. II size. These natural-wrapped cigars showcase Ecuadorian-grown leaf. Petrus is a mild-to-medium-bodied cigar with dense, spicy aromas and rich flavors.

PETRUS ETIQUETTE ROUGE
Handmade in Danli, Honduras.

Wrapper: Ecuador   *Binder: Honduras*   *Filler: Dom.Rep., Nicaragua*

Shape	Name	Lgth	Ring	Wrapper
Churchill	RCH 1	7	48	CC
Torpedo	RB 1	7	55	CC
Corona	RCR 1	5¾	44	CC
Robusto	RR 1	5	52	CC

HANDMADE CIGARS: BRAND LISTINGS

Here is a superior cigar, made in a limited production of 2,000 boxes per shape. Packed in exquisite Caoba wood boxes of 20 cigars, this is a medium-bodied, rich blend created to satisfy the most demanding cigar enthusiast.

PHEASANT
Handmade in Danli, Honduras.

Wrapper: USA/Connecticut   *Binder: Honduras*
Filler: Costa Rica, Honduras, Nicaragua

Shape	Name	Lgth	Ring	Wrapper
Double Corona	Churchill	7½	50	CC
Toro	Toro	6	50	CC
Robusto	Robusto	5¼	54	CC
Lonsdale	Corona	6½	42	CC

Here is a medium-bodied brand which was introduced in 1996 and complements the outstanding line of Spanish leather cigar and smoking accessories. Each of these styles is offered in elegant boxes of 25.

PHILLIPS & KING GUARDSMEN
Handmade in La Romana, Dominican Republic.

Wrapper: Indonesia/Java   *Binder: Dominican Republic*
Filler: Brazil, Dominican Republic, Mexico

Shape	Name	Lgth	Ring	Wrapper
Giant	No. 1	8	52	CM
Double Corona	No. 2	7½	50	CM
Toro	No. 3	6	50	CM
Robusto	No. 4	4¾	50	CM
Churchill	No. 5	7	48	CM
Corona	No. 6	5½	44	CM
Long Corona	No. 7	6	42	CM
Panatela	No. 8	6	36	CM

The Guardsmen series is the flagship of the famous cigar distribution firm of Phillips & King of Industry, California. It is mild in body, individually wrapped and offered in boxes of 25 cigars each.

HANDMADE CIGARS: BRAND LISTINGS

PINNACLE
Handmade in Santiago, Dominican Republic.

Wrapper: Indonesia   *Binder: Dom. Rep.*   *Filler: Dom. Rep.*

Shape	Name	Lgth	Ring	Wrapper
Churchill	Imperial Corona	6¾	46	CC
Robusto	Robusto	5	50	CC
Toro	Corona Gorda	6	50	CC

This is a new brand from the Dominican Republic, introduced in 1996. The medium-bodied taste is complemented by the unusual packaging: each cigar is banded, then presented in individual foil sleeves, which also bear the brand's band. The finished product is sold in elegant, all-cedar boxes of 25.

PLAYBOY
BY DON DIEGO
Handmade in La Romana, Dominican Republic.

Wrapper: USA/Connecticut   *Binder: Dom. Rep.*   *Filler: Dom. Rep.*

Shape	Name	Lgth	Ring	Wrapper
Double Corona	Churchill	7¾	50	CC
Toro	Double Corona	6	52	CC
Churchill	Gran Corona	6¾	48	CC
Robusto	Robusto	5	50	CC
Lonsdale	Lonsdale	6½	42	CC

Here is the long-awaited cigar, debuting in 1996, named for the famous magazine and entertainment company, produced in cooperation with Consolidated Cigar Company in its La Romana factory. The blend is medium in body and features a darker shade of Connecticut wrapper and the cigars are presented in elegant wooden box.

PLEIADES
Handmade in Santiago, Dominican Republic.

Wrapper: USA/Connecticut   *Binder: Dom. Rep.*   *Filler: Dom. Rep.*

Shape	Name	Lgth	Ring	Wrapper
Giant	Aldebaran	8½	50	CC

Giant	Saturne	8	46	CC
Giant Corona	Neptune	7½	42	CC
Churchill	Sirius	6⅞	46	CC-Ma
Corona	Centaurus	5¾	42	DC
Corona	Orion	5¾	42	CC
Panatela	Uranus	6⅞	34	CC
Corona	Antares	5½	40	CC
Robusto	Pluton	5	50	CC-Ma
Small Panatela	Perseus	5	34	CC
Cigarillo	Venus	5½	28	CC
Cigarillo	Mars	5	28	CC
	Machine-made:			
Cigarillo	Mini	3½	24	CC

Pleiades are exquisite cigars, imported from the Dominican Republic. They are created by hand, using only the finest long-leaf filler and smooth Connecticut Shade wrappers. Depending on the selection from the 12 available shapes, the richness, quality of taste and aroma will vary from mild and light to a bold, full-bodied flavor. The unusual packaging includes not only an all-cedar box, but each is equipped with a mini-humidifier to keep the cigars in perfect condition!

POR LARRAÑAGA
Handmade in La Romana, Dominican Republic.

Wrapper: USA/Connecticut   Binder: Dom. Rep.   Filler: Dom. Rep.

Shape	Name	Lgth	Ring	Wrapper
Lonsdale	Cetros	6⅞	42	CC
Panatela	Delicados	6½	36	CC
Double Corona	Fabulosos	7	50	CC
Corona	Nacionales	5½	42	CC
Short Panatela	Petit Cetro	5	38	CC
Pyramid	Pyramides	6	50	CC
Robusto	Robusto	5	50	CC

HANDMADE CIGARS: BRAND LISTINGS

This is an ancient brand, which first saw production in Cuba in 1834! Today's Dominican version is very mild and limited in production. It is generally available only to tobacconists who are members of the Tobacconists' Association of America (TAA).

POR MATAMOR
Handmade in Santiago, Dominican Republic.
Wrapper: USA/Connecticut   *Binder: Dom. Rep.*   *Filler: Dom. Rep.*

Shape	Name	Lgth	Ring	Wrapper
Double Corona	DJB	7	50	CC
Robusto	Amistad	4½	50	CC
Long Corona	Esperanza	6	43	CC
Toro	MQ	6	50	CC

Here is a new, limited production brand for 1996, introduced for the benefit of a discriminating few who appreciate a medium-bodied cigar with excellent construction. Por Matamor cigars are packed in all-cedar boxes of 25.

PORFIRIO
Handmade in Santiago, Dominican Republic.
Wrapper: USA/Connecticut   *Binder: Dom. Rep.*   *Filler: Dom. Rep.*

Shape	Name	Lgth	Ring	Wrapper
Corona	Coronas	5½	42	CC
Lonsdale	Lonsdale	6½	42	CC
Robusto	Robusto	5	50	CC
Double Corona	Churchill	7½	50	CC
Giant	Rubi	8½	52	CC

This is a new brand for 1996, with a mild body and an elegant Connecticut Shade wrapper surrounding Dominican tobaccos. Each cigar is presented in an individual cellophane sleeve and Porfirios are available in cedar cabinets of 25 cigars.

P L É I A D E S

HAND-ROLLED TO MEET THE HIGHEST EXPECTATIONS
OF CONNOISSEURS. MADE FROM THE CHOICEST LEAF
AND LONG FILLER IN THE DOMINICAN REPUBLIC.
THEY ARE HAND SELECTED FOR WRAPPER COLOR
AND PACKED IN FLAVOR-ENHANCING CEDAR BOXES.

Imported by Swisher International, Inc.

HANDMADE CIGARS: BRAND LISTINGS

PORTO BELLO
Handmade in Santiago, Dominican Republic.

Wrapper: USA/Connecticut *Binder: Mexico* *Filler: Dom. Rep., Honduras*

Shape	Name	Lgth	Ring	Wrapper
Giant	No. 1	8½	52	CC
Double Corona	No. 2	7½	50	CC
Churchill	No. 3	6⅞	46	CC
Toro	No. 4	6	50	CC
Lonsdale	No. 5	6¾	42	CC
Long Panatela	No. 6	7½	38	CC
Long Panatela	No. 7	7	36	CC
Corona	No. 8	5¾	42	CC
Robusto	No. 9	5	50	CC
Pyramid	Piramide	7	54	CC

Created in 1988, this is an economical, bundled brand which offers a mild taste in a handmade, all long-filler cigar – including a genuine Connecticut Shade wrapper!

PRIDE OF COPAN
Handmade in Honduras.

Wrapper: USA/Connecticut *Binder: Honduras* *Filler: Honduras*

Shape	Name	Lgth	Ring	Wrapper
Double Corona	Pride of Copan No. 1	6¾	50	CC
Long Corona	Pride of Copan No. 2	6	44	CC
Short Panatela	Pride of Copan No. 3	5⅜	38	CC
Panatela	Pride of Copan No. 4	5⅞	35	CC
Slim Panatela	Pride of Copan No. 5	6¼	30	CC
Small Panatela	Pride of Copan No. 6	4¾	30	CC
Cigarillo	Pride of Copan No. 7	4⅛	25	CC

HANDMADE CIGARS: BRAND LISTINGS

A quality, medium-to-full-bodied cigar, with quality construction. That's the story of Pride of Copan, created for those who want quality, consistency and value.

PRIDE OF JAMAICA
Handmade in Kingston, Jamaica.

Wrapper: USA/Connecticut   *Binder: Mexico*
Filler: Dominican Republic, Jamaica, Mexico

Shape	Name	Lgth	Ring	Wrapper
Double Corona	Churchill	7½	49	CC-Ma
Giant	Monarch	8	50	CC-Ma
Toro	Magnum	6	50	CC-Ma
Grand Corona	Petit Churchill	6	45	CC-Ma
Lonsdale	Lonsdale	6½	42	CC-Ma
Corona	Royal Corona	5½	42	CC-Ma
Panatela	President	6¾	38	CC-Ma

This famous brand continues to be created daily in Kingston, Jamaica and offered in boxes of 25 well-made, much-respected cigars. Connecticut Shade wrapper is used to help give the mild, rich flavor for which Pride of Jamaica is so well known.

PRIMERA DE NICARAGUA
Handmade in Ocotal, Nicaragua.

Wrapper: Nicaragua   *Binder: Honduras*   *Filler: Honduras, Nicaragua*

Shape	Name	Lgth	Ring	Wrapper
Lonsdale	No. 1	7	44	CM
Double Corona	Churchill	7	50	CM
Robusto	Rothschild	5	50	CM
Toro	Toro	6	50	CM
Giant	Viajante	8½	52	CM

Here is a mild-to-medium bodied cigar, produced from all long-filler tobaccos, introduced in 1990. This is one of the first brands to emerge after the civil unrest in Nicaragua and is presented in all-wood boxes of 25.

HANDMADE CIGARS: BRAND LISTINGS

PRIMO DEL CRISTO
Handmade in Danli, Honduras.

Wrapper: Honduras   *Binder: Honduras*   *Filler: Honduras*

Shape	Name	Lgth	Ring	Wrapper
Lonsdale	No. 1	6½	42	CC-Ma
Toro	Churchills	6½	50	CC-Ma
Corona	Coronas	5½	42	CC-Ma
Giant	Generals	8½	50	CC-Ma
Giant	Inmensos	8	54	CC
Long Panatela	Palmas Extra	7	36	CC
Long Panatela	Palmas Reales	8	36	CC
Petit Corona	Reyes	5	42	CC-Ma
Robusto	Rothschilds	5	50	CC-Ma
Toro	Toros	6	50	CC-Ma

These are well-made cigars that are offered in modestly-priced bundles of 25, with a medium-to-heavy body.

PRIMO DEL REY
Handmade in La Romana, Dominican Republic.

Wrapper: Indonesia   *Binder: Dom. Rep.*   *Filler: Dom. Rep.*

Shape	Name	Lgth	Ring	Wrapper
Robusto	No. 100	4½	50	CM
Giant	Aguilas	8	52	CM
Toro	Almirantes	6	50	CM-Ma
Long Corona	Cazadores	6	44	Ma
Lonsdale	Chavon	6½	41	CM
Toro	Churchill	6¼	48	CM
Slim Panatela	Panetela Extras	5⅞	34	CM
Slim Panatela	Panetelas	5⅝	34	CM
Lonsdale	Presidentes	6¾	44	CM-Ma

HANDMADE CIGARS: BRAND LISTINGS

Panatela	Reales	6⅛	36	CM
Lonsdale	Seleccion No. 1	6¾	42	CM
Long Corona	Seleccion No. 2	6¼	42	Cl-CM
Panatela	Seleccion No. 3	6¾	36	CM
Corona	Seleccion No. 4	5½	42	Cl-CM-Ma
Double Corona	Soberanos	7½	50	CM-Ma
	Machine-made, with short filler:			
Cigarillo	Cortos	4	28	CM

Primo del Rey are first-quality cigars first produced in 1961, offering a mild taste from a unique blend of leaves, notably including a Brazilian wrapper. An excellent value, the entire Primo del Rey series is very well constructed. Please note that some sizes are machine-bunched.

PRIMO DEL REY CLUB SELECTION
Handmade in La Romana, Dominican Republic.
Wrapper: USA/Connecticut   Binder: Dom. Rep.   Filler: Dom. Rep.

Shape	Name	Lgth	Ring	Wrapper
Long Corona	Nobles	6¼	44	CC
Churchill	Aristocrats	6¾	48	CC
Double Corona	Regals	7	50	CC
Giant	Barons	8½	52	CC

The Club Selection is a pleasant, mild smoke in four larger ring sizes for the experienced smoker. Offered in boxes of 25, the Connecticut Shade wrapper distinguishes this series from the standard Primo del Rey line.

PRIMO DEL REY GIFT PACK
Handmade in La Romana, Dominican Republic.
Wrapper: Indonesia   Binder: USA/Connecticut   Filler: Dom. Rep.

Shape	Name	Lgth	Ring	Wrapper
Lonsdale	Lonsdales	6½	42	CM-Ma
Grand Corona	Royal Corona	6	46	CM-Ma

| Double Corona | Soberanos | 7½ | 50 | CM-Ma |
| Giant | Aquilas | 8 | 52 | CM-Ma |

The third grouping of Primo del Rey combines tobaccos from three countries to produce a mild but distinctive taste. The packing is equally unique, as each size is offered only in 10-packs!

PRIVATE SELECTION
Handmade in Danli, Honduras.

Wrapper: Honduras *Binder: Honduras* *Filler: Honduras*

Shape	Name	Lgth	Ring	Wrapper
Giant	No. 100	8	50	CM
Robusto	No. 200	4¾	50	CM
Long Corona	No. 300	6¼	44	CM
Double Corona	No. 400	7¾	50	CM
Corona	No. 500	5⅝	42	CM
Long Corona	No. 600	6	42	CM

These cigars are new for 1996 and offer all long-filler tobacco combined with a natural wrapper for a medium-bodied taste.

PRIVATE STOCK
Handmade in Santiago, Dominican Republic.

Wrapper: USA/Connecticut *Binder: Dom. Rep.* *Filler: Dom. Rep.*

Shape	Name	Lgth	Ring	Wrapper
Double Corona	Private Stock No. 1	7¾	48	CC
Toro	Private Stock No. 2	6	48	CC
Slim Panatela	Private Stock No. 3	6½	33	CC
Panatela	Private Stock No. 4	5¾	38	CC
Corona	Private Stock No. 5	5¾	43	CC
Corona Extra	Private Stock No. 6	5¼	46	CC
Petit Corona	Private Stock No. 7	4¾	43	CC
Short Panatela	Private Stock No. 8	4⅝	35	CC

HANDMADE CIGARS: BRAND LISTINGS

Cigarillo	Private Stock No. 9	4⅝	26	CC
Petit Corona	Private Stock No. 10	4	40	CC
Robusto	Private Stock No. 11	4⅝	50	CC

These cigars are manufactured in one of the most exclusive factories in the world. High standards of quality make the Private Stock label an excellent value for cigars with a mild to medium body.

PROFESOR SILA
Handmade in Las Palmas, the Canary Islands of Spain.

Wrapper: USA/Connecticut   Binder: Canary Isl.   Filler: Canary Isl.

Shape	Name	Lgth	Ring	Wrapper
Robusto	Robusto	4⅝	50	CI
Corona Extra	Presidente	5⅝	45	CI
Long Panatela	Principe	7¼	38	CI
Grand Corona	Excellencia	6½	45	CI
Giant	Majestad	8	50	CI

This factory has been producing cigars since 1934 and, as practice makes perfect, are proud to present the new project for 1996, the Profesor Sila range. It is a light Connecticut wrapper and offers a mild-to-medium-bodied smoke in handy 5-packs or in boxes of 25.

PUNCH
Handmade in Cofradia, Honduras.

Wrapper: Ecuador, Indonesia/Sumatra   Binder: Honduras
Filler: Dominican Republic, Honduras, Nicaragua

Shape	Name	Lgth	Ring	Wrapper
Giant	Presidents	8½	52	DC-CM-Ma
Churchill	Double Coronas	6¾	48	DC-CM-Ma
Toro	Pitas	6⅛	50	DC-CM-Ma
Long Corona	Punch	6¼	44	DC-CM-Ma
Lonsdale	Lonsdales	6½	43	DC-CM-Ma
Robusto	Rothschilds	4½	50	DC-CM-Ma

HANDMADE CIGARS: BRAND LISTINGS

Churchill	Casa Grande		7¼	46	DC-CM-Ma
Corona	No. 75		5½	44	DC-CM-Ma
Long Corona	Amatistas		6¼	44	DC-CM-Ma
Slim Panatela	Largo Elegantes		7	32	DC-CM-Ma
Corona	Elites		5¼	44	DC-CM-Ma
Petit Corona	London Club		5	40	DC-CM-Ma
Lonsdale	After Dinner		7¼	45	DC-CM-Ma
Robusto	Super Rothschilds		5¼	50	DC-CM-Ma
Cigarillo	Slim Panatellas		4	28	DC-CM-Ma
Corona	Cafe Royal	*(tubed)*	5⅝	44	DC-CM-Ma
	Deluxe Series:				
Double Corona	Chateau "L"		7¼	54	DC-CM-Ma
Corona Extra	Chateau "M"		5¾	46	DC-CM-Ma
Grand Corona	Coronas		6¼	45	DC-CM-Ma
Corona	Royal Coronations	*(tubed)*	5¼	44	DC-CM-Ma
	Grand Cru Series:				
Toro	Britania		6¼	50	CM
Double Corona	Diademas		7¼	54	CC
Churchill	Monarcas	*(tubed)*	6¾	48	CM
Giant	Prince Consorts		8½	52	CM
Robusto	Robustos		5¼	50	CM-Ma
Robusto	Superiors		5½	48	CM
Torpedo	No. II		6	50	CM

The world-famous Punch brand is handmade in Honduras since 1969 from Cuban-seed tobaccos grown in Honduras, Nicaragua and the Dominican Republic. This range offers a magnificent, easy smoke with unsurpassed taste and bouquet. The Grand Cru series are made from vintage tobaccos aged from 3-5 years under the supervision of Villazon & Co.'s master blenders. Grand Cru cigars are robust in taste, yet sweet with a marvelous bouquet.

HANDMADE CIGARS: BRAND LISTINGS

Puro Nicaragua
Handmade in Ocotal, Nicaragua.

Wrapper: Ecuador　　　*Binder: Nicaragua*　　*Filler: Dom. Rep., Nicaragua*

Shape	Name	Lgth	Ring	Wrapper
Panatela	Lindas	5½	38	CC
Corona	No. 4	5½	42	CC
Robusto	Rothschild	5	50	CC
Panatela	Panatela Especial	6⅞	35	CC
Long Corona	Corona Gorda	6	44	CC
Lonsdale	No. 1	6⅝	44	CC
Toro	Toro	6	50	CC
Double Corona	Churchill	7	49	CC
Double Corona	Soberano	7¾	50	CC
Giant	Viajantes	8½	52	CC
Giant	Gigantes	8	54	CC

These heavy-bodied cigars are made by hand and use Nicaraguan-grown binder and filler tobaccos. Packaged in bundles of 25 cigars, they are an excellent value.

Puros Indios
Handmade in Danli, Honduras.

Wrapper: Ecuador　　　　　　　　　　　　　*Binder: Ecuador*
Filler: Brazil, Dominican Republic, Jamaica, Nicaragua

Shape	Name	Lgth	Ring	Wrapper
Double Corona	Churchill	7¼	53	CM-Ma
Churchill	Presidente	7¼	47	CM-Ma
Churchill	No. 1	7	48	CM-Ma
Grand Corona	No. 2	6½	46	CM
Lonsdale	Nacionales	6½	43	CM
Toro	Toro	6	50	CM-Ma
Robusto	Rothschild	5	50	CM

HANDMADE CIGARS: BRAND LISTINGS

Corona	No. 4	5½	44	CM-Ma
Long Panatela	Palmas Real	7	38	CM-Ma
Pyramid	Piramide No. 1	7½	60	CM-Ma
Pyramid	Piramide No. 2	6½	46	CM-Ma
Short Panatela	Petit Perla	5	38	CM-Ma
Pyramid	Gran Victoria	10	60	CM
Giant	Chief	18	66	CM

Introduced in 1995, the blending talents of Rolando Reyes are again at work in Puros Indios cigars. Leaves from five nations are blended by hand in Honduras to create a medium-bodied smoke in a wide variety of sizes, including the 18-inch Chief, which is the longest (along with the Cuba Aliados General) regular-production cigar marketed anywhere.

RAMAR
Handmade in Miami, Florida, USA.
Wrapper: Ecuador, Mexico, USA/Connecticut
Binder: Ecuador or Indonesia   Filler: Dom. Rep., Honduras, Nicaragua

Shape	Name	Lgth	Ring	Wrapper
Robusto	Robusto	5¼	50	CC-CM-Ma
Double Corona	Soberano	7½	50	CC-CM-Ma
Toro	Double Corona	6¼	50	CC-CM-Ma
Churchill	Churchill	7	48	CC-CM-Ma
Lonsdale	Seleccion No. 1	6¾	42	CC-CM-Ma
Long Corona	Seleccion No. 2	6¼	42	CC-CM-Ma
Panatela	Seleccion No. 3	6¾	36	CC-CM-Ma
Corona	Petit Corona	5¾	42	CC-CM-Ma
Giant Corona	Palmas	8	40	CC-CM-Ma
Panatela	Lauren	5¾	36	CC-CM-Ma
Pyramid	Piramides	7	60	CC-CM-Ma
Corona Extra	Adan	5½	46	CC-CM-Ma
Giant	Presidente	8¼	50	CC-CM-Ma

HANDMADE CIGARS: BRAND LISTINGS

Available since 1977, this cigar is getting wider notice in the 1990s, thanks to its high quality in construction and a mild-to-medium-bodied taste. Three wrapper shades are available: Connecticut tobacco for the lightest, Colorado-Claro wrappers, Ecuadorian leaves for the darker ''Cafe'' selection and Mexican-grown leaves for the maduro shade.

RAMON ALLONES
Handmade in Santiago, Dominican Republic.

Wrapper: Cameroon   *Binder: Mexico*   *Filler: Dom. Rep., Mexico*

Shape	Name		Lgth	Ring	Wrapper
Petit Corona	D		5	42	CM
Lonsdale	B		6½	42	CM
Lonsdale	A		7	45	CM
Double Corona	Redondos		7	49	CM
Lonsdale	Crystals	(tubed)	6¾	42	CM
Lonsdale	Trumps		6¾	43	CM
Robusto	Naturales		5½	50	CM
Small Panatela	Ramonitos		4¼	32	CM

This is a medium-to-heavy flavored cigar, manufactured in the same Santiago, Dominican Republic factory which produces famous Partagas cigars. It is exceptionally well made.

REGALOS
Handmade in Danli, Honduras.

Wrapper: Ecuador   *Binder: Dom. Rep.*   *Filler: Dom. Rep., Honduras*

Shape	Name	Lgth	Ring	Wrapper
Long Corona	Lonsdale	6	43	CC
Churchill	Churchill	7	47	CC
Robusto	Robusto	5	50	CC
Giant	Presidente	8½	52	CC
Toro	Toro	6	54	CC
Torpedo	Torpedo	6½	54	CC

HANDMADE CIGARS: BRAND LISTINGS

Double Corona	Especial	7½	64	CC

This is a beautiful cigar, well constructed and featuring an Ecuadorian-grown, Sumatra-seed wrapper. Introduced in 1996, it is full-bodied and offered in individual cellophane sleeves and all-wood boxes of 25.

REPEATER
Handmade, with mixed filler, in Danli, Honduras.

Wrapper: Honduras   *Binder: Honduras*   *Filler: Honduras*

Shape	Name	Lgth	Ring	Wrapper
Corona	Repeater 100	5½	43	CM
Long Corona	Repeater 200	6	43	CM
Lonsdale	Repeater 300	6½	43	CM
Lonsdale	Havana Twist	7	44	CM
Double Corona	Churchill	7	49	CM

This brand debuted in the late 1960s and utilizes medium-filler tobacco of all-Honduran origin, to produce an enjoyable smoke of medium-to-full body.

REPUBLICA DOMINICANA
Handmade in La Romana, Dominican Republic.

Wrapper: Indonesia   *Binder: Mexico*   *Filler: Proprietary*

Shape	Name	Lgth	Ring	Wrapper
Giant	No. 1	8	52	CC
Double Corona	No. 2	7½	50	CC
Toro	No. 3	6	50	CC
Robusto	No. 4	5	50	CC
Churchill	No. 5	7	48	CC
Lonsdale	No. 6	6⅝	44	CC
Long Corona	No. 7	6	42	CC
Panatela	No. 8	6⅞	38	CC

These bundled (25 per bundle) cigars have earned a growing following, thanks to its mild blend of Asian and Central/South American tobaccos.

HANDMADE CIGARS: BRAND LISTINGS

RIATA
Handmade in Danli, Honduras.

Wrapper: Mexico   Binder: Mexico   Filler: Honduras

Shape	Name	Lgth	Ring	Wrapper
Slim Panatela	No. 100	7	30	CC
Panatela	No. 200	6⅞	35	CC
Long Corona	No. 300	6	42	CC
Corona	No. 400	5½	44	CC
Lonsdale	No. 500	6⅝	44	CC
Churchill	No. 600	6⅞	48	CC
Robusto	No. 700	4¾	50	CC
Toro	No. 800	6¼	50	CC
Double Corona	No. 900	7½	50	CC
Giant	No. 1000	8	52	CC

These are handmade cigars offered in bundles of 25 cigars each. The construction is good and the blend is of mild body.

RICO HAVANA
Handmade in Danli, Honduras.

Wrapper: Ecuador   Binder: Honduras   Filler: Dom.Rep., Honduras

Shape	Name	Lgth	Ring	Wrapper
Giant	Rough Rider	9	50	CC-Ma
Churchill	Churchill	7½	48	CC-Ma
Lonsdale	Plaza	7	44	CC-Ma
Long Corona	Corona	6	42	CC-Ma
Robusto	Duke	5	50	CC-Ma
Corona	Habanero	5½	40	CC-Ma

A favorite since 1939, this medium-bodied blend of Cuban seed, Dominican-grown long-filler tobaccos combines with an Ecuadorian wrapper for great smoking flavor. Rico Havana is available in natural and maduro wrappers.

HANDMADE CIGARS: BRAND LISTINGS

RICOS DOMINICANOS
Handmade in Santiago, Dominican Republic.

Wrapper: USA/Connecticut   *Binder: Dominican Republic*
Filler: Brazil, Dominican Republic, Indonesia

Shape	Name	Lgth	Ring	Wrapper
Double Corona	Churchill	7	50	CC-Ma
Toro	Toro	6	50	CC-Ma
Corona	Breva	5½	44	CC-Ma
Lonsdale	Centro Largo	6¾	44	CC-Ma

This brand debuted in 1996 and offers a mild-to-medium bodied taste in either a natural or maduro wrapper. It has a rich aroma and, best of all, is an excellent value.

RIGOLETTO
Handmade in Santiago, Dominican Republic.

Wrapper: USA/Connecticut   *Binder: Dom. Rep.*   *Filler: Dom. Rep.*

Shape	Name	Lgth	Ring	Wrapper
Churchill	Black Magic	7½	46	CC-Ma
Lonsdale	Black Arrow	6¼	44	CC-Ma
Toro	Dominican Lights	6¼	48	CC-Ma

This brand, which debuted in 1905, are made by hand in the Dominican Republic, using Connecticut Shade leaves for natural wrappers and Connecticut Broadleaf tobaccos for the maduro style. Medium in body, it's an underrated smoke.

ROBALI
Handmade in San Jose, Costa Rica.

Wrapper: Ecuador   *Binder: Nicaragua*   *Filler: Nicaragua*

Shape	Name	Lgth	Ring	Wrapper
Giant	Viajante	8	54	CC
Churchill	Double Corona	7½	46	CC
Lonsdale	Linda	6½	41	CC

HANDMADE CIGARS: BRAND LISTINGS

Robusto	Robusto	4½	52	CC
Toro	Corona	6	50	CC
Corona	Senorita	5½	44	CC

New for 1996, Robali carries on the tradition of Costa Rican cigar making. A medium-bodied blend, these cigars are offered in boxes of 25 from the Robali de Centro America, S.A. factory.

RODRIGUEZ & MENENDEZ
Handmade in Tampa, Florida, USA.
Wrapper: Dom. Rep., Ecuador, Honduras, USA/Connecticut
Binder: Dom. Rep., Honduras, Nicaragua   Filler: Dom. Rep., Ecuador, Honduras

Shape	Name	Lgth	Ring	Wrapper
Churchill	Fuma	7¼	47	CC-Ma
Lonsdale	Palma	6½	43	CC
Robusto	Rothschild	4⅞	50	Ma
Churchill	Reyna	7¼	47	CC-Ma
Double Corona	No. 5	7	49	CC-Ma
Giant Corona	Imperiales	8	45	CC-Ma
Grand Corona	Gran Corona	6	47	CC-Ma
Slim Panatela	Panatela	5½	34	CC
Double Corona	Super Presidente	8¼	48	CC

Well respected since their introduction in 1981, these are medium-bodied cigars in the natural wrappers and full-bodied in maduro, produced in a small factory in the famous Tampa suburb of Ybor City.

ROLANDO
Handmade in Santiago, Dominican Republic.
Wrapper: USA/Connecticut   Binder: Dom. Rep.   Filler: Dom. Rep.

Shape	Name	Lgth	Ring	Wrapper
Churchill	No. 2	7½	48	CC
Toro	No. 3	6	50	CC

Long Corona	No. 4	6	43	CC
Robusto	Robusto	4¾	52	CC
Pyramid	Pyramid	6½	54	CC
Lonsdale	Perfecto	7	44	CC

Introduced in 1995, meticulously-selected tobaccos and extended aging contribute to the exquisite, mild-to-medium flavor of one of the world's finest cigars. Wrapped in the famous Connecticut Shade-grown wrapper, with Dominican filler leaf.

ROLLER'S CHOICE
Handmade in Santiago, Dominican Republic.
Wrapper: USA/Connecticut   Binder: Dom. Rep.   Filler: Dom. Rep.

Shape	Name	Lgth	Ring	Wrapper
Double Corona	RC Double Corona	7	50	CC
Long Corona	RC Corona	6	43	CC
Grand Corona	RC Lonsdale	6½	46	CC
Robusto	RC Robusto	5	50	CC
Petit Corona	RC Pequeno	4¼	40	CC
Corona	RC Fino	5½	41	CC
Torpedo	RC Torpedo	5½	56	CC
Toro	RC Toro	6	50	CC
Corona	RC Cetro	5½	43	CC

While not as well known as some other brands, Roller's Choice was introduced in 1992 and is a well-constructed, mild-bodied cigar produced in one of the Dominican Republic's most dependable factories.

ROMANTICOS
Handmade in Santiago, Dominican Republic
Wrapper: USA/Connecticut   Binder: Dom. Rep.   Filler: Dom. Rep.

Shape	Name	Lgth	Ring	Wrapper
Giant	Marc Anthony	8	52	Co

HANDMADE CIGARS: BRAND LISTINGS

Double Corona	Valentino	7	50	Co
Pyramid	Cyrano	6	52	Co
Corona	Cleopatra	5¾	43	Co
Robusto	Eros	5	50	Co
Short Panatela	Venus	5	36	Co

Introduced in 1996, this is a full-flavored, mild-to-medium bodied blend of long-filler tobaccos, offered in individual cellophane sleeves in elegant cedar cabinets of 25. Check out the shape names: some of the great lovers and love-gods in history!

ROMEO Y JULIETA
Handmade in Santiago, Dominican Republic.

Wrapper: Indonesia   *Binder: USA/Connecticut*   *Filler: Brazil, Dom. Rep.*

Shape	Name	Lgth	Ring	Wrapper
Giant	Monarcas	8	52	CM
Double Corona	Churchills	7	50	CM
Lonsdale	Presidentes	7	43	CM
Robusto	Rothschilds	5	50	CM-Ma
Lonsdale	Cetros	6½	44	CM-Ma
Long Corona	Palmas	6	43	CM
Corona	Coronas	5½	44	CM
Slim Panatela	Delgados	7	32	CM
Panatela	Brevas	5⅝	38	CM
Short Panatela	Panatelas	5¼	35	CM
Small Panatela	Chiquitas	4¼	32	CM
Pyramid	Romeos	6	46	CM

This famous brand originated in Cuba, and this version lives up to its heritage. Made by hand in the Dominican Republic, this line is medium in strength, using tobaccos from many nations to create a complex taste. The shortage of Cameroon wrappers often make these cigars hard to find.

HANDMADE CIGARS: BRAND LISTINGS

ROMEO Y JULIETA VINTAGE
Handmade in Santiago, Dominican Republic.

Wrapper: USA/Connecticut   Binder: Mexico   Filler: Dom. Rep.

Shape	Name	Lgth	Ring	Wrapper
Long Corona	I	6	43	CC
Grand Corona	II	6	46	CC
Robusto	III	4½	50	CC
Churchill	IV	7	48	CC
Double Corona	V	7½	50	CC
Pyramid	VI	7	60	CC

This is the ultimate cigar! Made with perfectly fermented tobacco, the wrapper is selected for a natural, oily sheen and silky appearance. The binder is aged Mexican leaf and the filler is superbly blended Cuban seed and long-leaf Dominican tobaccos. Introduced in 1993, this is a finesse cigar, mild with very round flavor and made in extremely limited supply.

ROSA CUBA
Handmade, with mixed filler, in Esteli, Nicaragua.

Wrapper: Ecuador   Binder: Dominican Republic
Filler: Dominican Republic, Honduras, Nicaragua

Shape	Name	Lgth	Ring	Wrapper
Robusto	Angels	4½	48	CC
Corona	Flor de Rosa	5½	44	CC
Toro	Governor	6⅛	48	CC
Robusto	Herencia	4½	52	CC
Churchill	Mille Fleurs	6¾	48	CC
Grand Corona	Media Noche	6½	46	CC
Toro	Ortiz y Laboy	6½	52	CC
Giant	President	8½	52	CC
Double Corona	Sultana	7½	54	CC
Lonsdale	Vargas	6½	44	CC

O Romeo, Romeo! wherefore Art Thou Romeo?

If you have been looking for our Romeo y Julieta® Vintage cigars and have been finding a lot of empty boxes like this... well, you're not alone. It seems that many discriminating cigar smokers are not able to find these cigars in stock at their local tobacconist.

So, why don't we make more? Believe me, we'd love to.

You see, the select Romeo y Julieta Vintage tobacco leaf takes a full three years to age and mature. This is what makes the cigars taste so... well, you know. That's probably why you were looking for them in the first place. And as much as we would like to make more, we simply cannot speed up the process that has produced such a rewarding flavor.

Just as Romeo found Julieta, you will find your true love, and the wait will be worth it.

HANDMADE CIGARS: BRAND LISTINGS

New for 1996, this line offers a medium-to-full-bodied flavor with a magnificent Ecuador-grown, Sumatra-seed wrapper, in economical bundles of 20.

ROSALONES
Handmade in Esteli, Nicaragua.

Wrapper: Nicaragua   *Binder: Nicaragua*   *Filler: Nicaragua*

Shape	Name	Lgth	Ring	Wrapper
Giant	Presidente	8	54	CC-Ma
Giant	Viajante	8½	52	CC-Ma
Double Corona	Presidente Corto	7¼	54	CC-Ma
Double Corona	Viajante Corto	7	52	CC-Ma
Double Corona	Emperador	7¾	50	CC-Ma
Double Corona	Emperador Corto	7½	50	CC-Ma
Churchill	Churchill	6⅞	48	CC-Ma
Churchill	No. 11	7½	46	CC-Ma
Toro	Duke	6	50	CC-Ma
Long Panatela	No. 9	8	38	CC-Ma
Long Panatela	No. 9 Corto	7	38	CC-Ma
Corona Extra	Corona Extra	5½	46	CC-Ma
Robusto	Consul	4½	52	CC-Ma
Lonsdale	No. 1	6⅝	44	CC-Ma
Lonsdale	No. 10	6½	43	CC-Ma
Long Corona	No. 3	6	44	CC-Ma
Corona	Nacional	5½	44	CC-Ma
Panatela	No. 5	6⅞	35	CC-Ma
Long Corona	No. 6	6	41	CC-Ma
Corona	Seleccion B	5½	42	CC-Ma
Slim Panatela	No. 7	7	30	CC-Ma
Panatela	Elegante	6½	38	CC-Ma
Petit Corona	No. 2	4½	42	CC-Ma

HANDMADE CIGARS: BRAND LISTINGS

Short Panatela	Petits	5½	38	CC-Ma
Slim Panatela	Senoritas	5½	34	CC-Ma
Small Panatela	Piccolino	4⅛	30	CC-Ma
Toro	Corona	5⅝	48	CC-Ma

This line, introduced in 1983, is primarily produced for the Nicaraguan home market, with some distribution reaching the United States. A 27-shape brand, it is a sister to the U.S.-marketed Flor de Nicaragua range. These are mild-bodied cigars, using filler and binder leaf from the Jalapa Valley of Nicaragua, with Nicaraguan wrappers.

ROYAL BARBADOS
Handmade in Bridgetown, Barbados.
Wrapper: Ecuador   *Binder & Filler: Caribbean blend*

Shape	Name	Lgth	Ring	Wrapper
Grand Corona	No. 2	6½	46	CC
Long Corona	No. 3	6⅛	42	CC
Corona	No. 4	5⅛	42	CC
Panatela	No. 6	6⅛	38	CC

This is a limited distribution, light-bodied cigar from Barbados, introduced in 1996 and offered in boxes of 25.

ROYAL COURT
Handmade in Danli, Honduras.
Wrapper: Ecuador   *Binder: Honduras*   *Filler: Honduras*

Shape	Name	Lgth	Ring	Wrapper
Panatela	No. 1 Petit Corona	5½	38	CC
Panatela	No. 2 Panatela	6⅞	36	CC
Long Corona	No. 3 Cetro	6	43	CC
Double Corona	No. 4 Presidente	7¾	50	CC
Giant	No. 5 Viajante	8½	52	CC

HANDMADE CIGARS: BRAND LISTINGS

Premium quality at modest prices. That's the story of this smooth, mild and flavorful cigar with a natural wrapper, which debuted in 1992. Each of the 25 cigars in this bundle is individually wrapped.

ROYAL DOMINICANA
Handmade in the Dominican Republic.

Wrapper: USA/Connecticut   *Binder: Mexico*   *Filler: Dom. Rep.*

Shape	Name	Lgth	Ring	Wrapper
Double Corona	Churchill	7¼	50	CC
Grand Corona	Corona	6	46	CC
Corona	Nacional	5½	43	CC
Lonsdale	No. 1	6¾	43	CC
Panatela	Super Fino	6	35	CC
Short Panatela	Mini	4	36	CC

This is a mild-to-medium bodied cigar, with a Connecticut wrapper and well-known for its quality construction and reasonable price.

ROYALES
Handmade in Santiago, Dominican Republic.

Wrapper: Indonesia/Java   *Binder: Brazil*   *Filler: Brazil, Dom. Rep.*

Shape	Name	Lgth	Ring	Wrapper
Giant	No. 1	8	52	CC
Double Corona	No. 2	7½	50	CC
Toro	No. 3	6	50	CC
Robusto	No. 4	5	50	CC
Lonsdale	No. 5	6⅝	44	CC
Long Corona	No. 6	6	42	CC
Panatela	No. 7	6⅞	38	CC

Introduced in 1992, Royales are a careful hand-blend of leaves that produces a mild cigar with a rich bouquet, produced in the Dominican Republic.

HANDMADE CIGARS: BRAND LISTINGS

ROYAL HONDURAS
Handmade in Danli, Honduras.

Wrapper: Indonesia/Sumatra *Binder: Dom. Rep.* *Filler: Honduras*

Shape	Name	Lgth	Ring	Wrapper
Giant	Czar	8	50	CC
Churchill	Sovereign	7	48	CC
Torpedo	Kings	6⅛	54	CC
Lonsdale	Prince	7	44	CC
Robusto	Majesty	5	50	CC
Corona	Joker	5½	42	CC
Pyramid	Princess	5	38	CC
Toro	Knight	6	50	CC

Royal Honduras is a new brand for 1996 and offers a mild to medium-bodied flavor in sizes named after characters in a royal court. All of these cigars are presented in cedarwood boxes. Please note that the two shaped cigars flare from 42 to 54 ring (Kings) and from 32 to 38 ring (Princess).

ROYAL JAMAICA
Handmade in La Romana, Dominican Republic
and in Maypen, Jamaica

Wrapper: Indonesia/Java *Binder: Cameroon* *Filler: Jamaica*

Shape	Name	Lgth	Ring	Wrapper
Slim Panatela	Buccaneer	5½	30	CM-Ma
Lonsdale	Corona Grande	6½	42	CM-Ma
Giant	Churchill	8	51	CM-Ma
Corona	Corona	5½	40	CM-Ma
Grand Corona	Director No. 1	6	45	CM
Lonsdale	Double Corona	7	45	CM
Slim Panatela	Doubloon	7	30	CM
Slim Panatela	Gaucho	5¼	33	CM
Double Corona	Giant Corona	7½	49	CM

HANDMADE CIGARS: BRAND LISTINGS

Giant	Goliath	9	64	CM
Slim Panatela	Navarro	6¾	34	CM
Long Corona	New York Plaza	6	40	CM
Grand Corona	Park Lane	6	47	CM
Petit Corona	Petit Corona	5	40	CM
Small Panatela	Pirate	4½	30	CM
Cigarillo	Rapier	6½	28	CM
Robusto	Robusto	4½	49	CM
Long Corona	Royal Corona	6	40	CM
Grand Corona	No. 1 Tube (tubed)	6	45	CM
Slim Panatela	No. 2 Tube (tubed)	6½	34	CM
Giant	No. 10 Downing Street	10	51	CM

Consistently ranked as one of the tastiest handmade cigars in the world, with an abundant variety of shapes and styles, Royal Jamaica is again being made in Jamaica. Transferred to the Dominican Republic in 1988 after Hurricane Gilbert destroyed the factory in Kingston, Consolidated Cigar has opened a new facility in Maypen, Jamaica and production began in late 1996. The filler is predominantly Jamaica-grown tobaccos, with a secret family additive applied during the fermentation process. The Cameroon binder combined with the Java wrapper results in a unique, spicy flavor. A dark Mexican maduro wrapper gives that series a rich taste with a hint of sweetness. The Mexican leaf is heated with steam and aged two weeks to result in a deep brown hue.

ROYAL MANNA
Handmade in Santa Rosa de Copan, Honduras.

Wrapper: Ecuador   *Binder: Honduras*   *Filler: Honduras*

Shape	Name	Lgth	Ring	Wrapper
Lonsdale	No. 1	7⅛	43	CM
Corona	No. 4	5⅛	42	CM
Panatela	Manchego	6¾	35	CM
Double Corona	Churchill	7½	50	CM
Long Panatela	Largo Extra Fino	8	38	CM

Robusto	Rothschild	4¾	50	CM
Toro	Toro	6	50	CM

This popular brand was introduced in 1972, originally made in the Canary Islands. It is well known for its Connecticut Shade-seed wrapper, excellent construction and a medium-bodied taste.

ROYAL NICARAGUAN
Handmade in Nicaragua.
(The distributor declined to provide any information on the origins of the tobaccos included in this brand.)

Shape	Name	Lgth	Ring	Wrapper
Giant	No. 2	8½	52	CC
Giant	No. 4	8	54	CC
Double Corona	No. 6	7½	52	CC
Double Corona	No. 8	7	49	CC
Lonsdale	No. 10	7	44	CC
Long Panatela	No. 12	7	36	CC
Toro	No. 14	6	50	CC
Long Corona	No. 16	6	43	CC
Corona	No. 18	5½	43	CC
Robusto	No. 20	5	50	CC

This is a medium-bodied cigar, with all long-filler tobacco, offered in modestly-priced bundles of 25.

RUBIROSA
Handmade in Santiago, Dominican Republic.

Wrapper: USA/Connecticut   Binder: Dom. Rep.   Filler: Dom. Rep.

Shape	Name	Lgth	Ring	Wrapper
Giant	Playboy	8½	50	CC
Churchill	Extasis	6⅞	46	CC
Robusto	Polo	5	50	CC

| Long Corona | Caribe | 6 | 44 | CC |
| Corona | Eros | 5¾ | 42 | CC |

Named for the famous Dominican playboy Porfirio Rubirosa (1909-65), who charmed, married and befriended many of the most famous and richest women in the world, this new line for 1996 offers a mild taste. Made completely by hand, these cigars are presented in boxes made only of Spanish cedar to enhance the aging process.

SABANA
Handmade in Cumana, Venezuela.

Wrapper: Ecuador   *Binder: Venezuela*   *Filler: Venezuela*

Shape	Name	Lgth	Ring	Wrapper
Panatela	Sabana No. 1	5½	38	CC
Corona	Sabana No. 2	5½	42	CC
Corona Extra	Sabana No. 3	5¾	46	CC
Petit Corona	Sabana Especial	4½	40	CC
Cigarillo	Sabanitas	4	26	CC

Here is a new brand from a nation which has more than 100 years of history in the growing and cultivation of tobacco. These cigars, introduced in 1996, offer a mild-to-medium bodied taste in elegant boxes of 25.

SABOR HABANO
Handmade in Esteli, Nicaragua.

Wrapper: Ecuador   *Binder: Nicaragua*   *Filler: Dom. Rep., Nicaragua*

Shape	Name	Lgth	Ring	Wrapper
Long Corona	Cetro	6	44	CC
Robusto	Rothchild	5	50	CC
Toro	Matador	6	50	CC
Double Corona	Churchill	7	49	CC
Giant	Presidente	8½	52	CC

Here is a medium-bodied cigar which matches a Connecticut-seed wrapper grown in Ecuador with a Havana-seed binder from Nicaragua and filler leaves

HANDMADE CIGARS: BRAND LISTINGS

from the Dominican Republic and Nicaragua. New for 1996, Sabor Habano is offered in boxes of 25 cigars each.

SABROSO
Handmade in Esteli, Nicaragua.

Wrapper: Ecuador *Binder: Nicaragua* *Filler: Nicaragua*

Shape	Name	Lgth	Ring	Wrapper
Robusto	Numero Uno	4¾	50	CC
Long Corona	Numero Dos	6	44	CC
Toro	Numero Tres	6	50	CC
Churchill	Numero Cuatro	7	48	CC
Giant	Numero Cinco	8½	52	CC

This new brand from Nicaragua offers a full-bodied taste and an excellent value. Sabroso cigars are packaged in bundles of 25 cigars each.

SAINT LUIS REY
Handmade in Danli, Honduras.

Wrapper: Honduras *Binder: Honduras* *Filler: Honduras*

Shape	Name	Lgth	Ring	Wrapper
Torpedo	Torpedo	6	54	CM
Double Corona	Churchill	7	50	CM
Toro	Serie A	6	50	CM
Lonsdale	Lonsdale	6½	44	CM

Introduced at LE CIGAR NOIR - BEVERLY HILLS on May 1, 1996, this Honduran version of an old Cuban brand was an immediate hit with everyone who tried it. Full-bodied but smooth on the draw, these cigars blend plenty of flavor with a slow-burning cadre of Honduran-grown, Cuban-seed tobaccos for a relaxing smoke. Saint Luis Rey cigars are individually cellophaned and packed in windowed boxes of 25.

SAN FERNANDO
Handmade in Santa Rosa de Copan, Honduras.

Wrapper: Honduras *Binder: Honduras* *Filler: Honduras*

HANDMADE CIGARS: BRAND LISTINGS

Shape	Name	Lgth	Ring	Wrapper
Churchill	Churchill	7	48	CM
Long Corona	Corona	6	44	CM
Robusto	Robusto	5	52	CM

This brand was introduced in 1975 and includes all-Honduran tobaccos. Named for one of Honduras's premier tobacco farms, San Fernando is a full-bodied blend.

SAN LUIS
Handmade, with mixed filler, in Honduras.
(The distributor declined to provide any information about the origin of the tobaccos in this brand.)

Shape	Name	Lgth	Ring	Wrapper
Double Corona	Soberanos	7½	50	CM
Lonsdale	Corona	6½	44	CM
Toro	Toro	6	50	CM
Panatela	Panatelas	6½	36	CM
Corona	Cetros	5⅜	42	CM

San Luis is a made-by-hand cigar, offered in value-priced bundles of 25 cigars. It is unusual for its double binder.

SAN MARCOS
Handmade in Danli, Honduras.

Wrapper: Ecuador   *Binder: Honduras*   *Filler: Honduras*

Shape	Name	Lgth	Ring	Wrapper
Giant	Embajadores	8½	52	CC
Churchill	Churchill	7	48	CC
Long Corona	Sabrosos	6	43	CC
Corona	Casa Blanca	5½	42	CC
Robusto	Rothschild	5	50	CC

HANDMADE CIGARS: BRAND LISTINGS

Here is a full-bodied blend which features a Connecticut-seed wrapper grown in Ecuador. The five classic shapes are offered in boxes of 25 cigars each.

SAN VICENTE
Handmade in Esteli, Nicaragua.

Wrapper: Nicaragua   *Binder: Honduras*
Filler: Brazil, Dominican Republic, Honduras, Nicaragua

Shape	Name	Lgth	Ring	Wrapper
Giant	Ruilovas	8½	52	CM-Ma
Double Corona	Prime Minster	7¼	54	CM-Ma
Toro	Barons	6⅛	50	CM-Ma
Robusto	Rothschilds	4½	50	CM-Ma
Churchill	Gran Corona	6¾	48	CM-Ma
Churchill	Gran Amigos	7¼	46	CM-Ma
Lonsdale	Numero Uno	6½	43	CM-Ma
Lonsdale	Exquisitos	7	42	CM-Ma
Corona	Royal Coronas	5½	42	CM-Ma
Cigarillo	Señoritas	5⅜	28	CM

This is the 50th anniversary of this respected brand, now made by hand in Nicaragua. The taste is medium-bodied, with mild spice flavors; San Vicente is offered in boxes of 25.

SANTA CLARA "1830"
Handmade in San Andres Tuxtula, Mexico.

Wrapper: Mexico   *Binder: Mexico*   *Filler: Mexico*

Shape	Name	Lgth	Ring	Wrapper
Double Corona	I	7	52	CC-Ma
Toro	II	6½	48	CC-Ma
Lonsdale	III	6⅝	43	CC
Corona	IV	5	44	CC-Ma
Long Corona	V	6	44	CC-Ma
Toro	VI	6	51	CC-Ma

HANDMADE CIGARS: BRAND LISTINGS

Cigarillo	VII		5½	25	CC
Slim Panatela	VIII		6	32	CC
Panatela	Premier Tubes	(tubed)	6¾	38	CC
Small Panatela	Quino		4¼	30	CC
Robusto	Robusto		4½	50	CC
Long Corona	Fiesta		6	42	CC-Ma

This is a medium-bodied cigar, of all-Mexican tobacco. The wrapper is a unique Sumatran-seed type, which gives this line a unique flavor in both the natural and maduro shades. The Fiesta features the "barber pole" double wrapper style.

SANTA DAMIANA
Handmade in La Romana, Dominican Republic.
Wrapper: USA/Connecticut   Binder: Dom. Rep.   Filler: Dom. Rep.

Shape	Name	Lgth	Ring	Wrapper
Churchill	Seleccion No. 100	6¾	48	Cl
Corona Extra	Seleccion No. 300	5½	46	Cl
Robusto	Seleccion No. 500	5	50	Cl
Lonsdale	Seleccion No. 700	6½	42	Cl
Double Corona	Seleccion No. 800	7	50	Cl

A beautifully-finished cigar that defines what a "claro" wrapper looks like, Santa Damiana is an elegant, medium-bodied smoke. This brand was originated in Cuba and today's Dominican-manufactured cigar was introduced in 1992. It is offered in attractive, slide-top, cedar boxes of 25.

SANTA ROSA
Handmade in Santa Rosa de Copan, Honduras.
Wrapper: Ecuador   Binder: Honduras   Filler: Honduras

Shape	Name	Lgth	Ring	Wrapper
Corona	No. 4	5½	42	CC-Ma
Long Corona	Cetros	6	42	CC-Ma
Giant	President	8½	50	CC

Double Corona	Churchill	7	49	CC-Ma
Lonsdale	Corona	6½	44	CC-Ma
Lonsdale	Elegante	7	43	CC-Ma
Slim Panatela	Finas	6½	30	CC
Panatela	Largos	6¾	35	CC
Corona Extra	Regulares	5½	46	CC
Robusto	Sancho Panza	4¾	50	CC-Ma
Torpedo	Torpedo	6½	54	CC-Ma
Toro	Toro	6	50	CC-Ma

Introduced in 1985, the Santa Rosa brand is marked by a beautiful new band, along with an expanded set of shapes. Made in the La Flor de Copan factory in Santa Rosa, Honduras, this is a mild brand with a smooth, easy taste that everyone can enjoy. The wrapper is particularly smooth Ecuadorian-grown leaf from Connecticut Shade seeds.

SANTIAGO
Handmade in Santiago, Dominican Republic.
Wrapper: USA/Connecticut   *Binder: Dom. Rep.*   *Filler: Dom. Rep.*

Shape	Name	Lgth	Ring	Wrapper
Churchill	No. 1	6¾	48	CC
Long Panatela	No. 2	7	36	CC
Grand Corona	No. 3	6½	46	CC
Corona Extra	No. 4	5½	46	CC
Petit Corona	No. 5	5	40	CC

A beautifully-boxed cigar, the Santiago brand blends mild tobaccos for a very mild body.

SAVINELLI EXTREMELY LIMITED RESERVE
Handmade in Santiago, Dominican Republic.
Wrapper: USA/Connecticut   *Binder: Dom. Rep.*   *Filler: Dom. Rep.*

HANDMADE CIGARS: BRAND LISTINGS

Shape	Name	Lgth	Ring	Wrapper
Churchill	No. 1 Churchill	7¼	48	CC
Grand Corona	No. 2 Corona Extra	6⅝	46	CC
Long Corona	No. 3 Lonsdale	6¼	43	CC
Toro	No. 4 Double Corona	6	50	CC
Corona	No. 5 Extraordinaire	5½	44	CC
Robusto	No. 6 Robusto	5	49	CC

"Extremely limited" is the key phrase in the name of this brand. Long famous for their high-quality pipes, the Savinelli tradition of craftsmanship is continued in this limited-distribution line of medium-bodied cigars, introduced in 1995.

SEGOVIA
Handmade in Segovia, Nicaragua.

Wrapper: Nicaragua   Binder: Nicaragua   Filler: Nicaragua

Shape	Name	Lgth	Ring	Wrapper
Double Corona	Crown Royal	7	52	CM
Long Corona	Primo Gorda	6	42	CM
Robusto	Robusto	5	52	CM
Toro	Toro	6	50	CM
Grand Corona	X-O	6¼	46	CM

Cuban seeds from the 1959 crop are the basis of this brand, which seeks to recreate the rich flavors of the Cuban heydey and escape the mediocrity of today's ultra-mild brands. Not surprisingly, this is a full, heavy-bodied cigar, with plenty of strong, ligero leaves inside.

SIGLO 21
Handmade in Santiago, Dominican Republic.

Wrapper: Ecuador   Binder: Dom. Rep.   Filler: Dom. Rep.

Shape	Name	Lgth	Ring	Wrapper
Robusto	No. 1	4½	50	CC
Lonsdale	No. 2	6½	44	CC

HANDMADE CIGARS: BRAND LISTINGS

Toro	No. 3	6	50	CC
Churchill	No. 4	7	48	CC
Giant	No. 5	8	50	CC

This is a new brand for 1996, saluting the 21st century ("siglo" in Spanish).
The cigars are medium-bodied, with excellent draw and a marvelous aroma.

SIGNATURE COLLECTION
Handmade in Miami, Florida, USA.

Wrapper: Ecuador   *Binder: Ecuador*
Filler: Dominican Republic, Honduras, Nicaragua

Shape	Name	Lgth	Ring	Wrapper
Torpedo	Chicas	5	38	Co
Corona	Caribe	5½	44	Co
Robusto	Robusto	5	50	Co
Lonsdale	Corona	6½	42	Co
Long Panatela	Lancero	7½	38	Co
Churchill	Double Corona	7½	46	Co
Double Corona	Churchill	7¼	50	Co
Double Corona	Presidente	7¾	54	Co
Torpedo	Torpedo	6½	54	Co

Introduced in 1994, the Signature Collection by Santiago Cabana cigars are
made in Florida exclusively by Cuban immigrant master rollers. These cigars
are made up of Cuban-seed tobaccos from the Dominican Republic, Ecuador,
Honduras and Nicaragua. The result is a medium-bodied cigar, with a slow and
even burn and a complex bouquet of taste and aroma.

SIGNET
Handmade in La Romana, Dominican Republic.

Wrapper: USA/Connecticut   *Binder: Dom. Rep.*   *Filler: Dom. Rep.*

Shape	Name	Lgth	Ring	Wrapper
Robusto	Bedford	4¾	50	CC
Long Corona	Berkeley	6	42	CC

Churchill	Buckingham	7	48	CC

This is a new brand in 1996, offered only in limited distribution. The brand has a mild, rich taste and is presented in cedar boxes of 25.

SILLEM'S LAS TERENAS
Handmade in Santiago, Dominican Republic.

Wrapper: USA/Connecticut   Binder: Dom. Rep.   Filler: Dom. Rep.

Shape	Name	Lgth	Ring	Wrapper
Lonsdale	Carabella	6⅝	42	CC
Toro	Hidalgo	6	50	CC
Robusto	Baraja	4½	50	CC
Double Corona	Levantado	7½	50	CC
Corona	Las Terenas	5⅝	42	CC

This brand was launched in mid-1996 from Sanitago, Dominican Republic. The Connecticut leaf wrapper and Dominican binder and filler combine for a mild taste.

660 RED
Handmade in Miami, Florida, USA.

Wrapper: Ecuador   Binder: Dom. Rep.   Filler: Honduras, Nicaragua

Shape	Name	Lgth	Ring	Wrapper
Toro	660 Red	6	60	CM

Wow! It's like holding a short police baton, more than a cigar. But light one up and you'll experience a powerful flavor. 660 Reds are offered - if you can find them - in bundles of 15.

SOL Y MAR
Handmade in Danli, Honduras.

Wrapper: Cameroon   Binder: Indonesia   Filler: Dom. Rep., Nicaragua

Shape	Name	Lgth	Ring	Wrapper
Double Corona	Churchill	7	50	CC
Torpedo	Torpedo	7	54	CC

HANDMADE CIGARS: BRAND LISTINGS

Toro	Toro	6	50	CC
Toro	Corona	6	48	CC
Robusto	Robusto	5	52	CC

Here is a new brand, with leaves from four nations combining to offer a medium-bodied smoke, with excellent construction. Sol y Mar cigars are presented in boxes of 25.

SOLO AROMA
Handmade in Danli, Honduras.

Wrapper: Ecuador　　　　Binder: Honduras　　　Filler: Dom. Rep., Honduras

Shape	Name	Lgth	Ring	Wrapper
Corona	No. 4	5½	42	CM
Long Corona	No. 2	6	43	CM
Lonsdale	Corona Gorda	6¼	44	CM
Robusto	Rothschild	5	50	CM
Lonsdale	No. 1	7	43	CM
Panatela	Panatela	6⅞	36	CM
Long Panatela	Palma de Mayorca	8	38	CM
Churchill	Corona Grande	7½	46	CM
Double Corona	Churchill	6⅞	49	CM
Toro	Toro	6	50	CM
Double Corona	Soberanos	7¾	50	CM
Giant	Viajante	8½	52	CM
	Handmade, with mixed filler:			
Lonsdale	Fumas	7	44	CM
Long Corona	Cazadores	6¼	44	CM

These cigars are handmade, using all Honduran tobaccos. Mild to medium in body, they are presented in bundles of 25 cigars each and modestly priced.

HANDMADE CIGARS: BRAND LISTINGS

SOSA
Handmade in Santiago, Dominican Republic.
Wrapper: Ecuador or USA/Connecticut

Binder: Honduras   *Filler: Brazil, Dominican Republic*

Shape	Name	Lgth	Ring	Wrapper
Churchill	Churchill	7	48	CC-Ma
Robusto	Wavell	4¾	50	CC-Ma
Lonsdale	Lonsdale	6½	43	CC-Ma
Corona	Brevas	5½	43	CC-Ma
Pyramid	Piramides	7	64	CC-Ma
Panatela	Santa Fe	6	35	CC-Ma
Double Corona	Magnums	7½	52	CC-Ma
Toro	Governor	6	50	CC-Ma

Juan Sosa is well known in the cigar trade for excellent products which are
modestly priced. Originally made in Miami in 1964 and then in the Dominican
Republic in 1974, this line bears his name and does it proud with a medium
bodied-smoke and a choice of an Ecuadorian-grown Sumatra-seed wrapper or,
for those who prefer maduro, well-aged Connecticut Broadleaf. Sosa cigars are
cellophaned and presented in slide-top cedar boxes.

SOSA FAMILY SELECTION
Handmade in Santiago, Dominican Republic.
Wrapper: USA/Connecticut   *Binder: Dom. Rep.*   *Filler: Dom. Rep.*

Shape	Name	Lgth	Ring	Wrapper
Lonsdale	No. 1	6¾	43	Co
Toro	No. 2	6¼	54	Co
Corona	No. 3	5¾	44	Co
Petit Corona	No. 4	5	40	Co
Robusto	No. 5	5	50	Co
Panatela	No. 6	6¼	38	Co
Toro	No. 7	6	50	Co
Churchill	No. 8	6¾	48	Co

HANDMADE CIGARS: BRAND LISTINGS

Double Corona	No. 9	7¾	52	Co
Slim Panatela	Intermezzo	5	32	Co

The Sosa family tradition of fine cigars is carried on in this line, first introduced in 1995. Medium to full-bodied in flavor, all of these cigars are round — not pressed — and are presented in elegant cabinet-selection boxes.

SPANISH HONDURAN RED LABEL
Handmade in Cofradia, Honduras.

Wrapper: Honduras   *Binder: Honduras*   *Filler: Honduras*

Shape	Name	Lgth	Ring	Wrapper
Giant Corona	Casino	8½	42	CM-Ma
Long Corona	Cetro	6	42	CM-Ma
Toro	Churchill Round	6	49	CM-Ma
Long Panatela	Elegante	7	38	Cl-CM-Ma
Giant	Emperadore	8½	52	CM-Ma
Lonsdale	Londre	7	40	Cl-CM-Ma
Churchill	Lonsdale	6¾	48	Cl-CM-Ma
Double Corona	Magnifico	7¼	54	Cl-CM-Ma
Giant Corona	Presidente	7½	45	Cl-CM-Ma
Robusto	Rothchild	4½	50	CM-Ma
Long Corona	Super Cetro	6¼	44	CM-Ma
Churchill	Wilshire *(glass jar)*	7¼	46	CM-Ma

These bundle-packed cigars are medium in body and easy to recognize thanks to the bright red label. The new Wilshire shape is packed in an elegant glass jar, completed by an enclosed cigar cutter.

SPECIAL JAMAICAN
Handmade in Santiago, Dominican Republic.

Wrapper: USA/Connecticut   *Binder: Mexico*   *Filler: Dom. Rep.*

Shape	Name	Lgth	Ring	Wrapper
Toro	Bonita	6	50	CC

HANDMADE CIGARS: BRAND LISTINGS

Double Corona	Churchill	7	52	CC
Lonsdale	Fancytale	6½	43	CC
Double Corona	Mayfair	7	60	CC-Ma
Double Corona	Nobles	7	50	CC
Small Panatela	Pica	5	32	CC
Pyramid	Pyramid	7	52	CC
Giant	Rey del Rey	9	60	CC-Ma
Lonsdale	A	6½	44	DC-CC-Ma
Long Corona	B	6	44	CC
Corona	C	5½	44	DC-CC
Toro	D	6	50	CC-Ma

This is a mild blend of tobaccos from three nations, combined to create a high-quality series of cigars, especially in the larger sizes. The huge "Rey del Rey" shape translates to "King of Kings."

ST. TROPEZ
Handmade in Danli, Honduras.

Wrapper: Ecuador   *Binder: Honduras*   *Filler: Honduras*

Shape	Name	Lgth	Ring	Wrapper
Lonsdale	Numero Uno	7	44	CC
Long Corona	Numero Dos	6	43	CC
Corona	Numero Tres	5½	42	CC

This is a new brand for 1996, offering a mild body and a modest price point. The quality of construction and leaf are all the more appreciated in cigars which are also affordable for an everyday smoke.

SUAVE
Handmade in Santiago, Dominican Republic.

Wrapper: USA/Connecticut   *Binder: Dom. Rep.*   *Filler: Dom. Rep.*

Shape	Name	Lgth	Ring	Wrapper
Long Corona	Corona	6	44	CC

HANDMADE CIGARS: BRAND LISTINGS

Robusto	Robusto	5	50	CC
Double Corona	Churchill	7½	50	CC

Introduced in 1996, this brand offers excellent construction and medium body from a blend of a Connecticut wrapper with two-year-old tobaccos from the Cibao Valley, the heart of the Dominican tobacco-growing zone. Suave cigars are presented either in all-cedar boxes of 25, or in bundles of 25 in individual cellophane sleeves.

SUERDIECK
Made in Cruz des Almas, Brazil.

Wrapper: Brazil   *Binder: Brazil*   *Filler: Brazil*

Shape	Name	Lgth	Ring	Wrapper
	Handmade cigars, made in Brazil:			
Slim Panatela	Brasilia	5½	30	CM
Slim Panatela	Caballeros	6	30	CM
Grand Corona	Finos	5¾	46	CM
Petit Corona	Mandarim Pai	5	42	CM
Slim Panatela	Nips	6	32	CM
Slim Panatela	Valencia	6	30	CC
Petit Corona	Viajantes	5	40	CM
	Premium series, handmade in Brazil:			
Corona Extra	Corona Brasil Luxo	5½	45	CM
Corona Extra	Corona Imperial Luxo	5½	45	CC
Corona	Mata Fina Especial	5¼	42	CM
Short Panatela	Panatella Fina	5⅝	36	CM
	Cigarillos, handmade in Brazil of 100% tobacco:			
Cigarillo	Beira Mar Finos	5¼	28	CM
Cigarillo	Copacabana	5	29	CC
	Cigarillos, machine-made in Brazil:			
Cigarillo	Palomitas	3½	32	CM

HANDMADE CIGARS: BRAND LISTINGS

Cigarillo	Palomitas Classics	3½	32	CM
Cigarillo	Palomitas Cherry	3½	32	CM
Cigarillo	Palomitas Clove	3½	32	CM
Cigarillo	Reynitas	3⅛	22	CC-CM

This well-known brand offers a unique, medium-bodied, flavorful taste of Brazilian tobacco in both handmade and machine-made shapes, famous since 1892. All use home-grown leaf, although the Corona Imperial, Palomitas, Panatela, Copacabana, Reynitas and Valencia shapes use Sumatran-seed tobaccos grown in Brazil.

TABACALERA
Handmade in Manila, the Philippines.
Wrapper: Indonesia/Java   Binder: Philippines   Filler: Dom. Rep., Philippines

Shape	Name	Lgth	Ring	Wrapper
Corona	Corona	5¼	42	CM
Lonsdale	Corona Largas	7	43	CM
Giant	Corona Largas Especiales	8	46	CM
Giant	Double Coronas	8½	50	CM
Short Panatela	Half Corona	4	37	CM
Short Panatela	Panatelas	5	35	CM
Robusto	Robusto	5	50	CM
Long Panatela	Banderellas	7¼	35	CM
Petit Corona	Brevas	5⅛	44	CM
Corona	Brevas a la Conserva	5¼	43	CM
Pyramid	Cortador	5	50	CM
Lonsdale	Don "Q"	7¼	41	CM
Lonsdale	El Conde de Guell Sr.	7	41	CM
Giant	Gigantes	14¼	60	CM
Slim Panatela	Panatela	5¼	34	CM
Slim Panatela	Panatela Largas	6	34	CM

HANDMADE CIGARS: BRAND LISTINGS

The famous history of cigar production in the Philippines is continued with the medium-bodied Tabacalera line, which dates to 1881. Using Southeast Asian tobaccos from the Indonesian island of Java for the wrapper, most of the filler and the binder is home-grown from the province of Isabela, located on the island of Luzon, also home to the Philippine capital of Manila.

TABACOS SAN JOSE
Handmade in Miami, Florida, USA.

Wrapper: Ecuador, USA/Connecticut *Binder: Dominican Republic*
Filler: Brazil, Dominican Republic, Honduras, Nicaragua

Shape	Name	Lgth	Ring	Wrapper
Corona	Corona	5½	44	Co-CC-Ma
Lonsdale	Lonsdale	6½	42	Co-CC-Ma
Robusto	Robusto	4⅞	50	Co-CC-Ma
Toro	Epicure	6	50	Co-CC-Ma
Churchill	Churchill	7	47	Co-CC-Ma
Double Corona	Double Corona	7⅝	50	Co-CC-Ma
Giant	Presidente	8	52	Co-CC-Ma
Torpedo	Torpedo	6½	54	Co-CC-Ma
Torpedo	Grand Torpedo	7½	60	Co-CC-Ma

Here is an exciting new brand for 1996, offered in three shades of wrapper: Natural and Rosado, both using an Ecuadorian-grown wrapper, and a maduro shade, utilizing Connecticut leaf. The result is a mild-to-medium bodied taste, offered in all-cedar boxes of 25 (except for the Gran Torpedo, offered in 10s).

TABACOS UNIVERSO
Handmade in Danli, Honduras.

Wrapper: Honduras *Binder: Honduras* *Filler: Honduras*

Shape	Name	Lgth	Ring	Wrapper
Corona	Numero 4	5½	42	CM
Long Panatela	Palma Fina	7	38	CM
Robusto	Rothschild	5	50	CM
Double Corona	Churchill	7	49	CM

HANDMADE CIGARS: BRAND LISTINGS

Giant	Soberano	8	50	CM

This is a 1996 introduction, handmade with long-filler tobaccos from Honduras. The body is medium and each shape is offered in boxes of 25.

TABAQUERO
Handmade in the Dominican Republic.

Wrapper: USA/Connecticut   *Binder: Proprietary*   *Filler: Dom. Rep.*

Shape	Name	Lgth	Ring	Wrapper
Giant	No. 850	8	50	CC
Torpedo	No. 754	7	54	CC
Churchill	No. 746	7	46	CC
Toro	No. 650	6	50	CC
Long Corona	No. 644	6	44	CC
Panatela	No. 638	6	38	CC
Petit Corona	No. 542	5	42	CC

Introduced in 1995, aged tobaccos are used to provide a this brand with a mild-to-medium bodied taste, offered in all-cedar boxes of 24.

TABANTILLAS
Handmade in the Dominican Republic.

Wrapper: Cameroon   *Binder: Dom. Rep.*   *Filler: Dom. Rep.*

Shape	Name	Lgth	Ring	Wrapper
Giant	A	10	50	CM
Giant	Gran Duque	8	50	CM
Long Panatela	Havana Club	7¼	38	CM
Panatela	1866 No. 1	6¾	38	CM
Toro	Torerro	6	50	CM
Corona Extra	Condado Real	5½	46	CM
Corona	No. 4	5¼	42	CM
Robusto	Romeo	4½	52	CM

HANDMADE CIGARS: BRAND LISTINGS

This is a new brand for 1996, offering a full-bodied smoke and the highest quality of construction. Offered in boxes of 25, except for the Tabantillas "A," which is offered singly.

TAMBORIL
Handmade in Tamboril, Dominican Republic.

Wrapper: USA/Connecticut   *Binder: Dom. Rep.*   *Filler: Dom. Rep.*

Shape	Name	Lgth	Ring	Wrapper
Giant	Double Corona	8	50	CC
Churchill	Churchill	7	47	CC
Churchill	Diablo	7	47	CC
Torpedo	Torpedo	6½	54	CC
Corona	Corona	6	44	CC
Robusto	Robusto	5	52	CC
Short Panatela	Cortadito	5	38	CC

Here is an exhaustingly produced cigar which offers a medium-to-full bodied taste. It features a Cuban-seed Domincan filler, Dominican Olor binder and genuine Connecticut wrapper. These are serious cigars made by serious smokers, and presented in boxes of 25.

TE-AMO
Handmade in San Andres Tuxtula, Mexico.

Wrapper: Mexico   *Binder: Mexico*   *Filler: Mexico*

Shape	Name	Lgth	Ring	Wrapper
Lonsdale	No. 1 Relaxation	6⅝	44	CC-CM-Ma
Long Corona	No. 2 Meditation	6	42	CC-CM-Ma
Panatela	No. 3 Torero	6½	35	CC-CM-Ma
Petit Corona	No. 4	5	42	CC-CM-Ma
Cigarillo	No. 5 Picador	7	27	CC-CM-Ma
Giant	No. 6 CEO	8½	52	CM-Ma
Cigarillo	No. 10 Epicure	5	27	CM
Cigarillo	No. 11 Elegante	5¾	27	CC-CM-Ma

Double Corona	No. 14 Churchill	7½	50	CC-CM-Ma
Double Corona	No. 17 Presidente	7	50	CM-Ma
Robusto	No. 18 Torito	4¾	50	CM-Ma
Toro	No. 19 Toro	6	50	CC-CM-Ma
Long Panatela	No. 24 Caballero	7	35	CM
Double Corona	No. 28 Maximo	7	54	CM-Ma
Grand Corona	No. 29 Satisfaction	6	46	CM-Ma
Robusto	Robusto	5½	54	CM-Ma
Torpedo	Figurado	6⅝	50	CM-Ma
Pyramid	Piramides	6¼	50	CM-Ma
Pyramid	Gran Piramides	7¾	54	CM-Ma
Lonsdale	Celebration (tubed)	6⅝	44	CM
Long Panatela	Caballero	7	35	CM
Perfecto	Double Perfecto	7	48	CM-Ma
	Made with short filler:			
Cigarillo	No. 26 Intermezzo	4	28	CC
Small Panatela	No. 27 Impulse	5	32	CC
Short Panatela	Pauser	5⅜	35	CM

This very popular brand, originated in the 1960s, is a product of the San Andres Valley, where all of the tobaccos for this brand are grown. Considered to be medium in strength, the enthusiast has a choice of natural or maduro wrappers, or can choose many of the shapes in the lighter-wrapped and lighter-bodied Te-Amo Lights.

TE-AMO SEGUNDO
Handmade in San Andres Tuxtla, Mexico.

Wrapper: Mexico   *Binder: Mexico*   *Filler: Mexico*

Shape	Name	Lgth	Ring	Wrapper
Panatela	No. 55 Torero	6½	35	CM-Ma
Long Corona	No. 60 Meditation	6	42	CM-Ma

HANDMADE CIGARS: BRAND LISTINGS

Lonsdale	No. 75 Relaxation	6⅝	44	CM-Ma
Double Corona	No. 90 Presidente	7	50	CM-Ma
Double Corona	No. 110 Churchill	7½	50	CM-Ma
Grand Corona	No. 120 Satisfaction	6	46	CM-Ma
Toro	No. 135 Toro	6	50	CM-Ma

These are just what the name suggests: seconds of the regular Te-Amo line, produced with the same San Andres Valley tobaccos. Offered in bundles of 20 cigars each, they are good cigars and an even better value.

TEMPLE HALL
Handmade in Kingston, Jamaica.
Wrapper: USA/Connecticut   Binder: Mexico   Filler: Dom. Rep., Mexico

Shape	Name	Lgth	Ring	Wrapper
Double Corona	No. 700	7	49	CC
Lonsdale	No. 675	6¾	45	CC
Robusto	No. 550	5½	49	CC
Long Corona	No. 625	6¼	42	CC
Small Panatela	No. 500	5	31	CC
Small Panatela	No. 450	4½	49	Ma
Torpedo	Belicoso	6	50	CC
Lonsdale	Trumps No. 1	6½	42	CC-Ma
Robusto	Trumps No. 2	5½	50	CC
Corona	Trumps No. 3	5½	42	CC-Ma
Double Corona	Trumps No. 4	7½	49	CC

A medium-strength cigar made in Jamaica since 1876, Temple Hall cigars are made and left in a natural, round shape - not pressed. It is an easy-drawing cigar which offers the connoisseur a choice of shapes, and in a few cases, the choice of a natural-shade or maduro-shade wrapper.

HANDMADE CIGARS: BRAND LISTINGS

TENA Y VEGA
Handmade in Danli, Honduras.

Wrapper: Cameroon   *Binder: Honduras*   *Filler: Honduras*

Shape	Name	Lgth	Ring	Wrapper
Long Corona	Cetros	6⅛	42	CM
Double Corona	Churchill	7	50	CM
Toro	Double Corona	6	50	CM
Lonsdale	No. 1	6¾	42	CM

These are rather medium-to-heavy bodied, all long-filler cigars. Its distinctive taste is produced by the blending of Honduran origin tobaccos and the hard-to-find, medium-brown Cameroon wrapper.

TESOROS DE COPAN
Handmade in Santa Rosa de Copan, Honduras.

Wrapper: Honduras   *Binder: Honduras*   *Filler: Honduras*

Shape	Name	Lgth	Ring	Wrapper
Double Corona	Churchill	7	50	CC
Long Corona	Cetros	6¼	44	CC
Toro	Toros	6	50	CC
Corona Extra	Corona	5¼	46	CC
Robusto	Yumbo	4¾	50	CC
Panatela	Lindas	5⅝	38	CC

Created in 1993, Tesoros de Copan cigars are much more than simply a mild-to-medium-bodied cigar with Honduran-grown Connecticut-seed wrappers. Part of the proceeds from the sale of these cigars supports the efforts of the La Ruta Maya Foundation, which is dedicated to the conservation of the Central American rain forests and historic preservation of the remains of the Mayans, who originated the use of tobacco many centuries ago.

THOMAS HINDS HONDURAN SELECTION
Handmade in Danli, Honduras.

Wrapper: Ecuador   *Binder: Honduras*   *Filler: Honduras*

HANDMADE CIGARS: BRAND LISTINGS

Shape	Name	Lgth	Ring	Wrapper
Giant	Presidente	8½	52	CM
Double Corona	Churchill	7	49	CM
Torpedo	Torpedo	6	52	CM
Toro	Short Churchill	6	50	CM
Lonsdale	Supremos	7	43	CM
Robusto	Robusto	5	50	CM
Long Corona	Royal Corona	6	43	CM
Corona	Corona	5½	42	CM

Introduced in the U.S. in 1994, Thomas Hinds Honduran Selection are premium, hand-rolled cigars. The long-leaf filler are double binder are of Honduran origin, while the wrapper is a slightly spicy Ecuadorian leaf.

THOMAS HINDS NICARAGUAN SELECTION
Handmade in Esteli, Nicaragua.

Wrapper: Ecuador   *Binder: Nicaragua*   *Filler: Nicaragua*

Shape	Name	Lgth	Ring	Wrapper
Torpedo	Torpedo	6	52	CC-Ma
Double Corona	Churchill	7	49	CC-Ma
Lonsdale	Lonsdale Extra	7	43	CC-Ma
Toro	Short Churchill	6	50	CC-Ma
Corona	Corona	5½	42	CC-Ma
Robusto	Robusto	5	50	CC-Ma

First offered in 1995, the Thomas Hinds Nicaraguan Selection showcases filler and binder tobaccos from the Jalapa region of Nicaragua. Easy to smoke thanks to top-quality construction, these cigars are elegantly packaged in handsome all-cedar boxes.

TIA MARTIA
Handmade in Santiago, Dominican Republic.

Wrapper: Honduras   *Binder: Mexico*   *Filler: Dom. Rep., Honduras*

HANDMADE CIGARS: BRAND LISTINGS

Shape	Name	Lgth	Ring	Wrapper
Lonsdale	No. 1	7	42	CM-Ma
Petit Corona	No. 4	5	42	CM-Ma
Double Corona	Churchill	7½	50	CM-Ma
Long Corona	Corona	6	42	CM-Ma
Panatela	Panatela	6	38	CM-Ma
Short Panatela	Petit	5	38	CM-Ma
Double Corona	Presidente	7	50	CM-Ma
Toro	Toro	6	50	CM-Ma

Created in 1978, this is a mild-to-medium blend of leaves from three nations, offered in modestly-priced bundles of 25.

TIBURON
Handmade in Danli, Honduras.

Wrapper: Ecuador   Binder: Indonesia/Sumatra
Filler: Dominican Republic, Honduras, Nicaragua

Shape	Name	Lgth	Ring	Wrapper
Slim Panatela	Tiger Shark	6¼	33	CC
Long Corona	Great White	6	42	CC
Corona	Mako	5¼	42	CC
Churchill	Black Tip	7	48	CC
Giant	Hammerhead	8½	50	CC

Despite the fierce names of the shapes, these are mild-bodied cigars. They are offered in bundles of 25 cigars each.

TODO EL MUNDO
Handmade in Villa Gonzales, Dominican Republic.

Wrapper: USA/Connecticut   Binder: Dom. Rep.   Filler: Dom. Rep.

Shape	Name	Lgth	Ring	Wrapper
Double Corona	Churchill	7½	50	CC
Toro	Grand Robusto	6	52	CC

HANDMADE CIGARS: BRAND LISTINGS

Churchill	Double Corona	7	48	CC
Long Corona	Corona	6	44	CC
Giant Corona	Petit Corona	7½	42	CC

Here is a 1996 introduction of a cigar whose names means "all over the world" in Spanish. Thanks to its mild-to-medium body and silky Connecticut wrapper, it probably will achieve popularity "todo el mundo."

TOOTH OF THE DOG
Handmade in Esteli, Nicaragua.

Wrapper: Nicaragua *Binder: Nicaragua* *Filler: Nicaragua*

Shape	Name	Lgth	Ring	Wrapper
Robusto	Rothchild	5	50	CM
Toro	Toro	6	50	CM
Double Corona	Churchill	7	52	CM
Long Corona	Cetros	6	44	CM

Here is a medium-bodied cigar of all-Nicaraguan origin, offered with an interesting name and an even more interesting box, each holding 20 Tooth of the Dog cigars . . . or is that Teeth of the Dog?

TOPPER CENTENNIAL
Handmade in Santiago, Dominican Republic.

Wrapper: Ecuador *Binder: Dom. Rep.* *Filler: Dom. Rep.*

Shape	Name	Lgth	Ring	Wrapper
Double Corona	Churchill	7½	52	CC
Toro	Toro	6	50	CC
Lonsdale	Lonsdale	6¾	43	CC
Pyramid	Pyramid	7½	50	CC

The Topper Cigar Company was founded in 1896, offering handmade cigars with imported long filler and Connecticut broadleaf wrappers. That tradition is now continued with the Topper Centennial, introduced in 1995, a handmade cigar manufactured in the Dominican Republic. This is a medium-bodied smoke, offered in three popular sizes.

HANDMADE CIGARS: BRAND LISTINGS

TOPPER GRANDE
Handmade in Esteli, Nicaragua.

Wrapper: Indonesia   *Binder: Nicaragua*   *Filler: Nicaragua*

Shape	Name	Lgth	Ring	Wrapper
Double Corona	Double Corona	7½	50	CM
Toro	Corona Gorda	6	50	CM
Robusto	Robusto	4½	50	CM
Lonsdale	Cetro	6½	43	CM
Corona	Corona	5½	43	CM

Here is a new handmade from an American institution among cigar makers, celebrating its 100th anniversary in 1996. This is a medium-to-full bodied smoke, featuring Indonesian wrappers around aged Nicaraguan leaves.

TORCEDOR
Handmade in Esteli, Nicaragua.

Wrapper: Nicaragua   *Binder: Nicaragua*   *Filler: Honduras*

Shape	Name	Lgth	Ring	Wrapper
Lonsdale	No. 1	7	44	CC
Double Corona	Churchill	7	50	CC
Robusto	Robusto	5	50	CC
Toro	Toro	6	50	CC
Giant	General	8	52	CC

"Torcedor" means cigar roller in Spanish and this 1996 brand salutes them with a mild blend of long-filler tobaccos from Honduras and Nicaragua.

TRESADO
Handmade in La Romana, Dominican Republic.

Wrapper: Indonesia   *Binder: Dom. Rep.*   *Filler: Dom. Rep.*

Shape	Name	Lgth	Ring	Wrapper
Giant	Seleccion No. 100	8	52	CC
Churchill	Seleccion No. 200	7	48	CC

Grand Corona	Seleccion No. 300	6	46	CC
Lonsdale	Seleccion No. 400	6⅝	44	CC
Corona	Seleccion No. 500	5½	42	CC

Tresado provides handmade quality at a value price. Introduced in 1988, the cigar starts with a Dominican blend and binder, then adds an Indonesian wrapper for a full-bodied, yet mild smoke.

TROYA
Handmade in Santiago, Dominican Republic.

Wrapper: USA/Connecticut   Binder: Dom. Rep.   Filler: Dom. Rep.

Shape	Name	Lgth	Ring	Wrapper
Torpedo	No. 81 Torpedo	7	54	CC-Ma
Double Corona	No. 72 Executive	7¾	50	CC-Ma
Churchill	No. 63 Churchill	6⅞	46	CC-Ma
Lonsdale	No. 54 Elegante	7	43	CC-Ma
Long Corona	No. 45 Cetro	6¼	44	CC-Ma
Long Panatela	No. 36 Palma Fina	7	36	CC
Corona	No. 27 Corona	5½	42	CC
Robusto	No. 18 Rothchild	4½	50	CC-Ma
	Troya Clasico:			
Double Corona	No. 72 Executive	7¾	50	CC
Corona	No. 27 Corona	5½	42	CC

Troya is a hand-crafted cigar of the highest quality, introduced in 1985. It has a medium body and a consistency in construction and draw that will reward the connoisseur every time. Troyas are offered in boxes of 25 cigars, in natural and maduro wrappers. The Clasico line of two shapes was created in 1991, and is produced only when truly superior leaves are available to create a fuller taste that is now encased in boxes of 20 cigars each. Look for a new Clasico band, and note that each box produced is sequentially numbered to ensure quality control and exclusivity.

HANDMADE CIGARS: BRAND LISTINGS

TULAS
Handmade in Danli, Honduras.

Wrapper: USA/Connecticut   *Binder: Mexico*   *Filler: Nicaragua*

Shape	Name	Lgth	Ring	Wrapper
Lonsdale	No. 1	6½	42	CC
Corona Extra	No. 2	5½	46	CC
Churchill	No. 3	7	48	CC
Giant	No. 4	8½	50	CC
Robusto	No. 5	5	52	CC
Toro	No. 6	6¾	54	CC

This is a mild-bodied cigar, modestly priced and offered in cellophane-wrapped bundles of 20 cigars each.

H. UPMANN
Handmade in the La Romana, Dominican Republic.

Wrapper: Indonesia   *Binder: Dom. Rep.*   *Filler: Dom. Rep.*

Shape	Name		Lgth	Ring	Wrapper
Grand Corona	Churchills		5⅝	46	CM
Churchill	Corona Imperiales		7	46	CM
Petit Corona	Corona Major	*(tubed)*	5	42	CM
Corona	Coronas		5½	42	CM
Corona	Corona Cristals	*(glass tube)*	5½	42	CM
Toro	Coronas Bravas		6½	48	CM
Lonsdale	Director Royales		6⅝	42	CM
Long Panatela	El Prado		7	36	CM
Lonsdale	Lonsdales		6⅝	42	CM
Churchill	Monarch	*(tubed)*	7	46	CM
Panatela	Naturales	*(tubed)*	6⅛	36	CM
Lonsdale	No. 2000		7	42	CM

Panatela	Panatela Cristal (glass tube)	6¾	38	CM
Robusto	Pequenos No. 100	4½	50	CM
Corona Extra	Pequenos No. 200	4½	46	CM
Petit Corona	Pequenos No. 300	4½	42	CM
Petit Corona	Petit Coronas	5	42	CM
Corona	Topacios	5¼	43	CM
Panatela	Extra Finos Gold (tubed)	6¾	38	CM
Panatela	Finos Gold (tubed)	6⅛	36	CM
Petit Corona	Tubos Gold (tubed)	5	42	CM
	Machine-made with short-filler:			
Cigarillo	Aperitif	4	28	CM
Small Panatela	Demi Tasse	4½	33	CM

Legendary is the only way to describe the H. Upmann brand, originated in Cuba in 1844. Today's Dominican-produced Upmann appeared in the U.S. for the first time in 1975 and combines a medium-bodied taste with first-class construction and a consistency – even through a change in wrapper tobacco from Cameroon to Indonesia – which makes this brand a dependable favorite of smokers everywhere.

H. UPMANN CABINET SELECTION
Handmade in La Romana, Dominican Republic.

Wrapper: Indonesia   *Binder: Dom. Rep.*   *Filler: Dom. Rep.*

Shape	*Name*	*Lgth*	*Ring*	*Wrapper*
Giant	Columbo	8	50	CM
Robusto	Corsario	5½	50	CM
Robusto	Robusto	4¾	50	CM

The larger girth of these marvelous cigars affords the smoker a full volume of smoke and a richness of taste and aroma that smaller-ring cigars cannot provide. The enthusiast will appreciate the "boite nature" packaging of 50 cigars per box.

HANDMADE CIGARS: BRAND LISTINGS

H. UPMANN CHAIRMAN'S RESERVE
Handmade in La Romana, Dominican Republic.
Wrapper: USA/Connecticut   Binder: Dom. Rep.   Filler: Brazil, Dom. Rep.

Shape	Name	Lgth	Ring	Wrapper
Long Panatela	Chairman's Reserve	7½	38	CC
Churchill	Churchill	6¾	48	CC
Double Corona	Double Corona	7	50	CC
Robusto	Robusto	5	50	CC
Torpedo	Torpedo	6	50	CC

This new brand, introduced in 1996, offers smokers a chance to sample the blend made for Consolidated Cigar Corporation's owner, Ron Perelman. It is medium-bodied and elegantly made; the Chairman's Reserve is individually boxed in a mahogany slide-top case! The other shapes are available in 20s.

V CENTENNIAL
Handmade in Danli, Honduras.
Wrapper: USA/Connecticut   Binder: Mexico
Filler: Dominican Republic, Honduras, Nicaragua

Shape	Name	Lgth	Ring	Wrapper
Torpedo	Torpedo	7	54	CC
Giant	Presidente	8	50	CC
Churchill	Churchill	7	48	CC-Ma
Long Panatela	No. 1	7½	38	CC
Toro	No. 2	6	50	CC-Ma
Lonsdale	Cetros	6¼	44	CC-Ma
Robusto	Robustos	5	50	CC-Ma
Corona	Coronas	5½	42	CC

V Centennial is handmade in Honduras using the finest tobacco from the Dominican Republic, Nicaragua, Honduras, Mexico and the United States. Selection and processing of this cigar began in 1992. It was introduced in November, 1993 and has become one of the top-rated cigars available today. It is considered a medium-bodied cigar.

HANDMADE CIGARS: BRAND LISTINGS

V.M. SANTANA COLLECTION
Handmade in Santiago, Dominican Republic.
Wrapper: USA/Connecticut   Binder: Dom. Rep.   Filler: Dom. Rep.

Shape	Name	Lgth	Ring	Wrapper
Robusto	Robusto	5½	50	CC
Long Corona	Corona Grande	6	44	CC
Double Corona	Churchill	7	50	CC
Pyramid	Pyramid	6	54	CC

This was a new brand for 1996, with a mild body and a smooth, genuine Connecticut wrapper, offered in limited distribution in boxes of 25 cigars each.

VARGAS
Handmade in Las Palmas, the Canary Islands of Spain.
Wrapper: Indonesia/Sumatra   Binder: Indonesia/Java   Filler: Canary Islands

Shape	Name	Lgth	Ring	Wrapper
Churchill	Presidentes	6¾	46	CM
Corona Extra	Senadores	5½	46	CM
Panatela	Diplomaticos	5½	36	CM
Double Corona	Churchill	7½	50	CM
Corona	Capitolios	5⅛	44	CM
Robusto	Robustos	4¾	50	CM

This is an old brand which is being re-introduced in 1996. It is mild in body and has excellent construction of primarily Indonesian leaves, offered in boxes of 25.

VERACRUZ
Handmade in San Andres Tuxtula, Mexico.
Wrapper: Mexico   Binder: Mexico   Filler: Mexico

Shape	Name	Lgth	Ring	Wrapper
Small Panatela	Flor de Veracruz Carinas	4⅝	34	CC
Long Corona	Mina de Veracruz *(tubed)*	6¼	42	CC

HANDMADE CIGARS: BRAND LISTINGS

Slim Panatela	Veracruz L'Operetta	4⅞	34	Ma
Lonsdale	Poemas de Veracruz*(tubed)*	6¼	42	Ma
Churchill	Veracruz Magnum *(tubed)*	7⅞	48	CC

Introduced in 1994, Veracruz ultra-premium cigars are hand-rolled from a selection of choice Mexican tobaccos. Remarkably mild, yet flavorful with hints of honey, spices and coffee, Veracruz are guaranteed fresh. In fact, each of the larger-sized cigars are individually encased in glass tubes for air-tight safety.

VICTOR SINCLAIR
Handmade in Santiago, Dominican Republic.
Wrapper: Indonesia, USA/Connecticut

Binder: Dominican Republic　　　　　　　*Filler: Dominican Republic*

Shape	Name	Lgth	Ring	Wrapper
Double Corona	Churchill	7½	50	CC-Ma
Robusto	Robusto No. 1	5½	50	CC-Ma
Robusto	Robusto No. 2	4½	50	CC-Ma
Long Corona	Lonsdale	6	44	CC-Ma
Pyramid	Pyramid	7	54	CC-Ma

Introduced in 1995, this handmade cigar offers two different shades of wrapper: a natural wrapper grown in Connecticut and a maduro wrapper from Indonesia. The blend is mild to medium in body and offered in boxes of 25.

VICTORY SPIRIT
Handmade in Esteli, Nicaragua.
Wrapper: Indonesia　　　　　　　　　　*Binder: Nicaragua*
Filler: Nicaragua and a proprietary Central American leaf

Shape	Name	Lgth	Ring	Wrapper
Corona	Champion	5¾	44	CC
Robusto	Victor	4¾	52	CC
Toro	Laureate	6	50	CC
Churchill	Conqueror	7	48	CC

HANDMADE CIGARS: BRAND LISTINGS

Here is a special cigar introduced in 1996 under license from the Olympic Council of Ireland. Featuring the five Olympic rings on its Collector's Edition boxes, this is a mild and flavorful blend which features shade-grown, Havana-seed wrappers grown in Indonesia. Victory Spirit cigars are available in commemorative cedar cabinets of 12 and in special cabinets of 24.

VILLAR Y VILLAR
Handmade in Esteli, Nicaragua.

Wrapper: Ecuador   *Binder: Honduras*
Filler: Dominican Republic, Honduras, Nicaragua

Shape	Name	Lgth	Ring	Wrapper
Giant	Bermejos	8½	52	CC
Grand Corona	Cazadores	6½	46	CC
Lonsdale	Figaros	6½	44	CC
Short Panatela	Half Coronas	4½	38	CC
Robusto	Laguitos	4½	52	CC
Pyramid	Pyramides	7	50	CC
Petit Corona	Remedios	4½	44	CC
Robusto	Robustos	4½	52	CC
Toro	Toros	6⅛	48	CC
Churchill	Valentinos	6¾	48	CC
Double Corona	754s	7	54	CC

The romance of the great days of the Cuban cigar industry are re-kindled immediately by the mere mention of this the name of this storied brand. For 1996, it re-appears as a modestly-priced, medium-bodied cigar with a Sumatra-seed wrapper grown in Ecuador. It is offered in bundles of 25.

VILLEGA REALES
Handmade in Moca, Dominican Republic.

Wrapper: Brazil   *Binder: Dom. Rep.*   *Filler: Dom. Rep.*

Shape	Name	Lgth	Ring	Wrapper
Corona	Corona	5½	43	CM
Churchill	Churchill	7	48	CM

HANDMADE CIGARS: BRAND LISTINGS

Lonsdale	Lonsdale	7	43	CM
Robusto	Robusto	4¾	52	CM
Toro	Toro	6	50	CM

These handmade cigars were introduced in late 1996 and feature Dominican-grown Piloto Cubano filler leaves and Olor binders, coupled with three-year-old Brazilian-grown Cameroon-seed wrappers. These is a medium-bodied brand produced under the supervision of Raul Diaz de Villega in the Montezuma factory in Moca, near Santiago, in the Dominican Republic.

VINTAGE HONDURAN
Handmade in Danli, Honduras.

Wrapper: Honduras　　　　　*Binder: Honduras*　　　　　*Filler: Honduras*

Shape	Name	Lgth	Ring	Wrapper
Lonsdale	Cetro	6½	44	CM-Ma
Toro	Governor	6	50	CM-Ma
Giant Corona	Imperial	8	44	CM
Corona	Matador	5½	42	CM-Ma
Panatela	Panatela	6	36	CM
Long Panatela	Panatela Larga	7	36	CM
Double Corona	President	7½	50	CM-Ma
Robusto	Rothschild	4½	50	CM-Ma
Giant	Sultans	8½	52	CM-Ma
Corona Extra	Toro	5½	46	CM-Ma

This is a medium-to-heavy bodied cigar, handmade in Danli, Honduras. Its robust, musky flavor is presented in oversized bundles of 50 cigars and is enhanced by its modest pricing!

VIRTUOSO TORAÑO
Handmade in Danli, Honduras.

Wrapper: Costa Rica, Ecuador　　　　　*Binder: Honduras*
Filler: Costa Rica, Honduras, Nicaragua

HANDMADE CIGARS: BRAND LISTINGS

Shape	Name	Lgth	Ring	Wrapper
Giant	Presidente	8	52	CC-Ma
Toro	Double Corona	6	50	CC-Ma
Robusto	Robusto	4¾	52	CC-Ma
Lonsdale	Lonsdale	7	44	CC
Long Corona	Cetros	6	43	CC

Introduced in 1995, Virtuoso is a long-filler, all hand-made cigar with a Colorado-Claro wrapper of Connecticut-seed origin grown in Ecuador. This and the blend of leaves from three nations in the filler and binder give this line a mild-to-medium body, but with plenty of taste. The maduro-wrapped shapes utilize leaf grown in Costa Rica.

VUELTABAJO
Handmade in Santiago, Dominican Republic.
Wrapper: USA/Connecticut   *Binder: Dom. Rep.*   *Filler: Dom. Rep.*

Shape	Name	Lgth	Ring	Wrapper
Giant	Gigante	8½	52	CC
Churchill	Churchill	7	48	CC
Robusto	Robusto	4¾	52	CC
Lonsdale	Lonsdale	7	43	CC
Toro	Toros	6	50	CC
Corona	Corona	5¾	42	CC
Pyramid	Pyramid	5	52	CC

Introduced in 1994, the Vueltabajo line is fine enough to bear the name of the most legendary tobacco-growing region in the world. Artfully crafted with a smooth Connecticut Shade wrapper, hand-selected Dominican Olor binder and the richest Dominican Piloto Cubano filler, this cigar is mild-to-medium in strength.

W & D BUNDLES
Handmade in Danli, Honduras.
Wrapper: Honduras, USA/Connecticut
Binder: Honduras   *Filler: Dominican Republic, Honduras*

Holy Smoke

They're that good.

Ask your favorite tobacconist for a Virtuoso, handmade in
Honduras, a Grand Nica, handmade in Nicaragua and a
Carlos Toraño, handmade in the Dominican Republic. All from the
fine line of Toraño cigars, a legendary name in smoking pleasure.

4631 Southwest 75th Avenue, Miami, Florida 33155

HANDMADE CIGARS: BRAND LISTINGS

Shape	Name	Lgth	Ring	Wrapper
Double Corona	Presidentes	7½	50	CM-Ma
Lonsdale	Cetros	6½	44	CM-Ma
Robusto	Coronas	5½	50	CM-Ma
Long Panatela	Panatele Larga	7	36	CM
Corona	Blunts	5	42	CM-Ma
Giant	Gigantes	8½	52	Ma

These cigars are mild, long-filler, handmade cigars manufactured in Honduras and offered in bundles of 25 cigars each. Two different wrappers are available to suit the taste of individual smokers: a Connecticut-seed grown in Honduras natural wrapper and Connecticut Broadleaf maduro wrapper.

WEST INDIES VANILLA
Handmade, with medium filler, in Miami, Florida, USA.
Wrapper: Brazil *Binder: Brazil*
Filler: Dominican Republic, Ecuador, Honduras, Nicaragua

Shape	Name	Lgth	Ring	Wrapper
Short Panatela	Carmelita	5	38	CM
Churchill	Carmella	7	46	CM

This is a vanilla-flavored cigar produced by the Caribbean Cigar Company and introduced in 1995. It is handmade using 100% tobacco, but with medium filler instead of long filler leaves. It has a full-bodied taste and is offered in boxes of 25 cigars each.

YAGO
Handmade in Danli, Honduras.
Wrapper: Honduras *Binder: Honduras* *Filler: Honduras*

Shape	Name	Lgth	Ring	Wrapper
Lonsdale	Fumas	7	44	CM
Lonsdale	Cazadores	7	44	CM
Double Corona	Churchill	7½	50	CM
Corona	Petite Cazadores	5½	44	CM

HANDMADE CIGARS: BRAND LISTINGS

Introduced in 1990, these cigars are made by hand, of all Honduran-grown tobaccos. The result is a medium-bodied cigar, which are offered in bundles of 10 or 25.

YUMURI
Handmade in Navarrete, Dominican Republic.
Wrapper: USA/Connecticut   Binder: Dom.Rep.   Filler: Dom.Rep.

Shape	Name	Lgth	Ring	Wrapper
Toro	Toro	6	50	CC
Churchill	Churchill	7	48	CC
Robusto	Robusto	4¾	52	CC
Corona	Corona	5½	43	CC
Lonsdale	Lonsdale	7	43	CC

This brand was introduced late in 1995 and continues to expand its distribution. Mild in body, it features Piloto Cubano filler leaves surrounded by an Olor binder and a Connecticut Shade wrapper. Individually sleeved in cellophane, Yumuri cigars are presented in a hand-varnished box of 25.

YUMURI 1492
Handmade in Navarrete, Dominican Republic.
Wrapper: Indonesia/Sumatra   Binder: Dom. Rep.   Filler: Dom. Rep.

Shape	Name	Lgth	Ring	Wrapper
Toro	Toro	6	50	CC
Churchill	Churchill	7	48	CC
Robusto	Robusto	4¾	52	CC
Corona	Corona	5½	43	CC
Pyramid	Piramid	6	54	CC
Lonsdale	Lonsdale	7	43	CC

This second Yumuri style substitutes a Sumatran wrapper, which helps to produce a mild to medium-bodied taste to the brand.

HANDMADE CIGARS: BRAND LISTINGS

ZINO
Handmade in Santa Rosa de Copan, Honduras.

Wrapper: USA/Connecticut   *Binder: Honduras*   *Filler: Honduras*

Shape	Name	Lgth	Ring	Wrapper
Cigarillo	Princesse	4¼	20	CC
Corona	Diamonds	5½	40	CC
Lonsdale	Tradition	6¼	44	CC
Slim Panatela	Juniors	6¾	30	CC
Panatela	Elegance	6¾	34	CC
Double Corona	Veritas	7	50	CC
Panatela	Tubos No. 1 *(tubed)*	6¾	34	CC
	Connoisseur Series:			
Double Corona	Connoisseur 100	7½	52	CC
Toro	Connoisseur 200	6½	48	CC
Grand Corona	Connoisseur 300	5¾	46	CC
	Mouton-Cadet Series:			
Lonsdale	Mouton-Cadet No. 1	6½	44	CC
Panatela	Mouton-Cadet No. 2	6	35	CC
Panatela	Mouton-Cadet No. 3	5¾	36	CC
Slim Panatela	Mouton-Cadet No. 4	5⅛	30	CC
Petit Corona	Mouton-Cadet No. 5	5	42	CC
Robusto	Mouton-Cadet No. 6	5	50	CC

The subtlety of Davidoff combined with the finest Honduran tobaccos and a Connecticut Shade wrapper is expressed in the Zino line. The Mouton-Cadet series was specially selected for Baronne Philippine de Rothschild, offering a rich aroma and a mild taste.

5.
MASS-MARKET CIGARS: INDEX

Here are 115 machine-made brands of cigars listed in a compact index to country of origin and shapes.

For each brand, a two-letter code designates the country of manufacture:

Be	Belgium	Mx	Mexico
Br	Brazil	Ne	Netherlands
CR	Costa Rica	Ni	Nicaragua
DR	Dominican Republic	PR	Puerto Rico
Ge	Germany	Sz	Switzerland
Ho	Honduras	US	United States
In	Indonesia		

In addition, each line lists the shape "groups" in which the brand is produced. The 19 standard shapes listed in section 1.03 are broken into ten groups, including:

1. Cigarillo
2. Panatela group
• Small Panatela
• Slim Panatela
• Short Panatela
• Panatela
• Long Panatela
3. Corona group
• Petit Corona
• Corona
• Long Corona
4. Lonsdale group
• Lonsdale
• Giant Corona

5. Grand Corona group
• Corona Extra
• Grand Corona
6. Figurado group
• Culebras
• Perfecto
• Pyramid
• Torpedo
7. Robusto-Toro group
• Robusto
• Toro
8. Churchill
9. Double Corona
10. Giant

MASS-MARKET CIGARS: INDEX

Additional, detailed information about each of these brands is available in the following section, offering brand listings.

Brand	Made in	Machine-made	Cigarillo	Panatela	Corona	Lonsdale	Grand Corona	Figurado	Robusto-Toro	Churchill	Double Corona	Giant
Antonio y Cleopatra	US	●	●	●	●				●			
Arango Sportsman	US	●	●	●		●			●	●		
As You Like It	US	●		●	●							
Balmoral	Ne	●	●	●	●							
B-H	US	●			●	●			●			
Bances	US	●		●	●		●		●			
Ben Bey	US	●			●							
Ben Franklin	US	●			●							
Black & Mild	US	●		●								
Black Hawk	US	●					●					
Budd Sweet	US	●		●	●							
Candlelight	Ge	●	●									
Caribbean Rounds	US	●		●		●						
Charles Denby	US	●			●							
Charles the Great	US	●		●	●						●	
Cherry Blend	US	●		●								
The Cigar Baron	US	●					●	●				
Cima	PR	●			●							
Clubmaster	Ge	●	●	●		●						

Brand	Made in	Machine-made	Cigarillo	Panatela	Corona	Lonsdale	Grand Corona	Figurado	Robusto-Toro	Churchill	Double Corona	Giant
J. Cortes	Be	●	●	●								
Cuesta-Rey	US	●		●	●	●						
Cyrilla	US	●		●	●					●		
Decision Maduro	US	●		●	●		●		●			
De Olifant	Ne	●	●	●	●							
Dexter Londres	US	●			●							
Directors	US	●	●	●	●							
Don Cesar	US	●			●							
Dry Slitz	US	●		●								
R.G. Dun	US	●	●	●	●							
Dutch Masters	PR	●	●	●	●		●		●			
1886	US	●			●							
El Cauto	DR	●			●	●	●					
El Macco	US	●					●					
El Producto	PR	●		●	●		●		●			
El Trelles	US	●			●		●	●				
El Verso	US	●	●	●			●					
Emerson	US	●			●							
Evermore	US	●			●		●					
Farnam Drive	US	●			●		●					
Figaro	US	●				●						
Flor de Borinquen	PR	●			●							

MASS-MARKET CIGARS: INDEX

Brand	Made in	Machine-made	Cigarillo	Panatela	Corona	Lonsdale	Grand Corona	Figurado	Robusto-Toro	Churchill	Double Corona	Giant
Florida	US	●			●							
Garcia Grande	US	●			●			●	●	●		
Garcia y Vega	US	●	●	●	●							
Gargoyle	US	●		●								
Gold & Mild	US	●		●								
Harvester	US	●			●							
Hauptmann's	US	●		●	●		●					
Havana Blend	US	●	●	●	●	●			●	●		
Hav-A-Tampa	US	●	●	●	●							
Heeren van Ruysdael	Ne	●		●								
Ibold	US	●	●	●	●				●			
Ideal	PR	●			●							
Jon Piedro	US	●		●		●	●					
Jose Melendi	US	●		●	●	●	●		●			
J-R Famous	US	●		●	●	●			●			
Keep Moving	US	●			●							
King Edward	US	●	●	●	●							
La Eminencia	US	●		●	●	●						
La Fendrich	US	●		●			●					
Lancer	US	●		●								
La Paz	Ne	●	●	●	●							
La Restina	PR	●			●					●		

MASS-MARKET CIGARS: INDEX

Brand	Made in	Machine-made	Cigarillo	Panatela	Corona	Lonsdale	Grand Corona	Figurado	Robusto-Toro	Churchill	Double Corona	Giant
Lord Beaconsfield	US	●		●	●					●		
Lord Clinton	US	●		●	●							
Marsh	US	●		●	●							
Miflin's Choice	US	●		●								
Moya	US	●		●	●	●						
Muniemaker	US	●		●			●	●	●			
Muriel	US	●	●	●	●		●					
Nat Cicco's	US	●		●	●	●				●		
National Cigar	US	●			●							
Odin	US	●			●							
Old Hermitage	US	●					●					
Optimo	US	●		●	●							
Palma	US	●				●						
Pancho Garcia	US	●			●							
Pedro Iglesias	US	●			●	●	●					
Phillies	US	●	●	●	●							
Pollack	US	●		●								
Red Dot	US	●		●	●							
Rigoletto	US	●		●	●		●					
Rio Hondo	PR	●			●							
Rivalo	PR	●	●		●							
Robert Burns	US	●	●		●							

MASS-MARKET CIGARS: INDEX

Brand	Made in	Machine-made	Cigarillo	Panatela	Corona	Lonsdale	Grand Corona	Figurado	Robusto-Toro	Churchill	Double Corona	Giant
Roi-Tan	US	●	●	●	●							
Rosedale	US	●					●	●				
Ruy Lopez	US	●		●	●		●					
San Felice	US	●			●							
Santa Fe	US	●		●	●							
San Vicente	US	●			●							
Schimmelpennick	Ne	●	●	●	●							
Sierra Sweet	US	●		●			●					
'63 Air-Flo	US	●			●							
Swisher Sweets	US	●	●	●	●							
Tampa Cub	US	●			●							
Tampa Nugget	US	●	●	●	●							
Tampa Sweet	US	●	●	●	●							
Tayo	PR	●			●							
Topper	US	●			●		●	●				
Topstone	US	●		●	●		●			●		
Travis Club	US	●		●	●				●	●		
Travis Club Premium	US	●		●		●	●	●			●	
Vasco da Gama	Ge	●			●							
Villa de Cuba	US	●			●	●						
Villazon Deluxe	US	●			●							

MASS-MARKET CIGARS: INDEX

Brand	Made in	Machine-made	Cigarillo	Panatela	Corona	Lonsdale	Grand Corona	Figurado	Robusto-Toro	Churchill	Double Corona	Giant
Villazon Deluxe Aromatics	US	●		●	●							
White Owl	US	●	●	●	●							
Willem II	Ne	●			●							
William Penn	US	●	●	●	●							
Windsor & Mark IV	US	●		●	●	●						
Wm. Ascot	US	●		●		●						
Wolf Bros.	US	●	●	●	●							
Y.B.	US	●			●							
Zino	Br	●		●								
	Ne	●	●	●	●							
	Sz	●		●	●							

Cigar Legends: Felipe Gregorio

"Being a cigar maker, you are an environmentalist by choice, because you are dealing with the Earth's riches. And I feel that you have to give back."

Phillip Wynne, better known by his "cigar name" of Felipe Gregorio, is the driving force behind Cigars of Honduras and an expanding line of high-quality cigars which celebrate the richness of the Central American soil and the ability of the artisans who plant, harvest, blend and roll some of the richest cigars available.

His comment about cigars and the environment came from his October 1995 interview in *The Cigar Monthly*. In his session with Publisher Robert Kemp, he reviewed his cigar-making career, which started only in 1990, but has taken off with the cigar boom and the high quality of his creations.

The son of an American foreign service officer, Felipe was introduced to Dr. Jorge Buesos in Santa Rosa de Copan, Honduras in the 1980s. In 1990, they began producing a middle-priced cigar to bring new tastes at an affordable level to a growing public interested in new tastes in cigars. The result was Petrus, soon to be followed by Felipe Gregorio, Habanica and a series of high-quality brands from Honduras and Nicaragua.

With success comes responsibility and the debut of Tesoros de Copan. The proceeds from this brand go in part to help the Rutamaya Foundation, dedicated to preserving the rainforest and helping the Mayan peoples of Central America. Thanks to Felipe, cigar lovers can help those who originated the cigar simply by enjoying their legacy.

6.
MASS-MARKET CIGARS

This section provides the details on 115 brands of mass-market cigars, generally made by machine for distribution to the widest possible audience in drug stores, supermarkets and, of course, tobacco stores.

Each brand listing includes notes on country of manufacture, shapes, names, lengths, ring gauges and wrapper color *as supplied by the manufacturers and/or distributors of these brands.* Ring gauges for some brands of cigarillos were not available.

Please note that while a cigar may be manufactured in one country, it may contain tobaccos from many nations. These cigars utilize short-filler tobaccos unless otherwise noted; a number of brands use homogenized (sheet) leaf for binders and/or filler.

Although manufacturers have recognized more than 70 shades of wrapper color, six major color groupings are used here. Their abbreviations include:

- ▸ DC = Double Claro: green, also known as "AMS."
- ▸ Cl = Claro: a very light tan color.
- ▸ CC = Colorado Claro: a medium brown common to many cigars on this list.
- ▸ Co = Colorado: reddish-brown.
- ▸ CM = Colorado Maduro: dark brown.
- ▸ Ma = Maduro: very dark brown or black (also known as "double Maduro" or "Oscuro.")

Many manufacturers call their wrapper colors "Natural" or "English Market Selection." These colors cover a wide range of browns and we have generally grouped them in the "CC" range. Darker wrappers such as those from Cameroon show up most often in the "CM" category.

Shape designations are based on our shape chart in section 1.03. Careful readers will note the freedom with which manufacturers attach names of shapes to cigars which do not resemble that shape at all! For easier comparison, all lengths were rounded to the shortest eighth of an inch, although some manufacturers list sizes in 16ths or even 32nds of an inch.

Readers who would like to see their favorite brand listed in the 1998 edition can call or write the compilers as noted after the Table of Contents.

ANTONIO Y CLEOPATRA

Machine-made in Puerto Rico.

Shape	*Name*	*Lgth*	*Ring*	*Wrapper*
Cigarillo	Grenadiers Whiffs	3⅝	23⅔	CM
Corona	Grenadiers Tubos	5⅝	42½	CM
Cigarillo	Grenadiers Minis	4½	28	CC-CM
Corona	Grenadiers Palma Maduro	5⅝	42½	Ma
Slim Panatela	Grenadiers	6¼	33½	CC-CM
Panatela	Panatelas Deluxe	5⅜	35½	CC-CM
Corona	Palma Maduro	5⅝	42	Ma
Corona	Classic Coronas	5⅝	42½	CC-CM
Toro	Churchills	5¾	50	CC
	Connecticut Shade Wrapper series:			
Cigarillo	Grenadiers Miniatures	4½	28	CC
Panatela	Grenadiers Panatelas	5⅜	35½	CC

MASS-MARKET CIGARS: BRAND LISTINGS

Corona	Grenadiers Presidentes	5⅝	42½	CC
Slim Panatela	Grenadiers	6¼	33½	CC
Toro	Churchills	5¾	50	Ma

This highly popular brand dates back to 1888. Today, it offers a fairly mild taste with Connecticut Broadleaf, Connecticut Shade and Indonesian Javan wrappers, sheet binders and Cuban-seed filler tobaccos.

ARANGO SPORTSMAN
Machine-made in Tampa, Florida, USA.

Shape	*Name*		*Lgth*	*Ring*	*Wrapper*
Slim Panatela	No. 100		5¾	34	CC-Ma
Lonsdale	No. 200		6¼	42	CC-Ma
Churchill	No. 300		7	46	CC-Ma
Robusto	No. 350		5¾	48	CC-Ma
Churchill	No. 400		7½	48	CC-Ma
Panatela	Tubes	*(tubed)*	6½	36	CC-Ma
Cigarillo	Tens		4½	28	CC

Popular since its introduction in 1984, this is a very mild and aromatic cigar, with a touch of vanilla flavoring. It offers an Ecuadorian wrapper, sheet binder and a filler blend of Dominican and Honduran tobaccos. It is offered in boxes of 25, except for No. 100 and Tens, which come in 50s.

AS YOU LIKE IT
Machine-made in Jacksonville, Florida, USA.

Shape	*Name*	*Lgth*	*Ring*	*Wrapper*
Long Corona	No. 18	6	41	DC-CC-Ma
Petit Corona	No. 22	4½	41	DC-CC
Long Corona	No. 32	6	43	DC-CC
Slim Panatela	No. 35	5¼	33	CC

MASS-MARKET CIGARS: BRAND LISTINGS

This popular brand offers a four-nation blend of tobaccos for a mild taste, presented in boxes of 50.

B-H

Machine-made in Yoe, Pennsylvania, USA.

Shape	*Name*	*Lgth*	*Ring*	*Wrapper*
Lonsdale	Boston Blunts	6½	44	CC
Lonsdale	Corona	6½	42	CC
Lonsdale	King Claro	6½	42	CC
Long Corona	Special 76	6½	42	CC
Robusto	Special 76 Oscuro	6½	44	Ma

This is a mild cigar made by the House of Windsor, featuring a Pennsylvania wrapper, sheet binder and a blend of several tobaccos in the filler, offered in boxes of 50.

BALMORAL

Machine-made in Duizel, the Netherlands.

Shape	*Name*	*Lgth*	*Ring*	*Wrapper*
Cigarillo	Diana	3⅜	20	CM
Cigarillo	Shetlands	3⅝	24	CM
Cigarillo	Sussex	4⅜	21	CM
Cigarillo	Midlands	4	30	CM
Cigarillo	Highlands	4⅜	28	CM
Petit Corona	Ideales	4⅝	40	CM
Slim Panatela	Overland	5¼	32	CM
Slim Panatela	Aristocrates	6¼	32	CM
Petit Corona	Corona de Luxe	4¾	42	CM

This is a new brand in the U.S. for 1996, offering an all-tobacco cigar with mild-to-medium body and outstanding quality. All of these cigars feature gorgeous sumatran wrappers, with Java binders and filler blends chosen from premium Brazilian, Javan and Sumatran leaves. The results are outstanding, as is the presentation: an all-cedar box of 10 or 25 cigars or a carton of 10s for the road.

MASS-MARKET CIGARS: BRAND LISTINGS

BANCES
Machine-made in Tampa, Florida, USA.

Shape	Name	Lgth	Ring	Wrapper
Robusto	Crowns	5¾	50	Ma
Small Panatela	Demi-Tasse	4	35	DC-CC-Ma
Slim Panatela	Havana Holders	6½	30	DC-CC-Ma
Long Corona	Palmas	6	42	DC-CC-Ma
Grand Corona	No. 3	5¾	46	DC-CC-Ma

BEN BEY
Machine-made in Frankfort, Indiana, USA.

Shape	Name		Lgth	Ring	Wrapper
Corona	Crystals	(tubed)	5⅝	44	CC

The Crystals are well named, as they are encased in a glass tube. The blend includes a Connecticut leaf wrapper, sheet binder and U.S. and Dominican tobaccos in the filler. Ben Beys are offered upright in specially-made cedar boxes of 50.

BEN FRANKLIN
Machine-made in the United States.

Shape	Name	Lgth	Ring	Wrapper
Petit Corona	Perfectos	4⅞	40	CC
Petit Corona	Blunts	5⅛	40	CC

BLACK & MILD
Machine-made in the United States.

Shape	Name	Lgth	Ring	Wrapper
Small Panatela	Pipe-Tobacco Cigars	5	30	Ma

MASS-MARKET CIGARS: BRAND LISTINGS

BLACK HAWK
Machine-made in Frankfort, Indiana, USA.

Shape	Name	Lgth	Ring	Wrapper
Corona Extra	Chief	5⅛	45	CM

The Chief has a medium body and uses a Connecticut leaf wrapper, a sheet binder and a blend of Dominican and U.S. tobaccos in the filler.

BUDD SWEET
Machine-made in Wheeling, West Virginia, USA.

Shape	Name	Lgth	Ring	Wrapper
Petit Corona	Perfecto	5	42½	CC
Slim Panatela	Panatela	5¼	34	CC

The Panatela boasts a genuine Connecticut leaf wrapper, sheet binder and U.S. and Dominican tobaccos in the filler for a medium-bodied taste. The Perfecto has the same binder and filler, but uses a homogenized sheet wrapper.

CANDLELIGHT
Machine-made in Dingelstadt, Germany.

Shape	Name	Lgth	Ring	Wrapper
Cigarillo	Mini Sumatra	2⅞	20	CC
Cigarillo	Mini Brazil	2⅞	20	Ma
Small Panatela	Senorita Sumatra	3¾	30	CC
Small Panatela	Senorita Brazil	3¾	30	Ma
Cigarillo	Panatela Sumatra	5¾	20	CC
Cigarillo	Panatela Brazil	5¾	20	Ma
Small Panatela	Corona Slim Sumatra	4	30	CC
Small Panatela	Corona Slim Brazil	4	30	Ma
Short Panatela	Block Corona Sumatra	4¾	38	CC
Short Panatela	Block Corona Brazil	4¾	38	Ma

MASS-MARKET CIGARS: BRAND LISTINGS

These small cigars are all-tobacco with a mild taste. The two types are puros; all of the tobacco in the Sumatra-named shapes is from Sumatra, likewise with the Brazilian shapes. Candlelights are offered in tins of 10, or boxes of 25 or 50.

CARIBBEAN ROUNDS
Machine-made in Yoe, Pennsylvania, USA.

Shape	Name	Lgth	Ring	Wrapper
Lonsdale	Casinos	6½	43	CI-CC-Ma
Short Panatela	Petites	4⅝	36	CC-Ma
Lonsdale	Rounds	7¼	45	CC-Ma
Long Panatela	Royales	6½	36	CC-Ma

Available in fairly large sizes for mass-market cigars, this brand offers a natural leaf wrapper, has a sheet binder and a blend of short-filler tobaccos. Most sizes are offered in wood boxes of 50.

CHARLES DENBY
Machine-made in Frankfort, Indiana, USA.

Shape	Name	Lgth	Ring	Wrapper
Corona	Invincible	5½	43	CI

Connecticut wrapper, sheet binders and a blended filler with American and Dominican tobaccos give this brand a medium body.

CHARLES THE GREAT
Machine-made in San Antonio, Texas, USA.

Shape	Name	Lgth	Ring	Wrapper
Double Corona	Churchill	7	50	CC-Ma
Long Corona	English Rounds	6	43	CC-Ma
Panatela	Classic	6	34	CC-Ma

MASS-MARKET CIGARS: BRAND LISTINGS

CHERRY BLEND
Machine-made in the United States.

Shape	Name	Lgth	Ring	Wrapper
Small Panatela	Pipe-Tobacco Cigars	5	30	Ma

THE CIGAR BARON
Machine-made in the United States.

Shape	Name	Lgth	Ring	Wrapper
Corona Extra	Corona Extra	5¾	45	CC-Ma
Figurado	Perfecto	4¼	43	CC-Ma

These all-tobacco, mild-to-medium bodied cigars feature genuine Connecticut Shade wrappers around a Connecticut Broadleaf binder and Dominican and Honduran fillers. Regularly available in boxes of 50, this brand also offers specially decorated boxes marked "Cigars for Dad" and a colorful holiday box featuring Santa Claus!

CIMA
Machine-made in Mayaguez, Puerto Rico.

Shape	Name	Lgth	Ring	Wrapper
Long Corona	Embajadores	6	42	CC
Long Corona	Brevas	6	42	CC
Long Corona	Swingers	6	42	CC

These cigars are machine made using all-tobacco blends. The wrappers and binders are grown in Puerto Rico, with the filler containing tobaccos from Puerto Rico, Mexico and the Dominican Republic. All of the shapes are offered in 5-packs and the Embajadores are also available in a box of 50.

CLUBMASTER
Machine-made in Bunde, Germany.

Shape	Name	Lgth	Ring	Wrapper
Cigarillo	Superior	3	22	CC
Short Panatela	Half Corona	5	35	CC

Lonsdale	Corona No. 1	6⅞	41	CC

Here is an elegant cigar which was introduced in 1973, with a mild body thanks to its Sumatran wrapper, German binder and filler tobaccos from Brazil and Indonesia.

J. CORTES
Machine-made in Moene, Belgium.

Shape	Name	Lgth	Ring	Wrapper
Small Panatela	Club	4½	30	CC
Cigarillo	Grand Luxe	4	25	CC
Short Panatela	High Class	5	38	CC
Panatela	Long Filler No. 1	5½	38	CC
Panatela	Long Filler No. 2	5½	38	CC
Small Panatela	Milord	4¼	30	CC
Cigarillo	Mini	3⅓	19	CC
Slim Panatela	Royal Class	5¼	30	CC

A European tradition since 1926, J. Cortes is gaining in popularity in the U.S. It is an all-tobacco brand, with Sumatran wrappers, Java binder and blended filler of tobaccos from Brazil and Indonesia. The J. Cortes "blue box" offers a mild taste in boxes of 10, 25 or 50 depending on shape.

CYRILLA
Machine-made in Tampa, Florida, USA.

Shape	Name	Lgth	Ring	Wrapper
Long Corona	Nationals	6	42	CC-Ma
Churchill	Kings	7	46	CC-Ma
Churchill	Senators	7½	48	CC-Ma
Panatela	Slims	6½	36	CC-Ma

These are mild cigars, offered in bundles of 25 cigars each. They feature either an Ecuadorian (natural) wrapper or a Connecticut Broadleaf in the maduro shade, a sheet binder and filler tobaccos from the Dominican and Honduras.

MASS-MARKET CIGARS: BRAND LISTINGS

DE OLIFANT
Machine-made in Kampen, the Netherlands.

Shape	Name	Lgth	Ring	Wrapper
Cigarillo	Fantje	3	20	CC
Small Panatela	Knakje	3½	31	CC
Short Panatela	Corona	4½	36	CC
Slim Panatela	Corona Panatela	5	34	CC
Corona	Ivory	5¾	41	CC
Cigarillo	Picabella	3	20	CC
Cigarillo	Panarillo	3½	26	CC

A famous all-tobacco, dry-cured brand in Holland since 1884, De Olifant's line of small cigars comes to the U.S. in 1996. The line offers a full-bodied taste in the smaller sizes and a medium-to-full flavor in the larger shapes. All of these cigars feature Sumatran "sand" wrappers and Javan binders, with filler tobaccos blended from leaves grown in Brazil, Java and Sumatra.

DECISION MADURO
Machine-made in Tampa, Florida, USA.

Shape	Name	Lgth	Ring	Wrapper
Robusto	No. 250	5½	49	Ma
Grand Corona	No. 350	6¼	45	Ma
Corona	No. 450	5	44	Ma
Short Panatela	No. 550	5⅜	37	Ma

This brand has been around since 1935 and today offers a mild to medium smoke at a great value. The all-maduro series features a Connecticut Broadleaf wrapper, with a sheet binder and filler tobaccos from the Dominican Republic. Each size is available in economical bundles of 20.

DEXTER LONDRES
Machine-made in Jacksonville, Florida, USA.

Shape	Name	Lgth	Ring	Wrapper
Corona	Dexter Londres	5¼	42	CC

Coronas Group

Here are examples of the corona-sized cigars, one of the most popular on the market. The corona-related shapes in this group include:

- Petit Corona   4-5 inches long; 40-44 ring.

- Corona   5¼-5¾ inches long; 40-44 ring.

- Long Corona   5⅞-6⅜ inches long; 40-44 ring.

Pictured opposite are:

▸ Peterson Hallmark Corona	5¾ x 43	Corona
▸ Pleiades Orion	5¾ x 42	Corona
▸ Orient Express No. 2415	5½ x 42	Corona
▸ Belinda Breva Conserva	5½ x 42	Corona
▸ Schimmelpennick VSOP Corona	4¼ x 41	Petit Corona

The Peterson Hallmark displays a Claro-shade wrapper, while the Pleiades' wrapper is slightly darker and classified as Colorado Claro. The Orient Express No. 2415 shows off a Colorado Maduro-shaded wrapper; the Belinda Breva Conserva's very dark brown is characteristic of a Maduro wrapper.

MASS-MARKET CIGARS: BRAND LISTINGS

This is a mild cigar, with a natural leaf wrapper and a four-nation filler blend. Dexters are available in handy five-packs and in boxes of 50.

DIRECTORS
Machine-made in Jacksonville, Florida, USA.

Shape	Name	Lgth	Ring	Wrapper
Cigarillo	Cigarillo	4⅜	27½	CM
Cigarillo	Coronella	5	27½	CM
Long Corona	Corona	6	42	CM
Short Panatela	Panatela	5⅝	36	CM

This range offers a mild taste, with a Wisconsin sun-grown wrapper, sheet binder and a blend of chopped filler tobaccos.

DON CESAR
Machine-made in Tampa, Florida, USA.

Shape	Name	Lgth	Ring	Wrapper
Corona	Palma	5⅝	42	CC

Here is a unique, machine-made cigar made from long-filler tobaccos, rather than the cut filler which is more common. The natural leaf wrapper surrounds filler leaves from the Dominican Republic and Honduras.

DRY SLITZ
Machine-made in Wheeling, West Virginia, USA.

Shape	Name	Lgth	Ring	Wrapper
Slim Panatela	Regular	5½	34	CC

This is a mild-bodied cigar with a homogenized wrapper, sheet binder and U.S. and Dominican tobaccos in the filler. The head of the cigar is finished with a small hole so that you can light it up without cutting!

R. G. DUN
Machine-made in Wheeling, West Virginia, USA.

MASS-MARKET CIGARS: BRAND LISTINGS

Shape	Name	Lgth	Ring	Wrapper
Petit Corona	Admiral	4¾	42½	CC
Petit Corona	Babies	4⅛	42	CC
Slim Panatela	Youngfellow	5¼	34	CC
Corona	Regal Blunt	5¼	43	CC
Corona	Bouquet	5½	42½	CC
Cigarillo	Cigarillo	4¼	29	CI

This is a medium-bodied cigar made by M. Marsh & Sons. It offers a Connecticut leaf wrapper, has a sheet binder and a blended filler of American and Dominican tobaccos.

DUTCH MASTERS
Machine-made in Puerto Rico.

Shape	Name	Lgth	Ring	Wrapper
Cigarillo	Cadet Regular	4¾	27½	CC
Cigarillo	Pipearillo /machine-made in the USA/	5⅛	27	CM
Petit Corona	Perfecto	4¾	44	CM
Panatela	Panatela	5½	36	CM
Slim Panatela	Cameroon Elite	6⅛	29½	CM
Corona Extra	Belvedere	4⅞	46½	CM
Corona	President	5⅝	40½	CM
Corona	Corona Deluxe	5¾	43	CM
Corona	Corona Maduro	5¾	43	Ma
Toro	Corona Grande	5¾	50	CM-Ma
	Masters Collection:			
Cigarillo	Cigarillos	4¾	27½	CC
Corona	Palmas	5⅝	42½	CC
Corona	Palmas Maduro	5⅝	42½	Ma

MASS-MARKET CIGARS: BRAND LISTINGS

Short Panatela	Panatelas Deluxe	5⅝	35½	CC

Remember the Dutch Masters television commercials of the 1960s, as the actors retired into the brand's trademark portrait at the end? The commercials are history, but the brand continues to do well, offering a mild smoke in both manufactured and natural wrapper styles. The filler in all shapes is a blend of Cuban-seed tobaccos.

1886
Machine-made in the United States.

Shape	*Name*	*Lgth*	*Ring*	*Wrapper*
Corona	Kings	5¾	43	CC
Corona	Queens	5⅝	42	CC

EL CAUTO
Machine-made in Miami, Florida, USA.

Shape	*Name*	*Lgth*	*Ring*	*Wrapper*
Long Corona	Blunt	6	43	CC
Long Corona	Corona Grande	6⅜	44	CC
Grand Corona	Fumas	6⅜	46	CC
Lonsdale	Super Fumas	7	44	CC

This brand includes one all-tobacco style (Corona Grande) and three others which use a sheet binder. El Cautos are offered in either boxes of 50 or bundles of 25.

EL MACCO
Machine-made in Frankfort, Indiana, USA.

Shape	*Name*	*Lgth*	*Ring*	*Wrapper*
Corona Extra	Puritano Dark	4¾	45	CM

This brand presents a medium-bodied taste and has a Connecticut leaf wrapper, sheet binder and a blend of Dominican and U.S. tobacco in the filler.

MASS-MARKET CIGARS: BRAND LISTINGS

EL PRODUCTO
Machine-made in Puerto Rico.

Shape	Name		Lgth	Ring	Wrapper
Small Panatela	Little Coronas		4⅝	31	CC
Corona	Blunts		5⅝	40½	CC
Petit Corona	Bouquets		4¾	44	CC
Petit Corona	Panatelas		5⅛	40½	CC
Corona Extra	Puritano Finos		4⅞	46½	CC
Corona	Coronas		5¾	43	CC
Robusto	Favoritas		5	48½	CC
Robusto	Escepcionales		5⅛	52½	CC
Corona	Queens	(tubed)	5⅝	42	CC

Introduced in 1916, this was the smoke of choice (in the Queens size) for decades for comedian George Burns and it continues to have many contemporary admirers. The many shapes are primarily clothed in manufactured wrappers; the Escepcionales and Queens feature a natural wrapper.

EL TRELLES
Machine-made in Jacksonville, Florida, USA.

Shape	Name	Lgth	Ring	Wrapper
Long Corona	Bankers	6	43	CC
Corona Extra	Blunt Extra	5¼	45	CC
Long Corona	Club House	6	41	Ma
Long Corona	Kings	6	41	CC
Pyramid	Tryangles Deluxe	5¼	45	CC

This is a very mild cigar, with a natural leaf wrapper and a four-nation filler blend, available in natural and maduro shades. El Trelles cigars are offered in convenient five-packs and by the box.

MASS-MARKET CIGARS: BRAND LISTINGS

EL VERSO
Machine-made in Frankfort, Indiana, USA.

Shape	Name	Lgth	Ring	Wrapper
Grand Corona	Corona Extra	5¾	47	CM
Corona Extra	Bouquet Dark	4¾	45	CM
Panatela	Commodore	6	36	CM
Corona Extra	Bouquet Light Leaf	4¾	45	CI
Cigarillo	Mellow	4¼	29	CI-CM

The sunny graphics on the El Verso box herald a medium-bodied cigar with a Connecticut wrapper, either a Connecticut or sheet wrapper depending on the model, and American and Dominican filler.

EMERSON
Machine-made in Wheeling, West Virginia, USA.

Shape	Name	Lgth	Ring	Wrapper
Petit Corona	Diplomat	4¾	42½	CI

American and Dominican filler tobaccos are at the heart of this one-shape brand. It offers a medium body and has a homogenized wrapper and sheet binder.

EVERMORE
Machine-made in Frankfort, Indiana, USA.

Shape	Name	Lgth	Ring	Wrapper
Corona Extra	Original	4⅝	45	CI-CC-CM
Long Corona	Palma	6	42	CI-CM
Grand Corona	Corona Grande	5¾	47	CI-CM

This is an all-tobacco cigar, with a Connecticut leaf wrapper, Connecticut binder and a blend of American and Dominican tobaccos in the filler.

MASS-MARKET CIGARS: BRAND LISTINGS

FARNAM DRIVE
Machine-made in Frankfort, Indiana, USA.

Shape	Name	Lgth	Ring	Wrapper
Corona Extra	Original	5⅛	45	CC-CC-Ma

This is an all-tobacco cigar that offers a medium-bodied taste and uses Connecticut leaves for the wrapper and binder and a blend of American and Dominican tobaccos in the filler.

FIGARO
Machine-made in San Antonio, Texas, USA.

Shape	Name	Lgth	Ring	Wrapper
Lonsdale	Figaro	6½	40	CC-Ma

This is a medium-bodied blend of 100% tobacco, which features a Connecticut wrapper and binder and filler tobaccos from the Dominican Republic. It is offered in colorful canisters of 25 each.

FLOR DE BORINQUEN
Machine-made in Mayaguez, Puerto Rico.

Shape	Name	Lgth	Ring	Wrapper
Long Corona	Flor de Borinquen	6	42	CC

This is an all-tobacco cigar with a Puerto Rican wrapper and filler tobaccos from Puerto Rico, the Dominican Republic and Mexico. It is offered only in boxes of 50.

FLORIDA
Machine-made in Wheeling, West Virginia, USA.

Shape	Name	Lgth	Ring	Wrapper
Petit Corona	Queen	5	42½	CC

Here is a medium-bodied cigar, made up of American and Dominican filler tobaccos, a sheet binder and a genuine Connecticut leaf wrapper.

MASS-MARKET CIGARS: BRAND LISTINGS

GARCIA GRANDE
Machine-made in Tampa, Florida, USA.

Shape	Name	Lgth	Ring	Wrapper
Corona	Corona	5½	44	CC-Ma
Toro	Laguitos	5⅝	48	CC-Ma
Long Corona	Pitas	6	43	CC-Ma
Pyramid	Pyramides	5¼	42	CC-Ma
Corona	Queens	5½	44	CC-Ma
Churchill	Trinidads	7¼	46	CC-Ma

This is a new cigar for 1996, with a medium body, an Ecuadorian wrapper, Honduran binder and filler tobaccos from the Dominican Republic, Honduras and Nicaragua. It is an excellent value, offered in bundles.

GARCIA Y VEGA
Machine-made in Dothan, Alabama, USA
and Santiago, Dominican Republic

Shape	Name		Lgth	Ring	Wrapper
Cigarillo	Cigarillos		4¼	27	DC
Cigarillo	Chicos		4¼	27	CC
Cigarillo	Miniatures		4⅝	29	CC
Cigarillo	Whiffs		3¾	23	CC
Slim Panatela	Tips	(tipped)	5¼	30	CC
Slim Panatela	Bravuras		5⅜	34	CC
Slim Panatela	Panatella Deluxe		5⅜	34	DC
Petit Corona	Senators		4½	41	DC
Petit Corona	Barons		4¾	41	CC
Petit Corona	Bouquets		4⅝	45	CC
Short Panatela	Delgado Panatela		5⅜	34	CC
Panatela	Elegantes		6⅜	34	DC
Panatela	Gallantes		6⅜	34	CC

MASS-MARKET CIGARS: BRAND LISTINGS

Corona	Presidente		5¾	41	CC
Corona	Napoleons		5¾	41	DC
Corona	English Coronas	(tubed)	5¼	41	CC
Slim Panatela	Granadas	(tubed)	6⅜	34	DC
Slim Panatela	Romeros	(tubed)	6⅜	34	CC
Long Corona	Gran Coronas	(tubed)	6⅛	41	DC
Long Corona	Gran Premios	(tubed)	6⅛	41	CC
Slim Panatela	Crystals No. 100	(tubed)	6⅜	34	CC
Long Corona	Crystals No. 200	(tubed)	6⅛	41	CC
Long Corona	Maduro		6⅛	41	Ma

Since 1882, this brand has been a favorite all across the United States, enjoyed more than 300,000 times daily nationwide. The natural leaf wrapper comes from Connecticut or Mexico and is combined with a sheet binder and a blend of filler tobaccos for the brand's characteristic mild taste. Please note that the Whiffs size offers two flavors: natural and Cavendish. Garcia y Vega cigars are always fresh thanks to in-the-pack pouches or tubes and are offered in packs of 3, 4 or 5 cigars or in boxes of 30, 40 or 50.

GARGOYLE
Machine-made in Frankfort, Indiana, USA.

Shape	*Name*	*Lgth*	*Ring*	*Wrapper*
Panatela	Lanza	6	38	Cl

The cigar is not as ugly as the brand name might imply! It's actually a medium-bodied smoke with a Connecticut wrapper, sheet binder and a blend of American and Dominican filler.

GOLD & MILD
Machine-made in the United States.

Shape	*Name*	*Lgth*	*Ring*	*Wrapper*
Small Panatela	Pipe-Tobacco Cigars	5	30	CC

MASS-MARKET CIGARS: BRAND LISTINGS

HARVESTER
Machine-made in the United States

Shape	Name	Lgth	Ring	Wrapper
Petit Corona	Perfecto	5	40½	CC
Corona	Record Breaker	5⅝	40½	CC

HAUPTMANN'S
Machine-made in Frankfort, Indiana, USA.

Shape	Name	Lgth	Ring	Wrapper
Corona Extra	Perfecto	5⅛	45	CI-CM
Corona	Broadleaf	5¼	43	CM
Corona	Corona	5¼	43	CI
Panatela	Panatela	5¾	38	CI-CM

This is a medium-bodied smoke, with a genuine Connecticut leaf wrapper, sheet binder and a blend of Dominican and U.S. tobaccos in the filler.

HAVANA BLEND
Machine-made in San Antonio, Texas, USA.

Shape	Name	Lgth	Ring	Wrapper
Short Panatela	Petit Corona	4¾	38	Ma
Cigarillo	Palma Fina	6½	29	Ma
Corona	Coronado	5	43	Ma
Corona	Delicado	5¾	43	Ma
Robusto	Rothschild	5	50	Ma
Lonsdale	Doubloon	6½	42	Ma
Churchill	Churchill	7	47	Ma

This is a medium-bodied blend of 100% tobacco, which includes Cuban tobacco from the 1959 crop, as well as Dominican tobacco, in the filler. The wrapper and binder are both Connecticut Broadleaf and the brand is offered in boxes of either 25 or 50 cigars.

MASS-MARKET CIGARS: BRAND LISTINGS

HAV-A-TAMPA
Machine-made in Tampa, Florida, USA.

Shape	Name		Lgth	Ring	Wrapper
Corona	Blunt		5	43	CC
Small Panatela	Cheroot		4¾	31	CC
Cigarillo	Jewel	(tipped)	5	29	CC
Cigarillo	Jewel Sweet	(tipped)	5	29	CC
Cigarillo	Jewel Classic	(tipped)	5	29	CC
Cigarillo	Jewel Black Gold		5	29	Ma
Cigarillo	Jewel Menthol		5	29	CC
Small Panatela	Junior		4½	31	CC
Panatela	Panatela		5½	36	CC
Petit Corona	Perfecto		4¾	43	CC
Petit Corona	Sublime		4¾	43	CC
Cigarillo	Tips Cigarillo	(tipped)	5	28	CC
Cigarillo	Tips	(tipped)	5	28	CC
Cigarillo	Tips Sweet	(tipped)	5	28	CC

This famous brand offers light, mild cigarillos with a manufactured wrapper and binder and a filler blend of Honduran and Dominican tobaccos.

HEEREN VAN RUYSDAEL
Machine-made in Valkenswaard, the Netherlands.

Shape	Name	Lgth	Ring	Wrapper
Panatela	Invincibles Grandes XO	6⅝	35	CC

This premium brand from Holland uses only the finest tobaccos from Indonesia (wrapper, binder and filler) and Brazil (filler) to create this medium-bodied masterpiece. Each all-cedar box is specially prepared to keep these cigars at their peak, including a special in-the-box humidifier!

MASS-MARKET CIGARS: BRAND LISTINGS

IBOLD
Machine-made in Frankfort, Indiana, USA.

Shape	Name	Lgth	Ring	Wrapper
Petit Corona	Blunt	4⅞	44	Cl-CM
Petit Corona	Black Pete	4⅞	44	CM
Robusto	Breva	5⅛	51	Cl-Ma
Cigarillo	Cigarillo	4¼	29	Cl-CM
Panatela	Ideals	5⅞	38	Cl-CM
Short Panatela	Slims	5¼	35	Cl-CM

Manufactured by the National Cigar Corporation, this brand offers a medium-bodied taste thanks to its Connecticut leaf wrapper, sheet or Connecticut binder – depending on the shape – and the filler blend of U.S. and Dominican leaves.

IDEAL
Machine-made in Mayaguez, Puerto Rico.

Shape	Name	Lgth	Ring	Wrapper
Long Corona	Cazadores	6	42	CC

This one-size brand is all-tobacco and includes a Puerto Rico wrapper and filler tobaccos from Puerto Rico, the Dominican Republic and Mexico. You can find it offered only in bundles of 25.

JON PIEDRO
Machine-made in Yoe, Pennsylvania, USA.

Shape	Name	Lgth	Ring	Wrapper
Lonsdale	Breva	6½	44	CM
Panatela	Slims	6½	44	CM
Grand Corona	Broadleaf Rounds	6½	44	CC-Ma

This is a mild cigar, offered in boxes of 50 in three popular sizes and in three wrapper shades. All of the wrappers are American-grown in Pennsylvania; a sheet binder is used, along with a blend of tobaccos in the filler.

MASS-MARKET CIGARS: BRAND LISTINGS

JOSE MELENDI
Machine-made in San Antonio, Texas, USA.

Shape	Name	Lgth	Ring	Wrapper
Short Panatela	Vega I	5⅝	37	CM
Corona	Vega II	5½	43	CM
Long Corona	Vega III	6	42	CM
Slim Panatela	Vega IV	6½	34	CM
Grand Corona	Vega V	6½	45	CM
Lonsdale	Vega VII	7	45	CM
Slim Panatela	Wild Maduro	6⅞	34	Ma
Robusto	Rothschild Maduro	5	50	Ma

This is a medium-to-full bodied, long-filler blend of 100% tobacco, with a Cameroon wrapper on the Vega series and Connecticut Broadleaf wrappers on the maduro styles. The binder is also Connecticut leaf, with the filler composed of tobaccos from Brazil and the Dominican Republic.

J-R FAMOUS
Machine-made in Tampa, Florida, USA.

Shape	Name	Lgth	Ring	Wrapper
Toro	Churchill	5¾	50	Cl-CM-Ma
Panatela	Delicados	6	39	Cl-CM-Ma
Long Corona	Plazas	6	42	Cl-CM-Ma
Lonsdale	Presidents	7⅛	44	Cl-CM-Ma

This is a medium-bodied, highly popular cigar with a Honduran wrapper, sheet binder and all-Honduran filler. It is an excellent value and offered in boxes of 50.

KEEP MOVING
Machine-made in Jacksonville, Florida, USA.

Shape	Name	Lgth	Ring	Wrapper
Petit Corona	Goodies	4½	41	CC

This one-size brand has a natural leaf wrapper and blends tobaccos of four nations in the filler. Look for Keep Moving in twin-packs, five-packs and in full boxes.

KING EDWARD
Machine-made in Jacksonville, Florida, USA.

Shape	Name	Lgth	Ring	Wrapper
Corona	Invincible Deluxe	5½	42	CC
Short Panatela	Panatela Deluxe	5¼	36	CC
Cigarillo	Cigarillo Deluxe	4¼	28½	CC
Petit Corona	Imperial	5	41	CC
Cigarillo	Specials	4⅜	28½	CC
Cigarillo	Tip Cigarillo *(tipped)*	4⅞	28	CC
Cigarillo	Wood Tip Cigarillo *(tipped)*	5½	29	CC
Cigarillo	Little Cigars	4⅜	29	CC

Britain's King Edward VII (1841-1910) is celebrated as the man who, with four words, revised the Victorian prohibition against tobacco soon after his ascension to the throne in 1901: "Gentlemen, you may smoke." This brand still bears his portrait and is now machine-made with a sheet wrapper and binder and a four-nation filler blend. Widely available in the U.S. and highly popular in England and 60 other countries, King Edward is offered in five-packs and boxes of 50.

LA EMINENCIA
Machine-made in Tampa, Florida, USA.

Shape	Name	Lgth	Ring	Wrapper
Lonsdale	Churchill Corona	6½	44	CC-Ma
Corona	Brevas	5½	44	CC-Ma
Long Corona	Plazas	6¼	42	CC-Ma
Panatela	Panetelas	6¼	38	CC-Ma

This is a mild-to-medium bodied brand of 100% tobacco, available in two wrapper shades. The wrappers are Ecuadorian-grown, with a Honduran binder and filler from the Dominican Republic, Honuras and Nicaragua.

MASS-MARKET CIGARS: BRAND LISTINGS

LA FENDRICH
Machine-made in Frankfort, Indiana, USA.

Shape	Name	Lgth	Ring	Wrapper
Corona Extra	Favorita	5⅛	45	Cl
Small Panatela	Buds	4¼	32	CC

La Fendrich cigars have a medium body, with a Connecticut wrapper, American and Dominican filler tobaccos and a sheet binder.

LA PAZ
Machine-made in Valkenswaard, the Netherlands.

Shape	Name		Lgth	Ring	Wrapper
Long Corona	Gran Corona	*(tubed)*	6	41	CC
Slim Panatela	Wilde Havana		4⅞	33	CC
Cigarillo	Wilde Cigarillos		4⅛	24	CC

The well-known La Paz brand, made of 100% tobacco, dates back to 1814. It is widely appreciated for the "Wilde" series which has an uncut end that provides a rich aroma from the first moment. Both of the Wilde shapes are full-bodied, while the Gran Corona offers a mild taste. The wrappers and binders are all Bazuki leaf from Indonesia, with filler blends of Brazilian and Indonesian tobacco.

LA RESTINA
Machine-made in Mayaguez, Puerto Rico.

Shape	Name	Lgth	Ring	Wrapper
Long Corona	Cazadores	6	44	Ma
Churchill	No. 1	7	46	Ma

These cigars are 100% tobacco and offer a medium bodied taste thanks to their Puerto Rican-grown wrapper and binder and a mixture of tobaccos from Puerto Rico, Mexico and the Dominican Republic in the filler. La Restinas are presented in bundles of 25.

MASS-MARKET CIGARS: BRAND LISTINGS

LANCER
Machine-made in San Antonio, Texas, USA.

Shape	Name	Lgth	Ring	Wrapper
Small Panatela	Havana Slims	6¼	29	CM

Here is a cigar made of 100% tobacco, including filler tobacco from the 1958 and 1959 Cuban crops. The wrapper and binder are both genuine Connecticut leaf; Lancers are offered in eight-cigar pocket packs.

LORD BEACONSFIELD
Machine-made in Tampa, Florida, USA.

Shape	Name	Lgth	Ring	Wrapper
Churchill	Rounds	7¼	46	DC-CC-Ma
Slim Panatela	Lords	7	34	DC-CC-Ma
Long Corona	Coronas Superba	6¼	42	DC-CC-Ma
Panatela	Lindas	6½	36	DC-CC-Ma
Corona	Cubanola	5½	44	DC-CC-Ma
Churchill	Directors	7¾	46	Ma

LORD CLINTON
Machine-made in Wheeling, West Virginia, USA.

Shape	Name	Lgth	Ring	Wrapper
Slim Panatela	Panatela	5¼	34	CC
Corona	Perfecto	5	42½	CI

The Panatela has a genuine Connecticut wrapper, sheet binder and a blend of filler tobaccos from the Dominican Republic and the United States. It has a medium-bodied taste. The Perfecto has the same filler tobaccos, but uses a sheet binder and wrapper.

MARSH
Machine-made in Wheeling, West Virginia, USA.

Shape	Name	Lgth	Ring	Wrapper
Slim Panatela	Mountaineer	5½	34	CC-Ma

MASS-MARKET CIGARS: BRAND LISTINGS

Panatela	Virginian	5½	37	CC
Panatela	Pioneer	5½	37	CC
Slim Panatela	Old Reliable	5½	33	Ma
Long Panatela	Deluxe	7	34	Ma
Long Panatela	Deluxe II	7	34	Ma
Corona	Corona	5	43	Ma
Long Panatela	Olde Style Stogies	7	34	Ma

This brand began back in 1840 and continues today as a popular mass-market cigar in many parts of the United States. All of the shapes are mild and all use genuine Connecticut-grown leaves for wrappers and sheet binders. Most of the shapes offer a U.S. and Dominican filler blend, except for the Old Reliable, which incorporates fire-cured Kentucky tobacco in its filler. The Deluxe and Old Style Stogies are finished with a pig-tail head. The heads of the Deluxe II and Corona shapes are pre-drilled with holes to allow instant ignition without cutting.

MIFLIN'S CHOICE
Machine-made in Wheeling, West Virginia, USA.

Shape	Name		Lgth	Ring	Wrapper
Panatela	Panatela	(tubed)	6⅜	32	CM

This small cigar uses a Cameroon wrapper, sheet binder and a blend of Caribbean tobaccos in the filler.

MOYA
Machine-made in Tampa, Florida, USA.

Shape	Name	Lgth	Ring	Wrapper
Lonsdale	Cazadores	6¼	44	CC-Ma
Corona	Deluxe	5⅜	44	CC-Ma
Lonsdale	Fumas	6¼	44	CC-Ma
Panatela	Panatela	6	34	CC

This brand is full-bodied and is 100% tobacco. The Deluxe and Panatela shapes are offered in boxes of 50; the others are packaged in bundles of 25.

MASS-MARKET CIGARS: BRAND LISTINGS

MUNIEMAKER
Machine-made in McSherrystown, Pennsylvania, USA.

Shape	Name	Lgth	Ring	Wrapper
Corona Extra	Regular	4½	47	Cl-CC-CM
Robusto	Straight	5⅛	48	CC
Grand Corona	Long	6	46	CC
Robusto	Breva 100's	5⅛	48	CC-Ma
Slim Panatela	Panatela 100's	6	33	CC-Ma
Grand Corona	Palma 100's	6	46	CC-Ma
Perfecto	Perfecto 100's	5¼	52	CC-Ma
Corona Extra	Cueto	4⅞	45	Cl-CC
Corona Extra	Bouquet Special *(tubed)*	5⅛	46	CC-Ma
Corona Extra	Judges Cave	4½	47	Cl-CC-Ma

F.D. Grave began this line in 1884 with the goal of making "the best possible cigars at prices cigar lovers could afford." Now, F.D. Grave & Sons continues this tradition of all-tobacco, medium-to-full-bodied cigars, featuring Connecticut Broadleaf wrappers and binders around a core of U.S. tobaccos in the filler. The Perfecto 100s and Bouquet Specials are boxed in 25s, while all of the other shapes are available in boxes of 50. Handy packs of four and five cigars each are also available of most sizes.

MURIEL
Machine-made in Puerto Rico.

Shape	Name	Lgth	Ring	Wrapper
Corona Extra	Magnum	4⅝	46½	CC
Small Panatela	Air Tips Regular *(tipped)*	5	30½	CC
Small Panatela	Air Tips Pipe Aroma *(tipped)*	5	30½	CC
Small Panatela	Air Tips Menthol *(tipped)*	5	30½	CC
Small Panatela	Air Tips Sweet *(tipped)*	5	30½	CC
Small Panatela	Coronella	4⅝	31	CC
Small Panatela	Coronella Pipe Aroma	4⅝	31	CC

MASS-MARKET CIGARS: BRAND LISTINGS

Small Panatela	Coronella Sweet	4⅝	31	CC
	Muriel Pipe Tobacco Cigars:			
Cigarillo	Black & Cherry	4⅛	27	CM
Cigarillo	Black & Sweet	4⅛	27	CM
	Muriel Sweets:			
Corona	Sweet Coronas	5⅝	40½	CC
Small Panatela	Sweet Minis	4	32	CC
Cigarillo	Sweet Tip Cigarillos *(tipped)*	5	27	CC

Muriels feature a manufactured wrapper and offer a variety of sizes for every smoker. The Coronella group includes all natural fillers, while the new Pipe Tobacco series includes pipe tobacco filler.

NAT CICCO'S
Machine-made in the United States.

Shape	Name	Lgth	Ring	Wrapper
Giant Corona	Churchill Rejects	8	46	Cl-CC-Ma
Long Corona	Governor	6	42	Cl
Churchill	Jamaican Rounds	7¼	46	CC-Ma
Long Corona	Plaza	6	42	Cl-CC-Ma
Lonsdale	Private Stock No. 35	6⅞	41	Cl-CC
Panatela	Rapier	6½	39	Cl-CC-Ma
	Aromatic and flavored series:			
Slim Panatela	Almond Liquer	6½	34	CC
Slim Panatela	Cuban Cafe	6½	34	CC
Long Corona	Plaza Aromatic	6	42	CC

MASS-MARKET CIGARS: BRAND LISTINGS

NATIONAL CIGAR
Machine-made in Frankfort, Indiana, USA.

Shape	Name	Lgth	Ring	Wrapper
Long Corona	Palma	6	42	Cl-CM

Made by the National Cigar Corporation, this medium-bodied blend incorporates a Connecticut wrapper, sheet binder and American and Dominican blended filler.

ODIN
Machine-made in Wheeling, West Virginia, USA.

Shape	Name	Lgth	Ring	Wrapper
Petit Corona	Viking	4¾	42½	CC

The Odin Viking offers a medium-bodied taste, with tobaccos from the Dominican Republic and the United States in the filler. The wrapper is homogenized tobacco leaf and a sheet binder is used.

OLD HERMITAGE
Machine-made in Hartford, Connecticut, USA.

Shape	Name	Lgth	Ring	Wrapper
Corona Extra	Golden Perfecto	5½	45	Cl

This brand was created in 1908 and is 100% tobacco. The wrapper and binder are Connecticut broadleaf, with the filler incorporating Brazilian, Dominican and U.S. tobaccos. The one shape has a perfecto-style tip and is offered in boxes of 50.

OPTIMO
Machine-made in Jacksonville, Florida, USA.

Shape	Name	Lgth	Ring	Wrapper
Panatela	Diplomat	6⅛	33	DC-CC
Long Corona	Admiral	6	41	DC-CC
Corona	Coronas	5¼	42	CC-Ma
Long Corona	Palmas	6	41	Ma

MASS-MARKET CIGARS: BRAND LISTINGS

| Slim Panatela | Panatela | 5¼ | 33 | DC-CC |
| Petit Corona | Sports | 4½ | 41 | DC-CC |

This popular brand was, at one time, made of Cuban tobacco, but is today a mass-market cigar. It offers a natural leaf wrapper and a four-nation blend in the filler, and is available in twin-packs, five-packs and, of course, full boxes of 50.

PALMA
Machine-made in the United States.

Shape	Name	Lgth	Ring	Wrapper
Lonsdale	Throwouts	6½	43	Cl-CC-Ma

PANCHO GARCIA
Machine-made in San Antonio, Texas, USA.

Shape	Name	Lgth	Ring	Wrapper
Long Corona	Impala	6	43	DC-Cl-CC-Ma
Corona	Royal No. 4	5⅝	43	DC-Cl-CC-Ma

Here is a quality mass-market cigar made from 100% tobacco, with a natural leaf wrapper available in four different shades! Pancho Garcia cigars are presented in individual cellophane sleeves in boxes of 50.

PEDRO IGLESIAS
Machine-made in Tampa, Florida, USA.

Shape	Name	Lgth	Ring	Wrapper
Corona Extra	Crowns	5	45	CC-Ma
Long Corona	Regents	6	44	CC-Ma
Lonsdale	Lonsdales	6½	44	CC

PHILLIES
Machine-made in Selma, Alabama, USA.

Shape	Name	Lgth	Ring	Wrapper
Corona	Perfecto	5¾	43	CC

MASS-MARKET CIGARS: BRAND LISTINGS

Long Corona	Titan		6¼	44	CC
Corona	Coronas		5⅝	41	CC
Petit Corona	Blunts		4¾	42	CC
Slim Panatela	Panatella		5½	34	CC
Corona	Sport		5¾	43	CC
Small Panatela	Cheroot		5	32	CC
Slim Panatela	King Cheroot		5½	32	CC
Small Panatela	Mexicali Slim		4⅝	32	CC
Petit Corona	Juniors		5	41	CC
Corona	Sweets		5¾	43	CC
Cigarillo	Tips	*(tipped)*	4½	28	CC
Cigarillo	Tip Sweet	*(tipped)*	4½	28	CC

This well-known brand is constructed with a sheet wrapper and binder, with the filler blend made from Dominican and Honduran tobaccos, to provide its mild-bodied taste.

POLLACK
Machine-made in Wheeling, West Virginia, USA.

Shape	Name	Lgth	Ring	Wrapper
Slim Panatela	Crown Drum	5½	33	Ma

The Crown Drum offers a mild taste with a Connecticut wrapper, sheet binder and U.S. and Dominican filler tobaccos.

RED DOT
Machine-made in Wheeling, West Virginia, USA.

Shape	Name	Lgth	Ring	Wrapper
Slim Panatela	Panatela	5¼	34	CC
Corona	Perfecto	5	42½	CC

This brand offers a medium body, with a Connecticut leaf wrapper, sheet binder and a blend of Domincan and flavored American tobaccos in the filler.

MASS-MARKET CIGARS: BRAND LISTINGS

RIGOLETTO
Machine-made in Tampa, Florida, USA.

Shape	Name	Lgth	Ring	Wrapper
Long Corona	Londonaire	6¼	43	CC
Corona Extra	Black Jack	5⅜	46	Ma
Long Corona	Natural Coronas	6	42	CC
Long Corona	Palma Grande	6	41	CI-CC
Slim Panatela	Natural Panatela	5	33	CC

This is a mild-to-medium brand produced in Tampa. First introduced in 1905, it features a Connecticut Broadleaf or Shade wrapper, a sheet binder and high-quality filler tobaccos from the Dominican Republic.

RIO HONDO
Machine-made in Mayaguez, Puerto Rico.

Shape	Name	Lgth	Ring	Wrapper
Long Corona	Caribe	6	42	CC
Long Corona	Churchill	6	42	CC
Long Corona	Alteza	6	42	CC

These are all-tobacco, machine-made cigars which offer a Puerto Rican wrapper and filler tobaccos from Mexico, the Dominican Republic and, of course, Puerto Rico. All of the sizes come in boxes of 25, plus the Churchill comes in a travel pack of three cigars.

RIVALO
Machine-made in Mayaguez, Puerto Rico.

Shape	Name	Lgth	Ring	Wrapper
Long Corona	Corona Imperiales	6	42	CC
Long Corona	Coronita	6	42	CC
Long Corona	Cazadores	6	42	CC
Cigarillo	Sabrosito	3½	26	CC
Cigarillo	Criollitos	3½	26	CC

MASS-MARKET CIGARS: BRAND LISTINGS

These cigars are made in Puerto Rico of 100% tobacco, with a Puerto Rican wrapper and fillers from Puerto Rico, Mexico and the Dominican Republic. The Corona Imperiales, Coronita and Criollitos are available in boxes of 50; the Cazadores in a box of 25; the Sabrosito in a box of 125 (!).

ROBERT BURNS
Machine-made in Santiago, Dominican Republic and Dothan, Alabama.

Shape	Name		Lgth	Ring	Wrapper
Corona	Black Watch	*(tubed)*	5⅝	41	CC
Cigarillo	Cigarillo		4½	27	CC

The Black Watch model is made in Santiago, the Dominican Republic, with a Connecticut Shade wrapper, sheet binder and a multi-nation blend of filler tobaccos in three-packs and boxes of 30. The famous Cigarillos are made in Dothan, Alabama with sheet wrappers and binders and blended filler, offered in five-packs and boxes of 50.

ROI-TAN
Machine-made in Puerto Rico.

Shape	Name	Lgth	Ring	Wrapper
Petit Corona	Bankers	5	40½	CI
Corona	Blunts	5⅝	40½	CI
Slim Panatela	Falcons	6¼	33½	CI
Panatela	Panatelas	5½	36	CI
Petit Corona	Perfecto Extras	5	40½	CI
Cigarillo	Tips	5⅛	27	CI

Here is a popular old brand which is now using a manufactured wrapper and binder with short filler tobaccos.

ROSEDALE
Machine-made in Hartford, Connecticut, USA.

Shape	Name	Lgth	Ring	Wrapper
Perfecto	Perfecto	4⅞	46	CM

MASS-MARKET CIGARS: BRAND LISTINGS

Corona Extra	Londres	5	46	CM

This brand, made continuously since the 1920s, is a part of the Topper cigar group, made of 100% tobacco. The genuine Connecticut Broadleaf wrapper surrounds a Connecticut binder and filler tobaccos from Brazil, the Dominican Republic and the U.S. Each shape is offered is packs of 5 or boxes of 50.

RUY LOPEZ
Machine-made in Tampa, Florida, USA.

Shape	Name	Lgth	Ring	Wrapper
Panatela	Panetelas	6	38	CC-Ma
Grand Corona	Corona Grande	5¾	45	CC-Ma
Corona	Vanilla Surprise	5½	42	CC-Ma

Here is a mild brand, made with 100% tobacco and featuring an Ecuadorian-grown wrapper, Honduran binder and Dominican, Honduran and Nicaraguan tobacco in the filler.

SAN FELICE
Machine-made in Wheeling, West Virginia, USA.

Shape	Name	Lgth	Ring	Wrapper
Petit Corona	Original	4¾	42½	CC

This brand has only one shape, but it's a popular corona thanks to its genuine Connecticut wrapper. The filler is a blend of American and Dominican tobaccos, surrounded by a sheet binder.

SAN VICENTE
Machine-made in the United States

Shape	Name	Lgth	Ring	Wrapper
Long Corona	Cazadores	6¼	44	DC-CC-Ma

MASS-MARKET CIGARS: BRAND LISTINGS

SANTA FE
Machine-made in Jacksonville, Florida, USA.

Shape	Name	Lgth	Ring	Wrapper
Long Corona	Biltmore	6	41	CC
Long Corona	Fairmont	6	43	CC
Slim Panatela	Panatela	5¼	33	CC
Corona	Patties	5½	42	CC

Tobaccos of four nations go into the blend of this mild cigar, which offers a natural leaf wrapper. The Patties model features a perfecto-style foot. Santa Fe cigars are offered in five-packs and full boxes.

SCHIMMELPENNICK V.S.O.P.
Machine-made in Wageningen, the Netherlands.

Shape	Name	Lgth	Ring	Wrapper
Petit Corona	Corona	4¼	41	CM
Corona	Grand Corona	5	41	CM
Small Panatela	Senorita	4	31	CM

Created in 1995, here is a fuller-sized Schimmelpennick cigar for those who enjoy the mild taste of this famous brand, founded in 1924. Named for a famous governor of Holland, Rutger Jan Schimmelpennick (1781-1825), these new sizes feature Sumatra sandleaf wrappers and a Java binder, combined with filler tobaccos from Brazil (Bahia type) and Indonesia (Bezuki). In its first year of distribution, it was named the "Cigar of the Year" in Holland and is offered in boxes of 25.

SIERRA SWEET
Machine-made in the United States.

Shape	Name	Lgth	Ring	Wrapper
Grand Corona	Renos	5⅝	45	CC-Ma
Small Panatela	Tahoes	4¾	32	CC-Ma

MASS-MARKET CIGARS: BRAND LISTINGS

'63 AIR-FLO
Machine-made in Wheeling, West Virginia, USA.

Shape	Name	Lgth	Ring	Wrapper
Petit Corona	Londres	5	42½	CC

One of the most unusual names in cigardom adorns this medium-bodied cigar, which has a sheet wrapper and binder and filler tobaccos from the United States and the Dominican Republic.

SWISHER SWEETS
Machine-made in Jacksonville, Florida, USA.

Shape	Name		Lgth	Ring	Wrapper
Corona	Kings		5½	42	CC
Petit Corona	Perfecto		5	41	CC
Panatela	Slims		5⅜	36	CC
Cigarillo	Coronella		5	27.5	CC
Small Panatela	Outlaw		4¾	32	CC
Cigarillo	Cigarillo		4⅜	28.5	CC
Cigarillo	Tip Cigarillo	*(tipped)*	4⅞	28	CC
Cigarillo	Wood Tip Cigarillo	*(tipped)*	4⅞	29	CC

Popular? Swisher Sweets are enjoyed everywhere, offering a mild, sweet taste with a manufactured wrapper and binder and a blend of filler tobaccos from four nations. You can find them in thousands of locations, in familiar red five-packs and in boxes of 50.

TAMPA CUB
Machine-made in Wheeling, West Virginia, USA.

Shape	Name	Lgth	Ring	Wrapper
Corona	Straights	5	42½	CC

There is only one shape in this brand, but it offers a medium body with American and Dominican filler tobaccos and a manufactured sheet binder and wrapper.

MASS-MARKET CIGARS: BRAND LISTINGS

TAMPA NUGGET
Machine-made in Tampa, Florida, USA.

Shape	Name		Lgth	Ring	Wrapper
Petit Corona	Sublime		4¾	43	CC
Petit Corona	Blunt		5	43	CC
Panatela	Panatela		5½	36	CC
Cigarillo	Tip Regular	*(tipped)*	5	28	CC
Cigarillo	Tip Sweet	*(tipped)*	5	28	CC
Small Panatela	Juniors		4½	31	CC
Small Panatela	Miniature		4½	31	CC

These "nuggets" incorporate sheet wrappers and binders with a blend of filler tobaccos from the Dominican Republic and Honduras for a mild and flavorful smoke.

TAMPA RESAGOS
Machine-made in Tampa, Florida, USA.

Shape	Name	Lgth	Ring	Wrapper
Corona	Regular	5¼	42	CC
Corona	Sweet	5¼	42	CC

These inexpensive cigars offer a mild taste, with homogenized wrappers and binders and filler tobaccos from the Dominican Republic. A favorite since 1951, Tampa Resagos are offered in bags of 20 cigars each.

TAMPA SWEET
Machine-made in Tampa, Florida, USA.

Shape	Name		Lgth	Ring	Wrapper
Petit Corona	Perfecto		4¾	43	CC
Small Panatela	Cheroot		4¾	31	CC
Cigarillo	Tip Cigarillo	*(tipped)*	5	28	CC

This three-shape brand features filler tobaccos from Colombia and Italy, surrounded by a homogenized wrapper and binder.

MASS-MARKET CIGARS: BRAND LISTINGS

TAYO
Machine-made in Mayaguez, Puerto Rico.

Shape	Name	Lgth	Ring	Wrapper
Long Corona	Princesa	6	42	CC
Long Corona	Gina	6	42	CC
Long Corona	Las Vegas	6	42	CC

These cigars are 100% tobacco, medium in strength and utilize a Puerto Rican wrapper and binder and a blend of Dominican, Mexican and Puerto Rican filler. All models are presented in boxes of 5.

TOPPER
Machine-made in McSherrystown, Pennsylvania, USA.

Shape	Name	Lgth	Ring	Wrapper
Long Corona	Grande Corona	6	46	CC
Corona Extra	Breva	5½	45	CI-CC-CM
Perfecto	Old Fashioned	4⅞	44	CI-CC-CM
Corona	Ebony	5½	46	Ma
Petit Corona	Broadleaf	4⅞	44	CM

Since 1896, Topper cigars gave offered a mild, flavorful taste with excellent value. Each of these models is made up of 100% tobacco and is offered in handy packs of 4-5 cigars, or in colorful boxes of 50. All feature genuine USA/Connecticut wrappers and binders and short filler from the Dominican Republic and the United States.

TOPSTONE
Machine-made in Tampa, Florida, USA.

Shape	Name	Lgth	Ring	Wrapper
	Connecticut Broadleaf series:			
Long Corona	Supreme	6	42	CC
Corona Extra	Extra Oscuro	5½	46	Ma
Grand Corona	Grande	5¾	46	CC-Ma

MASS-MARKET CIGARS: BRAND LISTINGS

Panatela	Panatela	6	39	CC-Ma
Corona Extra	Bouquet	5½	46	CC-Ma
Corona Extra	Oscuro	5½	46	Ma
Churchill	Directors	7¾	46	CC-Ma
	Natural Darks series:			
Churchill	Executives	7¼	47	Ma

These are well-known, 100% tobacco cigars made in Tampa, Florida and featuring dark-cured Connecticut Broadleaf wrappers. Each of the shapes is offered in boxes of 50, except for the Directors and Executives, which are available in boxes of 25.

TRAVIS CLUB
Machine-made in San Antonio, Texas, USA.

Shape	Name	Lgth	Ring	Wrapper
	Made with long filler:			
Perfecto	Especiales	5⅛	55	CC-Ma
	Made with long and short filler:			
Perfecto	Senators	5⅛	52	CC-Ma
Corona	Coronas	5⅝	43	CC-Ma
	Made with short filler:			
Panatela	Panatella	5½	38	CC-Ma
Long Corona	Plaza	6	43	CC-Ma
Robusto	Rothschild	4⅞	50	CC-Ma
Petit Corona	Sport Triangles	4¾	44	CC-Ma

These are outstanding U.S.-made cigars, in which the finest Connecticut Shade wrappers are combined with a Connecticut binder and filler leaves from Brazil, Connecticut and the Dominican Republic. They are offered in elegant boxes of 50 which picture the Travis Club building in San Antonio where this brand originated in 1893.

MASS-MARKET CIGARS: BRAND LISTINGS

TRAVIS CLUB PREMIUM
Machine-made in San Antonio, Texas, USA.

Shape	Name	Lgth	Ring	Wrapper
Double Corona	Churchill	7	50	CC
Grand Corona	Corona Extra	6¼	46	CC
Toro	Toro	6	50	CC
Long Corona	Palma	6	43	CC
Perfecto	Perfecto	5¼	52	CC
Robusto	Robusto	5	50	CC

Here is a beautiful cigar which features all-tobacco, all-long-filler construction and a mild-bodied taste. The elegant wrappers are genuine Connecticut Shade, the binders are also Connecticut-grown and the filler is composed of leaves from the Dominican Republic and Brazil. Travis Club Premium cigars are presented in individual cellophane sleeves inside elegant, varnished wooden cabinets.

VASCO DA GAMA
Machine-made in Bunde, Germany.

Shape	Name	Lgth	Ring	Wrapper
Long Corona	Vasco de Gama	6	42	CC

Named for the famed Portugese explorer who was the first to circle the Cape of Good Hope in 1497. The cigar dates from 1816 (!) and is a mild blend of Sumatra-seed Indonesian wrappers, with a German binder and Brazilian and Indonesian filler.

VILLA DE CUBA
Machine-made in Tampa, Florida, USA.

Shape	Name	Lgth	Ring	Wrapper
Corona	Brevas	5¾	44	CC-Ma
Long Corona	Majestics	6⅜	43	CC-Ma
Giant Corona	Corona Grande	7¼	45	CC-Ma

MASS-MARKET CIGARS: BRAND LISTINGS

Villazon Deluxe

Machine-made in Tampa, Florida, USA.

Shape	*Name*	*Lgth*	*Ring*	*Wrapper*
Giant Corona	Chairman	7¾	43	DC-CM-Ma
Lonsdale	Cetros	7⅛	44	DC-CM-Ma
Lonsdale	Senators	6¾	44	DC-CM-Ma

Villazon Deluxe Aromatics

Machine-made in Tampa, Florida, USA.

Shape	*Name*	*Lgth*	*Ring*	*Wrapper*
Long Corona	Commodores	6	42	DC-CM-Ma
Slim Panatela	Panatella	5¾	34	DC-CM-Ma

White Owl

Machine-made in Dothan, Alabama, USA.

Shape	*Name*	*Lgth*	*Ring*	*Wrapper*
Cigarillo	Coronetta	4⅝	29	CC
Short Panatela	Demi-Tip *(tipped)*	5⅛	32	CC
Cigarillo	Miniatures	4⅝	29	CC
Cigarillo	Miniatures Sweet	4⅝	29	CC
Slim Panatela	Panatela Deluxe	5¼	34	CC
Corona	Invincible	5⅜	41	CC
Corona	New Yorker	5⅝	41	CC
Slim Panatela	Ranger	6⅜	34	CC
Petit Corona	Sports	4¾	41	CC
	White Owl Select:			
Corona	Imperial	5⅝	41	CC
Petit Corona	Regent	4¾	41	CC
Cigarillo	Squire	4⅝	29	CC
Cigarillo	Darts	3¾	23	CC

MASS-MARKET CIGARS: BRAND LISTINGS

This brand started way back in 1887. Today, there are two lines: White Owl and White Owl Select. The regular line includes a sheet wrapper and binder around a five-nation blend of filler tobaccos, while the Select line has a Connecticut Shade wrapper and is offered in packs of four or five cigars. The regular line is offered in twin-packs, five-packs, six-packs or in boxes of 50.

WILLEM II
Machine-made in Valkenswaard, the Netherlands.

Shape	Name		Lgth	Ring	Wrapper
Corona	Optimum	*(tubed)*	5	41	CC

This is a medium-bodied cigar which dates back to 1916. It features an Indonesian wrapper and binder and Indonesian and Brazilian filler.

WILLIAM PENN
Machine-made in Dothan, Alabama, USA.

Shape	Name		Lgth	Ring	Wrapper
Cigarillo	Willow Tips	*(tipped)*	5	27	CC
Cigarillo	Willow Tips Sweets	*(tipped)*	5	27	CC
Cigarillo	Braves		4⅝	29	CC
Corona	Perfecto		5⅜	41	CC
Slim Panatela	Panatela		5¼	34	CC

Introduced in 1924, William Penn cigars offer mild taste thanks to a multi-nation blend of filler tobaccos, surrounded by homogenized wrappers and binders. The brand is offered in twin-packs, five-packs and boxes of 50 in the larger sizes.

WINDSOR & MARK IV
Machine-made in Yoe, Pennsylvania, USA.

Shape	Name	Lgth	Ring	Wrapper
Petit Corona	Crooks	5	40	CC
Giant Corona	Imperial	8	43	DC
Lonsdale	Maduro	6½	43	Ma
Lonsdale	Magnate	6½	43	DC

MASS-MARKET CIGARS: BRAND LISTINGS

Lonsdale	Palma	6½	43	DC
Slim Panatela	Panatela	6½	34	DC
Petit Corona	Sportsmen	5	43	DC

WM. ASCOT
Machine-made in Tampa, Florida, USA.

Shape	Name	Lgth	Ring	Wrapper
Lonsdale	Palma	6¼	42	DC-CC-Ma
Slim Panatela	Panatela	5¾	34	DC-CC-Ma

This is a very mild cigar, featuring an Ecuadorian wraper, sheet binder and Dominican and Honduran filler tobaccos. The Palma is offered in a variety of wrapper shades in boxes of 25 and the Panatela is available in boxes of 50.

WOLF BROS.
Machine-made in Yoe, Pennsylvania, USA.

Shape	Name	Lgth	Ring	Wrapper
Cigarillo	Nippers	3¼	20	CC
Small Panatela	Crookettes	4½	32	CC
Slim Panatela	Rum Crooks	5½	30	CC
Corona	Sweet Vanilla Crooks	5½	42	CC

Y.B.
Machine-made in Wheeling, West Virginia, USA.

Shape	Name	Lgth	Ring	Wrapper
Petit Corona	Squires	5	42½	CC

This old brand includes only one size, but it offers a medium body thanks to filler tobaccos from the Dominican Republic and the United States and a sheet binder and wrapper.

ZINO

Machine-made in Brazil, the Netherlands and Switzerland.

Shape	Name	Lgth	Ring	Wrapper
	Made in Brazil:			
Panatela	Santos	6½	34	CM
Small Panatela	Por Favor	4	30	CM
	Made in the Netherlands:			
Corona	Drie Cello	5¾	40	Co
Small Panatela	Jong	4¼	30	Co
Cigarillo	Cigarillos Brasil	3½	20	CM
Cigarillo	Panatellas Brasil	5½	22	CM
Cigarillo	Cigarillos Sumatra	3½	20	Co
Cigarillo	Panatellas Sumatra	5½	22	Co
	Made in Switzerland:			
Slim Panatela	Relax Brasil	5¾	30	CM
Petit Corona	Classic Brasil	4¾	41	CM
Slim Panatela	Relax Sumatra	5¾	30	Co
Petit Corona	Classic Sumatra	4¾	41	Co

Here are beautifully made, mild cigars which feature Brazilian or Indonesian tobaccos, offering outstanding quality and value in all-tobacco cigarillos and small cigars.

7.
SMALL CIGARS

This section provides the details on 51 brands of small cigars, generally made by machine for distribution to the widest possible audience in drug stores, supermarkets and, of course, tobacco stores.

For the purposes of this listing, small cigar "brands" are limited to those whose lines are dominated by (i.e., 67 percent or more of the shapes are) cigarillo or cheroot-shaped cigars. In addition, brands in the handmade or mass-market sections that offer the cigarillo shape in their lines include:

Handmade brands (43):
Abreu Anillo de Oro
Andujar
Antelo
Babalu
Carbonell
Celestino Vega
Cerdan
Crispin Patiño
Davidoff
Don Antonio
Don Diego
Don Xavier
El Rey del Mundo
El Valle
Excalibur
Hamiltons
Hamiltons Reserve
Havana Sunrise
Hoyo de Monterrey

Iracema
Jose Benito
Juan Clemente
La Gloria Cubana
La Herencia Cubana
Macanudo
Montecruz
Nat Sherman
Off Colors
Oscar
Partagas
Pleiades
Pride of Copan
Primo del Rey
Private Stock
Punch
Royal Jamaica
Sabana
San Vicente
Santa Clara 1830

SMALL CIGARS: BRAND LISTINGS

Suerdieck
Te-Amo

H. Upmann
Zino

Mass-market brands (30):

Antonio y Cleopatra	King Edward
Arango Sportsman	La Paz
Balmoral	Muriel
Candlelight	Phillies
Clubmaster	Rivalo
J. Cortes	Robert Burns
De Olifant	Roi-Tan
Directors	Schimmelpennick
R.G. Dun	Swisher Sweets
Dutch Masters	Tampa Nugget
El Verso	Tampa Sweet
Garcia y Vega	White Owl
Havana Blend	William Penn
Hav-A-Tampa	Wolf Bros.
Ibold	Zino

Each brand listing in this section includes notes on country of manufacture, shapes, names, lengths, ring gauges and wrapper color *as supplied by the manufacturers and/or distributors of these brands.* Ring gauges for some brands of cigarillos were not available.

When comparing and considering cigars listed in this category, it may be worthwhile to remember the standard dimensions of mass-produced cigarettes: almost always 7.9 mm in diameter (20 ring gauge) with lengths of 85 mm (approx. 3¼ inches) or 100 mm (approx. 3⅞ inches).

Please note that while a cigar may be manufactured in one country, it may contain tobaccos from many nations. These

SMALL CIGARS: BRAND LISTINGS

cigars utilize short-filler tobaccos unless otherwise noted; a number of brands use homogenized (sheet) leaf for binders and/or filler.

Although manufacturers have recognized more than 70 shades of wrapper color, six major color groupings are used here. Their abbreviations include:

- ▶ DC = Double Claro: green, also known as "AMS."
- ▶ Cl = Claro: a very light tan color.
- ▶ CC = Colorado Claro: a medium brown common to many cigars on this list.
- ▶ Co = Colorado: reddish-brown.
- ▶ CM = Colorado Maduro: dark brown.
- ▶ Ma = Maduro: very dark brown or black (also known as "double Maduro" or "Oscuro.")

Many manufacturers call their wrapper colors "Natural" or "English Market Selection." These colors cover a wide range of browns and we have generally grouped them in the "CC" range. Darker wrappers such as those from Cameroon show up most often in the "CM" category.

Readers who would like to see their favorite brand listed in the 1998 edition can call or write the compilers as noted after the Table of Contents.

AGIO
Machine-made in Geel, Belgium

Shape	Name	Lgth	Ring	Wrapper
Cigarillo	Biddies Brazil	3¼	20	Ma
Cigarillo	Biddies Sumatra	3¼	20	CC

SMALL CIGARS: BRAND LISTINGS

Cigarillo	Mehari's Sumatra	4	23	CC
Cigarillo	Mehari's Brasil	4	23	Ma
Cigarillo	Mehari's Mild & Light	4	23	Cl
Cigarillo	Mehari's Mild & Sweet	4	23	CM
Cigarillo	Mini Mehari's	2⅞	22	CC
Cigarillo	Mini Mehari's Mild & Light	2⅞	22	Cl
Cigarillo	Filter Tip *(tipped)*	3	21	CC
Cigarillo	Junior Tip *(tipped)*	3	21	CC
Cigarillo	Lights	3	21	CC
Small Panatela	Senoritas Red Label	4	31	CC
Small Panatela	Elegant	4⅛	32	CC

Here is one of the famous brands in cigarillos, offering dry-cured cigarillos and small cigars for almost every taste. Most of the shapes use wrapper leaves from Java; the Mini Mehari's Mild & Light and Mehari's Mild & Light use a Connecticut wrapper; the Mehari's Brasil features a Brazilian-grown wrapper; the Biddies Sumatra, Senoritas Red Label and Elegant have Sumatran wrappers; and the Mehari's wrapper is from the Cameroons. All use a sheet binder and a blend of mild tobaccos in the filler.

AL-CAPONE
Machine-made in Germany.

Shape	Name	Lgth	Ring	Wrapper
Cigarillo	Sweets	3¼		CC
Cigarillo	Pockets	2¾		CC

These cigarillos are made by the famous Dannemann firm and are offered in convenient packs of five (Sweets) and ten (Pockets).

ALAMO
Machine-made in the United States.

Shape	Name	Lgth	Ring	Wrapper
Cigarillo	Sweet Tip *(tipped)*	5	29	CC

SMALL CIGARS: BRAND LISTINGS

Cigarillo	Tip *(tipped)*	5	29	CC
Figurado	Perfecto	4¾	46	CC
Cigarillo	Cigarillo	4⅜	28	CC

ALTERNATIVOS GOLD
Machine-made in Miami, Florida, USA.

Shape	Name	Lgth	Ring	Wrapper
Cigarillo	Mild	3½	23	CC
Cigarillo	Mild & Light	3½	23	CC

Introduced in 1994, these small cigars offer a blend of Ecuador, Java and Malawi tobaccos. The Mild style presents a full flavor, while the Mild & Light style is medium in body.

G.A. ANDRON
Machine-made in Ireland.

Shape	Name	Lgth	Ring	Wrapper
Cigarillo	Brazil Cigarillo	3	23	CM
Cigarillo	Sumatra Cigarillo	3	23	CC

AVANTI
Machine-made in Scranton, Pennsylvania, USA.

Shape	Name	Lgth	Ring	Wrapper
Cheroot	Avanti	4½	34	Ma
Cheroot	Avanti Continental	5¾	34	Ma
Cheroot	Europa	5¾	34	Ma
Cheroot	Ipenema	5¾	34	Ma
Cheroot	Ramrod Deputy	4½	34	Ma
Cheroot	Ramrod Original	6½	34	Ma
Cheroot	Kentucky Cheroots	5¾	34	Ma

SMALL CIGARS: BRAND LISTINGS

Here is an all-tobacco, dry-cured, medium-bodied line of cigars, famous since their introduction in 1972. The ingredients are simple: fire-cured tobaccos from at least three different crop years of the finest farms in Kentucky and Tennessee, all barn-cured for at least four months. The Avanti and Avanti Continental are flavored with Anisette; the Ramrod Deputy and Ramrod Original are Bourbon flavored.

The Europa, introduced in 1994, uses a Kentucky dark-fired wrapper and binder and a blend of Belgian and Italian dark-fired tobacco for the filler.

BACKWOODS
Machine-made in Puerto Rico.

Shape	Name	Lgth	Ring	Wrapper
Cigarillo	Regular	4⅛	27	CC
Cigarillo	Sweet Aromatic	4⅛	27	CC
Cigarillo	Black & Sweet Aromatic	4⅛	27	Ma

This brand offers a mild taste but a surprise in its unfinished, "open" end. It has a natural or blackened wrapper and it presented in foil packs of 8.

BETWEEN THE ACTS
Machine-made in Tampa, Florida, USA.

Shape	Name	Lgth	Ring	Wrapper
Cigarillo	Between the Acts	3⅛	20	CC

Between the acts of your favorite show you can enjoy this mild, flavorful smoke, made up of a sheet wrapper and binder and filler tobaccos from Indonesia and the United States. Offered in packs of 20.

CAPTAIN BLACK LITTLE CIGARS
Machine-made in Tucker, Georgia, USA.

Shape	Name	Lgth	Ring	Wrapper
Cigarillo	Regular	3⅞	20	CC
Cigarillo	Sweets	3⅞	20	CC

Featuring the famous taste of Captain Black pipe tobacco, these little gems offer a mild taste, with a sheet wrapper and a blend of Indonesian, Philippine and United States tobaccos. Available in packs of 20.

CHARLES FAIRMORN
Machine-made in Dingelstadt, Germany.

Shape	Name	Lgth	Ring	Wrapper
Cigarillo	Piper's Mini Vanilla	3	20	CC
Cigarillo	Piper's Mini Cherry	3	20	CM
Cigarillo	Piper's Mini Plum	3	20	Ma
Small Panatela	Piper's Corona Vanilla	4¾	33	CC
Small Panatela	Piper's Corona Cherry	4¾	33	CM
Small Panatela	Piper's Corona Plum	4¾	33	Ma
Cigarillo	Piper's Panatela Vanilla	4½	25	CC
Cigarillo	Piper's Panatela Cherry	4½	25	CM
Cigarillo	Piper's Panatela Plum	4½	25	Ma

This line of cigarillos and small panatelas complements the handmade Charles Fairmorn line. These are all-tobacco, mild cigars available in three flavors and three wrappers: the Vanilla shapes all use Sumatran wrappers, while the Cherry range has Connecticut wrappers and the Plum group uses Brazilian Mata Fina tobacco for its wrappers. All sizes have Javan binders and fillers which are half pipe tobacco and half dry-cured tobacco of several types.

CHRISTIAN OF DENMARK
Machine-made in Denmark.

Shape	Name	Lgth	Ring	Wrapper
Cigarillo	Mini Cigarillos	3½	20	CM
Cigarillo	Long Cigarillos	3¾	20	CM
Cigarillo	Midi Cigarillos	4¾	23	CM

This mild cigarillo is made of dry-cured, 100% tobacco, wrapped in Indonesian leaf with Brazilian, Dominican and Indonesian tobacco inside. Christian cigarillos are offered in 20-packs.

SMALL CIGARS: BRAND LISTINGS

Corps Diplomatique

Machine-made in Belgium.

Shape	*Name*	*Lgth*	*Ring*	*Wrapper*
Cigarillo	Deauville	4		CC
Cigarillo	Panatela	4		CC
Cigarillo	After Dinner	5		CC

These cigarillos offer a mild taste, featuring an Indonesian (Sumatra) wrapper and Brazilian and Indonesian filler.

Dannemann

Machine-made in Germany and Switzerland.

Shape	*Name*	*Lgth*	*Ring*	*Wrapper*
	Made in Germany:			
Cigarillo	Moods	2⅞	20	CC
Cigarillo	Sweets	3⅝	20	CC
Cigarillo	Originale - Brazil	2⅞	20	Ma
Cigarillo	Originale - Sumatra	2⅞	20	CC
Cigarillo	Speciale - Brazil	2⅞	25	Ma
Cigarillo	Speciale - Sumatra	2⅞	25	CC
Cigarillo	Speciale - Lights	2⅞	25	Cl
Cigarillo	Imperial - Brazil	4¼	25	Ma
Cigarillo	Imperial - Sumatra	4¼	25	CC
Cigarillo	Lonja - Brazil	5⅜	25	Ma
Cigarillo	Lonja - Sumatra	5⅜	25	CC
Cigarillo	Menor - Sumatra	3⅞	28	CC
Cigarillo	Pierrot - Brazil	3⅞	28	Ma
	Made in Switzerland:			
Slim Panatela	Lights - Sumatra	6	34	CC
Slim Panatela	Lights - Brazil	6	34	Ma

SMALL CIGARS: BRAND LISTINGS

Corona Extra	Espada - Sumatra	5	45	CC
Corona Extra	Espada - Brazil	5	45	Ma
Cigarillo	Slims - Sumatra	6½	28	CC
Cigarillo	Slims - Brazil	6½	28	Ma

Geraldo Dannemann created this brand in 1873 and today, these famous all-tobacco, dry-cured cigarillos and small cigars feature primarily Sumatran and Brazilian tobaccos and are offered in a dizzying array of packs, tins and boxes of 25 for the small cigars.

DAVIDOFF CIGARILLOS
Machine-made in Denmark and the Netherlands.

Shape	Name	Lgth	Ring	Wrapper
	Made in Denmark:			
Cigarillo	Cigarillo Brasil	3½	20	CM
Cigarillo	Cigarillos Sumatra	3½	20	Co
	Made in the Netherlands:			
Cigarillo	Panatelas Brasil	5½	22	CM
Cigarillo	Panatelas Sumatra	5½	22	Co

These elegant cigars are all tobacco which use natural leaf and are dry-cured for smoothness and a mild or mild-to-medium bodied taste, depending on the wrapper.

DENOBILI
Machine-made in Scranton, Pennsylvania, USA.

Shape	Name	Lgth	Ring	Wrapper
Cheroot	DeNobili	3½	34	Ma
Cheroot	Twin Pack	4	34	Ma
Cheroot	Economy	4	34	Ma
Cheroot	Kings	4½	34	Ma
Cheroot	Toscani	6½	34	Ma

SMALL CIGARS: BRAND LISTINGS

Cheroot	Toscani Longs	6½	34	Ma

A wide variety of sizes marks this dry-cured, 100%-tobacco brand, which uses only dark-fired Kentucky and Tennessee tobaccos in its blend. A brand of distinction since 1896, the Denobili range is marked by a mellow, medium-bodied taste.

DON ANTONIO
Machine-made in Dingelstadt, Germany.

Shape	Name	Lgth	Ring	Wrapper
Cigarillo	Carmen Sumatra	4½	20	CC
Cigarillo	Carmen Brazil	4½	20	Ma
Cigarillo	El Cerro Sumatra	3½	25	CC
Cigarillo	El Cerro Brazil	3½	25	Ma
Cigarillo	El Lupo Sumatra	3	20	CC
Cigarillo	El Lupo Brazil	3	20	Ma

These cigarillos were introduced in 1992 and offer either Brazilian or Sumatran wrappers on each shape. The binder on all shapes is Indonesian, with filler tobacco from Brazil, the Dominican Republic, Germany, Honduras and Indonesia.

DUCADOS
Machine-made in Madrid, Spain.

Shape	Name	Lgth	Ring	Wrapper
Cigarillo	Ducados	3	26	CM

These cigarillos are fairly mild, thanks to the Sumatran wrapper. A sheet binder is used, along with a blended filler; Ducados are offered in tins of 10 and boxes of 50.

DUNHILL SMALL CIGARS
Machine-made in the Netherlands.

Shape	Name	Lgth	Ring	Wrapper
Cigarillo	Miniatures	3¼		CC

SMALL CIGARS: BRAND LISTINGS

Cigarillo	Senoritas	3⅞	32	CC
Cigarillo	Panatellas	5½	26	CC

These are elegant cigarillos fully worthy of the revered Dunhill name. Each uses a delicate Sumatra wrapper, Java binder and a combination of Brazilian Bahia and Java fillers to create a mild, flavorful taste. The Senoritas and Pantellas are offered in boxes of five, while the Miniatures are packaged in boxes of 10 cigars each.

DUTCH TREATS
Machine-made in McAdoo, Pennsylvania.

Shape	Name	Lgth	Ring	Wrapper
Cigarillo	Regular	3⅞	20	CC
Cigarillo	Menthol	3⅞	20	CC
Cigarillo	Pipe Aroma	3⅞	20	CC
Cigarillo	Sweet	3⅞	20	CC
Cigarillo	Ultra Lite	3⅞	20	CC

ERIK
Machine-made in Tampa, Florida, USA.

Shape	Name		Lgth	Ring	Wrapper
Cigarillo	Natural	(tipped)	3⅞	21	CM
Cigarillo	Menthol	(tipped)	3⅞	21	CM
Cigarillo	Cherry Flavor	(tipped)	3⅞	21	CM

The familiar Viking-ship logo adorns the ten-pack box of this filter-tipped brand, which features filler tobaccos from the Dominican Republic and the United States with a sheet wrapper and binder.

GESTY
Machine-made in Brazil.

Shape	Name	Lgth	Ring	Wrapper
Cigarillo	Muritiba	4¼		Ma

SMALL CIGARS: BRAND LISTINGS

Cigarillo	Mara Longo	5½		Ma

GOLD SEAL
Machine-made in Indonesia.

Shape	Name	Lgth	Ring	Wrapper
Cigarillo	Cigarillos	3½		CC
Cigarillo	Senoritas	4		CC

HAMLET SLIMS
Machine-made in the United States

Shape	Name	Lgth	Ring	Wrapper
Cigarillo	Panatellas	4¼	26	CC

HAVATAMPA LITTLE CIGARS
Machine-made in Tampa, Florida, USA.

Shape	Name	Lgth	Ring	Wrapper
Cigarillo	Naturale	3⅛	20	CC
Cigarillo	Sweet	3⅛	20	CC

This famous brand offers a little cigar with a sheet wrapper and binder and a blend of filler tobaccos from Honduras and the Dominican Republic.

HENRI WINTERMAN
Dry cured, machine-made in the Netherlands.

Shape	Name	Lgth	Ring	Wrapper
Cigarillo	Cafe Creme	2⅞	28	CC
Cigarillo	Cafe Creme Mini Mild	2⅞	28	CC
Cigarillo	Cafe Creme Mini	2⅞	28	CC
Cigarillo	Cafe Creme Plus Mild	2⅞	28	CC
Cigarillo	Cafe Creme Plus	2⅞	28	CC
Cigarillo	Scooters	3½	28	CC-Ma
Cigarillo	Cafe Noir	2⅞	28	Ma

SMALL CIGARS: BRAND LISTINGS

Cigarillo	Cafe Creme Mild	2⅞	28	CC
Cigarillo	Cafe Creme Tips	3⅞	28	CC
Cigarillo	Slim Panatella	6	26	CC
Cigarillo	Senoritas	4	32	CC

INDIANA SLIMS
Machine-made in Germany.

Shape	Name	Lgth	Ring	Wrapper
Cigarillo	Indiana Slims	3¼	26	Ma

Despite the American-sounding name, these rum-dipped cigars are made in Germany, dry-cured and offered in packages of 10 cigars each.

LA CORONA
Machine-made in Puerto Rico.

Shape	Name	Lgth	Ring	Wrapper
Cigarillo	Whiffs	3⅝	23⅔	Ma
Cigarillo	Whiffs Light	3⅝	23⅔	Cl

The famous La Corona brand continues with the Whiffs series, with the Light style added in 1995. Both sizes offer a natural Connecticut wrapper.

MADISON
Machine-made in Tampa, Florida, USA.

Shape	Name	Lgth	Ring	Wrapper
Cigarillo	Madison	3⅛	20	CC

The Madison taste is mild, with a filler blend of Indonesian and United States tobaccos, combined with a sheet wrapper and binder, offered in packs of 20.

MANIKIN
Dry cured, machine-made in England.

Shape	Name	Lgth	Ring	Wrapper
Cigarillo	Mild Blend	3⅞		CM

SMALL CIGARS: BRAND LISTINGS

NOBEL CIGARS
Machine-made in Copenhagen, Denmark.

Shape	Name	Lgth	Ring	Wrapper
Cigarillo	Petit Sumatra	3⅜	20	CC
Cigarillo	Medium Panatela Sumatra	3½	22	CC
Cigarillo	Grand Panatela Sumatra	5½	28	CC
Cigarillo	Petit Corona	3½	32	CC
Cigarillo	Petit Lights	3⅜	20	CC

Introduced in 1898, these elegant cigarillos are dry-cured and made of 100% tobacco, especially Indonesian Sumatran wrappers and Java binders in most sizes.

OMEGA
Machine-made in Tampa, Florida, USA.

Shape	Name	Lgth	Ring	Wrapper
Cigarillo	Omega (tipped)	3⅜	20	CC
Cigarillo	National Slims 100	3⅞	20	CC
Cigarillo	Cherry Flavor Slims 100	3⅞	20	CC
Cigarillo	Menthol Slims 100	3⅞	20	CC

Here's a mild-bodied smoke in a choice of flavors, with a sheet wrapper and binder and a blend of filler tobaccos from Indonesia and the United States.

PANTER
Machine-made in Geel, Belgium.

Shape	Name	Lgth	Ring	Wrapper
Cigarillo	Sprint	2⅞	21	CC
Cigarillo	Small	2⅞	21	CC
Cigarillo	Lights	2⅞	20	CI
Cigarillo	Silhouette	3⅜	20	CC
Cigarillo	Limbo	3⅞	24	CC

SMALL CIGARS: BRAND LISTINGS

Cigarillo	Mignon	3¾	25	CC
Cigarillo	Tango	3⅞	23	CC
Cigarillo	Vitesse	3¾	23	CC
Cigarillo	Mild Panatellas	5¾	21	CC

A famous brand in cigarillos for many years, the Panter is made by the highly-respected Agio Sigarfabrieken in Holland. The Silhouette, Bijou, Limbo and Panatellas shapes are all-tobacco cigars; the other shapes use a sheet binder. Wrappers come from Java (on Sprint, Small, Mignon and the Panatellas), Sumatra (Silhouette, Bijou and Limbo) and Connecticut (Lights). A new shape, the Mignon Deluxe, will soon feature an Ecuadorian wrapper.

PARODI
Machine-made in Scranton, Pennsylvania, USA.

Shape	*Name*	*Lgth*	*Ring*	*Wrapper*
Cheroot	Ammezzati	3½	34	Ma
Cheroot	Cello	4	34	Ma
Cheroot	Economy	4	34	Ma
Cheroot	Kings	4½	34	Ma

Here are famous dry-cured, 100% tobacco cigars which use only the finest, dark-fired tobaccos from Kentucky and Tennessee. Highly respected since their introduction in 1913, the blend of leaves always includes not less than three different crop years, which contributes to the medium-bodied flavor which Parodi is famous for.

PEDRONI
Machine-made in Switzerland.

Shape	*Name*	*Lgth*	*Ring*	*Wrapper*
Cheroot	Classico	3⅝	34	Ma
Cheroot	Anisette	3⅝	34	Ma

These small treats feature dry-cured, dark-fired leaves and are all tobacco; Pedronis are offered in twin-packs and five-packs.

SMALL CIGARS: BRAND LISTINGS

PETRI
Machine-made in Scranton, Pennsylvania, USA.

Shape	Name	Lgth	Ring	Wrapper
Cheroot	AA	3½	34	Ma
Cheroot	Sigaretto	3½	34	Ma
Cheroot	Sigaretto Kings	4	34	Ma
Cheroot	Toscanelli	4	34	Ma
Cheroot	Toscani	6½	34	Ma

Created in 1906, Petri offers all-tobacco, dry-cured cigars with a medium-bodied taste. The wrapper, binder and filler are all dark-fired Kentucky and Tennessee tobaccos from at least three different crop years.

PHILLIES LITTLE CIGARS
Machine-made in Selma, Alabama, USA.

Shape	Name	Lgth	Ring	Wrapper
Cigarillo	Natural	3⅛	20	CC
Cigarillo	Sweet	3⅛	20	CC

Here are little cigars with the mild taste of the famous Phillies line. The filler tobaccos are a combination of chopped Indonesian and United States leaves, surrounded by a sheet wrapper and binder.

PRINCE ALBERT
Machine-made in the United States.

Shape	Name		Lgth	Ring	Wrapper
Cigarillo	Soft & Sweet Vanilla	*(tipped)*	4⅞		CM
Cigarillo	Traditional	*(tipped)*	4⅞		CM
Cigarillo	Cool Mint	*(tipped)*	4⅞		CM

These tipped cigars are extremely mild and feature an all-pipe tobacco filler, aimed at providing pipe tobacco taste - and aroma - in cigar form.

Cigarillos, Cheroots and Panatelas

Here are examples of the smallest cigars available on the market today:

- Cigarillos and cheroots   6 or less inches long with a ring gauge of 29 or less.

- Panatela group, including
  - Small Panatela   4-5 inches long; 30-34 ring.
  - Slim Panatela   5 inches and more; 30-34 ring.
  - Short Panatela   4-5⅝ inches long; 35-39 ring.
  - Panatela   5½-6⅞ inches long; 35-39 ring.
  - Long Panatela   7 inches and more; 35-39 ring.

Pictured opposite are:

- Captain Black Sweet 3⅞ x 20   Little Cigar

- Davidoff Cigarillo   3½ x 20   Cigarillo

- Christian of Denmark
  Long Cigarillo   4 x 20   Cigarillo

- Toscanelli   3½ x 34   Cheroot

- Parodi Kings   4½ x 34   Cheroot

- El Rey del Mundo
  Elegantes   5¾ x 29   Cigarillo

- Don Tomas Special Edition
  No. 400   7 x 36   Long Panatela

SMALL CIGARS: BRAND LISTINGS

RUSTLERS
Machine-made in McAdoo, Pennsylvania, USA.

Shape	Name	Lgth	Ring	Wrapper
Cigarillo	Black 'n Cherry	3⅞	23	CC
Cigarillo	Menthol	3⅞	23	CC
Cigarillo	Sweets	3⅞	23	CC

This is a machine-made little cigar with a filter tip and a manufactured wrapper, offered in three flavored styles in flip-top boxes of seven cigars each.

ST. REGIS
Machine-made in Tampa, Florida, USA.

Shape	Name	Lgth	Ring	Wrapper
Cigarillo	Regular	3⅞	20	CC
Cigarillo	Menthol	3⅞	20	CC
Cigarillo	Pipe Bouquet	3⅞	20	CC

These little cigars have been around since 1951 and offer a mild taste, featuring a blend of U.S. tobaccos in the filler core. Available in packs of 20.

SCHIMMELPENNICK
Machine-made in Wageningen, the Netherlands.

Shape	Name		Lgth	Ring	Wrapper
Small Panatela	Florina		4	32	CC
Short Panatela	Half Corona		4	36	CC
Cigarillo	Nostra		3	20	CC
Cigarillo	Media		3	20	CC
Cigarillo	Media Brazil		3	20	Ma
Cigarillo	Mono		3	22	CC
Cigarillo	Mono Brazil		3	22	Ma
Small Panatela	Vada		4	32	CC
Cigarillo	Mini Tips	*(tipped)*	4	20	CC

SMALL CIGARS: BRAND LISTINGS

Cigarillo	Duet	6	26	CC
Cigarillo	Duet Brazil	6	24	Ma
Cigarillo	Duet Midi	4¾	26	CC
Cigarillo	Duet Plus	3½	26	CC
Cigarillo	Mini Cigar	3	20	CC
Cigarillo	Mini Cigar Milds	3	20	CC
Cigarillo	Havana Lights	3	20	CC
Cigarillo	Havana Milds	3	20	CC
Cigarillo	Swing	3	20	CC

One of the great names in cigarillos, enjoyed in more than 130 countries. These carefully-blended small cigars utilize tobaccos of a half-dozen nations to achieve their trademark mild-to-medium body and rich flavor. Highlights of the shapes include Indonesian wrappers on the Half Corona, Media, Mini Tip and Mono, Brazilian and Javan tobaccos in the Florina, a Cameroon wrapper and 12 types of filler tobaccos in the Vada, a combination of Brazilian, Indonesian and Cameroon leaves in the Duet, a Sumatran-seed wrapper grown in Brazil on the Mini and a Connecticut Shade wrapper on the Mini Mild. The only flavored cigar of the line is the Swing, which offers a surprising taste of mango!

SUERDIECK
Made in Cruz des Almas, Brazil.

Shape	Name	Lgth	Ring	Wrapper
	Handmade, with 100% tobacco:			
Cigarillo	Copacabana	5	29	CC
Cigarillo	Brasilia Petit	3⅛	22	CM
Cigarillo	Beira Mar Finos	5¼	28	CM
	Machine-made, with sheet binders:			
Cigarillo	Palomitas	3½	32	CM
Cigarillo	Reynitas	3⅛	22	CC-CM

SMALL CIGARS: BRAND LISTINGS

SUPER VALUE LITTLE CIGARS
Machine-made in McAdoo, Pennsylvania, USA.

Shape	Name	Lgth	Ring	Wrapper
Cigarillo	Cherry	3⅞	20	CC
Cigarillo	Sweet	3⅞	20	CC
Cigarillo	Menthol	3⅞	20	CC
Cigarillo	Ultra Mild	3⅞	20	CC
	Pipe Tobacco series:			
Cigarillo	Black & Sweet	4⅛	27	CM
Cigarillo	Black & Cherry	4⅛	27	CM

This brand uses manufactured wrappers and has filter tips. Super Values are offered in packs of 20.

SUPRE SWEETS
Machine-made in the United States.

Shape	Name		Lgth	Ring	Wrapper
Cigarillo	Tip Cigarillo	*(tipped)*	5⅛	27	CM
Cigarillo	Cigarillos		4¾	27½	CM
Petit Corona	Perfectos		4¾	44	CM
Cigarillo	Little Cigars		3⅞	20	CM

The tip Cigarillo and Little Cigars are made in McAdoo, Pennsylvania, while the Perfectos and Cigarillos are produced in Puerto Rico. All styles feature a manufactured wrapper.

TIJUANA SMALLS
Machine-made in Dothan, Alabama, USA.

Shape	Name		Lgth	Ring	Wrapper
Cigarillo	Aromatic	*(tipped)*	4¼	21	CC
Cigarillo	Cherry	*(tipped)*	4¼	21	CC
Cigarillo	Regular	*(tipped)*	4¼	21	CC

SMALL CIGARS: BRAND LISTINGS

Created in 1968, these mild cigars are tipped and made with sheet wrappers and binders and a blend of filler tobaccos. They are sold only in ten-packs.

TIPARILLO
Machine-made in Dothan, Alabama, USA.

Shape	Name		Lgth	Ring	Wrapper
Cigarillo	Mild Blend	(tipped)	5	27	CC
Cigarillo	Sweet Blend	(tipped)	5	27	CC
Cigarillo	Aromatic	(tipped)	5	27	CC
Cigarillo	Menthol	(tipped)	5	27	CC

These sleek cigars are made with sheet wrapper and binder and a blend of filler tobaccos; all of the sizes feature plastic tips. Tiparillos are offered in five-packs and boxes of 50.

THE TOBACCONIST CHOICE
Dry cured, machine-made in Yoe, Pennsylvania, USA.

Shape	Name	Lgth	Ring	Wrapper
Cigarillo	Sweet	3		CC

TOBAJARA
Machine-made in Germany.

Shape	Name	Lgth	Ring	Wrapper
Cigarillo	No. 1 Brazil	3¼	20	CM
Cigarillo	No. 2 Brazil	3⅝	26	CM
Cigarillo	Chicos Brazil	5½	28	CM

This is a medium-bodied, dry-cured cigarillo, offered in packs of 20 for the No. 1 and No. 2 models and in five-packs for the Chicos. This brand features a Brazilian wrapper, sheet binder and filler tobacco from Brazil and Indonesia.

SMALL CIGARS: BRAND LISTINGS

TORINO
Machine-made in Scranton, Pennsylvania, USA.

Shape	Name	Lgth	Ring	Wrapper
Cheroot	Twin	4	34	Ma
Cheroot	King	4½	34	Ma

This blend is 100% tobacco, using only dark-fired Kentucky and Tennessee leaves for a medium-bodied taste . . . but flavored with a touch of vanilla!

VICTORIA
Machine-made in Las Palmas, the Canary Islands of Spain.

Shape	Name	Lgth	Ring	Wrapper
Cigarillo	Mini	3¾	23	CC
Cigarillo	Cortados	3½	27	CC
Cigarillo	No. 5	4⅛	26	CC
Small Panatela	No. 10	4	30	CC
Small Panatela	No. 15	4¼	34	CC
Cigarillo	Coronas Reserve	3¼	20	CC
Cigarillo	Helios Capote Mini Club	4	23	CC

This light-bodied smoke features either a Connecticut wrapper (Cortados, Cigarro, No. 15, Coronas Reserve) or a Sheet wrapper (Mini, No. 10, Capote Mini Club), offered in 10-packs (except for the Coronas Reserve, in 20s).

VILLIGER
Machine-made in Germany and Switzerland.

Shape	Name		Lgth	Ring	Wrapper
Cigarillo	Bunte	*(tipped)*	4½	23	CC
Cigarillo	Curly		7¼	24	Co
Cigarillo	Villiger-Kiel Mild	*(tipped)*	6⅝	29	CI
Cigarillo	Villiger-Kiel Brasil	*(tipped)*	6⅝	29	CM

SMALL CIGARS: BRAND LISTINGS

Cigarillo	Villiger-Kiel Junior Mild *(tipped)*	4½	25	CI
Cigarillo	Villiger-Kiel Junior Brasil *(tipped)*	4½	25	CM
Short Panatela	Villiger Export	4	36	CC
Short Panatela	Villiger Export Kings	5⅛	36	CC
Cigarillo	Villiger Premium No. 3	6⅛	37	CI
Cigarillo	Villiger Premium No. 6	3¾	23	CI
Short Panatela	Villiger Premium No. 7	4	38	CI
Cigarillo	Villiger Premium No. 10	2¾	22	CI
Cigarillo	Rillos *(tipped)*	5	29	CC
Cigarillo	Braniff No. 2	4⅛	20	CI
Cigarillo	Braniff No. 3	4⅛	20	CM
Short Panatela	Braniff No. 8	4	38	CI
Cigarillo	Braniff Cortos Dark	3¼	20	CM
Cigarillo	Braniff Cortos Filter Light	3	20	CI

This famous brand began in 1888 and continues today as one of the world's most respected producers of cigarillos and small cigars. These models range in body from mild-to-medium to medium, using primarily Indonesian and Brazilian wrappers.

WINCHESTER LITTLE CIGARS
Machine-made in the United States.

Shape	Name	Lgth	Ring	Wrapper
Cigarillo	100s	3⅞	20	CC
Cigarillo	Light 100s	3⅞	20	CC
Cigarillo	Menthol 100s	3⅞	20	CC
Cigarillo	Sweet 100s	3⅞	20	CC
Cigarillo	Kings	3¼	20	CC
Cigarillo	Menthol Kings	3¼	20	CC

8.
INTERNATIONAL MEASUREMENT TABLE

For readers more conversant with cigar lengths in centimeters and ring gauges (diameter) expressed in millimeters, the following table will allow conversion of imperial measures into their metric equivalents.

Length	
In 1/8ths of an inch	Length in cm
2½	6.35
2⅝	6.68
2¾	6.99
2⅞	7.32
3	7.62
3⅛	7.94
3¼	8.25
3⅜	8.57
3½	8.89
3⅝	9.21
3¾	9.52
3⅞	9.84
4	10.16
4⅛	10.48
4¼	10.79
4⅜	11.11
4½	11.43
4⅝	11.75
4¾	12.06

Ring Gauge/Diameter	
In 1/64ths of an inch	Diameter in mm
20	7.9
21	8.3
22	8.7
23	9.1
24	9.5
25	9.9
26	10.3
27	10.7
28	11.1
29	11.5
30	11.9
31	12.3
32	12.7
33	13.1
34	13.5
35	13.9
36	14.3
37	14.7
38	15.1

MEASUREMENT CONVERSION TABLE

Length	
In 1/8ths of an inch	Length in cm
4⅞	12.38
5	12.70
5⅛	13.02
5¼	13.33
5⅜	13.65
5½	13.97
5⅝	14.29
5¾	14.61
5⅞	14.93
6	15.24
6⅛	15.56
6¼	15.87
6⅜	16.19
6½	16.51
6⅝	16.83
6¾	17.14
6⅞	17.46
7	17.78
7⅛	18.10
7¼	18.41
7⅜	18.73
7½	19.05
7⅝	19.37
7¾	19.68
7⅞	20.00

Ring Gauge/Diameter	
In 1/64ths of an inch	Diameter in mm
39	15.5
40	15.9
41	16.3
42	16.7
43	17.1
44	17.5
45	17.9
46	18.3
47	18.7
48	19.1
49	19.5
50	19.8
51	20.2
52	20.6
53	21.0
54	21.4
55	21.8
56	22.2
57	22.6
58	23.0
59	23.4
60	23.8
61	24.2
62	24.6
63	25.0

MEASUREMENT CONVERSION TABLE

Length	
In 1/8ths of an inch	Length in cm
8	20.32
8⅛	20.64
8¼	20.96
8⅜	21.28
8½	21.59
8⅝	21.92
8¾	22.23
8⅞	22.55
9	22.86
9⅛	23.18
9¼	23.50
9⅜	23.82
9½	24.13
9⅝	24.45
9¾	24.76
9⅞	25.08
10	25.40
11	27.94
12	30.48
13	33.02
14	35.56
15	38.10
16	40.64
17	43.18
18	45.72

Ring Gauge/Diameter	
In 1/64ths of an inch	Diameter in mm
64	25.4
65	25.8
66	26.2

9.
REFERENCES

For more information about cigars, these books make excellent and fun reading:

Bati, Anwer and Chase, Simon. *The Cigar Companion, A Connoisseur's Guide.* 2nd edition. Philadelphia: Running Press, 1995.

Davidoff, Zino with Gilles Lambert. *The Connoisseur's Book of the Cigar.* Trans. Harold Chester. New York: McGraw-Hill Book Co., 1984.

Dunhill, Alfred. *The Gentle Art of Smoking.* London: Max Reinhardt, Ltd., 1978.

Edmark, Tomima. *Cigar Chic: A Women's Perspective.* Arlington: Summit Publishing Group, 1995.

Garmirian, Paul B.K. *The Gourmet Guide to Cigars.* 3rd edition. McLean: Cedar Publications, 1994.

Hacker, Richard Carleton. *The Ultimate Cigar Book.* 2nd edition. Beverly Hills: Autumngold Publishing, 1996.

Jeffers, H. Paul and Gordon, Kevin. *The Good Cigar.* New York, New York: Lyons & Burford, 1996.

Kasper, Rhona. *A Woman's Guide to Cigar Smoking.* Lawrenceville: Cigar Savvy, Inc., 1996.

LeRoy, Bernard and Szafran, Maurice. *The Illustrated History of Cigars.* Trans. Lexus Translations Ltd. London: Harold Starke Publishers, Ltd., 1993.

REFERENCES

Rudman, Theo. *Rudman's Complete Pocket Guide to Cigars 1996.* Cape Town: Good Living Publishing, 1996.

Scott, Dale. *How to Select and Enjoy Premium Cigars . . . and Save Money!* 2nd edition. San Diego: Coast Creative Services, 1995.

NOTES

10.
RING GAUGE GUIDE

Use this handy guide to size up the girth of your cigars.
The illustrated ring sizes correspond to the following
shapes:

Ring: | 32-34 | Slim and Small Panatelas
       | 35-39 | Panatelas and Long Panatelas
       | 40-44 | Coronas and Lonsdales
       | 45-47 | Coronas Extra and Grand Coronas
       | 48-50+ | Robustos, Toros, Churchills, Double Coronas and Giants.

32 **33** **34** **35**

36 **37** **38**

39 **40** **41**

RING GAUGE GUIDE

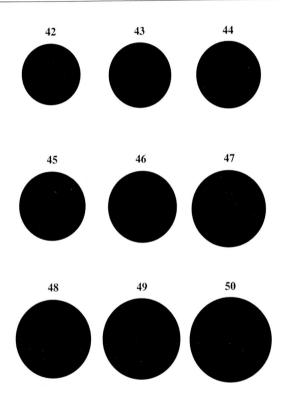

NOTES